W9-BCX-675

PACIFIST'S PROGRESS

Pacifist's progress

Norman Thomas and the decline of American socialism

by Bernard K. Johnpoll

Quadrangle Books

Chicago 1970

To David Karl Greenlee

Preface

Norman Thomas was the hero of my childhood and youth. When my contemporaries were extolling the glories of Tom Harmon or Johnny Mize or Max Carey or—if they had theatrical ambitions—of Katherine Cornell or Fred Allen or Leslie Howard, I was busy on street-corners singing the virtues of Norman Thomas and the placid revolution he exemplified. But that was many years ago. A war and an explosive peace which followed have exposed the dreams of my youth as nightmares or apparitions; in their stead have arisen new dreams, new hopes, and new lethargy. I am no longer a Socialist nor is the memory of Norman Thomas any longer quite so sacred to me. His philosophy appears today to be obsolete, even though this was not true when he espoused it. I suspect that Norman Thomas was no longer a Socialist in his latter days; his last book, *Choices*, far from seeming the work of a convinced Socialist, reads more like that of an ethicist pleading for the Golden Rule. Yet Thomas must be given his due. All his life, as he fought for civil liberties, for peace, and for an elusive ideal which he labeled democratic socialism, Thomas sought to improve the lot of "the least of these my brothers." He was a great, honest, and compassionate human being. Moreover, he was a man able to embody his views in action; he was a man who faced without fear a court injunction, an unfriendly crowd egged on by the corrupt mayor of Jersey City, or a lynch mob of Arkansas planters. He struggled without equivocation for what he believed to be the right. At times he erred, and being human he was less than eager to concede those errors. Yet, when I spoke with him in October 1963, he admitted that he had been wrong in his evaluation of communism and World War II—two of the major issues on which he took strong stands. If he had his life to live over again he would, he told me then, have changed some of his positions and, accordingly, some of his actions; but he would have followed the same path, for he believed he could do no other. He dedicated his life to peace, freedom, and justice, as he interpreted those terms, and he was then as much dedicated to these aspirations as he had been more than forty years earlier.

In its final assessment of Norman Thomas, after his death in December 1968, the *New York Times* called him a "mover and shaker" whose "moral fervor for social justice has contributed to a more just America." There can be no doubt that he was a "mover and shaker" or that he had great moral fervor. It was this moral fervor which led him into socialism, his own modified version of pacifism, and the struggle for civil rights and civil liberties. It was this same moral fervor which allowed him to attempt to influence the direction of his country during his fifty years of continuous political activity. Whether he succeeded is another matter—and it is to this question that I address myself in this book.

2

This is not a biography of Norman Thomas. Two biographies of him already exist, and a definitive biography is now being written. My sole interest in Norman Thomas in this book is in his role as a political actor. My own acquaintance with Thomas was limited. I met him only four times in my life: in 1942, when he discussed a report on Russia which I brought back from Archangel; in 1950, when he and I agreed on Socialist party policy at a national convention most of whose delegates disagreed with both of us; in 1963, when he was my guest during a speaking engagement in Oneonta, New York; and in 1967, when I acted as his host during a visit to the State University of New York at Albany. I make this point only to emphasize that I am neither a classical biographer nor a close friend writing Thomas's memoirs. All I propose in this work is to study Norman Thomas as a political figure, and to analyze what I take to be his role in the disintegration of American socialism. I write as a political scientist and an historian. My conclusions are based on as thorough an investigation of the available materials as appeared possible to me; it is in no way based on the opinions of others.

To accomplish this task I have used many sources—manuscript and published—over a period of six years. By far the most important of these was the Norman Thomas Collection in the New York Public Library, composed of more than 150 boxes

of letters, speeches, manuscripts, and political committee meeting minutes of various sorts, especially from 1933–1968. Thomas,
knowing the purpose of my research and my own critical view
of him, gave me permission to use the papers without restriction.
Without the Norman Thomas Collection it would have been
impossible to research this book.

The Socialist Party of America Collection, housed in the Perkins Memorial Library at Duke University, proved to be another invaluable source of material about Norman Thomas and
his leadership of the Socialist party from 1928 until his death in
1968. The collection has virtually all of the letters, statements,
and other manuscripts dealing with the party from its origins in
1901 until the present. It is particularly important for minutes of
meetings of national committees and the transcripts of national
party conventions. The collection is immense.

A third significant collection, particularly for filling in inter-
stices for the period 1924–1933, is the Daniel W. Hoan collection
in the Milwaukee County Historical Society Library. Hoan, who
was the Socialist mayor of Milwaukee from 1916 until 1940, had
an extensive correspondence both with Thomas and about him.
This collection is particularly valuable for its material about the
1928 campaign.

Also of importance is the Swarthmore College Peace Collection, especially the Henry Wadsworth Longfellow Dana papers
and the Fellowship of Reconciliation papers and minutes for
1916–1924 on microfilm. This is one of the two sources of material relating to Thomas's role during and soon after World
War I when he made his entry into the Socialist movement.
The Lusk Committee Collection at the New York State Library
in the State Education Department in Albany contains transcripts
of two major 1918–1919 speeches by Thomas as well as several
letters and other documents pertinent to his career during the
period immediately following World War I. The Lusk papers
fill in the gaps in the Socialist Party of America Collection, especially from 1917 to 1921.

Other manuscript collections which are of considerable importance are those in the Tamiment Institute Library at 7 East
15th Street, New York. Now part of the New York University
Libraries, Tamiment is without peer for Socialist materials. Of
special interest are the B. Charney Vladeck and James Oneal

papers, and the minute books of the Socialist party of New York City and State and of the Social Democratic Federation. The Norman Thomas narrative in the Columbia University Oral History project is basically a rambling series of recollections, none of which added much insight to the study and which, therefore, were not used.

Published material by and about Norman Thomas is extensive. Thomas wrote more than twenty full-length books, including among others: *The Church and the City*, 1917; *The Christian Patriot*, 1917; *Conscientious Objector in America*, 1923; *America's Way Out*, 1931; *The Choice Before Us*, 1934; *Socialism on the Defensive*, 1938; *We Have a Future*, 1941; *What Is Our Destiny*, 1944; *Appeal to the Nations*, 1947; *A Socialist's Faith*, 1952; *The Prerequisites for Peace*, 1959; *Socialism Re-Examined*, 1963; and *Choices*, 1969. He also wrote roughly 135 pamphlets, of which the most important are *War's Heretics*, 1917; *The New Deal: A Socialist Analysis*, 1933; and *Democratic Socialism: A New Appraisal*, 1953. Almost all of the pamphlets and books can be found in the Tamiment Institute Library. Thomas wrote a weekly column for *The New Leader* from 1925 to 1935, and for the *Socialist Call* from 1935 to 1953. Both of the weeklies covered Thomas's activities quite extensively during the periods noted. The *Jewish Daily Forward* also devoted considerable space to him, though it was not always friendly. The *World Tomorrow*, which Thomas edited from 1917 to 1921, is of considerable importance for that early period and from 1931 until its demise in 1934. The *American Socialist Quarterly*, later known as *American Socialist Monthly* and still later as *Socialist Review*, carried much material by and about Thomas and the Socialist party from 1932 to 1940. The *Intercollegiate Socialist* from 1917 to 1920 is another important source. Other magazines and journals which proved of significant help were the *Nation*, the *New Republic*, *Current History*, *Christian Century*, and *Commonweal*. Although I have not supplied a detailed bibliography, one may be constructed from the extensive notes at the end of this book.

The research for this book was made possible by a grant and a fellowship from the State University of New York Foundation and by a research grant from Hartwick College. I am deeply grateful to both.

For aid while using the Norman Thomas papers, I would like to thank Robert W. Hill, keeper of manuscripts at the New York Public Library, and his two able aides, Miss Jean R. McNiece and Paul R. Rugen. At Duke University, I was helped by Dr. Mattie Russell, curator of manuscripts, and her assistant curator, Dr. Virginia R. Gray. At Tamiment I received invaluable help from Mrs. Dorothy Swanson. I am, of course, particularly indebted to my wife, Lillian, whose editing made an unmanageable manuscript readable. I would also like to thank David Harrop, formerly of Princeton University Press, who suggested in 1963 that I enlarge my research on Thomas into a book. The editorial advice of Ivan Dee, editor of Quadrangle Books, proved invaluable. I am also indebted for advice and criticism to my friend Frank P. Zeidler, former Mayor of Milwaukee.

Despite the help of many friends and acquaintances, mentioned and unmentioned, I am of course solely responsible for any errors or misinterpretations in this book.

B.K.J.

Albany, New York
March 1970

Contents

PACIFIST'S PROGRESS

Introduction

For forty years, from 1928 until his death in 1968, Norman Thomas and the American Socialist party were virtually synonymous. Yet except for a short period during the 1930's Thomas was not a Marxist, though the party had long prided itself on its thoroughgoing Marxism. He was the political personification of the Protestant Social Gospel, in a party which included a great many Jews, Catholics, and nonbelievers; he was also an intellectual in a party which claimed to be of, by, and for the working class.

Thomas came to American socialism during World War I motivated by the poverty he witnessed in the neighborhood where he was a minister and by the Socialist party's opposition to the war. It was his pacifism that first led him into political action through his work with the pacifist Fellowship of Reconciliation, the American Union against Militarism, and the No-Conscription League; yet Thomas, who opposed the use of force, allied himself in the Socialist party during the 1930's with a faction that accepted, or at least refused to oppose, the use of armed insurrection as a means for achieving socialism.

Under Thomas's leadership the Socialist party withered and virtually disappeared. Internal disputes dominated the years he was its leader; and these disputes were at times sufficiently irreconcilable to rend the party with schisms. Each split had its own mass exodus of disaffected Socialists. And yet, despite the decline of the party's fortunes during his stewardship, particularly from 1932 to 1941, Thomas remained—and remains today —a popular figure in American political folklore. By the time of his death, it had become almost commonplace to give Thomas credit for many of the innovations—among others, social security, minimum-wage and maximum-hour laws, and public works —that were in fact enacted into law under Franklin D. Roosevelt. Yet these same reforms were propagated by the Socialist party campaigners at least as early as 1908, or more than ten years before Thomas joined the party.

What was Norman Thomas's role in the collapse and final

disintegration of the American Socialist party? And why has Norman Thomas been enshrined in the Valhalla of American political folk myths? These are two of the questions which this book will attempt to answer.

2

The political movement which Norman Thomas inherited was a mere shadow of its old self when he came to lead it in 1928. Organized in 1901 from a coalition of disparate regional and local Socialist organizations, the Socialist party ranged in ideology from dogmatic Marxist to Populist to municipal reformist to Christian ethicist; in political leadership, from big-city boss Victor Berger to the almost Christlike figure of Eugene Victor Debs, to the lackluster Marxian dialectician Morris Hillquit to the revolutionary orator and organizer William Haywood. From the beginning, the party was rent with dissension. Ostensibly, disagreements were almost always over questions of tactics and theory, but in reality they were caused by clashes of personality. The founders of the Socialist party in 1901 brought their own organizations into the party with them. Morris Hillquit and most of the Easterners from New York and Boston brought the remnants of the anti–De Leon forces of the Socialist Labor party, who had split from the older organization when the vituperative, vindictive Daniel De Leon gained complete dictatorial control of it. Victor Berger and his Germanic followers in Milwaukee brought a political organization which included hundreds of members. The saintly though hardly erudite Gene Debs brought the remnants of the Social Democracy of America, the Utopian foster child of his nearly successful attempt at organizing an industrial union of all railroad workers. George Herron, fresh from his battles for academic freedom in Iowa, brought a goodly number of his fellow Social Gospeleers. (By 1908 there were an estimated three hundred ministers in the ranks of the Socialist party, a source of embarrassment to the Marxists who relegated most clergymen to their own "materialistic" version of purgatory.) Other groups were involved as well; and, as the party developed, new factions arose continually, until the party was an unsteady coalition of minuscule sects each with its own prophet. Only rarely before 1918, however, did one group of

Socialists purge another; feuding was kept "within the family." True, there had been some splits, some schisms, some "bloodletting," but this was rare. The ouster of the IWW's "Big Bill" Haywood from the national executive committee in 1913 for his defense of sabotage as a possible weapon in the class war was the most significant; but this hardly constituted a purge in the classic sense.[1]

If there was a dominant philosophy in the Socialist party during its pre–Norman Thomas years, it was a simplistic Marxism best exemplified by Hillquit's *Socialism in Theory and Practice* and the 1908 Declaration of Principles and Electoral Platform. The latter was basically a pedantic reiteration of the classstruggle thesis coupled with appeals for working-class political action aimed at ending the capitalist system. "Capitalism," it declared, "keeps the masses of workingmen in poverty, destitution, physical exhaustion, and ignorance." Therefore, the "wageworking class . . . has the most direct interest in abolishing the capitalist system." To prevent the working class from seizing power, the Socialist declaration proclaimed, the capitalists "must keep in their pay all organs of the public powers, public mind and public conscience." The Socialists insisted, in effect, that the government of the United States, and all other political parties, served as the executive committee of the capitalist class. There could be no ultimate freedom, the Socialists declared, until "class rule" was destroyed by the working-class victory which would "free all humanity from class rule" and would "realize the international brotherhood of man." A victory of this kind could only come when the workingmen elected a Socialist government.

But until the achievement of the Marxian Utopia, the Socialists proposed social and economic reforms which would alleviate the sufferings of the mass of the workers of the United States. These reforms included public works for the unemployed; legal restrictions on hours of labor; abolition of child labor; factory inspection; compulsory insurance against unemployment, old age, illness, accident, invalidism, and death; the graduated income tax; steep and graduated inheritance taxes, and the establishment of a separate Department of Labor.[2] Although these demands were considered by most Socialists to be of only temporary importance, they were the basis for almost all campaigning; as a full-blown program, socialism was rarely, if ever, the theme of a campaigner's speech. Thus, the official call for a radical socialization of society, coupled with actual work aimed at reformation of the existing order, remained a hallmark of Socialist campaigning after the war, as well as during the early and most successful years of Thomas's leadership.

3

The Social Gospel movement was, to quote one of its historians, "the uniquely American movement toward the socializing and ethicizing of Protestantism." Its origins can be found in the social ethics of the Old Testament Prophets—particularly Isaiah —and in the social and ethical teachings of Jesus. Historically, both Jews and Christians had attempted to create a human society on earth which would be based on the Judeo-Christian ethic. Since the communism of the earliest Apostolic Christians, social redemption has been part of Christian doctrine. Certainly, it was among the dominant themes of the Puritans, who, rebelling against the socially-anesthetized formalism of the seventeenth-century Church in England, sought to build a new church and a new society in the New World.

The Social Gospel carried that tradition into industrial America of the latter half of the nineteenth and the first third of the twentieth centuries. Its immediate roots were primarily in New England Unitarianism, which "stressed the dignity and divine possibilities of man, the achievement of salvation through character . . . the unity and immanence of God, and the importance of the present life. . . ." The Social Gospel had other sources besides Unitarianism: the anti-slavery movement, particularly that part of the movement led by Wendell Phillips which saw in the economic or social exploitation of any human being a violation of Christianity; the liberalizing tendency in theology, best exemplified by such men as Frederick Maurice and Horace Bushell; the rising social consciousness among nontheologian scholars such as John R. Commons, Lester Ward, and Richard T. Ely; and the utopianism of Edward Bellamy and Laurence Gronlund.

Like the Socialist party, the Social Gospel was composed of several ideologies, ranging from philanthropism to socialism. Despite differences, however, a basic ideology permeated the movement. It was based on the passage in the Lord's Prayer, composed by Jesus in his Sermon on the Mount, "Thy will be done *on earth* as it is in heaven." Because the Social Gospeleers proposed that God's will be done on earth, they rejected as antithetical to Christianity the Augustinian assumption that life on this earth was merely transitory in preparation for some future existence in the City of God. It was on this earth, the Social Gospeleers insisted, that God's will should come to full fruition. In essence, the Social Gospel reasserted the basic Puritan "this worldliness," whose primary aim was the establishment of the "Kingdom of God on earth." Unlike their Calvinist precursors, however, the Social Gospeleers interpreted the "Kingdom of God" as a purely ethical society. Thus, to quote Socialist-Christian historian James Dombrowski, the "most prominent feature of the Social Gospel is its emphasis upon the saving of society rather than upon the salvation of individuals."

The Social Gospel was basically optimistic. It assumed that man was by nature good, that only the pressures of a venal society corrupted humanity. This assumption merely reiterated what most social scientists of the period were claiming. It led some of the Social Gospeleers to revolutionary conclusions (though not rebellion). Although some, possibly most, of the leaders of the movement were "liberals advocating the ethic of charity," there were some who believed that only a complete uprooting of the system, a full Socialist reconstruction of society, could bring about their dream of a Kingdom of God on earth. But even the most radical Socialist Christians were wedded to the concept of gradualism. This was natural in view of the pacifist nature of the religious base of the Social Gospel and the liberal Christian emphasis on moral persuasion, which was one of the keys to Social Gospel ideology.

The Socialist Christians agreed that a complete redistribution of economic, and hence of social, power was necessary if men were to live as brothers in the projected kingdom. They insisted that production for profit had to give way to production for use. They differed from their Marxian contemporaries primarily in the emphasis they placed on the means to be used to achieve their ends—and in their social origins. Whereas the Marxian Socialists were generally of working-class origin (although many of them rose into the middle class as attorneys, teachers, and physicians), most of the Social Gospel Socialists came out of the middle and upper classes, and almost all were ministers, publicists, or university professors.[3] The working-class oriented Marxian Socialists were less interested in means than in ends; because they came out of the working-class, or were still in it, their primary interests were still basically working class—the achievement of higher pay, shorter hours, protection against unemployment, old age, illness, and improved work conditions generally—regardless of the methods used to achieve them. The Social Gospel Socialists, being further removed from the working class, never lost their interest in means. Immediate alleviation of economic distress, though important, was of less significance to them than the methods used to achieve it. Thus the Social Gospel Socialists were more involved with civil liberties and civic betterment movements than were their Marxian comrades. The Christian Socialists fought against corrupt unionists, for example, whereas the so-called Marxians were ready to support them as long as they could "deliver the goods" for their members. The two groups could thus work harmoniously together only under limited conditions in which means were not at issue.

Norman Thomas was a Social Gospel Christian Socialist.

4

In 1844, Wendell Phillips, one of Norman Thomas's heroes, was sorely tempted to become a practical politician in the small anti-slavery Liberty party. But he refused because: "The politician must conceal half his principles to carry forth the other half—must regard, not rigid principle and strict right, but only such a degree of right as will allow him at the same time to secure *numbers*. His object is immediate success." Phillips considered himself a moral reformer who worshiped truth: "his object is duty, not success. He can wait, no matter how many desert, how few remain; he can trust always that the whole truth, however unpopular, can never harm the whole of virtue."[4] In sum, Phillips was reiterating the political truism that the practical politician must be willing to compromise to achieve his ends; the ideologue—whom he called a moral reformer—who has no expectation of achieving the goal he sets forth, need never compromise.

Like Wendell Phillips, Norman Thomas was a moral reformer, an ideologue. But unlike Wendell Phillips he also thought himself a politician. Indeed, during his entire political career, he was faced with the unpleasant choice of being a political failure or of compromising his ideals.

5

Norman Thomas's best friend, Roger Baldwin, has described him as "a great denouncer, aroused to indignation by one injustice or another." Yet he was more than that—he was also a great advocate pleading for a society based on the Social Gospel and unwilling to settle for less. Thomas was a great orator, an evangelist preaching the gospel of a better world free of hunger and despair and war and injustice, a world where all men would be brothers cooperating with one another in building an ever better tomorrow.

Tall and thin, inclining toward the gaunt, Thomas looked every bit the Old Testament prophet as he denounced the sins of society. Beginning with a reasoned critique of the society in which he lived, he would rise to thunderous heights of indignation as he assailed the inhumanity of a social order that condemned fully one-third of its population to poverty, permitted its young to die on far-off battlefields, consigned one-tenth of its population to ghettos lacking the minimal amenities of life, or which with one bomb slaughtered 100,000 human beings in a distant land. "He was," to quote Baldwin, "a crusader, an evangelist, a humanist to whom nothing mattered more than the search for the right road to abolish war, end poverty and create a world order of freedom and equality. His socialism was his search for the elusive road."[5]

The object of this book is to explore that search.

I
The making
of a socialist

There was little in the small city where Norman Thomas was born and raised or in the orthodox Presbyterian household of his parents to foretell his later role as a Socialist. Marion, Ohio, where Thomas was born on November 20, 1884, was a typical small county-seat with a population of about eight thousand, which served as the commercial center for a rich farming area about thirty-five miles north of Columbus. It was also a minor railroad center and had some small-scale, locally owned industries. In Marion, industries and locomotives belched smoke, most homes were plain and grey, and the town was a center for a number of unattractive stores. As in many other small industrial cities of that era, there were more saloons than churches. Not that there wasn't a multitude of churches, for the Roman Catholic Church and almost every Protestant denomination were represented. The Methodists had the largest congregation in town, but the Presbyterians, of whom the Reverend Welling Evan Thomas, Norman's father, was minister, had the second largest and the most prestigious.

There was an egalitarian air about Marion. The children of employers and workers went to the same public schools, and employees and the owners of factories were generally on first-name terms. But the apparent equality was in many ways a façade. One indication was that the different fraternal lodges, of which Marion had many, drew their memberships from different classes.

Politically, the Thomas family was Republican, as were most of the parishioners of the Presbyterian Church. Marion city and county, however, were Democratic. In 1900, William Jennings Bryan carried Marion County 4,141 to 3,770 for Republican William McKinley. Socialists were a rarity in Marion. In the same 1900 election, Eugene V. Debs, the Socialist candidate for President, polled one vote.

There was a strong sense of social obligation in the Thomas household, a sense of mission that Norman Thomas carried all his life. For he was the son, grandson, and great-grandson of Christian ministers. The Thomas home was naturally permeated with a strong Protestant tradition. His father and mother were orthodox Presbyterians who accepted Calvinism without question. But they were not humorless, nor bigoted, nor in any way fanatic. Thomas's father professed a belief in hell to which, according to his son, "I do not think that he would say . . . anyone was bound."

Thomas's paternal grandparents were Welsh immigrants who settled about 1820 in Bradford County in northeast Pennsylvania. Norman's paternal grandfather was an active minister in Pennsylvania well into his eighties.

Norman's father was a reserved man who had many friends but few intimates. He lived by a strict code in which duty, though exclusive of gloom, was the watchword. His orthodoxy was malleable. He supported liberalization of the Presbyterian creed during the great debate at the denomination's general convention in 1901. He was an extremely well-liked and highly successful minister. During his seventeen years in the Marion church —a period stretching from two months before Norman's birth until the summer of 1901—he more than doubled its membership, had a new $50,000 church edifice erected, and virtually retired the church's debt. His salary was $1,200 a year—high by Marion standards, but hardly sumptuous for a man with six children.

The most important influence on Norman during his childhood was his mother, who along with bringing up a family of six children, "helped a son with his Latin lesson while getting dinner—and a good one, too," and ran various church and civic groups. Mrs. Emma Mattoon Thomas was a descendant of pre-Revolutionary Scotch-Irish and Huguenot settlers in New York State. Her father, the Reverend Stephen Mattoon, had been a missionary in Siam for twenty years, after which he served for another twenty years as president of Biddle Institute (now Johnson C. Smith University), a Presbyterian college for Negroes in Charlotte, North Carolina. An unusually well-educated woman for her day (Mrs. Thomas was a graduate of Elmira Female College), she set little store by wealth, for which "she had more scorn than envy." She was primarily interested in her children's being healthy and educated, and growing up to be honest men and women. Although she accepted her husband's orthodoxy, she did so more out of loyalty to him than out of any unquestioning religious faith.

The eldest of the Thomas children, Norman was shy and introspective with a lively curiosity. An intense blue-eyed boy with a large head and spindly arms and legs, Norman was sickly during much of his childhood. He thus spent much of his time reading books from his father's extensive personal library; among the books he found there were such major classics as Lord Bryce's *American Commonwealth* and Edward Gibbons' *Decline and Fall of the Roman Empire*.

Norman's health improved after his twelfth birthday, and at this time he assumed the responsibility for earning his own spending money. He delivered the *Marion Star*, the local daily which was owned by a future President of the United States, Warren Gamaliel Harding. Norman was an able student, respected by teachers and fellow students alike, though not especially noted for being socially conscious.[1]

Immediately after Norman graduated from high school in 1901 his father resigned from the Marion church and accepted a call to Lewisburg, Pennsylvania. Because of family finances young Thomas was unable to enter Princeton University as he had desired. But the move to Lewisburg at least assured him of a university education, for Bucknell University, a Baptist institution which charged no tuition for ministers' children, was located there. He found the experience disappointing—he thought the teaching was poor and the school badly run. Fortunately, Thomas had a wealthy uncle who took an interest in him; he offered to pay his tuition at Princeton if Norman would pay for his other expenses. In 1902, then, Thomas entered Princeton as a sophomore to prepare for theological school. To earn his keep, he tutored students in the evenings, sold aluminum-ware door-to-door, and worked in a chair factory summers. He remained an honor student, doing particularly well in political economy, politics, and debate.

Although Thomas studied politics under Woodrow Wilson, whom he considered an excellent speaker, he was far more impressed with Winthrop M. Daniels, a conservative professor of political economy, and he was greatly influenced by Walter

Wyckoff, an assistant professor of political economy who had an affinity for the liberal Protestant Social Gospel. Daniels was a transportation economist whom Wilson was later to name to the Interstate Commerce Commission over the protest of Progressive senators. Wyckoff's main claim to fame was a two-volume work describing his experience as an unskilled migrant casual laborer during the 1890's, in which he showed sympathy for the workingman and respect, though not support, for moderate Socialists.

In 1905, Thomas graduated from Princeton with a bachelor of arts degree *magna cum laude*, membership in the national honorary fraternity Phi Beta Kappa, a first prize in history, and high honors in history, jurisprudence, and politics. He was class valedictorian.[2]

Although his parents expected him to enter theological seminary immediately after graduation from Princeton, Thomas was not certain that he wanted to make the ministry his career. He was more interested in politics. At the urging of his family, however, he accepted an appointment as a social worker at the Presbyterian Spring Street Settlement House in lower Manhattan. There he had his initial firsthand experience with the urban proletariat whom he had—on the basis of Wyckoff's writings—come to idealize. He soon discovered that the workers were less than the noble sons of toil whom the intellectuals were portraying in books and pamphlets. Social workers were scorned in the area, and most of Thomas's time was spent in attempting to bring "peace and enlightenment" by trying to talk longshoremen out of perforating one another with their hooks and by mediating gang fights.

Within a year after he went to Spring Street—where, incidentally, his salary was $500 per annum—two opportunities presented themselves. Princeton offered him an instructorship in oratory and debate, and a director of the settlement house offered to take him on a leisurely trip around the world. Thomas chose the trip, which he found intriguing. On his return to the United States he accepted an appointment as assistant minister at Christ Church (Presbyterian) in the 35th Street tenement neighborhood of New York, and entered Union Theological Seminary to prepare for the ministry.[3]

While Norman Thomas was a student there, Union was a center of the Social Gospel movement. Its God was more ethical than supernatural, its primary interest was in pragmatism, and it was more involved with religious psychology than with theological metaphysics. Its basic aim was the creation of a heaven on earth by nonviolent economic and social revolution. Among Thomas's teachers at Union were such leading exponents of the creed as Henry Sloane Coffin and Harry Emerson Fosdick; and it was at Union that Thomas first became acquainted with the works of Walter Rauschenbusch, prime mover of the Social Gospel movement and a nonparty Socialist. Thomas wrote to Rauschenbusch's biographer many years later that "insofar as any one book or series of books made me a Socialist, it was probably [by] Walter Rauschenbusch."

At Christ Church Thomas met Frances Violet Stewart, a social worker who had set up a tuberculosis clinic at the church. They were married in 1910 at fashionable Brick Church on Fifth Avenue, where Thomas had in the meantime become temporary minister. A year later, following his graduation from Union, and after a bitter argument with an orthodox examining board, Norman Thomas was ordained in the Presbyterian ministry.[4]

2

Thomas's first major involvement with social reform and the Socialist movement began after his ordination. His first (and only) assignment in the Presbyterian ministry was as the pastor of the East Harlem Parish and chairman of the American Parish Among Immigrants in New York, a federation of Presbyterian agencies under the Home Missions Committee whose aim was to promote "Christian life" among New York's foreign-born. Before this seven-year stay in East Harlem he had rejected entreaties from Socialist clergymen to join with them to achieve the "Kingdom of God" here on earth. As early as 1909, two years before Thomas moved to East Harlem, A. R. Williams, a Socialist minister in Boston, asked him, "What new anesthetic have you been putting on your soul to keep you from declaring your loyalty to the cooperative commonwealth . . . ?" Thomas did not reply. As for politics, Thomas supported his ex-professor Woodrow Wilson both times he ran for President—"with joy" in 1912, with some misgivings due to Wilson's preparedness program in 1916.

The East Harlem Parish was an immigrant area, primarily Italian and Hungarian. Gangs, crime, vice, and poverty were common in the neighborhood; violence was practically a way of life. There was little Thomas could do about these conditions, although he did try to alleviate the economic distress of some of his parishioners by establishing a workshop in which 450 men and women found work at fifty cents a day for a short period during 1914. Thomas found it "heartbreaking to turn hundreds of others away who applied. . . ." Most of the residents in the area were not only poor, they were also "in the grip of Roman Catholicism." And the Roman Catholicism was not, to quote Thomas, "of the fine type so often found in America, but rather that of Southern Europe, with its bigotry, superstition, and low ethics."

Much of Thomas's ministry at the American Parish consisted of social work rather than simple parish work. Perhaps his most interesting contribution to the area was the development of a summer camp at Oak Ridge, New Jersey, on land donated by William S. Coffin. It offered 101 boys and 100 girls from the tenement area a two-week respite in the open countryside. The camp was particularly valuable during the poliomyelitis epidemic that struck New York's tenement districts in 1916. Thomas's primary job was organizing the camp and raising funds for it, which he did successfully.

Thomas helped build his parish; its membership increased from 487 in 1911 when he became pastor to 1,582 in 1916; Sunday School enrollment rose during the same period from 536 to 1,114. But not all of East Harlem appreciated Thomas's work among the poor and the unemployed. An unsigned "poison pen" letter warned Thomas to keep the unemployed "bums" out of the neighborhood. "Your Bowery methods are good for that section of the city, thank God far away from here. . . . This is a respectable law-abiding street and you have no right to disgrace us by carrying the bad element of other streets up here. . . . We hope that you will hear this warning else we will be obliged to use some other methods Uncle Sam has taught us to use against undesirable cranks."[5] Nothing ever came of this "warning."

Besides his social ministry, Thomas helped organize a special graduate program at Teachers College, Columbia University to train people to work with immigrants in city churches. It attracted fifteen girls who held undergraduate degrees from such prestigious institutions as Vassar, Mount Holyoke, Northwestern, Wilson, California, and Illinois, and was considered a success. The courses ran the gamut from languages to Bible to industrial arts, with a master's degree offered at the conclusion of the course. Thomas himself taught a course in immigration and administered the program.

While at East Harlem Thomas also began his career as a writer. His first major assignment was the preparation of a paper, delivered at a conference organized by the New York Presbytery in January 1916, on the relation of Christian industrial work to trade unions. Shortly thereafter the New York Presbytery assigned Thomas to write a book on Presbyterian urban work in New York. Entitled *The Church and the City*, it marked the first time Thomas exhibited his turn toward socialism.[6]

3

Before the outbreak of World War I, while still at his ministry in East Harlem, Thomas began to consider himself a non-Marxian Christian Socialist. It is probable that Thomas would eventually have joined the Socialist party even had the war not occurred, although there were some things about it that he did not like. He found, for one thing, its propaganda methods too bombastic; and, for another, what little discipline the party had over its members seemed to him too much for a "free spirit."

Thomas's opposition to the war was the most important consideration in his joining the party, but it was not the sole reason for his finally coming into the movement. Of equal importance was his long "observation and experience of our existing capitalism as it operated on the Upper East Side where I lived and worked." In 1920, two years after he joined the party, Thomas testified: "I came to the conclusion [in East Harlem] that it was extraordinarily difficult under the existing economic structure for men and women of any class to carry out the ethics of Jesus. . . . I am not arguing that Jesus was a Socialist. That would be highly unhistoric and unscientific. . . . I am saying that there are certain very definite ethical principles set forth in the Bible, in the New Testament. They are very searching principles as I

ch to say, that was
h man entering the
ng unto others what
bitterest woes were
cks of the poor and
gave long prayers.
istic. Paul told his
uld not eat, a princi-
ngs that are ascribed,
sent time. I came to
ll whether the very
wet with the blood
men and women in
as that wage is com-
saw children stunted
and soul by that sys-
ildren of the world's
of proper nutrition.
ible for men to work
unto the dignity of
were desirable. I my-
n the . . . law or sys-
hich created classes;
. These things made
on. I finally came to
to me to be the ethics
revolutionary recon-
aught that we are all
d. And so, rather re-
. . . the best way of
ble to live according
peace and well-being
lizable would be the
Socialist economics."
the brunt of his edu-
East Harlem. For he
ced him to ask ques-
orced to question the
ocial, industrial, and

political problems of the time could be solved when so many workers could not, even under the most favorable conditions, earn a livelihood.[7]

The New York which Thomas had chosen as his home had become a city of the very rich—who could virtually buy their way out of its loneliness and corruption (for which they might indeed be to blame)—and the poor, who could not escape from the city's deleterious effects. The middle class fled to the suburbs. The basic cause of all the faults of New York, Thomas asserted, was economic, and "no diagnosis of New York can be adequate until we try to consider what our modern organization of life on a ruthless, competitive system has meant." Thomas's philosophy was now obviously Socialist, though still not Marxian. He remained a Christian, and a Social Gospeler, but he was now a Social Gospeler who rejected reform of the capitalistic order and proclaimed socialism as his gospel. "Our present economic order is based on competition rather than [on] cooperation and upon selfishness rather than [upon] brotherhood. Under it thousands of families live with that sword of Damocles, fear of unemployment, over their heads. In a so-called democracy, men exist under an industrial autocracy and are compelled to become cogs of machinery."[8]

In early 1917, Thomas was invited to deliver the William Penn Lecture in Philadelphia before the Young Friends Movement. It was in this lecture that Thomas, for the first time, proclaimed in detail his political-social creed, a creed that was to remain basically unchanged for the remainder of his life. He described Christianity as profoundly revolutionary. In place of competition it offered cooperation, in place of worldly gain it offered service, in place of acquisitiveness it offered "the blessedness of giving." The church, Thomas declared, had to strive to achieve a social order based on these Christian precepts; it was essential that the church "strive to conquer the whole of life for Christ." Jesus's ethics had to be accepted by the church as something more than merely a beautiful sentiment. Not only did the church have to accept Christ's anti-capitalist ethic, each individual Christian had the same responsibility. A Christian could not be a Christian in church only; his social, civic, and economic life had to reflect this revolutionary philosophy. Conditions of extreme poverty and great luxury set limits on the possible attainment of genuine Christian brotherhood. A Christian system could never be achieved in a social order dominated by the business ethic because "the God of business is unlimited profit, Mammon, not Christal. . . ."[9]

It was thus as a Socialist Christian that Norman Thomas faced America's entry into World War I.

4

The role the war played in the development of Norman Thomas's views can hardly be overemphasized. When he joined the Socialist party in 1918, he was a Christian pacifist whose hatred for war was intense, passionate, and deeply personal. War was a blunt denial of all the Christian principles he had always taken for granted.

Although his antipathy to war can be traced to earlier days, Thomas's first active participation in the pacifist movement came in 1914, when he and another young minister, Allen McCurdy, founded a short-lived association of anti-war clergymen. (Thomas and McCurdy, incidentally, were among the few clergymen who remained steadfast in their opposition to war even after the United States became involved.) At about the same time that Thomas and McCurdy were organizing their group, a larger Christian pacifist organization, the Fellowship of Reconciliation, was being formed. Originally organized in Great Britain in 1914, an American section of the Fellowship was founded a year later. An association of Christians who maintained that the teachings of Jesus were opposed to any social order which considered war a "natural" social activity, the Fellowship's primary objective was a "better way of life" free of war. Some of the members of the Fellowship were Socialists, others were not.

Thomas was not one of the founders of the Fellowship, yet within a year of its founding he was one of its guiding lights. He was elected a member of its council and led a group organized by the Fellowship (which included such notable clergymen as John Haynes Holmes, Henry Sloane Coffin, and John Nevin Sayre) to petition the House Committee on Military Affairs against conscription. By the beginning of 1917, Thomas was so involved with the Fellowship that he considered resigning his parish ministry in order to devote most of his time to the organization. Shortly after America entered the war, he became a part-time member of the Fellowship's staff, and from that time on he devoted much of his time to anti-war activity.

Thomas was also active in the No-Conscription League, which included among its leaders Rabbi Stephen S. Wise, Juliet Poyntz, and the Reverend John Haynes Holmes. After 1916 he was also a member of the governing council of the American Union Against Militarism. Thomas felt honored to be included in a group which claimed such notable citizens as Lillian Wald, Jane Addams, Oswald Garrison Villard, and Max Eastman. The Union opposed American intervention in Mexico and the Caribbean, and later fought against American entry into World War I. Thomas and Roger Baldwin later helped organize the Civil Liberties Bureau within the American Union Against Militarism; it was the Civil Liberties Bureau which eventually evolved into the American Civil Liberties Union. Thomas was "closely associated with this movement from the beginning."[10]

5

Before 1914, Thomas's opposition to war was based primarily on religion. Examining war in the light of Christian teaching, he decided that the two were irreconcilable. Regardless of its objective, war was incompatible with Christianity on either philosophical or ethical grounds. By Christianity, Thomas did not mean the visible church; he offered no apology for organized Christianity. He meant the spirit of Jesus as he understood it. It was in this sense that Thomas was a Christian pacifist.

But as America drew closer to becoming embroiled in the war, Thomas's rationale turned more political, economic, and social. "Is not this war after all a contest between different empires, and is there not a lust for empire manifested on both sides?" he asked rhetorically in 1916. The idea of empire was not invented by Germany, he pointed out, nor was Germany the first nation to use military force to collect debts from weaker nations. The roots of war were to be found in the un-Christian social order "of which we are a part." The roots were to be found in particular in surplus capital unmatched by morality. The dominant class, Thomas believed, coveted the profits that could be made from exploiting the peoples of China, India, Africa, Morocco, Mexico, and many other small nations. Capitalism was the social order which contained "in it the seeds of . . . world catastrophe. . . ."

Thomas reiterated his belief that capitalism's basic principles were a "self-seeking and . . . practical denial of brotherhood"; and these basic principles were the cause of war. He also decried capitalism's militant patriotism. He agreed that "we owe what we are to society," yet denied that society and the state were the same. Man, in his view, owed what he was to all humanity, not merely to his own country. "Nations are but creatures of a day —humanity endures; and to make me transfer to my nation all the debt I owe mankind is fundamentally unjust."

Despite his pacifism, Thomas acknowledged that there were occasions when physical force might be justified, "but not the hideous violence of war." To be justifiable, force had to serve a redemptive purpose for the individual; and this could never be true of the wholesale slaughter of war. War was, in Thomas's view, anarchic, lacking the direction of police force, for example, which is employed against a known offender for his own ultimate redemption if possible. Thomas summed up his position on war when he said: "No righteous end can justify unholy means; no righteous end can be permanently attained by such means."[11]

6

When America declared war in 1917, churches throughout the nation announced suport of this country's military effort. This made Thomas furious. He assailed the churches for preaching the gospel of war in the name of the "Pacifist of Nazareth," and he derided the ecclesiastical authorities for preaching hatred of the Germans in the name of Jesus, who preached love of one's enemies. Thomas accused the churches of giving man a thoroughgoing religion of the state when they "beat the drums outside the recruiting offices."

Thomas was unsparing in his criticism of church support of the war. The error lay, he maintained, in a failure of most of the churches to understand the crisis which confronted mankind. Churches sent missionaries to the far reaches of the world to keep the heathens from perishing; yet their own sons were killing one another in a murderous war. The concept that the ends justify the means was, Thomas reiterated, the supreme ethical heresy; yet churches blessed the war as a means of achieving righteous aims. "How can we accept Christ as Lord and Master and deny his spirit by sharing responsibility for the unutterable horrors of war? Shall we cast out Satan by Satan?" he asked. The churches might at least have called an international conference to pray that "God might no longer be grieved by the spectacle of men, professing faith in the same Christ, killing one another. . . ."

Some churchmen charged that a victory for Germany would mean the death of Christianity and democracy, and that it was thus necessary to declare a moratorium on both. Thomas replied that if neither would work in the greatest crisis in history, it would be difficult for men to trust them once the war was over. How could men be sure that a dictator would yield his power after the war crisis had passed? Besides, "A victory based on espionage and poison gas would be no victory for Christianity."

Thomas conceded that liberation had followed some wars. But the cost had invariably been enormous, for war is a wasteful and destructive way of getting results. Its very nature is incompatible with the sense of universal comradeship and the power of sober thought needed to fulfill the dream of those who fought to end all fighting. Thomas believed in a universal moral law which made it impossible to win the Kingdom of Heaven on earth by war, for war is essentially an immoral means. Even if the question of means were ignored, he doubted that war could achieve the desired ends. "What terrible evils have followed even the noblest wars. One has gone, another has arisen. All the centuries of war have brought us to this end. Violence has not cast out violence."

After America's entry into the war, some of the clergy who had belonged to the Fellowship of Reconciliation resigned. One of these, the Reverend Ralph Harlow, defended his position by citing the democratic American war aims and the threat of Prussianism. Thomas firmly rejected Harlow's arguments: "It is absurd . . . to say we as a nation are animated in this war purely by love of democracy. Do you really think that our great papers like *The New York Times* which prate about war for democracy are fighting for democracy when they have devoted all their strength to oppose political and industrial democracy at home? Do you think this is a pure love of humanity when they have been the open defenders of a system which produces the unnumbered inhumanities of the industrial life? Do you think Americans in general, with their shameful record of race riots, are purely disinterested redressers of the crimes of Belgium and Armenia?"[12]

7

One of Thomas's major anti-war activities was the fight against the maltreatment of conscientious objectors. He had a personal interest in this problem since his brother, Evan, was one of the few "absolutist objectors" who refused to do any service —even work that was not connected with the war effort—under conscription. Evan was sentenced to twenty-five years in military prison for refusing to report for duty. While at the Fort Riley, Kansas, military stockade he led a hunger strike and was court-martialed for refusing to obey an order—to eat. He was then placed in solitary confinement and suffered corporal punishment. Other conscientious objectors were similarly maltreated, particularly members of obscure religious sects who refused, on theological grounds, to register for the draft or to accept any duty once conscripted, or those who objected on nonreligious philosophical or political grounds. This persecution led Thomas to write: "Men's affairs are in a sorry plight if it serves society to compel the individual to be true to his fellows by being untrue to himself."

Thomas agreed that the conscientious objector might be mistaken. But, he pointed out, democracy necessarily involved the right of a man to be mistaken without penalty. In a democracy each man has the right to decide for himself what is right or wrong. This is not a generous tolerance; it is a fundamental right. Thomas believed that it was the essence of democracy that the state exist for the individual, that conscience should be above the state. The assumption that the individual exists for the state he equated with Prussianism. Democracy implies an accommodation between the individual and society. Should the state be able to control men's convictions, it would become dangerous to society as well as to the individual. Should the state try to force a man who believes war is wrong to fight, he could in justice raise the cry: "We ought to obey God rather than man." Jesus had ruled that man should "render unto Caesar the things that are Caesar's and unto God the things that are God's"; and Thomas maintained that conscience is always God's.

Thomas was very much aware of the tragic effect of war upon the men who fought in it. History proved, he said, that war made possible the ascendance of man's bestial nature. Immorality and violation of the sanctity of the home were increased by war and the conditions in military camps. The events were so grave that they endangered Western civilization.

One of the causes of this degrading effect of war, according to Thomas, was the fact that few soldiers fought because they were crusading for a cause or desired to prove that they were bold. Most went unwillingly, either from a stern sense of duty or fear of public opinion. Those who served against their inner desire took it as a personal injury if another man escaped the draft. Men stationed in bases within the United States were, in Thomas's opinion, more virulent in their resentment against those who escaped service completely than were men who fought abroad. The effects of war were "a characteristic of the crowd mind."[13]

Not all conscientious objectors refused to bear arms on religious grounds; some refused because of political antipathy toward the war and the system which they considered its underlying cause. Although men who refused to accept military duty for religious reasons were given the privilege of asking for conscientious-objector status—which meant they could either avoid military service or work to enhance the war effort—political objectors had no such right. Thomas defended their position; their moral objection was as valid as objection for religious reasons. A political objector, persuaded that the ends of war did not justify the means, could be as much repelled by it, and as much entitled to consideration, he maintained, as was his religious counterpart.

The primary significance of the conscientious objector, in Thomas's view, was his refusal to concede to the state the right to dispose of him as it saw fit, even in time of war. Essentially, conscientious objectors were more effective against the idea of the divinity of the state—an idea which Thomas abhorred—than they were against war. They rejected the state's attempts to control men's consciences while affirming that under certain conditions civil disobedience was a duty no matter how severe the penalty. Although Thomas agreed with their position, he warned that civil disobedience was not to be undertaken lightly; it was not to be used as a "cloak for cynical contempt for the law." It was instead the "last recourse of brave and sincere souls" under trying conditions.

Looking back five years later, Thomas wrote of the conscientious objectors: "This insignificant fraction of the youth of America challenged the power of the state when it was mightiest and the philosophy of war when it was most pervasive. They didn't court martyrdom, but served principle. They didn't despise the state but merely refused to make it god." There were few objectors, "but the memory of their defiance may some day help break the spell which holds the patient masses like dumb driven cattle in obedience to the financiers and diplomats for whose intrigues they pay with their lives under the grip of the homicidal mania called patriotism."[14]

8

Even before America entered World War I, the Socialist party was in a period of electoral decline. Its vote had fallen from more than 900,000 in 1912 to approximately 500,000 in 1916. Internecine strife was rampant. Most European Socialists had already abandoned internationalism for nationalism, which in many cases led to a split in party ranks. With the United States involved in the war, the American party was facing the same problem. Would American Socialists support the war, or would they oppose it and hazard the consequences?

The American Socialists' answer was not long in coming. Rightly or wrongly, the party showed remarkable courage, for its position was to cost it many of its more prominent members (including Allan L. Benson, the 1916 Socialist presidential candidate) and bring persecution to many others at the hands of the federal government and self-appointed patriots. Sticking by its internationalism, the party officially opposed the war. After acrimonious debate the day after the United States declared war on Germany, the Socialist Party Emergency Convention in St. Louis voted 140 to 36 in favor of a resolution opposing the war.

The resolution proclaimed the party to be: ". . . unalterably opposed to the system of exploitation and class rule which is upheld and strengthened by military power and sham national patriotism. We, therefore, call upon the workers of all countries to refuse to support their governments in their wars. The wars of contending groups of capitalists are not the concern of the workers. . . . The working class of the United States has no quarrel with the working class of Germany or any other country. They have been thrown into this war by the trickery and treachery of the ruling class through its representatives. . . . We brand the declaration of war by our government a crime against the nations of the world. . . . It is not a war to advance democracy. . . . Democracy can never be imposed on any country by force of arms."

A pledge to offer "unyielding opposition to all proposed legislation for military conscription" and to support all "mass movements in opposition to conscription" was the center of a particularly heated debate. Most of the native-born intellectuals, like John Spargo, the multi-millionaire J. Phelps Stokes, and William English Walling, a leader of its left wing, deserted the party.

Its position on the war being compatible with his own, Thomas now drew nearer to the Socialist party. But neither Thomas nor most Socialists were as unequivocally opposed to the war as might appear on the surface. Meyer London of New York, the only Socialist in Congress, voted against American participation in the war but supported almost all measures for its prosecution—except the repressive Espionage Act under which radicals were persecuted. Algernon Lee, director of the Socialist Rand School of Social Science and a member of the New York Board of Aldermen, supported both the resolution against war and an appropriation for construction of the "artistic monstrosity" called the Victory Arch on Fifth Avenue. Thomas wrote Lillian Wald in 1918: "Frankly my own feeling with regard to the war is undergoing something of a change. On religious grounds I am still obliged to think that war is a hideously unsatisfactory method of righteousness, but the Russian situation and the progressive abandonment of imperialistic aims by the allies, under pressure from the President and British Labor, remove the reproach of hypocrisy from us, while the German people seem to be more completely under the dominance of their Junker class than I had thought."[15]

9

Given the direction in which Thomas's thinking was evolving, it is probable that he would have joined the Socialist party even if World War I had not come. But it was Thomas's Christian pacifism that propelled him into the party. America's entry into the war led Thomas into pacifist groups in which he became involved with members of the Socialist party. Moreover, the Socialist campaign in the 1917 New York elections was fought on the issues that Thomas considered crucial. The party's leading figure in New York, Morris Hillquit, made a special effort to bring Thomas into the party. Most of the native-born intellectuals resigned from the party when it adopted its anti-war resolution; of those left in the party leadership only Eugene V. Debs, an excellent agitator but certainly no intellectual, was a native-born American. Hillquit was born in Latvia, Victor Berger was a native of Austria-Hungary. Hillquit believed it was essential to bring "bright, young American" leaders into the party. He realized that a party based on immigrants could hardly become a major movement. He therefore paid special attention to Thomas, in whom he saw intellectual qualities and a charisma which he believed would attract young people to the movement.

Hillquit was the Socialist candidate for Mayor in New York in the 1917 election. Although he attacked the inequities of the political and economic system during the campaign, his main thrust was against the war. Thomas, impressed with Hillquit and with the anti-war character of his campaign, announced his support of Hillquit and became an active figure in his campaign.

The Socialists saw great significance in Thomas's coming out for Hillquit. Their spirits were buoyed because a native-born minister supported their candidate in a campaign in which Socialist speakers were assailed as "yellows" by Theodore Roosevelt, in which meetings were broken up by gangs of "patriots," and at a time when Postmaster General Albert S. Burleson was using his office to destroy the Socialist press. Thomas's letter pledging his support to Hillquit was reprinted on page one of the Socialist *New York Call;* he was named to the Hillquit Non-Partisan Board; and he was among the featured speakers at a Madison Square Garden rally for Hillquit.[16]

Thomas's support for Hillquit and his opposition to the war made his position at the American Parish untenable. The Parish was not self-sustaining; it required gifts from wealthy Presbyterians. His actions made it likely that many of the Parish's financial supporters would now withhold their gifts. He therefore resigned from his position in early 1918 to become full-time secretary of the Fellowship of Reconciliation and editor of its monthly journal, *The World Tomorrow*.[17]

Thomas was not yet a member of the party, for he still had serious doubts about political socialism. "How shall we then [under political socialism] protect individual initiative and freedom from the deadly weight, if not the actual tyranny, of an unsympathetic and unimaginative bureaucracy?" he asked. Despite his fears of bureaucratic domination, Thomas became active in the Intercollegiate Socialist Society—an organization of college-educated Socialists—because, "More and more it is becoming a choice with the thinking intellectual between alliance with the forces of conservatism or of socialism."

As late as September 1918, Thomas rejected those who importuned him to join the party. "What thus far deters me from membership in the party," he answered one Socialist, "is a fear of its tendency to trust to coercion rather than persuasion. The ultimate values in the world are those of personality, and no theory of the state, whether socialistic or capitalistic, is valid which makes it master, not servant, of man."[18]

Yet within a month Thomas decided to join the party. "Perhaps to certain members of the party my socialism would not be the most orthodox variety," he wrote Alexander Trachtenberg, party secretary. He told Trachtenberg that he was interested in the party only as an instrument for furthering ideals, and that he accepted the party platform in principle only, reserving the right to reject details. Moreover, he insisted that if he were a Midwestern farmer he would support the Non-Partisan League—a semi-Socialist agrarian political movement which attempted with some success to capture the Republican party in the Prairie States—despite the fact that this would mean his expulsion from the party. Despite his pacifism, he rejected some of the more bombastic passages of the party's anti-war St. Louis resolution.[19]

10

Norman Thomas's anti-war journalism soon attracted official notice. Postmaster General Albert S. Burleson, who tried to destroy the Socialist press during World War I, considered Thomas "more insidious" than even Debs. He held up mailings of many radical journals, including *The World Tomorrow*, and attempted to have Thomas indicted under the Espionage Act. John Nevin Sayre intervened successfully with his father-in-law, President Wilson, to prevent Thomas's indictment, but not before a federal judge had decried *The World Tomorrow* for talking too much about policies and for being anti-Wilson.[20]

After joining the Socialist party, Thomas became more and more alienated from his church. His opposition to the war was now based less on Christian ethics than on political socialism. Churchmen had criticized the use of violence by organized labor during the industrial strife which preceded the war. These same churchmen were now supporting organized international war. Thomas considered this incongruous because, he felt, revolutionary violence is less indiscriminate and more clearly directed against specific injustices than is modern international war. Revolutionary violence is also less likely to perpetuate itself in armies and militarism.

He now accepted the simplistic Socialist view of the cause of war: "The tap root of war is economic." It was the threat to American trade implied in the submarine blockade, and not the reported atrocities in Belgium and Armenia or the sinking of the Lusitania, that led America into the conflict. If conditions had been reversed and American trade had been conducted mainly with the Central Powers rather than with the Allies, "it is questionable whether the moral condemnation of Germany would have been so keen or the acceptance of Allied imperialism so uncritical."

After 1918, Thomas argued that in early times the origin of war lay in the impelling need to assure food supplies for growing populations. This caused migrations from Asia to Europe and the conflicts which accompanied them. By the seventeenth and eighteenth centuries military action was aimed at protecting markets. Britain in the eighteenth and nineteenth centuries, with her well-developed industries and empire, had no need for war, although she participated in the Opium War to force her trade upon China. Japan was opened for trade by veiled threats from the United States fleet. The Balkan wars were linked to arms-makers in need of greater markets. Armed conflicts in modern times have as their chief prize, Thomas said, control of raw materials. Investors are the modern makers of war. With saturation reached in home investments, these possessors of "surplus capital wrung out of the exploitation of the working class" must seek higher rates of interest in foreign investments or in loans to corrupt foreign rulers. It was this fiscal and economic rivalry between Britain, France, and Germany which, Thomas believed, caused World War I. Thomas deduced that it was fear of German industrial hegemony on the continent, along with the effect of German exports on French and British investment markets, particularly in the Near East, which were the real underlying causes of the war. No single nation was totally responsible; each shared responsibility. Thus, Thomas reasoned, whole nations stumbled into war in support of their investors.[21]

Thomas's conversion to socialism did not bring with it an immediate total rejection of Christianity. He remained an ethical Christian and a pacifist for some time afterward. He believed that the labor and Socialist movements had replaced the church as the moving force for internationalism and brotherhood. He also believed that in the end men would have to turn to Christ to achieve universal brotherhood. "From the destruction of greed and selfishness and fear, from the emptiness of ecclesiastical form and ceremony, from a mere humanitarianism working through economic and social readjustment, men will yet turn to Christ that they may find life more abundant." As a Socialist, Thomas summed up his position in 1920 when he said that only a positive pacifism, which added class-consciousness to its religious anti-war philosophy, could have averted World War I. He still rejected violence as a means for achieving the ultimate victory of humanity; a left-wing Armageddon was not part of his theology. He doubted that any change in the social order could compensate for a world-wide Civil War, the legacy of which would be misery and general chaos. Unless man could find a way to a revolutionary social order without violence, there could be no "City of God" or Utopia on earth.[22]

11

Thomas's path to the Socialist party was long and tortuous. It began in a conservative manse in a little county seat in Ohio; it wound its way through Princeton, social work, Union Theological Seminary, and East Harlem until it reached the Social Gospel, which foretold a heaven on earth. Yet it was only normal that, having chosen the gospel of salvation on earth through a reorientation of society from competition to cooperation, Norman Thomas should accept the need for political action to achieve that end. The only political road he could find that led to the end he sought was that of the Socialist party.

Thomas's philosophy when he entered the Socialist party contained elements of Marxist, anarchist, and Christian thought. He accepted the Marxian interpretation of history in his analysis of the economic basis for war; his ethical revulsion against the competitive capitalistic system and against violence was basically Christian. His rejection of the supremacy of the state over the individual was primarily individualistic anarchist. Like George Lansbury in Great Britain, during this period Thomas was basically a Christian-Libertarian Socialist.

II
Road to
leadership

The Socialist party of the 1920's, the decade during which Norman Thomas emerged as its nominal leader, was a weak and declining organization. Membership had fallen from 118,000 in 1919 to 12,474 in 1923. More than thirty thousand left-wing members resigned in 1919 to join one of the new Communist groups which came into being as a result of the Bolshevik Revolution. The once-thriving Socialist press was fast disappearing; the *New York Call*, the party's leading daily organ, had collapsed in 1923. Of seventy Socialist newspapers published in 1912, only seven remained in 1923. Abraham Cahan, a founder of the party and editor of the pro-Socialist *Jewish Daily Forward*, conceded by 1923 that the Socialists had failed to become a major force in American political life. David Karsner, the former managing editor of the *Call*, called the Socialist party of the early 1920's "a political ghost stalking in the graveyard of current events seeking respectable burial." The party, he said with justification, had been reduced to a "debating society, whose remaining members are not particularly conscientious in attendance."[1]

2

Internal disputes developed in inverse proportion to the party's strength. Behind these factional fights was the revolution in Russia more than five thousand miles away. No issue had ever before so completely captured the imagination of Socialists as had the Bolshevik seizure of power, nor had any so disrupted the American Socialist party.

The continual bickering in the party irked Thomas; he was, after all, a reasonably new member not yet inured to the incessant dispute over fine points of dogma which had become the hallmark of Socialist organizations. Thomas was not unsympathetic with the Russian Revolution—he had, in fact, lent his home for a pro-Soviet meeting in 1919—but he did oppose any attempt to transport that revolution to the United States with its unique social, economic, and political system and history.

The internal feuding in the Socialist party resulted in 1919 in its division into three parts—the Socialist party, the Communist Labor party, and the Communist party. There were thus four distinct socialist parties in the United States, the old, small, and doctrinaire Socialist Labor party being the fourth. Writing of the 1919 situation, Thomas noted the similarity between these splits and the various schisms in the history of the Christian church. The Communist party and the Communist Labor party, he found, were more obsessed with the proletarian dictatorship and "Revolution and a capital 'R'" than they were with socialism. The only difference between the two Communist parties, he observed, was the "rather arbitrary fashion" by which the Communist party was dominated by members whose native language was Russian. Both, he said sarcastically, were "more Bolshevik than Lenin." Moreover, he was annoyed at their carping criticisms of the Socialist party for being too much interested in reform measures, despite the fact that the latter had adopted a manifesto "which gives in clear and unmistakable language an uncompromisingly Socialist exposition of the war and the peace, of capitalism and imperialism."

The one good effect of the split, Thomas discerned, was to drive from the Socialist movement many "pathological cases," persons who dreamt of future violence and possible revolutionary greatness, and who loved mystery and intrigue. He did not deny that the Communists had also drawn many younger, "ardent spirits" whom the Socialist party could not afford to lose, that the continuing wrangling in the radical movement had disgusted thousands of former supporters who now dropped out of the radical movement completely. "The Communist fight against us has not made Communists, but Democrats and Republicans." If only the left-wing parties would stop hurling vile epithets at each other and get busy in the educational and industrial fields, "they might later be in a position to work out the tactics of revolution."[2]

3

During the "Red Scare" of 1919–1921, Thomas was honored by having his name listed by the arch red-hunter Archibald Stevenson among sixty-two "dangerous enemies" of the United States. Among the organizations with which Thomas was affiliated—and which Stevenson cited in documenting Thomas's radicalism—were the American Union Against Militarism, the National Civil Liberties Bureau, the Liberty Defense Union, the Fellowship of Reconciliation, and the National Conference of Labor. Listed with Thomas were Jane Addams, Henry J. Cadbury, Roger Baldwin, Charles A. Beard, Morris Hillquit, Reverend John Haynes Holmes, Episcopal Bishop Paul Jones, Rabbi Judah Magnes, James Maurer, Amos Pinchot, Oswald Garrison Villard, Lillian Wald, James P. Warbasse, and Eugene Victor Debs.

Thomas's activities during the early 1920's might have given Stevenson some justification. Thomas was, in fact, active on three fronts: civil liberties, labor, and international affairs. He was a delegate to the 1921 Amnesty Congress in Washington, whose objective was to win freedom for radicals and other opponents of the war still held in prison. He spoke at a mass rally in Madison Square Garden in opposition to United States intervention in Russia, calling the members of the expeditionary force "mercenaries." He was active in the 1919 textile strikes in Passaic and Paterson, New Jersey. He was also instrumental in raising a relief fund for striking miners, and helped organize Pullman porters, paper-box workers, and insurance company employees.

During the Passaic textile strike, the local authorities, in an effort to keep Thomas from speaking, turned out the lights in the auditorium—and so he read the Declaration of Independence in the dark, prefacing his reading by remarking: "This consigning of the Declaration of Independence to outer darkness is exactly what is happening in Passaic." In Mount Vernon, New York, Thomas, John Haynes Holmes, and Rose Schneiderman, leader of the Women's Trade Union League, were arrested for reading the Bill of Rights and the New York State Constitution at a street-corner in defiance of a local ban against such meetings. The case against them was finally dismissed, though it was not until seventeen years later that the principle that street meetings are a right was established in another case in which Thomas played a role.[3]

Thomas continued to divorce himself from the organized Christian Church. He resigned from the board of the Philadelphia Society, a Princeton Christian group, because "my own views are so much more radical than those of the [other members of] the Board that my presence on it might not be wholly desirable. . . ." Nor was he particularly impressed with the interfaith movements aimed at developing tolerance and understanding between the religions. He was invited to attend one of the organizational meetings of the National Conference of Christians and Jews. After listening to several explanations of how religion had made men feel more "brotherly" and how religion had made for unity in America, Thomas spoke up: "I remember my somewhat distant connection with Doubting Thomas," he remarked, and went on to question the historical accuracy of the speakers who preceded him. "For as I read history it was a simple fact that the Jews were the chosen people. God said so, God did it; it wasn't their fault; they were the chosen people and the others weren't chosen. Period. It is a well-known and essential doctrine of the Catholic Church that 'outside the [Catholic] church there is no salvation. . . .' As for the Protestant sects . . . their record is not good. The liberty they sought for themselves in religion they rarely extended gladly to others. . . . [Although] the Protestants were not sure that other Protestants could not get to heaven, they were quite sure that they, Methodists, Presbyterians, what have you, had priority and that it was a little unfortunate for people to waste their time on these secondary sects since they had to learn so much over again when they got to Paradise." It was the last time he was invited to a meeting of the National Conference of Christians and Jews.[4]

Now determined to devote his life to the radical movement, Thomas also severed all ties with the most bourgeois part of his past—among other things, his membership in the upper-class Colonial Club at Princeton to which he was elected in 1904. In his letter of resignation, he wrote: "I am persuaded after long thought that the whole club system of Princeton is not for the best interests of the University, still less is it appropriate to that new era of democracy which it is my profound hope will dawn upon the earth."[5]

4

Many of the views Thomas held when he entered the Socialist party underwent major changes during his early years as a member. Most significant among these changes was his position on war. Thomas was still basically a pacifist during the 1920's; but he no longer considered pacifism an end in itself, and now believed that political action was a necessary part of effective opposition to war. It was useless simply to point out the horror and futility of war, he argued. It was necessary to work for the establishment of a fellowship of free men capable of bringing about an enduring peace. More important, he insisted, pacifism must not be mistaken for passivism. Thomas thus argued that it was necessary to develop effective nonviolent means which would preclude war. Such means, he believed, would be found in the use of electoral politics and in the organization of labor in powerful trade unions.

Despite his pro-labor activity, Thomas was not blind to the weaknesses of trade unions. He found factionalization, machine rule, coercion, hypocrisy, and overcentralization as prevalent in unions as in the state. Moreover, the ruling factions within unions disregarded democratic processes. "The problem," Thomas believed, "is not the problem of one form of organization but of organization in general. In our modern world, more than ever before we must have organization, and efficient organization, but neither in church nor state nor labor unions has man learned how to organize without some loss of brotherhood and freedom. . . ."[6]

No topic was more heatedly discussed among Socialists than the pros and cons of bolshevism. In the early days immediately after the Russian Revolution, Thomas found much in bolshevism that met with his approval. He was, in particular, favorably inclined toward bolshevism's insistence on "the democratization of industry and expropriation of landlords." He was similarly impressed with the cultural autonomy offered the non-Russian minorities and the independence granted Finland. But on one issue Thomas was vehemently opposed to the Bolshevik regime—the issue of civil liberties. "Men cannot . . . justify the coercion of personality by military conscription by calling the new idol the proletariat instead of the state. . . . [We] are unalterably persuaded that if the Bolshevik power can live on no other basis than by the suppression of discussion its days are numbered. . . . [We] are persuaded of one firm truth, that if the workers of the world have set before their eyes the ideals of freedom and brotherhood the last way to attain their goal is by the road of dictatorship, proletarian or otherwise." Not all of the Social Gospel Socialists agreed; a bishop once told Thomas: "Of course, when I pray to God I am really thinking of Lenin and Trotsky and all the workers of the world."[7]

An issue often ignored by Socialists in 1919 was race, but Thomas refused to ignore it. Nor did he suggest that it could be solved by a simple change of the economic order, as did most Socialists, although he considered such a change to be essential to ending race hatred and persecution. Race prejudice was, Thomas maintained, a sign of cultural deprivation; the Southern states, where race relations were at their worst, were also the states where culture was least developed. "You cannot deny to your fellow man elementary justice; you cannot be brutal and hypocritical and manage to sustain for yourself real freedom of body or mind or spirit, you cannot be creators of civilization or art or music or beauty or discoverers of truth, while . . . the common life is poisoned by injustice and inequity and oppression." The real victim of the persecution of the black man was thus not the Negro alone; the white man was an equal sufferer: ". . . although we have been the master race and the dominant race our souls have been defiled, and . . . our body politic has been corrupted and poisoned by the atrocity and cruelty of our attitude toward our black fellow citizens."[8]

5

Thomas's rise in the Socialist movement began almost as soon as he became a party member. Within a matter of weeks he was a featured speaker at the tenth annual convention of the Intercollegiate Socialist Society. The rise was natural; Thomas was one of the few native-born intellectuals left in the party. Most of the others resigned to support the war; by 1919 the lure of the Communist movement had attracted most of those who remained Socialists. In 1921, Thomas was considered one of the likely candidates for Mayor of New York City (along with James Oneal, Judge Jacob Panken, Scott Nearing, and Charles Ervin), but he refused to allow himself to be considered because of persistent illness in his family. After resigning the editorship of *The World Tomorrow* in 1921, Thomas devoted most of his energy to the Intercollegiate Socialist Society and its successor, the League for Industrial Democracy. The ISS was founded in 1905 by a group of college-educated Socialists, because, as its first president, Upton Sinclair, said, "since the professors would not educate the students, it was up to the students to educate the professors." Within a year there were college chapters at the best schools, including Wesleyan and Columbia. From its earliest days the ISS published a journal, the *Intercollegiate Socialist*, and held large meetings at which Socialist ideas were expounded by such noted lecturers as Sinclair, Jack London, and Harry W. Laidler. In 1910, Laidler became secretary of the ISS, a post he was to hold for almost half a century. The internal schisms created by the war and the Russian Revolution caused the ISS to fall into serious decline. By 1921, it was necessary for the ISS to reorganize itself into the broader-based League for Industrial Democracy, which was open to noncollegians. In 1922, Thomas and Laidler became the co-executive directors of the renamed organization whose professed aim was: "Production for use, not for profit."[9]

6

After Thomas resigned as editor of *The World Tomorrow*, he accepted an appointment as associate editor of the *Nation*, one of the leading liberal weeklies in the country. He was by then established as an able journalist and editor. Therefore, in 1923 when the *New York Call* was replaced by the pro-labor, though officially non-Socialist, *New York Leader*, Thomas was the logical choice for editor.

The *Call* had never been a successful newspaper; its circulation reached its apex at fifty thousand in 1917. By 1923, that circulation had fallen to less than ten thousand. The internal disputes, the continual splits, the persecution during the war had all taken their toll. The needle trades unions—the International Ladies Garment Workers Union and the Amalgamated Clothing Workers Union, both of which had been the mainstays of Socialist support in New York—joined with a few local organizations and formed a corporation which attempted to salvage what they could of the *Call*. With their own funds, plus a sizable grant from the American Fund for Public Service, they reorganized the old *Call* and renamed it the *New York Leader*. With Thomas as editor, and Heber Blankenhorn, an experienced newspaper- man, as managing editor, the *Leader* was born.

The *Leader* was a newspaper designed for popular taste with standard features and standard news coverage. Its sports pages, among the best in the city, were edited by Ed Sullivan, who was later to gain fame as a columnist for the *New York Daily News* and as a television star. But it finally never got off the ground. Its circulation never reached thirty thousand, despite the fact that the unions affiliated with it had more than 300,000 members. It had virtually no advertising. In three months the unions had poured $80,000 into the newspaper, and they refused to put any more funds into it. Thus, the *Leader* died after a short three months' life.

Why did the *Leader* fail? Thomas blamed it on the internal feud between left and right in the unions. Under orders from Thomas the *Leader* remained neutral in internal union squabbles; he demanded fairness and accuracy of his reporters and writers in coverage of internal union news. This was the opposite of what the labor leaders wanted. They had expected the newspa- per to attack the left-wingers.

While he was editor of the *Leader*, Thomas also tried his hand at organizing a union of newspapermen. He founded the Press Writers Union, but it was denied an AFL charter, and the orga- nization was still-born.[10]

7

The Socialist election campaign of 1920 in which Eugene V. Debs ran for President while a convict in the Atlanta Federal Penitentiary was, on the surface, a success. Debs had polled his highest vote, though it was a lower percentage of the total vote than in 1912. But almost all Socialists knew that the 1920 vote was not a Socialist vote—it was basically a protest against the anti-Red repressions of the day and a personal tribute to Debs. Moreover, few local Socialist candidates made respectable show- ings. It was now apparent that the Socialist party had little future as an independent, unaffiliated electoral force.

A special Socialist party convention in 1921 therefore decided to "ascertain the degree of readiness to be found in liberal, progressive, and radical groups for independent political action." Thus, in a complete reversal of their traditional opposition to the formation of a federated, independent labor party similar to that in Britain, American Socialists decided to undertake the preliminary work aimed at forming such a party. In this instance necessity was, apparently, the mother of concession.

The party's new stance was in line with Thomas's thinking. He had for some time believed that a labor party could play a significant role in establishing socialism in the United States. To be of genuine value a labor party, Thomas insisted, would require a program that went beyond immediate economic and political demands; it had, in fact, to have a philosophy close to socialism. As early as 1919, when it was still considered a heresy among Socialists, Thomas had favored a labor party, even if it had no pro-Socialist philosophy, providing it barred coalitions with the major parties. The role of the Socialist party in such a labor party, Thomas felt, should be that of a constituent member. The Socialists would thus be able to maintain their separate identity while supporting labor party candidates in elections.[11]

The Socialists changed their stance at a propitious time, for a major move toward independent political action was underway independent of the Socialists. A group of progressive politicians and railroad labor men had already begun preliminary discussions from which was to emerge the Conference for Progressive Political Action and the LaFollette Campaign of 1924.

8

The 1924 election was the first in which Thomas ran for public office; it was also the first in the party's history in which the Socialists did not run their own presidential ticket.

The Socialists were active in the organization of the Conference for Progressive Political Action, almost from its inception. They participated in the 1922 February meeting at which the CPPA was formally organized by a combination of progressive political organizations and the Socialist party. The Socialists were particularly interested in turning the CPPA into "an independent party of labor and farmers," and in excluding from its ranks the

Communists, who had become a disruptive factor in labor and left-wing politics.

By early 1924, "labor party fever" was high in Socialist ranks. In Britain, the Labor party had made sensational gains and had formed a minority government. "If British labor can do it, why can't we?" Thomas asked. Certainly, he argued, the American workingman was as capable of realizing his political power as was his British counterpart. Perhaps the new American labor party might not elect a President in 1924; but then it was not necessary that a labor party be "born fully grown and fully armored for conflict." He believed the new labor party could capture some state and local governments and in time could, undoubtedly, hold the balance of power nationally. The end result would be that the workers and farmers would exert an influence far beyond any they had previously exerted. "[Until] labor makes its influence felt in politics, government will remain on the side of privilege." Thomas ridiculed the American Federation of Labor's insistence that it would reward its friends and punish its enemies, on a nonpartisan basis, at the ballot box within the context of the two major parties. That, he said, was as ridiculous as assuming that labor could win in the industrial field "by rewarding good employers and punishing bad." Thomas and his fellow Socialists were not alone in assuming that an American labor party was in the making. Harold Lord Varney, a labor journalist, agreed that Samuel Gompers' "nonpartisan" policy for the American Federation of Labor was dying: "With the star of the incredible British Labor victory before the eyes of the American unions, the old nonpartisan achievements of the American Federation of Labor must seem pale and inadequate in comparison. Perhaps in the Conference for Progressive Political Action we already have the embryo form of the great adventure of the American trade unions."[12]

The *Nation* sent Thomas as its reporter to the February 1924 preparatory meeting of the CPPA in St. Louis. His enthusiasm was reinforced: the program adopted by the organization was everything he—and most Socialists—had hoped for. It called for public ownership and democratic control of the railroads and for public ownership of water power; public control of natural resources, including oil and coal; a limit on the use of injunctions in industrial disputes; federal farm marketing; and trial by jury in contempt of court cases. Most important—to Thomas, at least —it took a firm stand against war and imperialism. Thomas was hopeful that the real beginning of a labor party was about to be made.

Not all Socialists were as enthusiastic as Thomas and the other Socialist party leaders. Some rejected an alliance with the Progressives: "If they [the Progressives] want a change, a real third party, let them come into the Socialist party. There is no middle ground. The system under which we live must either be Capitalistic or Socialistic, consequently there should be no compromise on the part of the Socialist movement." Others were less than enthusiastic about the man who was the obvious choice of the CPPA for President, Senator Robert M. LaFollette of Wisconsin. One Socialist charged that "LaFollette is not interested in the fundamental cause of the Labor movement. He is interested in his ambition and everything must be subordinated to this aim." Socialists had good reason to question LaFollette; he was no Socialist, nor was he even a labor man. He was instead an old-school Western radical whose ideas were basically those of the Populist party of the turn of the century.[13]

The Socialist opposition to LaFollette was not limited to rank-and-file members or to small, unimportant segments of the party. At the Wisconsin state convention, Daniel Hoan, Socialist Mayor of Milwaukee, attempted to instruct that state's delegation to support LaFollette only if he pledged to support the formation of a permanent labor party.

The division within their party caused the Socialists to call their convention for two days after the CPPA meeting. The reasoning was obvious: If the CPPA named a ticket independent of the two major parties and voted to organize a new party, the Socialists would support that ticket. If, on the contrary, the CPPA named two "old-party men," or backed one or the other of the major candidates, the Socialists would name their own ticket.

Even among the Socialist delegates to the July 4 CPPA convention in Cleveland at which LaFollette was nominated, there was serious division. A minority felt that unless a labor party were formed immediately the Socialists should name their own ticket. The majority, including Norman Thomas, who was a delegate from the League for Industrial Democracy, wanted to back LaFollette under any conditions. They noted that the British Labor party had for some years functioned as the Labor Representation Committee within the Liberal party. The final decision at the Socialist caucus supported the latter, majority, view.[14]

The CPPA convention nominated LaFollette and adopted a platform that almost duplicated the Socialist program—except for its ultimate goal. The delegates also agreed to instruct the national committee to call a meeting for January 1925 to decide on organizing a permanent national party. The Joint Executive Council of the CPPA elected at the convention included William H. Johnston, of the Machinists Union; Edward Keating, of the railroad brotherhoods; Morris Hillquit, of the Socialist party; Lynn J. Frazier, of the Non-Partisan League; and chairman John M. Nelson and vice-chairman Robert M. LaFollette, Jr. One other name was added shortly after the convention had adjourned—Norman Thomas of New York, representing the League for Industrial Democracy. The choice of a vice-presidential candidate was left to LaFollette.

The Socialist convention was stormy. The majority, to which Thomas belonged, wanted to endorse LaFollette, and was led by Hillquit and Berger; the larger minority group, headed by William H. Henry of Indiana, insisted that the CPPA was no labor party and that the Socialists should nominate their own ticket; a second, smaller minority, led by New York Municipal Court Judge Jacob Panken, wanted to withhold support from LaFollette until it was known who the vice-presidential candidate would be. A telegram from Debs urging the convention not to nominate a candidate for President but to keep the party intact "and the Red flag flying," which was read to the convention just before it voted on the issue, caused all opposition to collapse. By a vote of 115 to 17 the Socialist party endorsed LaFollette.[15]

The Socialists hoped that the vice-presidential nomination would go to a Socialist or, at least, to a labor man. William M. Feigenbaum, associate editor of the Socialist weekly *New Leader*, had said only a week before the convention that although Socialists would back LaFollette they would expect a labor man of the stature of James H. Maurer, Socialist President of the Pennsylvania State Federation of Labor, to be the vice-presidential candidate. If, on the contrary, "the Vice Presidential candidate is merely a political insurgent like Senator Wheeler . . .

the Socialists are hardly likely to support" the Progressive ticket. LaFollette chose Senator Burton K. Wheeler, a progressive Democrat from Montana, as his running mate, and, despite Feigenbaum's statement to the contrary, the Socialists supported him.[16]

Once committed to the CPPA and LaFollette's candidacy, the Socialists gave, to quote LaFollette's son, Robert Jr., yeoman service even where such service might have been against their own plans. But it was apparent from the outset that the Socialists were to give much but get little in return.[17]

9

By supporting LaFollette for President and Wheeler for Vice-President the Socialists had obviated the necessity of naming a national ticket; but the Socialists were still responsible for state and local candidates where they were strong enough to field such tickets. In New York, after considerable coaxing, Norman Thomas was nominated for Governor. Thomas knew he had no chance of defeating Liberal Democrat Alfred E. Smith, but he accepted the nomination because he thought it would give him an opportunity to stump New York State for LaFollette and Wheeler, "the most hopeful event in American politics in our generation," and because it would give him a chance to work for a farmer-labor party. But not all LaFollette supporters were ready to back Thomas. Most made it clear that they intended to support Smith. So seriously did some of the LaFollette people feel about supporting Smith that it was necessary for the LaFollette-Wheeler campaign committee in New York to order "that all speakers appearing under the auspices of this committee . . . confine themselves to the LaFollette-Wheeler national ticket and its national platform." One LaFollette supporter tried to form a LaFollette-Smith Non-Partisan League, which would circulate advisory ballots on how to split a ballot and vote for both candidates. He expressed the hope that Thomas would drop his candidacy, but he feared Hillquit and Thomas "are far too romantic for that."

There was genuine fear among many progressives that Thomas was going to cut deeply into Smith's vote and thus cause his defeat. (There was some basis for this fear on the part of the

Smith supporters; in 1920 the Socialists had polled 169,000 votes, while Smith was defeated by 109,000 votes.)[18] Labor leaders, except for a few Socialist local union officials in Salamanca and Buffalo, the leaders of the needle trades unions, officers in a few small building craft locals and Dr. Henry B. Linville, president of the Teachers' Union, opposed Thomas. The state conference of the CPPA, which accorded Hillquit and Fiorello LaGuardia, progressive congressman from New York City, standing ovations, virtually ignored Thomas. A spokesman for the railroad unions made clear that "under no circumstances would any of the Brotherhoods endorse the Socialist state ticket."[19]

Thomas campaigned actively, making an average of three speeches a day—on some days five or six—and visiting virtually every city in the state. But he ignored his own candidacy and campaigned for the national LaFollette-Wheeler ticket. The most impressive single meeting of the campaign was the LaFollette rally at Madison Square Garden. Until that time the largest political rally in New York history, it drew fourteen thousand people, of whom seven thousand paid from fifty-five cents to two dollars for seats (charging for seats was a Socialist innovation). Another six to seven thousand could not get in because the hall was overcrowded, and had to hear the speeches over amplifiers outside. Norman Thomas, who received an ovation second only to that accorded LaFollette, struck out at the national Democratic and Republican parties: he assailed the Democrats as "the party of the Espionage Law, the cruel and illegal anti-Red raids, the spy system, the war frauds, child labor in the South, A. Mitchell Palmer [Attorney General under Wilson] and his anti-labor injunctions"; and he labeled the Republicans the party of "Forbes, Fall, and Dougherty [principals in the Teapot Dome Scandal], the party of Judge Gary and company-owned towns, the party of big business and big injunctions against labor."[20]

On election day, LaFollette polled 4,800,000 votes, Norman Thomas fewer than 100,000. LaFollette had run particularly well in the Midwest, the Rocky Mountain states, and the Pacific Coast (he carried only his home state of Wisconsin). Two Socialist candidates were elected to Congress, Victor Berger of Wisconsin and Fiorello LaGuardia of New York City. (LaGuardia was, in fact, a progressive Republican who supported LaFollette, and thus ran on the Socialist and Independent tickets.)

The Socialist contribution to the LaFollette vote was significant. In New York City, for example, LaFollette did extremely well in the districts Socialists had historically dominated. In the same districts, the progressive vote went for Smith; throughout the city Thomas ran more than 40 per cent behind the rest of the ticket.[21]

Despite his own poor showing, Thomas was elated at the La-Follette vote. It was "proof of the existence of a sentiment in the United States plenty strong enough to warrant a new party." But within a month it was apparent that the dream of a labor party was going up in smoke. The American Federation of Labor at its El Paso convention rejected overwhelmingly a motion by ex-Socialist Max Hayes of Cleveland that it begin to organize such a party. Judge Panken, who had doubts about the LaFollette campaign from the very outset, was now bitter. "We expected a Labor party out of the Cleveland [CPPA] convention. What did we get?" He noted that labor unions, which had formerly financed Socialist campaigns, had given their money instead to the CPPA. "We gave everything and gained nothing," Panken concluded. The final blow fell at the CPPA's last meeting on February 21–22, 1925. Three of the four railroad unions at the CPPA's final convention opposed the formation of a labor party; LaFollette's followers wanted another Progressive party, which the Socialists rejected out of hand. Only the Socialists, William H. Johnston of the Machinists Union, and the spokesmen for the needle trades unions, favored a labor party. The CPPA died at that meeting in Chicago, and the dream of an American equivalent to the British Labor party died with it.[22]

In retrospect, why did the Socialists support LaFollette? They knew he had no genuine commitment to a labor party; they knew the American labor movement was basically opposed to the concept of independent political action. The truth was that the Socialist party leadership knew they had no alternative. The party was in such weakened condition, after the war persecutions and the Communist schisms, that it could not run a national ticket of its own. Looking back, Thomas agreed that the party had wasted its energies on the campaign, but he also noted that there was no alternative. The net effect of the LaFollette campaign on the Socialist party was catastrophic. Between 1924 and 1925 it suffered a loss of almost two thousand members.

Thomas noted that the Socialists had become so involved in the LaFollette campaign that the party organization was collapsing. Yet, twenty-five years later, Thomas still maintained that the risk of backing LaFollette in 1924 in the hope of forming a labor party "was worth taking even though we lost." Thomas did concede, however, that the party suffered because of his "own folly in throwing everything into the national election to the neglect" of his own state organization and campaign.[23]

10

Yet the LaFollette debacle did not dampen Thomas's Socialist ardor. He remained active in a movement that was in the doldrums, but his activity was limited primarily to fighting for civil liberties and appealing to middle-class intellectuals like himself for support of the party. In 1925, for example, he spoke on twenty-nine college campuses in New England, the Middle Atlantic states, and the Midwest. In that same year he also edited the League for Industrial Democracy's biweekly news service. In 1926, he addressed more than 45,000 persons in 175 speeches and lectures, primarily at colleges and universities. It would be unfair to ignore Thomas's activity for the working class, but this involvement was primarily in defense of civil liberties and came basically out of a feeling of *noblesse oblige*. The high point of his work for labor was reached during the 1926 textile strike in Passaic, New Jersey.

Textile workers were generally among the most exploited in the United States. Wages were low, hours of labor long, and they were denied basic constitutional rights by local governments which were virtually controlled by mill owners. Among textile hands, the Botany Mills in Passaic had a reputation as the worst in the industry. Moreover, the United Textile Workers of the AFL made little effort to organize the workers in the mill, most of whom were unskilled. A new union was formed by Harvard-educated Albert Weisbord, who resigned as Socialist organizer in Massachusetts in 1924 to join the Communist party. In April 1926, the thirteen thousand employees at Botany went out on strike.

The police and courts of Passaic and adjacent Garfield were used to terrorize the strikers. Justice of the Peace Lewis M.

Hargreaves, a bill-collector by trade, declared himself a martial-law court despite the fact that there had, in fact, been no declaration of martial law. Arthur Garfield Hays, a leading civil liberties attorney, found it "perfectly evident that strikers cannot get justice. . . . Never have I seen anything equal to this." Arrested strikers were forced to raise unusually high bail, defendants were denied right to counsel, and Justice Hargreaves prohibited the taking of notes in his court. To add insult to injury, the mill and the city administration made it impossible for the union to rent a meeting hall in Passaic or Garfield.

It was to fight these breaches of civil liberties that Thomas became involved in the Passaic strike. He rented a vacant lot in Garfield to hold a mass meeting which attracted three hundred strikers and supporters. The local sheriff read the riot act, which Thomas ignored as he began speaking from the stump of an old apple tree. "We have come here to test our rights as American citizens to hold a peaceful meeting for a legal and legitimate purpose," Thomas said. He congratulated the assembled strikers on their forebearance and peaceful behavior. Then, suddenly, before Thomas could finish his speech, a sheriff blew a whistle, cried "Clear 'em out," routed the crowd, and arrested Thomas.

The deputies (there were at least fifty at the meeting) whisked Thomas off. Attempts to locate him were futile; reporters for the *Nation* and the *New York Times* who tried to find him were forcibly ousted from police headquarters. Finally, hours later, after he was denied an opportunity to consult with an attorney, Thomas was held in $10,000 bail and charged with disorderly conduct. The bail was set so late at night that the sheriff would not accept it until the following morning, so Thomas spent the night in jail.

The police conceded that the meeting had been peaceful before the sheriff's men interrupted it; still they maintained that Thomas had been disorderly because he had ignored the riot act. Thomas's attorney, a conservative civil libertarian named John Larkin Hughes, noted that there was no riot law in New Jersey, that such a law was "a figment of the imagination of somebody in this county." In October, almost six months later, with the strikers defeated and too late to salvage the constitutional right to free assembly and speech, the Bergen County grand jury cleared Thomas.

Thomas's growing disillusionment with the church was but-
tressed by his strike experience. Within a week after his arrest,
Thomas attempted, as a Presbyterian minister, to discuss the
strike situation at a meeting of the Presbytery of Hudson, Passaic, and Bergen Counties at the Passaic Presbyterian Church.
After a stormy debate, he was denied the floor. Disgusted,
Thomas warned the churchmen that "the attitude of the churches
in the crisis only serves to convince the laboring class that the
terms Christian charity, fair play, and constitutional rights are
nothing but bunk," and thus was turning the workers to communism.[24]

III
Emergence of
the leader

The Socialist party's decline continued at an accelerated rate in the decade after the war. Its membership, which had totaled more than 118,000 less than ten years before, by 1928 fell to 7,793. Many of its members were enrolled in foreign-language federations which had a greater loyalty to Socialist movements in other lands than to the Socialist Party of America. Max Eastman, who had gone from the Socialist to the Communist movements and then out of both during the 1920's, complained that "our Socialist movement is so weak and ineffectual, thirty or so years after its birth, that there is nothing for it to do than be born again."

Faced with these crippling losses in its popular base, the party's leaders seriously considered a proposal in 1928 that no national ticket be nominated. As late as May there was no assurance that the party would name a presidential candidate. It was only after William H. Henry, the party's semi-literate national secretary, completed a survey indicating that no independent third party planned to enter the race that the national executive committee decided to offer a ticket. Even so, the decision was made with misgivings; the committee members recognized that the Socialist party was in no condition to run a credible campaign. Moreover, the party leaders hoped that a labor party, even a nonlabor progressive party, would emerge before election day so that the Socialists would not have to enter the field. Even those who, like Thomas, favored a campaign were less interested in winning votes than they were in the opportunity to do educational work aimed at the organization of a new political party.[1]

The party's weakened condition was caused by a combination of the internecine strife of the past ten years and the inability of Socialists to cope with economic prosperity. Internal feuding had sapped the party's strength, and prosperity made it almost impossible for the Socialists to attract converts and thus gain new strength.

It would be unfair to accuse the Socialists, or Thomas, of misjudging the effect of prosperity, or of ignoring the few opportunities for party activity that developed. On the rare occasions when funds were available, the party was active. But it was hard to convince the American public that the prosperity they were enjoying was an illusion, or that Socialists could solve problems which major parties either found insoluble or ignored.

Faced with working-class defections, the Socialists began to appeal to intellectuals. With this shift in emphasis toward the educated class, party leadership was moving from the old-line labor-oriented party bureaucracy to the middle-class, university-trained intelligentsia. Although intellectuals had always been welcomed into the Socialist party, they had never before been the focus of the party's appeal. It was in large part this shift in emphasis, a shift that emerged clearly during the 1928 election campaign, that allowed Thomas to rise to the leadership. Unlike the old-line Socialist officials, he was able to reach the intellectuals; he was one of them, they understood each other.

2

There were three major issues that divided American Socialists during the latter part of the 1920's: the League of Nations, Prohibition, and the Soviet Union. The dispute over the Socialist position on the League had divided party members since 1919. It was not until 1926, however, that the question created an irreconcilable conflict. At the national convention that year, disagreement over the issue of the League was so sharp that it was necessary to delay taking any position for two years lest the party be splintered anew.

The leaders of both sides in this controversy had been closely identified for many years with the party's right wing. The pro-League faction was dominated by Morris Hillquit, intellectual leader of the conservative wing and an orthodox Marxian Social Democrat; the anti-League faction was headed by Representative Victor Berger, leader of the powerful Milwaukee local, the only Socialist in Congress, and one of the party's least radical figures. Thomas supported Hillquit's position—but with some qualms.

He conceded that the League of Nations was valuable as a force for peace in Europe; but he feared that outside of Europe it was little more than a cover for Western imperialism. The absence of the United States and Soviet Russia was, he felt, one of the League's most serious weaknesses. Although Thomas could understand the League's pressing on even though the United States did not join, its failure to invite Soviet Russia annoyed him. How could a nation covering one-sixth of the land area of the world, the scene of "the most dramatic experiment in the world," be excluded from the world body, he asked? As for the United States, Thomas wanted it to join, but only under conditions that would make the League more "positively an agency of peace and justice."

Berger and his supporters (including such party luminaries as James Graham, president of the Montana Federation of Labor) insisted that the League was a smokescreen to hide the pillage by the victors of Versailles. They saw it as a plot by which the Big-Four powers, Britain, France, Japan, and the United States (even though it was not a member), were trying to rule the world.

The Hillquit view was accepted at the 1928 national convention when the Socialist party officially declared for American participation in the League of Nations. But the resolution was adopted only after a secret agreement had been worked out in which Hillquit and his lieutenants agreed that party spokesmen would not press for American membership in the League. The party was thus committed in principle, though not in practice, to American participation in a world organization. The agreement, for which he was responsible, reflected Thomas's position, and was a foretaste of his isolationist pseudo-internationalism of the years immediately preceding American entry into World War II.[2]

On the domestic scene, no issue was more studiously avoided by the Socialists than Prohibition. Thomas recognized the divisive threat posed by the issue because of the religious and regional makeup of the party. Protestants from the West were strongly in favor of retaining Prohibition, while nearly all of the predominantly Catholic and Jewish membership of the Eastern and Midwestern states demanded repeal. Thomas insisted that the question be divorced from politics and that the party take no stand on it. The conventions in 1926 and 1928 adopted his position, though with disastrous effect.[3]

3

The most contentious issue among Socialists during the 1920's, more significant than Prohibition or the League, was the attitude of party leaders toward the Soviet Union. Some, like Hillquit, early considered the Bolshevik regime to be non-Socialist and oppressive; others, including Thomas, admired Soviet accomplishments while condemning their denial of political democracy. Thus when the anti-Soviet Jewish Socialist Verband held a rally to welcome to New York Alexander Kerensky, the last democratic premier of Russia, Thomas protested. He conceded that Kerensky was entitled to a fair hearing, but he argued that the Socialists should not have arranged the meeting. "The Socialist party," he wrote, "can well afford to be generous in praise of Russian achievements even while it pleads the cause of Russian political prisoners. Do not forget that the average worker would regard the collapse of the Russian experiment as the collapse of Socialism as well as Communism."

The debate on the Soviet issue reached its climax at a discussion of "What Shall Be the Attitude of Socialists Toward the Soviet Union," at the fourth anniversary dinner of the *New Leader*. The participants included the Rand School president, Algernon Lee, and Morris Hillquit for the anti-Soviet faction, and Norman Thomas and James H. Maurer, president of the Pennsylvania Federation of Labor, for the pro-Soviet wing.

Maurer, who was subjected to merciless heckling during his speech, had just returned from a trip to Russia at the head of a trade-union delegation. He defended the Soviet system without reservation: "If what they have over there is communism, I don't care if they call me a Communist. . . . This is a fight of workers, and I don't care what kind of fight the workers are in, I'm with the workers first, last, and all the time." Thomas was somewhat less fervent in his defense of the Soviet system. Failure of the "experiment," he feared, would be a disaster for socialism; Socialists should therefore be sympathetic to the Soviet regime.

"Simply to denounce the Russian Revolution, as Edmund Burke denounced the French, plays into the hands of black reaction," he argued.

Lee, who fancied himself a theoretician but who has more aptly been described as a Talmudist, assailed the Soviet Union as a police state and placed the blame for the oppressive nature of that regime on the nature of bolshevism. It remained for Hillquit to answer Thomas and Maurer. The Soviet regime, he declared, "has been the greatest disaster and calamity that has occurred to the Socialist movement." Then, turning to Thomas, he said: "Comrade Thomas has expressed fears of what might happen if the [Soviet] experiment fails. I say the experiment has already failed."[4] Although Thomas would agree within ten years time that Hillquit and Lee had been correct in their assessment of the Soviet regime, at the moment he insisted that they had formed a conclusion too soon on the true nature of the Soviet state.[5] Thomas rarely admitted that he might have erred.

4

A weak and divided Socialist party convened in New York in late May 1928. No presidential candidate of any standing was available to it. The three logical contenders should have been Hillquit, Berger, and Mayor Daniel W. Hoan. But both Hillquit and Berger, having been born abroad, were constitutionally ineligible to be President; Hoan was too busy as Mayor of Milwaukee to consider the thankless task of being the Socialist presidential candidate. Maurer, who was in many ways similar to Debs, was a fourth possible choice; but he was eliminated because his vehemently pro-Soviet views were unacceptable to the party's dominant anti-Soviet wing. This inability to find a suitable candidate created a dilemma for party leaders. They were still committed to nominating a national ticket. Shortly before the convention, Hillquit intervened to suggest that 1928 might be a good year to nominate a virtual unknown. This, he argued, would give the party an opportunity to develop new leadership. It would also help attract new and younger members. He conceded that the Socialists could not hope to win many votes, but he argued that the election could be used to help rebuild the party with a strong intellectual base. Hillquit therefore proposed that the party nominate Norman Thomas, whose ability as a speaker capable of reaching intellectuals impressed him. Berger agreed with Hillquit's assessment, though he was loathe to nominate an Easterner—conceding to support Thomas only after he was assured that Thomas, a native of Ohio, was really a Midwesterner. Thomas, who had misgivings about running, accepted the nomination only after Hillquit pleaded with him for two full days.

Thomas was barely known outside the New York area; he was not considered a likely successor to Debs, and he was a relative newcomer to the party, having been a member for less than ten years. Yet he was nominated without opposition, and the speeches at the nominating sessions made it appear that the Socialists had found a new Messiah. Louis Waldman, who placed Thomas's name in nomination, compared him favorably with Abraham Lincoln, Wendell Phillips, William Lloyd Garrison, and Eugene Victor Debs. In seconding the nomination, Berger recalled that Thomas "came to us at a time when it was dangerous to join the Socialist party. . . . [He] was one of the few intellectuals who instead of running away from us, came to us." It remained for a delegate from California to tell the convention the truth: "We looked the country over; we found leaders, but as presidential candidates some of them were, unfortunately, by accident of birth, ineligible."[6]

As soon as Thomas was chosen he began an extensive campaign. His first major address was before an audience of three thousand striking textile workers in New Bedford, Massachusetts, a few days after his nomination. Thereafter he delivered more than 150 speeches to audiences ranging in size from thirty to more than ten thousand. He spoke in such diverse places as Winston-Salem, Baltimore, Paterson, Cheyenne, St. Louis, Los Angeles, New York, and Chicago. In Salt Lake City, Thomas spoke in a Congregational Church; in Pocatello, Idaho, he addressed a crowd in the Union Pacific yards. Three times he spoke on radio networks. Although his first campaign speech was to strikers, he focused his efforts not on the working class but on the middle-class liberals who had supported LaFollette in 1924.

Thomas's speeches varied with his audience. One professor of rhetoric who heard him recalled that he had "a certain knack for dignified showmanship." His basic technique was to denounce the two old parties with a minimum of rancor and then offer an idealistic and "plausible" alternative. He appealed as a thoughtful liberal to other thoughtful liberals.

The *Christian Century*, the liberal Protestant weekly, found Thomas to be "one of the clearest minded and most attractive leaders of liberal thought in the country." But it questioned whether he would appeal to the working class. The *Christian Century's* editors agreed, however, that if the Socialists "wished to appeal to the intellectuals" they could have made no better choice than Thomas. The *Christian Century* proved to be a good prophet. Thomas-for-President clubs sprouted on university campuses; the Socialist candidate was given a rousing welcome at Harvard's Liberal Club; thirty-six leading educators—including Paul H. Douglas, of the University of Chicago, Jesse H. Holmes, of Swarthmore College, S. Ralph Harlow and Granville Hicks, of Smith College, LeRoy E. Bowman, of Columbia University, and Harry F. Ward and Arthur Swift, of Union Theological Seminary—announced their support of the Socialist presidential ticket. A committee of 120 intellectuals, including W. E. B. DuBois, Fola LaFollette, Benjamin A. Javits, Freda Kirchway, and seventy-five ministers headed by Bishop Paul Jones, was formed to support Thomas.[7]

The Democrats' nomination of New York Governor Alfred E. Smith, a Catholic who favored the repeal of Prohibition, short-circuited any attempt to win significant liberal Protestant support for Thomas. Even the *Christian Century* supported the Republican Herbert Hoover, while conceding that he was the most conservative of the candidates. Citing Smith's stand for the repeal of Prohibition, the ostensibly liberal journal commented: "The choice lies between Smith and Sahara! The *Christian Century* is for Sahara!" Moreover, the weekly's editorial staff rationalized that the political ambitions of the Roman Catholic Church made experiment with a Catholic President dangerous.

The religious prejudice that played a significant role in the campaign roused Thomas's ire. Prohibition, he argued, was being used as a mask for religious partisanship. Religious prejudice, he warned, was being dragged into the campaign "in a degree that is profoundly hurtful to our democracy." But his appeal was almost completely ignored by the nation's press as well as by most church leaders.

Despite this stand, Thomas's chief campaign target was Smith, whom he saw as a pseudo-progressive wedded to the corrupt Tammany machine of New York City. Thomas's own campaign was aimed at the progressives, who were also one of Smith's targets. They were thus competing for the same constituency.

Thomas's campaign oratory was hardly revolutionary; most of it was little more than old populism and progressivism warmed over. Actually, Thomas conceded that his aim was less the immediate establishment of socialism than it was the amelioration of social ills. As the campaign was being waged at the height of prosperity, neither Smith nor Hoover made any serious proposals for dealing with economic crises. Thomas, on the contrary, addressed himself to the growing problem of unemployment. He proposed public works, public employment bureaus, and unemployment insurance as reasonable solutions to the problem. These were radical (though hardly revolutionary) suggestions for 1928, even though Socialists had proposed these or similar solutions since the latter half of the nineteenth century and a Democratic president was to enact them within a decade. On foreign policy issues, Thomas was hardly more revolutionary than on domestic ones; he favored a reduction, but not the elimination, of tariffs, American participation in the League of Nations, and a withdrawal of American Marines from Nicaragua, where they were battling Augusto Sandino's nationalist rebels. On almost all issues his position was typical of most right-wing Socialists. He called for a gradualist approach to nondoctrinaire socialism rooted in social reform.[8]

Although few intellectuals voted for Thomas, many were impressed by him. The liberal Social Gospel Protestant churchmen in particular liked Thomas, though most of them voted for Hoover out of fear of "Rum and Romanism." Trade unionists, on the contrary, neither voted for Thomas nor were they impressed with him. This was true even of those who had previously supported the Socialist party. Only $8,000 of the party's campaign funds of almost $100,000 came from trade-union sources. Most labor leaders supported Smith.

When the results were in, Thomas received only 267,420 votes, considerably less than 1 per cent of the almost 37 million votes cast. Hoover polled 21,391,993 while 15,016,169 voters supported Smith. Thomas had polled the smallest Socialist vote since 1900 and the smallest percentage of the vote ever recorded by an American Socialist in a presidential election.

Indicative of the woeful state of American socialism was the distribution of the vote. Almost a fourth of the Socialist vote was polled in New York City, though less than $3,500 had been spent on the campaign in the entire state. In Wisconsin, which had long been considered the Socialist stronghold, Thomas polled only 18,213 votes; and Berger, though he received 42,000 votes in a single district, lost his seat in Congress. The Wisconsin Socialist organization had raised less than $1,000 toward the national campaign.

The huge difference between the Thomas and the Berger vote and the lack of interest in the national campaign among Wisconsin Socialists irritated Thomas. It indicated to him that there was something wrong with Wisconsin socialism. Moreover, Thomas claimed he was not welcome in Milwaukee during the campaign; he had been invited there only once between May and October. In a letter to Thomas, Mayor Hoan blamed the low vote on the failure of the Socialists to take a firm stand against Prohibition. "This is the home of the breweries," Hoan wrote. "The brewery workers were originally more nearly 100 per cent Socialist than any other unions. . . . They have been thrown out of employment and naturally are deeply incensed at the Prohibition law. . . . They were so incensed at remarks made against Smith in the [*Milwaukee Daily*] *Leader* and by Victor [Berger] that they deliberately and intentionally voted for Smith and many of them deliberately voted the straight Democratic ticket."[9]

Although neither Thomas nor any other Socialist leader was encouraged by the 1928 presidential vote, they did see some bright spots. Thomas was particularly pleased with the resounding defeat of Smith and the Democratic party. He believed that the Democrats' extremely poor showing indicated that the party of Jefferson, Jackson, the Southern Bourbons, and Tammany was dead, and that American politics was in the process of realignment into a conservative party—the Republican—and a new farmer-labor-progressive party in which Socialists would play a decisive role.

Moreover, the Socialists had found a new leader in Thomas— one who could develop a following. From the outset Thomas had recognized that his job was as much to rejuvenate the party organization as it was to garner votes. He therefore spent more time reviving dormant or dead party branches and locals than he did in appealing to the public. As a result, party membership, which had been in constant decline since 1922, showed a net gain of 368 during the campaign.[10]

5

Most of the new members who entered the Socialist party during the 1928 campaign were young, middle-class, and well educated. Almost all of them were primarily attracted by Thomas—for he was essentially one of them and spoke in their idiom. The new party members were anxious to follow his leadership, and gave him a base from which he could remold the party in terms of his own ideas. The weakness of the party's organization gave him the opportunity to remake it.

The weakest link in the party's organization was its national secretary, William H. Henry, who was, at best, an incompetent. Uncultured, unintellectual, semi-literate, Henry was involved in nativist, anti–New York, and anti-Semitic activities in a party which, despite its rhetoric and its relatively large Jewish membership, had a substantial amount of Midwestern nativist sentiment. Henry was a lazy man whose sole asset was his long membership in the party. Thomas's experience with Henry during the 1928 campaign led him to insist that the party get rid of him. In a confidential memorandum to party leaders throughout the nation, Thomas wrote: "The party as it existed prior to this campaign under the leadership or lack of leadership of its national office cannot do the job [of holding gains made during the campaign]. . . . Everything else is useless unless we can get . . . a group of young and energetic people as a general staff. . . . I am never so discouraged about Socialism as when I am talking to Comrade Henry. . . . If Henry cannot be removed until next May [when his appointment would come up for renewal] he must immediately be supplemented and more or less shelved." Without a new national secretary, Thomas feared, the party could not hope to make any appreciable headway. Henry's tenure as secretary ended in May 1929, but not because of his incompetence; Socialists rarely fired anyone for incompetence. He lost his job because of marital problems. His wife Emma, a party bureaucrat in her own right, brought suit for divorce against him in early 1929; and, because of a strong puritanical streak among most Socialists, he was precluded from continuing in the post.[11]

After a short period of interim secretaries, the national executive committee named Clarence Senior to the post. A twenty-seven-year-old university-educated disciple of Thomas, only two years out of the University of Kansas where he had been active in the Student League for Industrial Democracy, Senior had since his graduation been an official of the Cleveland Federation of Teachers. The national executive committee said of Senior's appointment that it indicated "a definite trend within the party toward the placing of greater responsibility on its younger element." The committee failed to note that it also signified that actual operational control of the party was being placed in the hands of a middle-class intellectual, and that the national office was being cast in Norman Thomas's image.

The shift of administration from a working-class to a middle-class base was the first in a series of changes that Thomas tried to effect in the party. The most important of these changes was the deletion of that part of the application for party membership that affirmed the applicant's belief in the class struggle. This led to considerable debate and disagreement within the party before it was finally adopted. With the deletion of the affirmation, the party moved away from its Marxian ideology and closer to Thomas's "nondoctrinaire socialism." The elimination of the pledge was a major gain for Thomas, whose primary theme in party debate had been, "There is no use in our talking revolution."[12]

There were other significant internal party debates in which Thomas played a leading role. He opposed a proposal, which had considerable support, that the party change its name because "Socialist" was a near-dirty word in America. He favored a move to delete the requirement that members always vote the full Socialist ticket, no matter what the circumstances. It was his own reluctance to sign such a pledge which had kept him out of the party for more than a year during 1917–1918.

No internal party dispute generated as much heat as the question of the location of party headquarters. Thomas and most Eastern Socialists favored moving the headquarters from Chicago to New York. There was considerable argument against the move, particularly in Wisconsin. In part, opposition was based on a genuine fear that the New York Socialists would ignore the needs of the party's members in the Western states. But basically the opposition was anti-Semitic and nativist in nature, a fact that angered Thomas.[13]

Another major internal problem that bothered Thomas was the party's inability, or at least unwillingness, to act against labor union officials who were also party members and whose actions in their unions were ethically reprehensible. This had been a serious problem since the party's earliest days, but no action was taken because Socialist campaigns received their principal financial support from these labor union officials before 1928. When these same union officials ignored the Socialist campaign in 1928, the party moved to discipline some of them. Its New York City Central Committee ordered an investigation of the trade union tactics of "some nominal Socialists." Although this action cheered Thomas, little came of it, and "Socialist" trade unionists continued to ignore the party and its leader with impunity.[14]

In any case, it was clear that the party was in the process of being remade. It was no longer a Marxian working-class party, despite the rhetoric of some of its leaders. With Thomas in command, the Socialist party was moving in the direction of simple progressivism. It appealed for social justice rather than revolution; it cried out for immediate ameliorative social reform rather than full-blown socialism; its ethical precepts were dominant over its radical rhetoric; its bureaucracy boasted university degrees rather than union cards. By 1929, the Socialist Party of America had become, in fact, the party of Norman Thomas.

6

One of Thomas's most significant contributions was in the field of municipal reform in New York City. Beginning in 1925, when he was the Socialist nominee in the New York mayoralty election, Thomas had been active in denouncing the corruption and waste then rampant in the Tammany-run city administration. After a gruelling campaign in which he pleaded for an end to slums, graft, and inefficiency and for construction of publicly owned low-rent housing, he had polled fewer than forty thousand votes. Four years later, in 1929, he again accepted the nomination and, in what was to be his most effective campaign, led the drive for municipal housing, unification and municipal ownership of the city's transit lines, and an end to the corruption that was then endemic in the city. He was not elected, but all of the proposals he advocated during that campaign were eventually enacted, and his exposures of corruption helped end the reign of Tammany Hall.

In view of the disastrous results of 1925, Thomas had been less than anxious to run again four years later. Shortly after the 1928 presidential race he proposed that the Socialists attempt to create a coalition of labor and progressive forces to win control of the city government. Attempts were being made at fusing various anti-Tammany forces in the city, but Thomas opposed these because they assumed the inclusion of the city's Republicans, whom he described as "Tammany's jackals." If the alliance Thomas proposed could not be formed—and it was obvious to most Socialists that it could not—he wanted the Socialists to nominate Morris Hillquit as candidate for Mayor. Harry W. Laidler and Louis Waldman agreed with Thomas that Hillquit would be the ideal candidate, but Hillquit ruled himself out for personal reasons.

That Thomas was the best candidate available was apparent. Not only had be begun to make a reputation for integrity and intellect, but he had also shown a grasp of the city's problems and a sincere interest in them. During the 1928 presidential campaign, Thomas took time out to argue against a proposed increase in the city's five-cent subway fare as well as to testify for public housing before the city's aldermen. With virtually no dissent, the Socialists nominated Thomas for Mayor and adopted a platform that emphasized the need for social reform in the city. The dominant theme of the campaign was struck in the platform, which cited the sewer, bus, milk, street-cleaning, pushcart, and marketing scandals and the unsolved murder of the racketeer Arnold Rothstein in a mid-town hotel. "Scarcely a department of the Walker administration is without a scandal," the platform declared, and it promised to clean up the city. The platform would have done any progressive proud. It called for a unified city-owned transit system, reorganization of the police department, election of magistrates, a system of public defenders, scien-

tific zoning, rent controls, the razing of slums and their replacement with municipally owned housing, a nonpartisan board of
education, the merit system for appointments, more vocational
training, better training for teachers, scholarships for the poor,
new school construction, academic freedom for all teachers, public or cooperatively owned markets, "just and scientific evaluation of property for taxation," and unemployment aid.

The Republicans nominated Fiorello LaGuardia, who had left
the Republican party in 1924 to be elected to Congress as a Socialist and progressive. He returned to the Republican party in
1926 and was re-elected to Congress as a Republican. Although
LaGuardia had a well-deserved record as a genuine progressive,
Thomas was adamant in his opposition to him: ". . . no matter
how progressive Major LaGuardia talks in or out of Congress,
he can only be elected with the support of the working Republican district leaders and he knows it. These men average worse
than Tammany leaders on the principle that a jackal is worse
than a lion. . . ."

In the course of the campaign, Thomas publicized long-
smoldering scandals. His exposures were to a great extent responsible for the celebrated investigations under Judge Samuel
Seabury which resulted in the ouster of Mayor James J. Walker
in 1932 and the demise of Tammany Hall in 1933. His charges
of corruption in the city's magistrate courts were instrumental
in a Bar Association probe in 1930 which first brought these
scandals to light. He was also responsible for the exposure of the
municipal transit scandal, which involved Walker directly with
the graft.

Thomas's muckraking progressivism was appreciated by the
good-government forces. "The only redeeming feature of the
election is the candidacy of Norman Thomas," the *Nation* remarked. The Scripps-Howard *New York Evening Telegram*
supported him. The nonpartisan Citizens Union, without a single
Socialist on its board, endorsed Thomas in a statement which
paid tribute to his sincerity and fearlessness. "He would bring
dignity and character to the mayor's office," the statement declared. A nonpartisan league, headed by the Reverend John
Haynes Holmes and including the philosopher John Dewey,
Rabbi Stephen S. Wise, the Reverend Harry Emerson Fosdick,

the Reverend John Howard Melish, the columnist Heywood Broun, and Dr. Henry Neumann, leader of the Ethical Culture Society, was organized to back Thomas's candidacy.

Although Thomas had thus won the support of the middle-class intellectual progressives, he was again ignored by organized labor. The Central Trades and Labor Council, the city's official American Federation of Labor body, endorsed Tammany's candidate, James J. Walker. The *New Leader* called the Central Trades and Labor Council an auxiliary of Tammany Hall—justifiably, since historically it had almost invariably supported the Tammany candidates in New York City. "The greatest tragedy of New York," Thomas wrote, ". . . is that *official* labor so largely seems even to its own rank and file [to be] on the side of privilege and allied with the powers that prey."

If Thomas's war against Tammany corruption won him support from the city's good-government elements, his campaign was hardly likely to drive the most anti-Socialist of them away. John Dewey remarked: "Although Norman Thomas was nominated by the Socialist party, he is the only genuine nonpartisan candidate in the present campaign." Thomas spoke of reform, of making New York a better place in which to raise a family. He called for reducing municipal expenditures, eliminating needless offices. At the forefront of his proposals was muncipal housing aimed at "rooting out nurseries of crime and disease." He also spoke of planning, hospitals, transit, unemployment relief, and public markets. To the home owner Thomas promised "honest assessments and the use of taxes for the public, not the politicians good."

Thomas also favored a far-reaching reorganization of the governments of the greater New York area. "If we were commissioned by a Socialist government of the United States to establish governmental efficiency in the New York region," he wrote in collaboration with Paul Blanshard, "we would erase the state lines that now surround New York City altogether and create a new unit with half of the overlapping machinery of government abolished."[15]

Election day results amazed even optimistic Socialists. Although Tammany's Mayor Walker was easily re-elected, Thomas polled 174,931 votes, or almost four-and-a-half times his 1925 total. His gains were centered in middle-class areas: in the well-to-do 8th Assembly District in the West Bronx his vote increased from 1,074 to 9,283; in the Jewish middle-class 21st Assembly District in Brooklyn, it increased from 586 to 5,573; and in suburban Queens, it increased from 1,943 to 24,761. More than five hundred new members joined the party in the city during this short period.[16]

As was typical among Socialists, even happy events led to serious differences. The Reverend John Haynes Holmes proposed at the rally celebrating the large Thomas vote that the party give up its name, delete the reference to socialism in its platform, and devote all of its energies to electing Norman Thomas Mayor of New York. Hillquit and Thomas were both incensed by the proposal. "Drop your name, drop part of your program," Hillquit parodied Holmes. "Why Norman Thomas would not take the mayoralty on a gold platter on those terms." "Not on a silver one, either," Thomas humorously added. Holmes persisted. He urged Thomas to be the "Moses" of a "general nonpartisan mass movement of righteousness in New York." But Thomas was firm in his rejection: "You cannot defeat Tammany, far less build the City Beautiful without a philosophy, a program, and organization; that is to say without a party. . . . New York needs not a good man but a good party. . . . We shall not be saved by a political Messiah. . . ." Holmes repeated his proposal a week later at the Community Church, of which he was minister. He now suggested that a federation of Socialists, trade unionists, settlement-house social workers, independents, and liberals form a coalition with Thomas as its leader aimed at wresting control of the city from Tammany. Trade unionists and settlement-house leaders, Hillquit answered, were hardly likely to enter a party with the Socialists, so long as the latter refused to surrender their principles. As for liberals and nonpartisans, Hillquit suggested they form their own party and work with the Socialists on the city and national levels. Although Hillquit and Thomas both rejected Holmes's suggestion, they were not in total agreement with each other. Thomas wanted the Socialists to invite labor people and intellectuals to a conference "to talk over this situation; rather than demand that they accept our party . . . and program." Hillquit wanted the party to open its doors to all interested labor men and professionals, but added: "I would certainly hesitate to organize them as a separate group holding themselves aloof. Company of this kind, after all, is very uncertain."

Basically, Thomas favored a progressive approach divorced from the two major parties, but he was not opposed to coalitions with non-Socialists interested in genuine social reforms. Simply to fight Tammany's corruption without offering a program of major reforms was, in Thomas's view, the height of futility. Those good government movements that were organized around no program except the end of Tammany he considered useless. Nor was he interested in efficiency in government *per se*. "Efficient for what?" he asked. "Good for whom? For real estate interests and public utilities? For its own ends, and the ends of the privileged groups generally, Tammany is amazingly efficient."[17]

Shortly after the 1929 election, Thomas, Holmes, Rabbi Stephen S. Wise, John Dewey, and the Methodist Bishop Francis J. McConnell formed the City Affairs Committee, a nonpartisan group whose aim was to win the support of non-Socialists for the Socialists' municipal efforts. The organization was staffed by Paul Blanshard, Henry J. Rosner, and E. Michael White, who four years later became major officials of the LaGuardia administration. The City Affairs Committee brought charges of corruption against Mayor Walker in 1931. The charges were rejected out of hand by Governor Franklin D. Roosevelt without allowing the committee's two spokesmen, Rabbi Wise and Dr. Holmes, to make rebuttal. A year later a second state investigation under Judge Seabury proved the accuracy of the charges and Walker was forced to resign. Roosevelt's high-handed treatment of the City Affairs Committee and its charges was one cause of Thomas's personal disdain for him.[18]

Socialism, Thomas maintained in 1931, "has a peculiar applicability to municipal problems, and nothing but the Socialist ideal and programs will shake off the alliance of politics and privilege which Tammany typifies." But Thomas's campaign that year for borough president of Manhattan was hardly Socialist. He stressed municipal reform and won the support of all of the good-government leaders of that borough. Even the conservative Republican Congressman Hamilton Fish called Thomas "an ideal leader to rally all the forces of reform, regardless of class, for a cleanup of the New York City government." In that campaign, Thomas's last on a municipal level, he polled a record 48,438 votes, about 13 per cent of the total. The Tammany borough president, a man named Samuel Levy, was re-elected with 247,110 votes, or almost five times as many as Thomas. Even the scandals then being exposed by the Seabury investigation that Thomas had triggered were not enough, at least in 1931, to defeat Tammany in New York.[19]

Thomas's municipal campaigns laid the foundations for the LaGuardia upheaval of 1933 that resulted in the defeat of Tammany Hall, but they were hardly Socialist. They were, in fact, little more than municipal social reform campaigns along the lines made famous by such progressives as "Honest" Tom Johnson of Cleveland and "Golden Rule" Sam Jones of Toledo. Early in the Thomas era, the American Socialist party had moved away from socialism into progressivism.

7

When in October 1929 the prosperity bubble burst, neither Norman Thomas nor any other Socialist leader was surprised. They had been expecting economic collapse since the period of apparent prosperity had begun. In April 1929, only six months before the crash of the stock market, the national executive committee of the Socialist party warned that unemployment was rising to dangerous levels and that mass suffering was likely before winter unless the government took immediate action. The committee urged party branches to organize the unemployed into councils "to formulate measures of relief."

Thomas believed that the collapse in the price of stocks did not indicate a genuine diminution of America's wealth. Three days after the market crashed he wrote: "To my mind the mad stampede of the bulls which was later matched by a wild stampede by the bears was essentially gambling. . . . Let it be observed that all this increase and decrease of paper value had little reflection in real wealth. . . . Real values are made by labor by hand and brain. There may be 'easy money' apart from work but not true wealth." Thomas's socialism still bore a striking resemblance to the Protestant ethic, for he had little compassion for speculators. But when general economic distress followed the stock market crash, Thomas cited it as proof that the capitalist system had collapsed. "Before our eyes," he told his fellow party members, "the Socialist prediction of the breakdown of capitalism is being fulfilled with a rapidity and completeness which not even the most convinced Socialist expected to see in 1928." The basic cause of the depression was, Thomas believed, underconsumption. In particular cases, he agreed that overproduction may have been genuine, "but in sum total what we suffer from is underconsumption. . . ." If overproduction was economically indefensible, underconsumption, he felt, was morally outrageous. Abject destitution in the midst of an abundance of food "is not a failure to understand," he told a Princeton audience, "but rather an ethical or moral failure." The inhumanity of the depression was more important to Thomas than the proof it offered that the Socialists were justified in their criticism of the capitalist system. True, it confirmed the Socialist case; it emphasized the inadequacies of a system based on production for profit rather than for use. But, more important for Thomas, it exposed the un-Christian character of the capitalist society of 1930. Thomas cried out that "the wage system is even more heartless than chattel slavery. The owner of slaves could scarcely afford to let them starve when he had no work for them. But our industrialists expect to hire and fire at need with precious little corporate responsibility."[20]

In early 1930 Thomas and Louis Waldman proposed a "coherent and practical" program of relief for New York City's unemployed. The program called primarily for works projects financed by the city. Mayor Walker rejected the proposal on the specious legal grounds that the city did not have the power to spend money on work relief except for veterans and the blind. Even a ruling by the state attorney general to the contrary failed to move Walker.

Thomas also proposed a six-point national program for alleviating the conditions of the growing army of unemployed. The program called for: (1) accurate statistics on unemployment; (2) a coordinated system of public employment offices; (3) retraining of workers in overcrowded or obsolete fields; (4) public works projects; (5) unemployment insurance; and (6) shorter working hours. All of this program was to become law within the next seven years under a Democratic President intent on saving the capitalist system. This was so because the program, though designed by a Socialist, was in fact designed to operate under the capitalist system. Like most of Thomas's other programs, it was designed to reform capitalism rather than to replace it.

The depression which followed the stock market debacle offered the Socialist party its first opportunity in a decade for growth, and Socialists were quick to grab the opportunity. Although most Socialists continued to use the rhetoric of anti-capitalism, their primary efforts were aimed at amelioration. In May 1930 the Women's Section of the party in New York set up a soup kitchen which for several months offered food to unemployed who otherwise faced starvation. About a year later, Thomas, at the insistence of the other members of the party's committee on unemployment, made a radio appeal for financial contributions to a private charity scheme called the "Block-Aid Plan." Essentially a help-your-neighbor service, the plan proved patently futile. Thomas recognized that it was unlikely to have much effect in alleviating hunger in New York, but he answered Socialists who objected to his support of the plan by saying that "failure to raise any money at this juncture would mean that a great many men . . . would be utterly without help."

Thomas's interest in alleviating the suffering of the unemployed was ridiculed by the Communists, who believed all remedies for relief of unemployment short of revolution were futile. This concept was alien to Thomas. In the first place, he was not convinced that unemployment could be avoided during the period of transition from capitalism to socialism; as Soviet farms became more mechanized, he believed, Russia too would face a rising problem of technological unemployment. Moreover, Thomas favored government action to alleviate the suffering caused by unemployment on purely humanitarian grounds, and because "broken men and their hungry children do not make the best material for the cooperative commonwealth."[21]

Thomas's early reaction to the depression underlined the fact that, despite his occasional use of quasi-Marxist rhetoric, he was primarily pleading for amelioration of the conditions of the poor. His proposals were moderate and always attainable within the context of the capitalist system.

8

Two organizations whose primary goal was the building of a new political alignment in the United States emerged during the last two years of the 1920's. They were to cause further dissension within the Socialist party and were to help lay the ground for the internal disintegration of the party during the 1930's. The first of these organizations, the League for Independent Political Action (LIPA), appealed to intellectuals and was chiefly interested in organizing them into a semi-Socialist progressive party. The second organization, the Conference for Progressive Labor Action (CPLA), directed its activities at the trade-union movement, which it hoped to radicalize and politicize into a mass party of labor.

The LIPA was organized in December 1928 by Norman Thomas, Paul H. Douglas, then professor of economics at the University of Chicago, and Sherwood Eddy, a Social Gospeleer. Its stated purpose was to form a "permeative fellowship" which would be bound together by the idea of a Socialist America and which would be pledged to work for a labor party in the United States. Its opening meeting, at New York's International House, drew only fifty-three intellectuals. Yet by May 1929 they had generated sufficient interest to be in a position to name an executive committee of twenty-five, including John Dewey as national chairman, Zona Gale, Jim Maurer, and W. E. B. DuBois as vice-chairmen, and Oswald Garrison Villard, Devere Allen, Kirby Page, Reinhold Niebuhr, Harry W. Laidler, Douglas, Eddy, and Thomas as executive members. Howard Y. Williams, a Congregational minister from St. Paul, Minnesota, was named executive secretary. The LIPA membership was made up mainly of Social Gospel ministers, university professors, and left-wing journalists. Its leaders expected the LIPA to become the American equivalent of the British Fabian Society.

There was considerable duplication of membership; many of the most active LIPA members belonged to the Socialist party. Besides Thomas and Maurer, influential Socialists in the LIPA included Joseph Schlossberg, secretary-treasurer of the Amalgamated Clothing Workers, Paul Blanshard, of the City Affairs Committee, the mine union organizer Powers Hapgood, the publicists Nathan Fine and MacAllister Coleman, and Professor Vida Scudder, a leading Christian Socialist.

In 1930 the LIPA threw the support of its 4,500 members behind Socialist candidates in New York City, Milwaukee, and Reading, Pennsylvania. It officially supported Labor party tickets in Buffalo, New Bedford, and North Dakota, and the Farmer-

Labor party candidates in Minnesota. In Brooklyn, the LIPA ran Thomas's campaign for Congress in the upper-middle-class district which included the predominantly Jewish Flatbush and the Protestant-Yankee Bedford-Stuyvesant neighborhoods. The LIPA campaign won Thomas unexpected support; the *New York World* noted that "Mr. Thomas may be expected to obtain a large vote from citizens who have no interest in his Socialist platform but who respect him as a man and wish to administer a telling rebuke to the obtuse and myopic leaders of both major political parties in New York City."

The result of the election exceeded the expectations of almost all Socialists. Thomas polled 21,983 votes, or almost three times the 1928 vote of the Socialist candidate in that district. The vote of the Democratic incumbent, Andrew Somers, declined from 70,953 to 46,681, and the Republican vote fell from 53,700 to 29,862.[22]

Other LIPA-endorsed candidates did almost as well in other New York City districts. Ostensibly, the outlook for the LIPA becoming an effective electoral instrument should have been high. Unfortunately, a dispute developed within the organization almost immediately after the election. The fight centered around a Christmas letter by the League's chairman, John Dewey, to Senator George Norris, the progressive Republican from Nebraska, inviting him to resign from the Republican party and help form a new party aimed at "building happier lives, a more just society, and the peaceful world which was the dream of him whose birthday we celebrate this Christmas day." Norris rejected the proposal because, he said, "the people will not respond to a demand for a new party except in case of a great emergency when there is practically a political revolution."

The invitation to Norris set off political fireworks. A. J. Muste, the leading figure in the Conference for Progressive Labor Action, who was also a member of the executive committee of the LIPA, resigned from the latter. James Oneal, editor of the *New Leader*, who had been friendly to the LIPA, now wanted all Socialists to withdraw *en masse*. Harry Laidler told the twenty-fifth anniversary dinner of the League for Industrial Democracy: "A party which cannot be launched unless some U.S. senator waves his magic wand is hardly worth launching and has no assurance of permanence or of helping in fundamental change." Norman Thomas joined the chorus of opponents of the Dewey action, though in milder terms than Laidler. The executive committee, faced with a potential splintering of the League, dissociated itself from the Dewey invitation in terms similar to those of Laidler.

It was apparent by 1931 that there was considerable disenchantment with the LIPA among Socialists. Hillquit in particular opposed the League, primarily because he despaired of organized labor forming a party in America, and disapproved of a middle-class-oriented progressive party. The increased Socialist vote of 1930 led Hillquit to say: "There is no need for the creation of a new party in the United States fashioned along the lines of the British Labor party." When the executive secretary of the LIPA proposed a joint conference with the Socialist party to discuss the 1932 election, Hillquit rejected the suggestion out of hand. Nor was Hillquit alone in his disdain for the LIPA; Milwaukee's Socialist Mayor Daniel W. Hoan also turned down a similar invitation in terms as harsh as Hillquit's.

At the time less emotionally wedded to the Socialist party than either Hillquit or Hoan, Thomas disagreed with their actions. He still saw the LIPA as a useful organization, and remained a firm believer in the idea of a labor party. Thus, when in late 1931 the LIPA proposed a four-year program aimed at winning power in 1936, Thomas was impressed. The LIPA program was composed primarily of the so-called "immediate demands" which had been part of all Socialist election platforms since the party was founded in 1901.

"I think the LIPA . . . has done valuable educational work," he told the eighth annual dinner of the *New Leader* in March 1932. ". . . [Although] its present four-year program . . . omits some things I think very important . . . it is a useful elaboration of an immediate program."[23]

Thomas's support was based on two considerations. First, he was genuinely interested in organizing a labor party. Second, he had reason to believe that a labor, farmer-labor, or progressive party would come into existence before the 1936 election and could win that election. Thomas knew that he was the most likely leader of that party—especially if it were to be organized by the LIPA.

The assumption that the LIPA would lead to a major labor

party with Thomas as its leader had one major flaw: the LIPA had only 6,062 members by 1932. But the idea was not completely irrational. Conditions appeared propitious for the rise of a third party, and there could be little doubt that Thomas would be the LIPA's choice. Paul Douglas dedicated his book *The Coming of a New Party* "To Norman Thomas . . . who is, to my mind, the best representative of the new spirit in American political life." In the book, which was the bible of the LIPA, Douglas also paid homage to other Socialist leaders, including Oscar Ameringer, Hillquit, Maurer, and Hoan, and to the Socialists generally, but he reserved his primary accolades for Thomas.[24]

The LIPA indicated in 1932 that Thomas was in fact its leader. When Thomas complained that some of Dewey's statements made it appear that the LIPA's intention was the organization of an amorphous middle-class party of protest of which he, Thomas, did not approve, Executive Secretary Williams assured him that the LIPA leadership believed "that no diluted philosophy of government or economics will do for this day." Noting that the four-year program included almost all of the Socialists' immediate demands, he concluded: "There will be no compromise with these declared principles."

Events over the next eighteen months were to prove that the LIPA's protestations were little more than rhetoric. In the 1932 campaign the League officially supported Thomas for President, but its efforts were of little consequence; if anything, its activities helped to further divide the party. Many LIPA members voted for Roosevelt while proclaiming Thomas the best candidate. By mid-1933, most of the LIPA members abandoned the fight for a new party and moved into the New Deal camp. By September 1933, the LIPA withdrew from national politics and vanished.[25]

9

The ultimate objectives of the Conference for Progressive Labor Action and the LIPA differed little, and much the same people made up the membership of the two movements. Unlike the LIPA, the CPLA addressed itself to the labor movement, and it used the rhetoric of revolution rather than the semantics of moderate, progressive intellectualism.

Although Thomas was directly involved in the formation of

the CPLA, he was not its leading figure. That man was Thomas's long-time friend and associate, the Reverend A. J. Muste. Muste originally planned to become a Fundamentalist Calvinist minister of the Dutch Reformed Church, but somewhere along the road he rejected fundamentalism and turned to his own version of the Social Gospel, an amalgam of pacifism and Marxism. Muste dedicated his ministry to the labor movement, and in 1922 helped organize the Brookwood Labor College, a school for training trade-union bureaucrats imbued with genuine social consciences, of which he was president.

Supported primarily by the progressive, pro-Socialist needle trades unions, Brookwood was detested by most AFL leaders, particularly Matthew Woll, president of the Photo-Engravers International Union and a vice-president of the AFL. Woll was also acting president of the conservative National Civic Federation, an organization of business and labor leaders opposed to old-age pensions and aggressive labor unions. Woll fought Brookwood because its aim was a militant, aggressive labor movement. In 1928, Woll accused Brookwood of inculcating disloyalty to the AFL, fostering sympathy with the Communist party, criticizing religion, and preaching sexual liberty. The charges were patently false: except for a single teacher, the entire Brookwood faculty was hostile to the Communist party; most of Brookwood's support came from AFL unions; and far from sexual liberty, an air of Puritanism, reflecting the religious values of its president, permeated Brookwood's campus in the New York suburb of Katonah. It was apparent that Woll's charges were based on Brookwood's threat to his own view of a labor utopia: docile, conservative unions, based on crafts and limited to the most highly skilled artisans using tactics totally devoid of militancy.

Since most AFL officials were in basic agreement with Woll's views, he had little difficulty in having Brookwood condemned by the labor federation's executive council. The *New Leader*, which like most official Socialist newspapers had ignored internal union disputes—except to condemn Communists who took up cudgels against established leadership—now opened a campaign against Woll and the National Civic Federation. Thomas, who had been a close friend of Muste since 1913 when they met at a Union Theological Seminary graduate seminar, led the assault on

Woll. Some Socialists who were also union officials found it expedient to support Woll. They attempted to convince the editor of the *New Leader* to drop his attack. This led Thomas to explode: "Our desire to cooperate [with conservative trade unionists such as Woll] . . . has gone too far. It has been misunderstood. We have lost, not gained, influence in the AFL and among unorganized workers by our failure to take and push a more vigorous line distinguished on the one hand from Communism and on the other from Wollism. . . . No party can win workers to independent political action which gives them the impression of accepting Wollism in the unions. . . ."

The strong stand taken by the new Socialist leader, and supported by the Eastern organ of the party, indicated to Muste that the time was ripe to begin a drive for the radicalization of American labor and for the formation of a labor party. In the early part of 1929, *Labor Age*, Muste's monthly journal, published a sixteen-point program for a progressive labor movement. The program, little more than a rehash of old Socialist proposals, some dating back to 1901, called for among other things organization of the unorganized workers into industrial unions open to all regardless of race, religion, or political belief; democratization of the labor unions; struggle against the National Civic Federation's influence in the labor movement; a fight against the use of injunctions in labor disputes and against "yellow dog contracts," which made union membership a cause for discharge from employment; and a system of social insurance against the economic consequences of unemployment and old age. There were also planks calling for recognition of Soviet Russia, opposition to imperialism and militarism, and the organization of a labor party based on organization of industrial workers.

The program struck an immediately responsive chord among many Socialists. Thomas wrote: "The more I think over it, the more important does it seem to me to make it the work of the Socialist party." Nor was Thomas alone. A conference called almost immediately by Muste and attended by 151 delegates from seventeen states formed the CPLA in May 1929. Accepting the sixteen-point program, the CPLA, after condemning both the Communists and the AFL leadership, proclaimed that its aim was to convert the AFL "to progressive policies and to infuse it with a new fighting spirit." Among the leading figures of the

new organization were several moderate Socialists, including Al-
gernon Lee, James Oneal, Abraham Lefkowitz, leader of the
New York Teachers Union, Winston Dancis, pacifist leader of
the Young People's Socialist League, and Frank Crosswaith, the
Negro labor organizer. Thomas hailed the organization of the
CPLA as "one of the most heartening things I have seen."

The AFL leadership was quick to counterattack. John Spargo,
who left the Socialist party in 1917 to support the war and who
now earned his living writing for anti-labor journals, led the assault in a two-column letter to the *New York Times* on June 13,
1929. He called the CPLA a collection of "professional radicals
whose eminence in leadership of attack is . . . proportionate to
their lack of experience in bona fide unions, either as members or
officials. Their ignorance of the practical movement is their principal qualification. . : ." Spargo made Thomas the principal target
of his assault. "What, pray," he asked, "are the qualifications of
Norman Thomas for judging and condemning the course of action adopted by such an experienced leader as William Green
and for setting himself up as judge of the Executive Council of
the American Federation of Labor? When did he work at any
manual occupation, know unionism from the inside, and share its
difficulties?" The letter was reprinted and distributed to all labor
union publications by the AFL-controlled International Labor
Press Service. Oneal and Thomas replied in the *New Leader*,
whose readership was, at best, a minuscule part of that reached
by Spargo.[26]

A circular letter was also sent out by the AFL to all of its affiliates warning them against contributing to Communist groups or
to the CPLA. In New York, the crucial fight occurred in the
United Hebrew Trades (UHT), a federation of unions with
predominantly Jewish memberships which was organized late in
the nineteenth century by Socialists and which still considered
itself friendly to the Socialist party. Despite a plea by B. Charney
Vladeck, one of the most popular figures in the Jewish labor
movement, after a heated debate the UHT voted 36 to 4 to condemn the CPLA as a dual union movement. The Labor Committee of the New York City Socialist party read the situation accurately: the CPLA had no labor following worth counting. The
committee therefore attempted to salvage what it could for the
party's future finances, and invited Woll to speak under its aus-

pices. Morris Hillquit joined in the chorus, calling the CPLA "half-Communist, half-IWW, half-liberal," and he urged Socialists to end their continuous hunt for a "will-of-the-wisp of a new labor party."[27]

The ambivalence of the Socialists alienated Muste, who moved toward a completely independent stance. At the 1931 CPLA convention, Muste and three of his followers, Louis Budenz, J. C. Kennedy, and Benjamin Mandel, won control of the organization and announced the immediate formation of a new revolutionary, non-Communist party. All Socialists then withdrew from the CPLA. The Conference itself eventually became the short-lived American Workers party.[28]

The formation of the CPLA was another in the chain of events by which the Social Gospeleers helped tear the Socialist party asunder in their futile hunt for a viable, democratic method for achieving power in an apathetic America, whose working-class had little interest in the message of the Social Gospel or of socialism.

10

The Militant–Old Guard confrontation in the Socialist party, which began in 1930, was more a struggle between generations than between ideologies. The ideological content of the struggle did not develop until the disagreement was almost two years old, and the issues over which the fight developed had little connection with objective reality. By 1930, the average party activist who had lived through the war years, the Communist schisms, and the decline in Socialist fortunes was in his sixties: Julius Gerber, the secretary of the New York local, for example, was born in 1871, and Morris Hillquit was born in 1869. Few of the other old-line Socialists were under fifty; many were closer to seventy. The "new breed," many of whom had become interested in socialism during the 1928 and 1929 campaigns, were generally in their twenties and thirties. Thomas, who was then in his mid-forties, was considerably older than most of them.

The basic differences between the old-line Socialists, who were labeled the "Old Guard," and the new breed, who were called "Militants," were over tactics rather than principles. Actually, the adherents of the Old Guard were, if anything, more

Marxist than the Militants. Gerber complained in 1931 that the
Militants had accused the Old Guard of being dogmatic Socialists and "old fogies" because they "would rather swear by the
whiskers of Karl Marx than see the party grow." Gerber pointed
out that, since the Militants had come into the party, Socialists
"spent more time advocating civic virtue than the class struggle."
Most Militant Socialists of 1930–1931 were also members of the
League for Independent Political Action or the City Affairs
Committee.

The earliest Militant group, organized in New York in April
1930, had a three-point program aimed at making the Socialist
party a more active rather than a more radical organization. The
program called upon party members to form Socialist caucuses
in labor unions; urged more mass propaganda by the party; and
proposed the organization of a new Socialist daily newspaper.
The Militant movement was centered primarily in the New York
local; it attempted, therefore, to control the city convention of
the party. Although the convention voted in favor of the Militant proposal for a daily newspaper, the decision was never acted
upon. The convention took no notice of the mass propaganda
issue. But on the motion that Socialists form caucuses in the trade
unions, the convention, dominated by the Old Guard, voted
"No"; the idea horrified the Old Guard, even though all that
was proposed was that the Socialists in trade unions caucus "not
for the purpose of capturing the unions but for the purpose of
organizing them [the Socialists] . . . so that they can carry on
Socialist agitation in the unions." The Old Guard wanted the
Socialists to maintain their historic hands-off policy with regard
to the trade unions.

At the New York City convention, the Militants had more
support in the party than had generally been assumed. On the
trade-union issue, the Old Guard, which controlled all of the
bureaucratic apparatus of the city party organization, was barely
able to defeat the Militants. But the apparent strength of the Militants did not upset the Old Guard.

While disagreeing with the Militants' basic tenets, Hillquit
told the convention that he believed they might actually be a
valuable asset to the party because they brought new life into
discussion of party issues. He added, however, that the Militants
were deluding themselves when they assumed that they were

radicals; their views more nearly approximated progressivism or populism. Hillquit's remark led one Militant to interject: "You're confusing us with Norman Thomas." To which Hillquit replied with justification: "He has had your full support on this matter."

Some Militants did occasionally declaim against the Fabian belief in the "inevitability of gradualness." But they offered no blueprint for cataclysmic revolution, nor were they seriously opposed to the evolutionary process that most Socialists favored. What they really opposed was the "inevitability of stagnation," which had become the unstated policy of the New York Socialist local. The movement in New York City was still living in the past; the staff was composed entirely of older men, many of whom treated their positions in the party hierarchy as sinecures in lieu of retirement benefits for a lifetime devoted to preaching an unpopular cause. Moreover, they refused to consider possible alternatives to the "tried-and-true" methods that Socialists had employed in New York from one failure to the next. There had been opposition to the stultification of the New York office for some years; but before the rise of Norman Thomas there had been no leader around whom the potential activists could gather.

On one other apparently substantial issue, that of the Soviet Union, the Militants and Old Guard disagreed. The Militants did not, however, adopt a more radical position; theirs was merely a more pro-Soviet one. This pro-Sovietism reflected the liberalism which pervaded the Militant wing of the party. Most liberals of the 1930's tended to be uncritically pro-Soviet; on the contrary, most non-Communist radicals, from Emma Goldman to Morris Hillquit, were highly critical of Stalin's regime.

At the December 1930 session of the New York City convention, Theodore Shapiro, a spokesman for the Militants, attempted to have a pro-Soviet resolution adopted. It was a typical liberal resolution: it hailed Soviet achievements and compared them with the "failures" of the German Social Democrats. Murray Baron, another young Militant, told the convention that capitalism feared nothing more than a Soviet success. A third bright, young Militant, Max Delson, ridiculed the contention that the Soviet regime was oppressive because it was dictatorial. The Soviet people, he contended, were far less interested in ephemeral political democracy than they were in bread. Then Baron, almost accidentally, opened an ideological Pandora's box when, in an effort to defend the Soviet dictatorship, he cried out, "Socialists might have to resort to dictatorship in some countries."

This was too much for Thomas. Although he had defended the Soviet regime against Hillquit only two and a half years previously, he refused to support the endorsement of the dictatorship in 1930. As he had in 1928, Thomas still rejected the violent anti-Soviet attitude of the ultra-conservatives; but he conceded now that the Soviet use of terror was becoming a permanent fixture and that the Russian trade unions were little more than "company unions." All he would grant to the Soviet dictatorship was that it was "the only dictatorship not working for its own profit." He also insisted that the Socialists had to offer "something better than the hard dictatorship of communism." In the end, the convention supported a resolution—endorsed by both Thomas and Hillquit—which was anti-Soviet. The delegates rejected both a violently anti-Soviet resolution, proposed by a group of East European émigré Social Democrats, and the Militants' pro-Soviet proposal.

Although he disagreed with the Militants on the Soviet issue, Thomas remained closely identified with that group for two reasons: first, his distaste for the Old Guard bureaucrats, and, second, his desire to be identified with the younger, more aggressive element in the party.

The Militants were neither monolithic nor well organized. There were disagreements among them on both issues and on tactics. Some of the Militants wanted the party to move further away from Marxian rhetoric and become more of a reformist party—among them, Thomas, Blanshard, and Rosner. Another element among the Militants wanted the party to maintain its Social-Democratic ideology intact while employing more agressive tactics—in this group were Jack Altman, Harry Laidler, and McAlister Coleman. A third segment, which included Samuel DeWitt, Max and Bob Delson, Leonard Bright, and Theodore Shapiro, wanted to turn the party into a more revolutionary Marxist organization.

The divergences in the Militant movement were not considered detrimental by the members of the faction; most enjoyed the discussions that resulted from the disagreements. Most of the Militants were recent college graduates. Intellectual dialogue had become virtually a way of life for them. To expand the dialogue a group of Militants called a conference in the summer of 1931 at the Jewish Socialist Verband camp. The long-range effects of this conference were to be catastrophic for the party, and were to lead to an irreconcilable conflict three years later.

The conference itself produced little that was startling. The discussions were long-winded, replete with radical verbiage as meaningless as it was tedious. The primary targets of the speakers, including Norman Thomas, were the leaders of the nation's trade unions, who were assailed for their subservience to employers, their corruptibility, and their support of capitalist politicians, particularly their alliance with Tammany Hall in New York. The Militants were especially critical of so-called Socialist trade unionists who were unwilling or unable to oppose the non-Socialist orientation of their organizations. There was some revolutionary semantics, but the participants accepted the moderation that American Socialists had been preaching since the anti-sabotage resolution of 1912. True, Norman Thomas declaimed: "It is not our Socialist duty to subordinate socialism to democracy." But in the next breath he was insisting that democracy was the more perfect way to make the revolution.

Although the meeting itself offered nothing to upset even the most moderate of Socialists, immediately after the sessions a small group of Militants took precipitous action which was to change what had been a friendly dialogue on tactics into an interminable internal party squabble which was to sap what strength the party had left. This small group formed a formal Militant factional organization which declared "open warfare" on the party leadership and planned to publish and disseminate "left-wing" material within the party. Support for the Militant cause slipped rapidly after formation of the factional organization. Where barely ten votes separated the Militants from the Old Guard at the 1930–1931 city convention, the Old Guard polled 80 to the Militants' 40 at the 1931–1932 convention.[29]

The Militant–Old Guard dialogue might have been helpful to the party had it continued at the level of 1930–1931. It gave a voice to the party's younger members and it allowed the old-timers, who had spent the greater part of a lifetime in the movement, an opportunity to offer their answers. But the formal organization of the faction turned the friendly discussion into a catastrophic squabble and spelled disaster for the party. One of the few men who might have reconciled the conflict, even after it had become formalized, was Norman Thomas. Unfortunately, he associated himself with the Militant wing and thus eliminated himself as a potential healer of party wounds.

11

Thomas's rapid rise to leadership was resented by many of the older Socialist leaders, particularly Morris Hillquit, who was primarily responsible for it in the first place. Moreover, many of Thomas's actions were hardly designed to ease internal party frictions. There was a holier-than-thou attitude about Thomas which acted as an abrasive. In 1931, this attitude, and the reciprocal animosity it engendered among old-line Socialists, caused a major dispute to erupt which very nearly resulted in a new party split.

This dispute involved a law suit against the Soviet government in which Hillquit acted as attorney for anti-Soviet plaintiffs. It was one of a number of cases involving the Soviet Union in which Hillquit had participated. His success in these cases had built his law practice and made him a wealthy man, which irritated many Socialists. Some of them believed Hillquit was "betraying the working class" by accepting clients who challenged Soviet nationalization decrees. Thomas was particularly annoyed at Hillquit's actions because he believed they could be interpreted as anti-Soviet and thus anti-Socialist. Hillquit ignored most of these private criticisms.

In 1930, Hillquit accepted a case which resulted in a public dispute. This case involved a group of Russian refugees whose oil lands had been seized by the Soviet government and then leased to two American oil companies. The Russian refugees sued for a share in the profits. Although Hillquit denied that his clients' case challenged the authority of a government to nationalize a natural resource, it was obvious to most Socialists that the principle was, in fact, under attack. Hillquit had another strong argument in favor of his taking the case: he was an attorney, and as such had to work within the framework of existing law. The case was a simple one involving a dispute over property rights, the sort of suit that makes up "90 per cent of the regular work of the general practitioner in the legal profession." Unfortunately,

Hillquit was not a mere general legal practitioner—he was also national chairman of the Socialist party.

Thomas saw in the court suit an opportunity to challenge Hillquit's position as a rival for leadership of the party. In 1931, with Hillquit in Europe, Thomas opened his attack. Claiming that "many people inside and outside the party" had asked him about it, he questioned the propriety of Hillquit accepting this type of case. "Cases . . . like the one which Comrade Hillquit has taken up," Thomas wrote in his weekly column in the *New Leader*, "emphatically seem to me to have a political significance contrary to the well-established Socialist position on the right of nationalization and the duty of the United States government to recognize Soviet Russia."[30]

Thomas's attack on Hillquit was resented by the *New Leader's* editor, James Oneal, who attempted unsuccessfully to prevent its publication. Even a capitalist court would not attack a man when he is not around to defend himself, Oneal complained. Although Hillquit may not have been around, he was able to defend himself. "I am frankly at a loss to understand why all these eager questions should have been addressed to Comrade Thomas, who is not responsible for my actions, and why he should consider himself obligated or competent to make public answer to them," Hillquit wrote from Vienna. He further questioned the honesty of Thomas's motives, citing internal party machinery for investigating charges. Moreover, Hillquit did not believe it was Thomas's duty to justify or condemn Hillquit's actions. "It seems to me [that] if I were asked questions concerning Comrade Thomas's conduct in any private undertaking of his, I would, as a matter of common comradely courtesy, refer to him for the answer."

Old Guard Socialists as well as Militants opposed Hillquit's role in the so-called Russian oil cases. Even Oneal, a vehement anti-Militant, agreed that Hillquit had erred in taking the case and wanted him to withdraw for ethical considerations.

Although the lines were not drawn on sharp factional lines, the loudest outcry against Hillquit came from the Militants, who saw an opportunity to eliminate the leading figure in the Old Guard. The loudest outcry against Thomas's tactics came from the Old Guard, who feared Thomas's power in the party. Both Thomas and Hillquit early recognized the potential danger in the situation; Hillquit had in fact made arrangements to withdraw from the case in June 1931. The Thomas attack delayed his formal withdrawal until August. Hillquit's withdrawal did alleviate the immediate danger of a split in the party. But it only delayed the open rupture.

The schism involved few substantive issues. Hillquit saw the disagreement revolving around the issue of "Thomasism," which he described as a movement by Thomas and some of his followers to seize political and intellectual control of the party. To achieve this end, Hillquit realized that the pro-Thomas faction had to undermine Hillquit's leadership. He believed that the pro-Thomas wing wanted to set Thomas up "as a sort of national and international Socialist Pope." The oil suits were merely an excuse for Thomas and his followers to attack Hillquit, the Old Guard leader believed. The Russian oil suit incident pointed up the growing dispute between the old-line labor-oriented Socialists, and the new, Social Gospel–oriented group led by Thomas. "If we let matters drift another year, our divinity students will be insisting that each branch meeting be opened by prayer," Oneal wrote in 1931. Although he was exaggerating the situation, the intellectuals, many of whom were ministers and divinity students, were attempting with considerable success to recast the party; it was becoming apparent that the Socialist party could not continue much longer divided between the lethargic Marxism of the Old Guard and the aggressive Social Gospel progressivism of the pro-Thomas Militants. One or the other would have to drive its rival out.[31]

12

By 1932 Norman Thomas had become the chief Socialist party spokesman on major issues. His influence among new, younger, generally educated middle-class party members was immense. Yet he was disliked and mistrusted by the old-line Socialist leaders who had nurtured the party during the preceding thirty years through occasional success and frequent failure.

To the Old Guard, Thomas was a liberal rather than a Socialist. Certainly, the rhetoric of what he was preaching was hardly socialism as they understood it. To men like Hillquit, Oneal, and Lee, socialism was coextensive with what they defined as Marxism. To Thomas, Marxism and socialism were related but not coextensive. It was this static Marxism of the Old Guard which repelled Thomas, and it was Thomas's non-Marxian "liberalism" which alienated the Old Guard.

Thomas wanted to appeal to the intelligentsia rather than to the working class. "We need their brains and their 'respectability,' " he wrote to Mayor Hoan, "not only because they are valuable in general but because the American workers in their present psychology are likely to follow their lead politically." To the Old Guard this was rank heresy; they still wanted the party to "assert its labor character."

Despite these apparent differences, there was little that separated Thomas's objectives from the objectives of Oneal or Lee or Hillquit. Thomas agreed with the Old Guard that the Socialist revolution would best be achieved without violence. Nor was his view of democracy at variance with that of any other Social Democrat. Both Thomas and the Old Guard agreed that it was necessary to defend parliamentary democracy. Despite disagreements with Hillquit and Lee about some aspects of the Soviet system, Thomas agreed with them that the denial of political liberty by the Stalin regime was creating "precisely the sort of servile state anti-Socialists have always prophesied and which we have indignantly denied we should tolerate."[32]

Yet Thomas and the Old Guard did not speak the same revolutionary language. While they proposed to use the same evolutionary road to the same type socialism, the Old Guard employed Marxian rhetoric and Thomas preferred to use the language of the middle-class intellectual liberal. Hillquit could claim that capitalism was outmoded because "it is not today giving men the bread, the security, the peace, the freedom, the brotherhood which they have a right to expect." He could cite that a million Americans were unemployed even at the height of the prosperity; and those without jobs had to accept "meager and contemptuous charity." Thus, where the so-called Marxists in the Socialist party could condemn capitalism as being historically in error, Thomas condemned it for the ethical and humanitarian price it exacted.

The socialism which Thomas preached was the same as that which Socialists had been preaching for decades in the Western world. He favored public ownership and control of land, natural resources, and the principal means of production and distribution; the use of peaceful, parliamentary means for achieving the transformation of a capitalist into a Socialist society; and the preservation of the democratic state. He doubted that socialism was an infallible panacea for all the wrongs in the world. He did, however, believe it offered the best hope for a "fellowship of free men, which is the only Utopia worthwhile. . . ."

Thomas's Socialism was a dynamic amalgam of Henry George, Karl Marx, and the Social Gospel. He agreed with George that the rental value of land belonged to society and not to the individual. But he questioned that the single tax on unearned increment from land values would by itself erase the world's economic inequities. Thomas admitted that Socialists owed a great debt to Karl Marx, but he urged Socialists to treat Marx with the "attitude scientists take to a Newton or a Darwin, not the attitude Orthodox Jewish Talmudists or Christian theologians take to their Scriptures." He warned Socialists that they would err if they accepted much of the Victorian optimism that permeated Marx, or if they ignored the technological changes which had made much of what he had to say no longer relevant. The class struggle, which Thomas accepted as a fact of history, was not so simple as Marx had painted it. Nor did he believe it implied literal class war. He saw the class struggle as a social myth, as a unifying force. As a concomitant to his view of the class struggle, Thomas wanted the Socialists to appeal to workers as consumers rather than as producers, which marked another of his departures from classical Marxism. The materialistic conception of history he considered poor philosophy and worse psychology. He dismissed the labor theory of value "as least important of all [Marxian theories] for the nonacademic citizen." Yet he recognized that there was no available wealth without work.

Thomas, who resigned his ordination in 1931, remained a Social Gospel Christian. He was elated by such "victories" as the fact that the New York East Conference of the Methodist Church had taken liberal positions with regard to social insurance, civil liberties, and militarism. He called for a new higher relation "of intelligent cooperation in the use of the world's wealth for the abolition of war and the realization of freedom and brotherhood" to replace the "rather shabby capitalist religion of Babbitt and the Rotary Clubs. . . ."[33] Thomas was basically a Social Gospel minister preaching from a nation-wide pulpit to a limitless congregation. Unfortunately, internal parish politics was consuming more and more of his time.

IV
Socialism
in our time,
1932–1934

Between 1932 and 1942, a period of intense political and economic crisis in the United States, the Socialist party, which could have profited, fell apart and disintegrated into a minuscule sect. Twenty years later, Thomas was to blame the Socialist collapse on the popularity of the New Deal. But this was an oversimplification; actually, the party's demise was caused by at least seven different developments. Some of the causes of the party's collapse were beyond the control of Norman Thomas and his followers; but errors of both omission and commission by Thomas played a significant role in the party's demise.

The causes for the disintegration included:

1. The internal struggle between the young Militant, or "left," wing and the entrenched Old Guard, or "right" wing;

2. The New Deal, which enacted almost the entire Socialist program of ameliorative measures;

3. The rise of major reform movements within the two-party system, particularly under Fiorello LaGuardia in New York and Upton Sinclair in California;

4. The Communist drive for a united front with the Socialists;

5. The Spanish Civil War;

6. The "Trojan Horse" activities of the Trotskyites and other Communist sects within the party;

7. Thomas's isolationism (which he labeled noninterventionism) during the pre–Pearl Harbor period of World War II.

There were other, less significant, reasons for the party's demise; but in one way or another all were related with the seven basic causes.

2

In early 1932, the outlook for the Socialist party was hopeful. Membership had increased to 15,332. Admittedly, this was 643 fewer members than the party had had in 1903, but it was almost double the membership in 1928. Moreover, only a relatively small proportion of the party membership was in foreign-language branches with dual loyalties, although this was less the result of Socialist design than of harsh new immigration laws enacted during the 1920's. The circulation of pro-Socialist periodicals rose from 301,000 in 1928 to 700,144 in 1932. Ninety-six new party locals were organized during 1931; and another 114 were formed during the first five months of 1932.

Despite these optimistic signs, the party's national secretary, Clarence Senior, reported to the 1932 national convention: "Unfortunately it [the Socialist party] is not growing as fast as conditions and activity might warrant us to expect." Among other difficulties, state legislatures were making it extremely difficult for Socialists to get on the ballot in key states such as Illinois and Ohio.[1]

Growing factionalism was an additional problem. It was absorbing more of the party activists' time than organizational and electoral work. Not only had the factional disputes grown more intense by 1932, there were also more factions involved. In 1930–1931 there were only two factions, the Old Guard and the Militants. By 1932 there were two new factions—the Reformers and the Pragmatists.

Nor were the factions solid or monolithic groups; they were themselves divided into sub-factions. The most extreme "right wing" sub-faction within the Old Guard was linked with the *Jewish Daily Forward* and its editor, Abraham Cahan, who had been one of the founders of the party but whose socialism had become steadily more diluted until by 1932 it was hardly distinguishable from conservative trade unionism. The more moderate of the Old Guard preached "a social democracy with the accent on the last word." As a whole, the Old Guard was well described by an unfriendly contemporary as composed of "complacent, over-cautious" men who "lack imagination, initiative, and energy." Most of them had been members of the party for twenty years or more.

The ideas of the Reformers and the Pragmatists were identical, except that the Reformers were vehemently anti-Soviet whereas the Pragmatists were sympathetic to the Russian experiment. Neither the Reformers nor the Pragmatists considered themselves Marxists; both believed in appealing to voters as consumers rather than as producers. They were particularly active in agitating for clean municipal government, municipal ownership of public utilities, and the formation of a new labor or Progressive party. B. Charney Vladeck, business manager of the *Forward* and an old antagonist of Cahan, and Mayor Daniel W. Hoan of Milwaukee were the leading figures among the Reformers; Thomas was the leading figure among the Pragmatists. Most of the young Militants, who "would rather be wrong with Thomas than right with Hillquit," had by 1932 come to think of themselves as Marxists; Thomas had not. Many of them conceded that the "old-time Marxians in the party [the Old Guard] unquestionably have a case against Thomas" for his non-Marxist reformism. They looked upon Thomas as a Moses who could lead the party out of Old Guard control, but hardly as the man who could lead America to socialism.

The leaders of the Militant faction included Franz Daniel, of Union Theological Seminary, Professor Maynard Krueger of the University of Chicago, Max Delson, a New York attorney, and Paul Porter, fresh from the University of Pennsylvania. The Militants were almost all younger professional men; many were ministers recently graduated from Union, Vanderbilt, Crozer, or Harvard; some were professors at Harvard, Smith, or Union, and a few were attorneys. Most had been in the party less than two years, and their clarion cry was "Socialism in our time."

The ideological differences among the Militants were at times greater than their differences with the Old Guard. To the older members of the faction, such as McAlister Coleman, militancy meant "going to the workers with concrete evidence of our alliance with their cause. I mean living out our struggle where the struggle is hottest." In essence, Coleman favored a program of organizing the unorganized workers. His militancy was basically a form of activism not unlike the position of the Militants of 1930–1931. The "Revolutionary Marxism" of most of the other Militants was a concoction composed of Marxism, elitism, and syndicalism. They opposed liberal or reformist tendencies within the party, though their choice for party spokesman, Norman Thomas, was a pragmatic reformer. They wanted the party to place its reliance primarily on working-class elements, even if they themselves were mainly middle-class intellectuals. They favored the party's adopting a noncritical pro-Soviet stance. They wanted the Socialists formally to condemn craft unions and endorse industrial unions which would organize the unorganized.

Most important, the Militants of 1932 opposed "naive reliance on bourgeois 'democratic' institutions." In their view, "Capitalist democracy is in reality the property of the capitalist class. . . . [which] can be viewed as a game between capital and labor in which the capitalist is at liberty to make the rules, count the points, or suspend the rules entirely. . . ." The Militants accused the members of other factions of making a fetish of "capitalist democracy," whereas "we, revolutionary Marxists . . . want socialism, not democracy."

The attack on democracy nearly splintered the Militant faction. Anna Bercowitz, the editor of the pro-Militant *American Socialist Quarterly*, denounced the demand for immediate socialism at the cost of democracy. She told the Militants that they did not realize that "in democracy the working class, the deadly enemy of capitalism, has a wonderful weapon for itself. If the workers only understood how to use this weapon, it would become the most dangerous thing for capitalism. . . ." Thomas, who agreed with the Bercowitz position, was irritated by the antidemocratic statement of the Militant faction, and in fact considered severing his ties with the Militants because of it. But his antipathy for the Old Guard and the adulation of the young "revolutionaries" led him to continue his close relationship.[2]

3

So severe had the feuding become by mid-1932 that Socialists could only hope that the various elements within the party would somehow work together during the forthcoming presidential campaign. It turned out to be a futile hope. The May 1932 national convention in Milwaukee, at which Thomas was nominated for President for the second time, was the most unruly and factionalized in twenty years, with delegates involved in internal squabbling from the start.

The convention could have been a high point in Socialist history. Consider the context. There were at least ten million Americans out of work; farm prices were nearing all-time lows; banks were closing, some permanently. The United States was in the depths of the depression, and Americans should have been receptive to the Socialist message. But Socialists were more interested in their internal squabbles than in influencing American politics. Mayor Hoan's welcoming address, in which he pleaded that "we devote our time to building the Socialist party . . . and waste no time in bickering . . ." was virtually ignored by the assembled delegates. They were too busy caucusing to hear him. Almost immediately after the address the convention got down to the business of the day—feuding.

There were at least two diametrically opposed resolutions on each issue of substance. The pro-Soviet resolution proposed by the Militants was adopted after it had been modified by Thomas into a simple demand that the Stalin regime be recognized. The Militant resolution on trade unions, which called for party control of Socialists in trade unions and an effective organizing campaign, was defeated after hours of debate. All the other Militant resolutions met the same fate. Four separate planks were proposed on Prohibition: (1) to ignore the issue completely; (2) to call for a popular referendum; (3) to demand repeal and government ownership of liquor production and distribution; and (4) to denounce the major parties for raising the issue in an effort to divert attention from social injustice. The convention voted 84 to 77 for repeal after an intemperate debate which cut across factional lines.

Thomas's nomination, which was opposed by only one delegate, was, in effect, the eye of the hurricane. It came immediately after the vituperative debates on program and platform and immediately before the even more heated fight over the attempt to oust Morris Hillquit from the national chairmanship. It was the latter issue—over an honorary, powerless position—which pointed up the ideological emptiness of the party struggle.

Hillquit succeeded Victor Berger as national chairman after the latter's death in 1929, and it soon became clear that he had been a poor choice. His health was failing; his lucrative law practice had made him suspect in the eyes of many Socialists; he spent much of his time in Europe at international Socialist conferences and virtually ignored the problems of organization; as a foreigner and a long-time resident of New York, he was suspect in the eyes of many Midwestern party members who mistrusted New Yorkers in general and foreigners in particular.

Thomas played the leading role in the effort to oust Hillquit. Their antipathy for each other had been growing since 1928. Thomas believed that Hillquit acted as a brake on Socialist activity nationally at a time when Thomas's protégé, Clarence Senior, was trying to make the party an effective organization. Thomas also considered Hillquit his chief rival for party leadership. For these reasons, Thomas was instrumental in arranging for a coalition of all anti-Hillquit elements in an effort to wrest the national chairmanship from him. He brought together the Reformers, the Pragmatists, and the Militants into an alliance whose sole interest was the removal of Hillquit. Their choice for his replacement was Mayor Hoan, the least militant of the party leaders. Hoan was friendly with most of the Old Guard, but he had detested Hillquit since the days of World War I when the *Milwaukee Daily Leader* lost its mail privileges and was struggling for life. All of the *Leader's* creditors—except Hillquit—had agreed to forgo interest payments; Hillquit collected his interest regularly. (Years later, Hoan learned that it was not Hillquit, who was at the time ill in a sanatorium, who insisted on the interest payments; it was a New York bank which was handling all of his accounts.) Hoan's distaste for Hillquit was reinforced when they worked together during the LaFollette campaign of 1924. Hoan found Hillquit to be "self-important," dogmatic, unpleasant, egotistical, and "a great student of international problems, but woefully weak on matters of organizational tactics." Despite his antipathy for Hillquit, Hoan refused to run until Thomas convinced him that he was the only one who could defeat the incumbent.

Jim Maurer, Thomas's 1928 running mate, tried in vain to work out a compromise. He used his personal friendship with Thomas, Hoan, and Hillquit to mediate the antagonism. But it was too late; none was willing to settle the dispute amicably. The debate was bitter. Socialists accused other Socialists of Ku Kluxism, nativism, and anti-Semitism. Joseph Sharts of Ohio charged that the "formula of the Hoan supporters is that no Jew can lead the Socialist party." (Even the pro-Hillquit *Jewish Daily Forward* labeled the Sharts charges false.) Hillquit won the election with a minority of the vote: he polled 7,526 votes cast by 105 delegates, Hoan received 6,985 votes from 80 delegates, with nine delegates representing approximately 730 votes abstaining. Hillquit carried only the New Jersey, California, and Ohio delegations unanimously and won a majority of the vote in New York, Connecticut, and Pennsylvania. Hoan carried all of the other states.

Hillquit used his acceptance speech to excoriate his opponents, especially Thomas and Hoan. He told the delegates: "I do not belong to the Daniel Hoan group to whom socialism consists of merely providing clean sewers of Milwaukee. . . . I am also against practical socialism [which Thomas had called for in his acceptance speech], for I am above all else a Marxian Socialist. . . ."

The Old Guard's victory in the fight over the national chairmanship was to be its last. The very next day they lost control of the national party machinery. The anti–Old Guard factions elected five members—Leo Krzycki of Wisconsin, Powers Hapgood of Indiana, Darlington Hoopes of Pennsylvania, Albert Sprague Coolidge of Massachusetts, and Norman Thomas—to the previously Old Guard–dominated national executive committee. The Old Guard elected only three: Jasper McLevy, the future mayor of Bridgeport, Connecticut, Lilith Wilson of Pennsylvania, and John C. Packard of California. Two of the new committeemen—Hoan and James Graham of Montana—were ambivalent, though they leaned toward the anti–Old Guard faction.

Hillquit's victory soon proved to be a hollow one for the Old Guard, when he died in October 1933. Fearful that Thomas would succeed him, the leaders of the Old Guard attempted to convince Hoan to run for the post. But Hoan refused, and Thomas was not interested in the empty honor. The post then went to Leo Krzycki of Milwaukee, a vice-president of the Amalgamated Clothing Workers, who was considered more of a Militant than either Thomas or Hoan.[3]

4

Despite the ill-will engendered by the convention struggle over the national chairmanship and the intensification of the factional fight in the party, many Socialists were hopeful of polling a record vote in the 1932 presidential election. Shortly after he was nominated, Thomas wrote: "Everybody agrees that this year is a year of Socialist opportunity. Socialist interest and even Socialist locals are springing up in unexpected places in gratifying fashion." Nor were Socialists alone in assuming that they would get a record vote; many non-Socialists agreed with them. One Republican journalist predicted that Thomas would get two million votes; and the Democratic campaign committee feared that Thomas was endangering a Roosevelt victory in New York and three other key states.

Thomas proved an inexhaustible campaigner. He spoke as many as six times a day, seven days a week. His audiences were huge; where in 1928 he addressed crowds of four to five hundred, in 1932 he had audiences of eight to ten thousand. In New York he attracted more than twenty thousand persons to Madison Square Garden, and in Milwaukee fourteen thousand flocked to hear him. Record crowds were reported from coast to coast. He was a favorite among collegians throughout the country. He led in straw polls at Pennsylvania, Columbia, and New York Universities, among others; he ran second to Hoover at the Universities of Chicago and Minnesota, and at Vassar, Jamestown, and Hiram Colleges; at Notre Dame and Milwaukee State College he ran ahead of Hoover but behind Roosevelt. Forty-six members of the Harvard faculty supported him publicly; and the editor of *Christian Century* called him "the best informed, deepest thinking, and most morally courageous political leader now playing a major role in our national life."

Thomas was held in high esteem even by some of capitalism's staunchest defenders. Claude Moore Fuess, a conservative journalist, reported that it had become fashionable among the more affluent to say that they would vote for Thomas as a protest against the failure of the government to act in the worsening economic crisis. Fuess was himself impressed with Thomas, whom he described as resembling Woodrow Wilson in depending more on logic than on emotions in his appeal. He noted that Thomas's "manner is faintly academic," and suggested that he would "fit naturally into the atmosphere of an English house party with Balfour and Asquith." Such a man was hardly likely to be a dangerous radical, certainly not a bomb-throwing enemy of established society. Fuess likened Thomas to St. Francis of Assisi, Tolstoy, and Gandhi, "the immaculate idealists of the race."

Although Thomas won support and respect from middle-class intellectuals, he did poorly within the ranks of labor. Even nominally Socialist labor-union officials gave his campaign a minimum of support. Only one national union, the American Federation of Full-Fashioned Hosiery Workers, and one state federation of labor, that in Vermont, endorsed Thomas. The unions which normally supplied the finances for Socialist campaigns were particularly niggardly in 1932. Only $26,000 was raised from all sources, compared with $110,000 in 1928. Few local unions supported Thomas, who had to rely on some 267 *ad hoc* campus-based Thomas-for-President clubs and the six hundred Socialist party branches to do the day-to-day work of carrying on a campaign at the local level.

In New York, the labor unions were particularly antipathetic to the Thomas campaign. The New York State Federation of Labor and the Central Trades and Labor Council of New York City were political appendages of the Tammany Hall Democratic machine. When Governor Roosevelt, after interminable procrastination, finally forced Mayor Walker to resign in 1932, on the basis of charges made in 1929 by Thomas, the state federation voted its confidence in Walker. At the same meeting the federation voted, with little opposition, to support Roosevelt for President. The only active opposition came from Herman Woskow, a pro-Thomas Socialist who was the delegate from the Pressmen's Union; the nominally Socialist delegates from the International Ladies Garment Workers and other needle trades unions were absent. Woskow charged that they had absented themselves by design.

Thomas's campaign was directed primarily against Roosevelt, whom he accused of "parading under the false colors of liberalism." Thomas charged that Roosevelt was "playing ball" with Tammany, that he had no program, and that he took his orders on foreign affairs from publisher William Randolph Hearst, a jingoistic enemy of the League of Nations. Thomas indicated that he had more respect for Hoover than he did for Roosevelt, since, as he noted, Hoover had the advantage of consistency. Both major party platforms came under Thomas's fire for their conservatism. Brevity was the only advantage he found in the Democratic platform. As between the two parties, Thomas had no preference, finding one as bad as the other. In practice, however, Thomas saved his heaviest ammunition for the Democrats.

He charged that it was the "party which debars Negroes from the polls in the South and makes it difficult for white workers to vote by poll-tax; the party of machine-made corrupt politics in Northern cities. . . ." Thomas's attacks on the Democrats can be explained by the fact that both he and they were appealing to the same constituency of disenchanted Americans; he had little hope of reaching solid Republicans, the only voters who could be expected to support Hoover in 1932.

The primary theme of Thomas's campaign was social reform within the context of capitalism. He did say that the capitalist system was no longer viable and that a socialist structure based on production for use and not for profit would have to replace it; but he said it rarely, and without much conviction. He paid lip service to the young Militants within the party by saying, "We are not democrats at the price of socialism," but he was quick to add that there was no reason to use undemocratic means in a country which, like America, had a democratic tradition. He said Socialists were revolutionists, but in the next breath added that this did not mean that he or the party favored cataclysm; it meant rather that they wanted to overhaul the system completely "without the wholesale mass violence which in this age of economic complexity and destructiveness . . . would prove so incredibly deadly. . . ."

Thomas knew he could not win the 1932 election; his primary objective in the campaign was to bring the party's message before the public. He was acting in the role of an evangelist hoping to influence the American people to accept as part of their salvation such things as minimum-wage laws, maximum-hour laws, unemployment insurance, and old-age pensions. To a woman who wrote offering to support him personally, he replied, "I would not for a moment solicit the support of voters as a personal matter, since it is my emphatic belief that the 'good man' theory in politics is quite misleading. . . . [My] own personal views . . . are of far less importance than the official declaration of the Socialist party, as expressed in the platform and declaration of principles."

Despite a spirited campaign and huge crowds, despite economic and political indications of a record Socialist vote, Thomas polled only 884,781 votes, or barely 2.5 per cent of the nearly 40 million cast. Roosevelt won with 22,809,638 votes to 15,758,901 for Hoover. Thomas blamed his small vote on the liberal constituency's fear that Hoover might win, and to a great extent this was true. Yet dissent within the party played a major role in his electoral failure. In Old Guard–dominated districts, Thomas ran considerably behind the rest of the Socialist ticket; in Militant districts, he ran extremely well. In New York, the Old Guard stronghold, for example, Thomas polled only 122,565 votes, while Hillquit, who was the Socialist candidate for Mayor, polled 251,656. Socialist congressional candidates in New York City, who normally run far behind the presidential candidate, polled 139,419 votes.

The feuds which disrupted the campaign were caused by minor irritations. Most were mere symptoms of the malaise of factionalism. When two Militants, Amicus Most and Mary Hillyer, were employed by the national office to do campaign work, there was serious complaint from the Old Guard, particularly from William Feigenbaum, associate editor of the *New Leader*. Another incident was caused by the party's national campaign committee's organization of a Thomas-for-President Committee in New York, which was composed of intellectuals who supported the national ticket. The New York state organization complained that the committee was being set up in an effort to bypass the state and local organizations, and charged that it would hinder the party's work for the rest of the ticket. The argument was specious, for the reverse was actually true, the committee having been set up to raise funds for the Thomas campaign and thus release the New York party to devote its primary energies to the local campaigns. The Old Guard–controlled New York party virtually ignored Thomas's campaign, and placed obstacles in the path of the committee at every opportunity.

The feud reached its climax a few days before the election when a letter from Paul H. Douglas, chairman of the Thomas-for-President Committee, appeared in the *Nation*. It suggested a plan by which voters could cast their ballots for Thomas and still be assured they were not helping the major party candidate they most disliked. The plan, similar to pairing in Congress, called for the pairing of anti-Roosevelt voters, who preferred Thomas but were voting for Hoover, with anti-Hoover voters, who preferred Thomas but were voting for Roosevelt, thus free-

ing each to vote for Thomas. It attracted no attention from potential voters. But it was another excuse for the Old Guard to
vent its anger on Thomas and his followers. Julius Gerber, the
executive secretary of the New York party and a member of the
Old Guard who loathed Thomas, sent a letter to Mayor Hoan,
the national campaign director, demanding that he take immediate action. "Let us not pervert our party, the Socialist party,
from a party of labor to a party of reform," Gerber wrote. Trying to placate both sides, Hoan sent a letter to the *Nation* which
proved, primarily, that he, like most Socialists, did not understand the Douglas plan.

There were other instances of irritation; charges and counter-
charges flew, almost all of them irrelevant or tangential. But it
was apparent that the animosities engendered by the internal dispute had reached a point where insignificant incidents now took
on major proportions. The result was an ineffective campaign
and a low vote for Thomas.

The election results were disappointing to Thomas. Yet there
were some hopeful signs. Thomas was convinced that there were
884,781 "convinced Socialist voters"; the protest vote had gone
to Roosevelt. Moreover, neither FDR nor the Democrats generally had indicated to Thomas's satisfaction that they could
solve the depression, thus "Democratic [party] failure, which is
inevitable, will be bound to play into our hands. . . ."[4] Thomas
was also certain that the Socialist party, or a new labor or Progressive party, would rise to victory from the ashes of the 1932
election.

5

The election did not affect the party's growth adversely.
Senior had feared that a Socialist vote of less than 5 million would
result in a sharp decline in membership. Instead, the rate of increase accelerated immediately after the election. By the end of
1932 there were six thousand more members in the party than
there had been the previous year. Long dormant organizations
were coming back to life, and new party centers were mush-
rooming. After a fourteen-year hiatus, there was once again a
Socialist party organization in Oklahoma, a pre-war pillar of Socialist strength. There were new state units in Arizona and West

Virginia. This new growth was due in great part to Thomas's campaign. Wherever he spoke, he spent considerable effort rejuvenating dormant party organizations and uniting sympathetic individuals into Socialist units.

There was scant expectation among Socialists or their sympathizers that the party could hope to gain power in the foreseeable future. At least one significant Socialist supporter, the radio news commentator Gabriel Heatter, blamed the bleak outlook on the failure of the old-line Socialists to "amend outworn and impossible tenets." Heatter suggested that the word "Socialism" was repugnant to most Americans, and proposed that the party change its name and reconstruct itself into a "real third party movement unencumbered by the handicaps which the socialist Party labors under today." If it reorganized itself into such a party, and stripped its program bare of the verbiage gathered through the ages, Heatter suggested, the party could gain millions of new followers. Heatter's proposal was rejected by Thomas; yet his own program was remarkably similar to it. "Our immediate business," Thomas wrote, "is to unite in a party, socialist in objective and program, whatever its name, the men and women who want substantially what we want but go on voting for a Norris or a LaFollette in the old parties because they admire them and understand their language as they do not understand us. These men in the old parties never can achieve what we want." What Thomas could not accept in the Heatter proposal, however, was the suggestion that the Socialist party divest itself of an ultimate goal. He insisted that the party required such a goal as a myth, or a mystique, which would appeal "very definitely and specifically to the exploited workers with hand and brain. . . ."

Thomas was unalterably opposed to any creed which would, in effect, require every Socialist speaker to "shout class conflict in Marxian language." This reiteration of dogma, in language that was alien to most American workers, was one of the causes to which Thomas ascribed the failure of the Socialist party. His opposition to dogma extended to both the lethargic Marxism of the Old Guard and the hyper-revolutionary Marxism of the various Communist parties and sects. He accused the Old Guard of using its Marxism as a cover for inaction: "I protest when certain self-proclaimed Marxists act as if to believe in the class struggle was a kind of mystic act of faith, which almost absolves them from hard and intelligent work."

Thomas's objection to the quietism of the Old Guard and to the bluster of the Communists and so-called revolutionary Socialists placed him outside the Marxist pale. Yet he was not rejecting Marxism *per se*. He agreed that in "the historical development of socialism, Marx and the Marxist school hold first place." The economic crisis was proof to Thomas that the Marxian theory of recurring crises under capitalism had merit, and he accepted Marx's prophecy that capitalism would be destroyed "by doom that it carried within it." Similarly, he agreed that the class struggle was an actual fact both in the sense of an ongoing struggle between groups with conflicting interests and as "*the* class struggle between an owning and a working class. . . ."

But to Thomas the fact of class struggle did not imply—as it did to most Communists—that there could be no social salvation without catastrophe, confusion, and disorder. Nor did it follow that because he rejected the Communist faith in violence that he wanted the Socialists to be committed to absolute pacifism. It meant simply that he wanted Socialists to seek "earnestly to preserve international peace and to utilize democratic methods." It was, in his view, childish to assume that present and future events in America would "conform absolutely to the Russian model." Thomas insisted that it would be better to use democratic methods where they were available than to overthrow a democratic parliamentary regime "for the sake of an uncertain chance of developing out of catastrophe an effective Communist dictatorship."

If Thomas had little faith in the traditional Marxists, by 1932 —one year after he resigned his ordination—he had even less faith in the Christian Church. "Christianity, after nineteen centuries, has not yet been tried," he wrote. Yet he still believed in the need for a Christian social order, and was convinced that socialism was the best way to achieve it. "The ethics of Christianity and the kind of God it professes to accept as Lord of Life are . . . wholly incompatible with capitalism and its god profit," he urged. To achieve the good Christian life, he said, would require a revolution in the Church, for it has "in the main been an opiate" while its sacred book has within it "so much dynamite." No longer a minister, but now the leader of a radical political movement, Thomas was still basically a Social Christian pleading for a world based on the Social Gospel.

Thomas was even more disillusioned with the labor-union movement, which he accused of lacking idealism. The result, he maintained, was corruption and intimidation of members by labor officials. "In union after union, men and women think of themselves not as citizens of the Republic of Labor but as subjects to a more or less useful labor oligarchy which gets them favors."[5]

6

The program of social reform inaugurated by Franklin D. Roosevelt immediately after he took office as President was one of the chief causes for the disintegration of the American Socialist party. The New Deal enacted most of the Socialist proposals for amelioration of conditions of working people under a capitalist system. Many of the Socialists and progressives, who had supported Norman Thomas, now backed Roosevelt. Among them were most of the Socialist trade-union officials, almost all of the founders of the League for Independent Political Action, and great numbers of intellectuals, who began their government careers working for the various agencies established by Roosevelt during his first two terms in office. Among those who supported the Socialist ticket in 1932 and were later to serve in the Congress as New Deal Democrats were Paul H. Douglas of Illinois, Andrew Biemiller of Wisconsin, and George Rhodes of Pennsylvania. Even Norman Thomas seriously considered supporting Roosevelt for a short period in late 1933 and early 1934.

Immediately before Roosevelt was inaugurated, Thomas feared that the economic crisis would worsen, and that there would be further deflation as Democratic congressmen attempted to balance the budget as promised in their platform. He feared the result would be a demand for wild inflation, followed by a cry for stabilization, and thence dictatorship. Thomas was not alone in assuming the worst; other political figures despaired for American democracy and thought America could easily become a fascist state. Thomas pointed out that there existed in America such social phenomena as "abominable racial and national prejudices"; a willingness to worship a strong man; an impatience with democracy; extremely weak and poorly organized labor and Socialist movements; and a powerful group of conservative, anti-democratic industrialists.

Thomas was more optimistic after Roosevelt's inauguration. On March 13, 1933, he and Hillquit visited Roosevelt; both were impressed by the new President's action of closing all banks temporarily in order to avert a financial crisis. Roosevelt, unlike previous Presidents who ignored radicals, listened attentively as the two Socialist leaders proposed that Roosevelt socialize the Federal Reserve System, establish a public banking system, turn all banks that the government rescued from bankruptcy over to the public system, direct tighter Federal Reserve Board controls of solvent banks, and establish a National Credit Board and a National Economic Council to control credit. Thomas and Hillquit also recommended that Roosevelt propose that Congress guarantee each family $10 a week and each single person $5 a week and appropriate $6 billion in public works, half of which would be used for building public-housing units.

Four weeks after Roosevelt's inauguration, Thomas was elated with the administration's accomplishments. FDR had shown "an energy and directness of purpose surpassing anything his earlier record had led us to expect." Thomas conceded that Roosevelt's program was "hopelessly inadequate" for 1933, but it was at least a start in the right direction. Whether what he did was good, bad, or indifferent, it was, said Thomas, "at least action which temporarily restored hope and confidence and lifted the country out of the depths of depression." Thomas attributed much of the slight economic improvement which was noted by late 1933 to the New Deal, though he feared "there has not been enough improvement to really make a great difference in the living conditions of the workers." To Socialists and other radicals who charged that the New Deal had simply replaced laissez faire with state capitalism, he replied that even if this were true it did not "deny the magnitude of some of the achievements or the considerable measure of social idealism behind them." The truth was, Thomas told his fellow Socialists, that Roosevelt's program "far more nearly resembled the Socialist . . . than his own platform." He was basically correct. Where Socialists called for a thirty-hour week, most codes under Roosevelt's National Industrial Recovery Act established thirty-five to forty-hour weeks. Socialists asked for $10 billion in relief and public works funds; FDR had appropriated $3.8 billion. Socialists called for the abolition of sweatshops and child labor; the NIRA codes abolished most sweatshop conditions and did away with child labor except in some agricultural work and newspaper vending. "Without [the New Deal]," Thomas wrote, ". . . no one knows what stage of disintegration we should have reached." The lack of organization of workers and farmers, he warned, made it likely that the chaos would have led to riots, confusion, and probably fascism. He believed that the New Deal gave labor and Socialists time to build for a new society.

After eight months, Thomas believed that under "the Roosevelt administration the workers have won much." He was convinced that Roosevelt's program was not socialism, but it did indicate that democracy could be made to work, and it represented progress. Not all Socialists agreed with Thomas's analysis. The super-revolutionists, who were by late 1933 and early 1934 moving into the Socialist party from small and exotic Communist sects, and many of the Old Guard agreed on little except their antagonism toward the New Deal. Within a year after the Inauguration, the Old Guard figure James Oneal insisted that Roosevelt had failed. As proof he cited the decline of the middle class, many of whose members were becoming working men. An official party pronouncement, written by Oneal, declared the only virtue of the New Deal to be that it offered a technique for the organization of labor. Although Thomas was favorably inclined toward Roosevelt, he agreed with the party's Marxists that the New Deal was not socialism. But where they considered it rank heresy to praise the New Deal, he called it "an immensely bold attempt to stabilize capitalism," and he thought the attempt worth making. Moreover, instead of assailing Roosevelt as an agent of the capitalist class who was attempting to blind the workers to their enslavement under capitalism, Thomas was impressed with Roosevelt as a President "who has courage, political shrewdness, a liberal point of view, and a willingness to act. . . ."

At the outset, Thomas did fear that the New Deal might lead to fascism. "It is by no means certain that the job [which the Roosevelt administration set for itself] can be done at all," Thomas wrote a month after Roosevelt took office; "it is certain that if it is done it will be at the price of a definite transi-

tion to a fascist stage of capitalism. . . ." Yet a month later
Thomas had changed his mind; he could now report that "I do
not think that . . . America has gone dangerously far along the
line of making the President a dictator. Indeed, that someone
can lead is heartening. . . . We Socialists in power would have to
emulate the President's vigor in getting things done. . . ." Although the Civilian Conservation Corps, composed of young unemployed men assigned under semi-military conditions to jobs
in the nation's forest preserves, was too similar to the Mussolini
youth groups for comfort, Thomas doubted that there was any
danger of Roosevelt becoming a fascist dictator. The lack of a
definite philosophy on Roosevelt's part was what most disturbed
Thomas about the New Deal. Nor were its ultimate aims discernible to him. He claimed that Roosevelt took seemingly drastic
action amid a fanfare of propaganda, and then after "extensive
use of government credit to back big business . . . we have met
another crisis and are right back where we started from."
Thomas criticized the Roosevelt administration for what he considered its extravagant use of propaganda and threats, and its lack
of "positive action." He was unhappy that the New Deal operated to protect the capitalist system. Yet Thomas conceded that
his own actions, should he have been elected, would have been
substantially the same as Roosevelt's during his first hundred days
in office; the difference would have been one of ultimate philosophy. Unlike Roosevelt and his "grand adventure in opportunism," Thomas would have wanted, ultimately, to launch a "direct attack on the all-important question of the redistribution of
national income. . . ." Except its lack of a long-range philosophy,
there was little about the New Deal which Thomas criticized.

He was particularly pleased with Section 7A of the National
Industrial Recovery Act, which allowed labor to organize and
bargain collectively. The President had done for labor all he
could have done, Thomas wrote; the rest was up to labor itself.
He doubted that most of the labor unions were capable of making
proper use of the new law in organizing the unskilled and the
Negroes, but there was nothing more the President or Congress
could do. The organization of labor by crafts rather than by industries, or the jurisdictional warfare between various unions,
were matters that could only be solved by working men themselves. They could be accomplished either by reforming the

AFL, which Thomas favored, or by the formation of new unions, which he opposed. Most Socialists agreed with Thomas, but there were some who had grown impatient and were pressing for new aggressive industrial unions, and others who showed what Thomas labeled "undue servility to AFL officialdom."

The Securities and Exchange Act would be of little help to workers and farmers, but Thomas agreed that it was a worthwhile law for the protection of small investors. Despite defects in the Home Owners Loan Act—particularly the lack of coercive power over banks and the 80 per cent of true value limit on loans—he did not oppose it. The one piece of New Deal legislation which Thomas most favored was the basically socialist Tennessee Valley Authority. The one piece of New Deal legislation that most disturbed him was the Agricultural Adjustment Act, which paid farmers "from the proceeds of a tax on consumers to destroy that abundance of foodstuffs which men had struggled thousands upon thousands of years to be able to create. And this . . . in the midst of a cold and hungry world."

The height of labor and Socialist adulation of the New Deal came at a victory meeting of the International Ladies Garment Workers Union, which had just settled a strike, at New York's Madison Square Garden in October 1933. Abraham Cahan, one of the speakers, delivered a long eulogy of Roosevelt and his administration, which concluded: "President Roosevelt has earned the gratitude of every thinking man in the country. He should be a Socialist; if anybody is entitled to membership in our party he is." Thomas, who also spoke, was only slightly less enthusiastic than Cahan. He said he would second Cahan's nomination of FDR for membership in the Socialist party if Roosevelt would propose to nationalize coal mining and banking. In the light of Roosevelt's actions, his championing of TVA, and the continuing economic crises in the coal and banking industries, it was not farfetched to assume that Roosevelt might attempt such nationalization.[6]

7

Thomas's activity in New York municipal affairs, particularly his candidacy for Mayor in 1929, had earned him a considerable following among civic reformers. Some were sorely disappointed that he was running for President and thus not available as the mayoralty candidate in the 1932 election, which was to choose a one-year successor to James J. Walker. Thus, when the planning for the 1933 regular municipal campaign was being organized, Raymond V. Ingersoll, leader of the Brooklyn reformers, asked Thomas to be the mayoralty candidate of an anti-Tammany fusion movement then being formed. The proposed fusion movement was to have been composed of the New York City Republican party and other elements that might be willing to unite with it to fight Tammany Hall. Thomas was sorely tempted by Ingersoll's offer, but his position as nominal national leader of the Socialist party, and his refusal to work with the New York Republican organization, which he considered the "jackal" of city politics, made it necessary for him to refuse the offer.

The Socialists, no less than the civic reformers, recognized that with Thomas as their candidate they might capture the most coveted mayoralty in the nation. The Seabury disclosures were beginning to have their effect, and Thomas was exceedingly popular because of his role in exposing the municipal scandals under Tammany. The party's leaders, particularly Louis Waldman and Harry W. Laidler, wanted Thomas to be the Socialist candidate for Mayor. But Thomas's antipathy for the Old Guard bureaucrats who controlled the party machinery in New York was so strong that he refused. He doubted, too, that any Socialist could win against a fusion candidate dedicated to reform, and besides he wanted to limit himself to national issues.

The Socialists therefore nominated Charles Solomon, a labor lawyer and party war-horse. He ran a disheartening campaign against three major opponents, two of whom called themselves reformers. The Republican-Fusionists nominated Fiorello LaGuardia, progressive Republican congressman from East Harlem and a friend of Thomas; the Tammany Democrats renominated colorless, if uncorrupted, Mayor John P. O'Brien, and the dissident Democrats under Bronx boss Edward Flynn nominated Joseph V. McKee, the president of the Board of Aldermen. It was apparent from the start that Solomon's vote would be woefully small. Most of the reformers who would have favored Thomas were now supporting LaGuardia. Thomas was inactive during the campaign; on the few occasions when he did speak for Solomon, he refused to assail LaGuardia, reserving his fire instead for McKee and O'Brien. The Solomon campaign received a body blow in September when Paul Blanshard, former secretary of the League for Industrial Democracy, former editor of the *Nation*, Militant Socialist, and close friend and literary collaborator of Norman Thomas, resigned from the Socialist party to support LaGuardia. Other Socialists interested in immediate civic reform, notably John Haynes Holmes, threatened to follow suit. Only an appeal by Thomas prevented Holmes's defection, though he told Thomas he could see no reason why the Socialists did not join the fusion movement "under such conditions of local interest as exist in New York today."

Defections, threats of defections, lack of interest in the campaign within the faction-ridden party, a shortage of funds, a luckluster candidate, and a fusion ticket which attracted the anti-Tammany voters who would normally have supported Thomas—all these combined to cut the Socialist vote in New York to less than half of what it had been four years earlier. Solomon polled only 63,450 votes and ran a poor fourth. The remainder of the Socialist ticket in the city did as poorly. Thomas was upset, and wrote to Clarence Senior saying that the poor showing raised serious questions about the future of the party in New York City. True, Socialists had done well in other cities; they had, under Jasper McLevy, swept all offices in Bridgeport, Connecticut; the two major parties had found it necessary to run a single ticket to defeat Socialist J. Henry Stump in Reading, Pennsylvania; and major gains were recorded by Socialists in Olean, New York, and Toledo, Ohio, among other cities. But in New York City, which was Thomas's primary interest, the party was in poor shape after the disastrous showing in the municipal election.

LaGuardia invited Thomas to become a member of his municipal cabinet, but Thomas refused. Other Socialists were less reticent about accepting high-level positions with the non-Socialist municipal government. Blanshard accepted the post of commissioner of investigations. Henry Rosner and Michael White, two of the party's experts on civic affairs, joined LaGuardia's staff after resigning from the party. Jacob Panken was named to the Domestic Relations Court bench. Solomon was named a magistrate in an appointment that particularly annoyed Thomas because it "makes us look like a job bargaining party."

At the suggestion of LaGuardia, Thomas was named a member, without pay, of the Charter Revision Commission, the only political position Thomas ever held. He was active on this commission in proposing the legalization of muncipal ownership of public utilities and proportional representation in the city legislature. Although the commission dissolved in 1934 without any clear accomplishments, its real achievements became apparent four years after its demise when Thomas's proposals came to fruition with the municipal ownership of the huge transit system and the enactment of proportional representation in elections to the City Council.[7]

8

Because Thomas had an active record of aid to labor unions, because his honesty was above suspicion, and because he was nominal leader of the Socialist party and thus accepted as a non-Communist, his aid was sought by trade unionists fighting racketeering or conservative control of their organizations. Thomas's involvement in several union squabbles during the early 1930's resulted in serious friction between the Old Guard and himself, and played a significant role in the disintegration of the Socialist party.

The most serious disagreement developed in 1933 over Thomas's actions in the struggle for power between the AFL Fur Workers International Union, controlled by Old Guard Socialists, and the Communist-controlled Fur Workers Union of the Needle Trades Workers Industrial Union. In this battle, one of the bloodiest in New York labor history, both sides used tactics that were reminiscent of gang warfare. The Communists used physical violence and employed such gangsters as Arnold Rothstein against their opponents. The right-wing AFL union used political deals and court injunctions against the Communist-controlled union. By the time Thomas became involved in the dispute, the physical assaults had ceased temporarily; the AFL union had obtained an injunction prohibiting employers from bargaining with the left-wing union, or the left-wingers from bargaining with the employers. "Communist or Communist-controlled dual unions have uniformly failed to meet the needs of the mass of workers," Thomas wrote. "Communist tactics deliberately have made it impossible for non-Communists over any long period of time to work with their organizations. But to use an injunction directly or indirectly against a dual union, even a Communist-controlled dual union, is to go far to justify the existence of such a union in the minds of the workers." Although Thomas wanted the furriers to be organized in "one strong, clean union . . . affiliated with the AFL" and opposed dual unions on principle, he believed that under some conditions, particularly where racketeering or subservience by union leaders existed, dual unions were unavoidable.

In order to register his displeasure with the injunction obtained by the right-wing AFL union and to investigate the conditions in the fur market in mid-town New York, Thomas visited the offices of the Communist-controlled union. The visit, which was reported in the Communist press as evidence that Thomas supported their union, set off angry attacks against him by members of the Old Guard bureaucracy and among Socialist union officials. Samuel Shore, president and manager of the AFL union as well as a member of the Socialist party, demanded that the party labor committee take immediate action against Thomas. William Feigenbaum, who considered himself a personal friend of Thomas, pleaded with him to support the AFL union in order not to expose to public view the division within the party. Julius Gerber sent Thomas an official party letter deploring his action. Thomas ignored the letters and wrote instead to Nathan Chanin, an old friend and leader of the Jewish Socialist Verband, whose opinions he respected. Chanin agreed with Thomas that the right-wing unionists' tactics were reprehensible, but he noted that "similar tactics were used by the left wing. . . . The right wing enlisted the aid of Dudley Field Malone [a noted lawyer closely tied to the New York Democratic machine], the left wing used, prior to this, the services of gangster Arnold Rothstein." Chanin told Thomas that he understood his position but disapproved of his appearance before the left-wing union because it "gave a new hold" to the Communists.

Although Thomas was impressed with Chanin's arguments, he still believed party officials should protest the actions of the right-wing leaders of the AFL union. He therefore sent out a memorandum to all party branches explaining that he was not in sympathy with the pro-Communist union, but insisting that the present right-wing leadership was using tactics designed to prevent the organization of an honorable and democratic non-Communist union in the fur industry. Complaints against Thomas by officials of the AFL union resulted in the denunciation by the party's City Central Committee of the tactics used by the right-wing fur union officials, whom they blamed for the rise of the Communist union. At the same time they disapproved of Thomas's visit to the left-wing union headquarters because it had "the unintentional effect of creating in the minds of the fur workers an impression of support for the Communist union."

The *New Leader,* which sided with the AFL union officials, refused to print articles by Thomas dealing with the situation. For a month Thomas withdrew his weekly column from the *New Leader.* A second time, in the fall of 1933, he agreed to tone his column down only after pleas by party members who feared that the column might hurt Solomon's campaign for Mayor. But Thomas did not yield completely; instead he sent a letter castigating the *New Leader's* actions to the secretaries of all party branches. "If we are going to connive with any sort of action which makes unions allies to government and users of injunctions and the like against other unions, we are conniving on the beginnings of fascism." Eventually Thomas agreed to drop his demand that the party's City Labor Committee formally assail the AFL union's actions in the dispute. The AFL furriers' officials, in turn, issued a statement in which they denied any animosity toward Thomas, despite his actions, because they agreed that he was "prompted solely by his desire to serve the labor movement and to instill into all branches of it the spirit of genuine democracy, class-conscious militancy, and vigorous activism." But the union officials refused to withdraw the injunction unless official representations against it were made by the labor and Socialist movement. Within two years, the AFL union virtually died of atrophy, and the issue became moot. But the strife engendered by Thomas's behavior in the fur workers' dispute helped to aggravate the internal struggle for control of the party which was then approaching open warfare.

Nor was the furriers union strife the only internecine labor struggle in which Thomas took part. He was instrumental in exposing the dictatorial rule of James C. Petrillo, president of the American Federation of Musicians, over the New York local, thus helping to restore democracy to that local. His advice helped to steer the anti-racketeering dissidents in the AFL Waiters Union in New York City away from dual unionism. He was also deeply involved in an internal struggle between two unions in the boot and shoe industry. The *Jewish Daily Forward*, which had a penchant for supporting corrupt unions so long as they were affiliated with the AFL, backed the corrupt, stolid, and ineffectual Boot and Shoe Union, while Norman Thomas used his column in the *New Leader* to support the young, aggressive, United Shoe and Leather Workers Union. The Labor Committee of the New York party appealed to the *Forward* to give both unions fair coverage, and urged Thomas to drop his "merciless attack upon the Boot and Shoe Union." The *Forward* and Thomas both ignored the committee—and the committee took action against neither.

Because Thomas had a strong sense of Christian ethics, the Communist tactics appalled him. But he was even more repelled by the racketeering element in labor unions and dishonest and undemocratic methods used by some Socialist labor officials to keep Communists and dissidents from seizing power. He was involved in the struggle against racketeers in the Taxi Drivers Union, and against the undemocratic behavior of the officials of Local 10 of the International Ladies Garment Workers Union in denying the vote to dissident members. The local's leader, David Dubinsky, was then a member of the party and his local was one of the party's financial mainstays, but that did not prevent Thomas from speaking out.[8]

9

The Socialist attitude toward the Communists during the early 1930's was unfriendly, but it was not hostile. Most Socialists looked upon the Communists as overactive, unkempt ideological cousins with vile mouths and misdirected zeal. But they generally hoped that the two movements could soon unite, at least on crucial issues. The Communists, on the contrary, considered the Socialists the "particular betrayers of the working class," and directed their principal attacks against Thomas, Hillquit, Cahan, and the other Socialist leaders. Since honesty and fair play were bourgeois virtues to the Communists, they ignored them and used any calumny, no matter how contrived, to attack the Socialists. As one observer noted, "the extent and variety of their attacks is bounded only by the fertility of their imaginations." The Communists made no secret of their antipathy for the Socialists; it was broadcast by the *Daily Worker* and repeated incessantly in speeches, pamphlets, and broadsides by Earl Browder, Moisaye Olgin, Clarence Hathaway, William Z. Foster, Robert Minor, and the other Communist leaders. Despite their attacks, the Communists at the same time proclaimed their desire for a "united front," or joint action, with the Socialists on major issues.

The Communists were not, however, seeking genuine unity on specific issues. They wanted instead joint action during which they would be able to reach the rank-and-file Socialists and "expose" their leaders. The chief purpose of the united front was thus the disruption of the Socialist party, by whatever means. The American Communist party and the Young Communist League had been instructed by the Communist International to devote their chief attention during the 1932 election campaign to "unmasking and combatting the Socialists." The technique was simple: Communists were instructed to heckle every Socialist speaker and to break up every Socialist election meeting by shouting irrelevant questions. If shouting and heckling were not successful, physical violence was used. In Lawrence, Massachusetts, for example, a mob of Communists attempted to assault Norman Thomas. They rushed the stage on which he was speaking, and only speedy action by police prevented him from suffering serious injury. The leader of the Communist mob, a woman, was arrested; but Thomas refused to press charges because it would have been uncomradely to use police power against fellow radicals, and because "we don't want any martyrs." Again and again Thomas was the target of Communist vilification. James Ford, a Negro candidate for Vice-President on the Communist ticket in 1932, charged that Thomas "actually incites and justifies lynching by the white upper classes"—this because Thomas opposed an outlandish Communist plan for establishing a semi-independent Negro republic in the South. "Sniveling, yellow Socialist faker" and "Social Fascist sky pilot" were two of the other more colorful expletives used against Thomas.

Despite the Communists' open boast of their intention to destroy the Socialist party, Thomas hoped that the Socialists and Communists could unite on some issues. But as Communist tactics became more violent, even he despaired. Then a series of events, culminating in Hitler's victory in Germany, led to an ostensible shift in the Communist line which gave Thomas hope that a genuine united front was indeed possible. Most Socialists agreed that the Communist shift in position was more apparent than real, but some, like Thomas, decided that it was worth negotiating with the Communists. In March 1933, within weeks after the inauguration of President Roosevelt in America and the ascension to absolute power by Adolf Hitler in Germany, the Communists sent out a call for a united front against Roosevelt, war, and fascism. It was directed to: "The Toiling Masses of the United States; the National Executive Council of the American Federation of Labor; the National Committee of the Socialist Party; the National Committee of the Conference for Progressive Labor Action; the National Committee of the Trade Union Unity League; all other National Trade Unions and Working Class Organizations, National and Local, Negro and White." It was ludicrous to expect AFL leaders to accept an invitation from the Communist party, with whom it had been warring, or to unite with the Trade Union Unity League, a Communist-controlled federation of minuscule and nonexistent unions whose primary function was to irritate AFL affiliates in the same fields. Its six-point program was also unlikely to win unanimous approval from the invited organizations. First, the Communists wanted unity against "Roosevelt's hunger and war program," a program that was then barely spelled out, let alone underway. Second, they called for unemployment insurance, which was not then uniformly supported by labor leaders. Third, they demanded the release of Tom Mooney and the nine Scottsboro boys jailed in Alabama on a questionable charge of rape. The fourth point, which could have won unanimous support, urged united action against Hitler's anti-Semitic fascist rule in Germany. The last two points were the usual demands for an end to Japanese and American imperialism and for defense of the Soviet Union from impending imperialist attack.

The Communist call to a united front also included a gratuitous attack on Socialist leaders, both in America and in Germany. It accused the American Socialists of congratulating Roosevelt on his banking acts, "which have already wiped out the savings of many small depositors . . ." and the German Socialists of having carried out "acts of capitulation to Hitler," which the American Socialists either ignored or approved. Despite these failings, the Communists offered to unite with the Socialists and even to cease all attacks on the Socialist party during the period of the united front, a condition all Socialists insisted upon. But the Communists soon proved they could not halt their anti-Socialist diatribes. Another appeal for a united front, from the New York District of the Communist party, falsely accused Mayor Hoan of using Milwaukee police to assault Communist-led marchers demanding unemployment relief, and Socialist leaders generally of "aiding the war plans of the bosses and their preparations for attack on the Workers' Fatherland [Soviet Russia]."

Although the Communist appeals were filled with anti-Socialist diatribes, they were considered by the Socialists' national executive committee at its next meeting. Thomas proposed that a three-man Socialist sub-committee meet with a Communist sub-committee "on the feasibility of better relations between the parties, including possible terms of united action on specific issues. . . ." The motion set off a hot debate, with Thomas arguing that the alternative was *ad hoc* united fronts between inexperienced and undisciplined Socialists and experienced, highly disciplined Communists. The Thomas argument carried the day; by a vote of five to three the national executive committee decided to name a sub-committee to negotiate with a similar sub-committee of the Communist party on a possible united front. Within a matter of days, however, there were new Communist attacks, verbal and physical, against Socialists, and the national executive committee was forced to reverse itself.

Despite the preponderance of evidence that the Communists were not interested in a genuine united front, as late as January 1934 Thomas believed that the Socialist national executive committee should make "some try at it." Nor was Thomas alone. In California, the 1934 Socialist state convention barely rejected a motion for an immediate united front. The agitation for a united front would probably have borne fruit within the year were it not for a wild fist, bottle, and knife-swinging riot in New York's Madison Square Garden. The prelude to the riot came in February 1934 when the Austrian Social Democrats rose against the

Clerical-Fascist Dollfuss regime. The American Socialists and their trade-union allies rallied to the defense of their Austrian comrades. As a demonstration of their support, the Socialist party and the needle trades unions called a mass meeting at Madison Square Garden. The Communists, who were neither involved in the Austrian fighting nor invited to the rally, decided to attend and "capture" the meeting. No sooner had the meeting begun than a mob of well-organized Communists, mainly furriers, forced their way into Madison Square Garden, raised a din so loud that speakers could not be heard, and then started attacking Socialists with fists, bottles, and knives. An attempt to rush the platform was repulsed, but the meeting broke up in pandemonium. It was one of the worst riots in New York history; and there could be no doubt who was at fault. The Communists had organized the disruption and had succeeded in wrecking a Socialist meeting.

The Old Guard, which had opposed all attempts at a united front, now believed itself justified. Julius Gerber said: "If you do not want fascism in the United States, you must fight bolshevism." Party branches and Young People's Socialist League groups were instructed to cut off further dealings with Communists; they were not to attend or participate in any debates, symposia, conferences, or meetings of any kind with Communists. Even Norman Thomas, up to this point the eternal optimist about the Communists, conceded that there was little hope of united action "with these irresponsible destroyers of the labor movement." In despair, he wrote his old friend and fellow civil libertarian Roger Baldwin: "I'm convinced [on the basis of the Madison Square Garden affair] that a united front with Communists is impossible...." Yet two months after the bloody riot, Thomas modified his stance: "Sorrowfully I am compelled to believe that the Madison Square Garden meeting was the final proof that we cannot have a formal united front with the official Communist party ... so long as the chief aim of the Communist party is to destroy the Socialist party by lies and slander and even violence. ... So important, however, is it going to be to get inclusive action of all groups opposed to war and fascism, and to the tyranny of employers in a labor dispute, that we dare not neglect any opportunity to bring about a better state of affairs. ... And the various committees which pass on party tactics must not take the position that never can we have any sort of intercourse with Communists. . . ."⁹

The united front was one of the issues on which the Socialist party was to destroy itself. Norman Thomas's naiveté with regard to the Communists, even after their true intentions were totally obvious, helped steer the party toward its destruction.

10

The rise of Adolf Hitler to power in Germany in 1933 was particularly shocking to most Socialists. The German Social Democratic party had been the most powerful in the world; the German Communist party had similarly been a major force. The news that the Reichstag had given control to Hitler and his fascist, anti-Semitic National Socialists caused Thomas great anguish: "I am distressed," he wrote Clarence Senior, "and so is Hillquit. . . ." In part, Thomas held the United States to blame for the calamitous event. By insisting that the war debts owed to the United States by its 1917–1918 allies be repaid, he charged, the administration in Washington forced the Allied powers to insist that Germany pay reparations for World War I, thus undermining the German economy. Moreover, Thomas believed that because the United States had done little for disarmament, it had contributed to the conditions which allowed Hitlerism to grow. Hitler's victory drained Thomas's normal optimism. The German Social Democrats had forsaken socialism for constitutionalism, he argued, and were left with neither. "To vote for [Marshal Paul von] Hindenberg [for president of Germany] to block Hitler," as the German Socialists had done, "and then get both— that is a tragedy."

Because of the German debacle, a special conference of the Labor and Socialist International to meet in Paris was called for August 1933. Elected as the American delegates were two supporters of the Old Guard, Hermann Kobbe and Jacob Panken, and four Militants, Paul Blanshard, a Philadelphia attorney named David H. H. Felix, Professor Maynard Krueger of the University of Chicago economics department, and Clarence Senior. At the conference the majority of American delegates allied themselves with the more radical European Socialists—particularly with the delegates from the General Jewish Workers Bund of

Poland and the left-wing delegates from the French, Belgian, and Estonian parties—to support a quasi-Communist resolution written by Henryk Erlich and Victor Alter of the Bund and endorsed by Marceau Pivert of France and Paul-Henri Spaak of Belgium. It called for what was euphemistically termed "workers' democracy," but what was in effect a Soviet-style dictatorship. Panken, the spokesman for the two-man Old Guard minority, was appalled by the anti-democratic tenor of the Militant delegates. Along with most other delegates, he was opposed to the Erlich-Alter resolution, which was defeated by a vote of 291 to 18.

Thomas was placed in a particularly awkward position by the Militant delegates at the Paris conference. He did not approve of the Erlich-Alter resolution, particularly its anti-democratic rhetoric. But he feared that he would be aiding the Old Guard if he publicized his differences with the majority delegates, all of whom were closely aligned with him. At the party's national conference in Detroit in June 1934, Thomas attempted to salvage what he could from a bad situation. He proposed that the convention vote its support of the majority of American delegates, while voicing its disapproval of all inferences of dictatorship in the Erlich-Alter resolution. The convention, however, voted its lack of confidence in the majority of the American delegation and opposed the Erlich-Alter resolution *in toto*.[10]

11

The factional fights of 1930–1932 seemed pale by comparison with the almost incessant strife which swept the party beginning in 1933. Division within the party grew more complicated; there were now splits within the ranks of each of the wings. James Oneal listed six factions; he could well have listed eight or nine. They ranged from the semi-Populist Oklahoma group, which wanted little to do with theory, to the Old Guard, which wanted little to do with action. In addition there were the Militants, some pro-Thomas and others anti-Thomas; a large group of independent Socialists, led by Mayor Hoan, Darlington Hoopes, and James Graham of Montana, who tried to ignore intra-party differences; and a small, highly vocal group of extreme revolutionists calling itself the Revolutionary Policy Committee. The divisions within each of these factions at times exceeded the differences among them. The Old Guard was divided between a virtually non-Socialist wing, headed by Cahan and Joseph Shaplen, who reported Socialist party affairs for the *New York Times*, and a more moderate wing which included Jacob Panken, Louis P. Goldberg, and Matthew Levy. Similar groupings existed in the ranks of the more radical wings. "We multiply parties, leagues, would-be parties, and God knows what," Thomas said, "and yet none of them has been strong enough to capture ten seats in Congress or to gain a considerable voice in the ranks of organized labor. Russia had one Lenin. We, if we can believe some of our enthusiasts, have anywhere from three to half a dozen. All they lack is followers."

The influence of the Communists—Stalinite and Lovestoneite—on the Revolutionary Policy Committee was apparent from the organization's beginning. The rhetoric of its statements, manifestoes, appeals, and publications was unmistakably Communist. In its official "Appeal to the Membership of the Socialist Party," the committee proclaimed that "it is necessary [for the Socialist party] to acquire possession of the state power so as to transform capitalist society into Socialist society by means of the dictatorship of the proletariat." The appeal proposed the organization of workers' councils, or soviets, which were "historically suited to serve as organs of liberation." It favored the violent overthrow of capitalism and rejected the "fetish of legality," and wanted the Socialist party to take the initiative in working for united action with the Communists.

The Revolutionary Policy Committee Appeal horrified many Socialists. If the "general analysis of this document is correct," Reinhold Niebuhr said, "then the Communist party has essentially the right line and is bound to prevail. . . ." Devere Allen, another Militant, accused the authors of the Appeal of substituting bombast for fact. The most caustic comment came from Kirby Page, editor of the *World Tomorrow*, the Social Gospel journal in which the Appeal was printed: "If the Socialist party desires to commit suicide, it has only to accept their communistic proposals." Yet, aside from their rhetoric, the members of the Revolutionary Policy Committee, apart from the Lovestoneites and Stalinites who helped form it, were hardly revolutionary. Many of them were little more than zealous Social Gospeleers who would have been horrified had they realized the implications of what they were saying. One of the committee's leading lights, Francis Henson, the young executive secretary of the National Religion and Labor Foundation in New Haven, spoke in grandiose revolutionary terms but favored nonviolent tactics, meant missionaries when he spoke of disciplined professional revolutionists, and wanted all good "revolutionists" to dedicate their lives to building the new society. "This might entail active membership in the Socialist party for the present, hearty support of efforts looking toward the formation of a revolutionary labor party . . . editing revolutionary pamphlets, directing working-class dramas, etc. . . ." The Militant faction, like the Revolutionary Policy Committee, spoke of revolution and dictatorship of the proletariat, but its members did not relish dictatorship, even rhetorically. "The first task of the Socialist movement is the achievement of state power," the official Militant program proclaimed, "and the question of the means to be followed is one of expediency."

Thomas belonged to no organized faction. He felt that his position as the nominal spokesman for the party precluded his membership in any of its various groupings. Moreover, he wrote to Franz Daniel, the former theologian who vacillated between the Militants and the Revolutionary Policy Committee: "I do not believe any of us should be bound by caucus action. . . ." On most issues Thomas was ideologically closest to the more moderate Old Guard group, but spiritually he was closest to the Militants. The ideological and tactical rhetoric of the Revolutionary Policy Committee was completely alien to Thomas, who was unalterably opposed to the dictatorship of the proletariat. "If we declare for it," he wrote, "we shall have lost our reason for existence and will be ground between the upper and nether millstones of fascism and communism." He agreed that the party should not give democracy a higher priority than it gave socialism, but he insisted that a democratic society was the true goal of socialism. Thomas opposed advocacy of armed insurrection which "can only invite a plague of stool-pigeons, provoke a tyranny of repression, and act as a stimulus to fascism." In his view, armed insurrection was the least desirable route to socialism, though he agreed it might become necessary if all other methods should be barred. Both the right and the left wings of the party were, he charged, being overly romantic; both ignored the magnitude of the task facing the party—the task of awakening an apathetic people to the need for socialism.[11]

12

The Socialists gathered in national convention in Detroit on May 31, 1934, under less than optimal conditions. In fourteen months in the White House, Roosevelt had won the backing of most of the progressives and labor-union officials upon whom the Socialists traditionally relied for support. Hitler, in power since March 1933, had virtually eliminated the German Social Democratic party, the pride of the Socialist world, without resistance. Within the American Socialist party, dissension interfered with organizational and agitational work to the point where both became virtually nonexistent. Roosevelt was an important factor in the party's woes; in some cities—Kenosha, Wisconsin, for example—Socialist party members spent more time "boosting Roosevelt and the New Deal program" than they did propagandizing for socialism. This was particularly true in areas where the Socialist party was dominated by labor-union officials, though later in the year FDR's opposition to Senator Robert Wagner's labor relations bill would temporarily cool their ardor. Hitler's destruction of the German Social Democrats, and the failure of the German party's leaders to resist, caused considerable soul searching among American Socialists; but the resistance by the Austrian party in February 1934 and the failure of the Communists to resist Hitler's takeover with anything more substantial than empty rhetoric, stilled even that issue. Party feuds grew more heated the longer they continued; and the more heated the arguments, the less discernible became the issues that set them off. The struggle for the soul of a party involved few issues but many personalities.

It was almost universally agreed that Thomas held the key to control of the 1934 convention. His position would sway the votes of enough delegates to give control to one wing or the other. The Militants and the Old Guard were almost equal in delegate strength. Thomas was thus the chief target of pleas from all sides. His pacifist friends implored him to oppose violence in any form. To S. Ralph Harlow, a minister, friend, and a leader of the party in western Massachusetts, he confided that he had lost his faith in pacifism, though he still vehemently rejected violence and "dogmatic speculation about future violence." Jacob Panken appealed to Thomas to use his position to oppose Militant and Revolutionary Policy Committee resolutions calling for dictatorship and civil war. Thomas replied with a column in the *New Leader* assailing both dictatorship and violence—a column Panken mistakenly took to be an endorsement of his own group in the party dispute. Thomas still opposed the Old Guard and its "blind ties to the AFL leadership." The Militants moderated their official statement because Norman Thomas opposed "completely or by implication almost all of the substance of a left-wing position." Even the modified resolution failed to win his approval; he disliked its inference that violence would be necessary to achieve socialism. Thomas appeared to be refusing to ally himself even temporarily with any group.

Despite all these problems, the convention found the party membership at its highest point in fourteen years. Two days before the convention assembled, the national office reported 23,-600 members, a gain of more than five thousand since January. Yet it would be wrong to assume that the party had grown because it had won new and vital support for its policies. Much of the gain merely represented new members who joined temporarily during the mad scramble for delegates. Shortly after the convention, the party's membership declined by more than 2,500 to 20,951. The gain from 1933 was still remarkable, but it was more accurate than that reported immediately before the convention assembled. Thomas tried to set the theme of the convention; he wanted it to dedicate itself to the fight against fascism, "the last stage of disintegrating capitalism." He described this as the outstanding task before all lovers of peace, freedom, and justice. There was no time to be lost, Thomas warned, because there were signs of an incipient fascism in the United States: "Both Mussolini and Hitler on the way to power talked a good deal the way Huey Long and Father Coughlin talk today." Even while attempting to set a constructive tone for what appeared certain to be a destructive convention, Thomas could not ignore internal party disputes; he deviated from his theme long enough to warn that the talk of violence and dictatorship rampant in left-wing circles "is exactly the best way to help the fascists."

Thomas's proposed convention theme was almost completely ignored by the delegates. They were intent on getting down to the infighting in which many on both sides seemed to revel. Lines were drawn on almost every issue as well as in the elections to the various committees which were named at the start of the meeting. From the beginning, it was apparent that the Old Guard was to be rebuffed. A coalition of the Revolutionary Policy Committee, the Militants, the independents, and the followers of Norman Thomas was in control.

The major struggle at the convention was over a new Declaration of Principles, which was to be the formal statement of the party's philosophy. Because the platform committee charged with writing it was composed of members of three disparate groups—pacifists, Militants, and supporters of Thomas—it labored interminably attempting to agree on basic principles. Since it soon became apparent that it was impossible for the committee to reach any agreement, the night before debate was to begin it was decided to have Devere Allen, a Social Gospel pacifist journalist, write the declaration for presentation the next morning. Allen labored through the night and into the morning, but the result was a poorly written document. Most of the leading delegates, particularly Hoan and Thomas, assumed that it would be amended on the floor of the convention. The Allen declaration was made available to the committee only one hour before it was to be debated. It was evident to anyone who read the declaration that it was hastily conceived and even more hastily written.

The declaration stated: "War cannot be tolerated by Socialists, or preparations for war. They [Socialists] will unitedly seek to develop trustworthy working-class instruments for the peaceable settlement of international disputes and conflicts. They will seek to eliminate military training from schools, colleges, and camps. They will oppose military reviews, displays, and expenditures, whether for direct war preparedness or for militaristic propaganda, both in wartime and in peacetime. They will loyally support, in the tragic event of war, any of their comrades who for anti-war activities or refusal to perform war service, come into conflict with public opinion or the law." Thus far, the declaration could easily have been the product of any pacifist group. It was a simple, noncontroversial statement of the pacifists' position. But this was followed by a paragraph, doubtless inserted to please the Militants, which was to be one of the main factors in the fatal warfare that rent the party for the next two years. "They will meet war and the detailed plans for war already mapped out by the war-making arms of the government," the declaration noted, "by massed war resistance, organized as far as possible in a general strike of labor unions and professional groups in a united effort to make the waging of war a practical impossibility and to convert the capitalist war crisis into a victory for socialism."

If this section of the declaration was neither pacifist nor Militant, even though attempting to be both, it was even more contradictory in its stand on revolution and democracy. "In its struggle for a new society," Allen pontificated, "the Socialist party seeks to attain its objective by peaceful and orderly means." But if fascists were to use force to keep Socialists out of power, the party planned to use all means, "which will not merely serve as a defense against fascist counter-revolution but will carry the revolutionary struggle into the camp of the enemy." After proclaiming anew the party's faith in democracy, the declaration proclaimed that Socialists saw for themselves "the task of replacing the *bogus* democracy of capitalist parliamentarianism by a genuine workers' democracy." "If capitalism can be superseded by a majority vote, the Socialist party will rejoice. . . . If the capitalist system should collapse in a general chaos and confusion . . . the Socialist party, whether or not in such a case it is a majority, will not shrink from the responsibility of organizing and maintaining a government under the workers' rule." The declaration said different things to different people. It was at once pacifist and militant, committed to democratic processes and dedicated to seizure of power by any means available whether or not the party had majority support. Attempting to appeal to everybody, it satisfied no one.

The distribution of delegate strength was about 35 per cent Old Guard, 20 per cent Militant, 5 per cent Revolutionary Policy Committee, and 40 per cent prepared to support Thomas. Thus Thomas could swing the convention in any direction he chose. Since he and Hoan wanted to tone down the rhetorical militancy of the declaration, they agreed that Hoan would propose amendments that Thomas would support. But before Hoan could get the floor, Charles Solomon blocked his move. "I think it is high time that we stop trying to straddle and compromise on basic propositions," Solomon declared. "I am not satisfied to make this document acceptable to those who are basically opposed to it." Andrew Biemiller, the chairman of the session and a Militant, ruled that Solomon was parliamentarily justified. B. C. Vladeck, who followed Biemiller in the chair, refused to allow amendments by Matthew Levy, and was upheld by the delegates. Significantly, it was Solomon's insistence that there could be no amendments which cost the Old Guard, of which he was a member, victory. Hoan and Thomas, who held the balance of power, wanted the declaration rewritten into an aggressive restatement of Social Democratic principles.

Debate on the declaration was long-winded and ill-tempered. When Louis Waldman, who led the Old Guard attack, reached the dais, he was booed. He called the declaration "bombastic," "unreal," and "unconvincing," and implied that he would feel compelled to resign from the party if the declaration were approved. He refused to "subscribe in advance . . . to such a maniacal attitude. . . ." Moreover, he insisted that the declaration was unclear: "What do you mean by 'general collapse'? Who is to define it? Under what circumstances will you set up your revolutionary government . . . ? How much chaos must there be?" Solomon assailed the declaration "not because it is too radical but because it is too reckless." George Kirkpatrick, author of *War, What For,* who was persecuted for his anti-war activity in the First World War, opposed the declaration because he believed it was "putting swords and ropes in the hands of our enemies." Joseph Sharts, the Socialist candidate for Governor of Ohio, who had become a jingoist, anti-pacifist, anti-labor, anti-social-legislation reactionary, denounced the whole declaration. "I, as an American, loving America above all nations of the earth, hereby register my declaration that I will stand by America. . . . I will not yield to those red internationalists who have written into this platform the right to say I must attack my country under all circumstances that they select."

Speaking in favor of the declaration, Allen denied that it was illegal: "The question of whether or not our actions are legal will be decided not by ourselves but by the opposition." Powers Hapgood, a mine-union organizer and a hero of the party's left wing, won loud and long applause when he pleaded for a more radical declaration. "The working class in this country," he declared, "is waiting at the present time for a political party which will not quibble about these phrases." Biemiller, who was chairman of the platform committee, joined in the chorus of the left: "There is a philosophy involved in it [the declaration], we make no bones about it; it is the philosophy of revolutionary Socialism. . . ." Thomas, his efforts to have the declaration amended stymied, rose to support a statement with which he was clearly not in accord. His plea for the declaration made it evident that he interpreted it from the least revolutionary angle possible. He claimed he had expected the left wing, rather than the right wing, to assail it. The declaration, he said, merely repeated what Socialists had always said—that they would use violence when all other means were denied them. Only fear of mass sentiment would avert war, he declared. Then, in an emotional appeal, he roared: "This is the way to break that thing: to say we will not fight, you lords and rulers of men."

Voting on the declaration came late on the third day of the convention. Tempers were frayed, nerves were on edge; the debate had aggravated the already substantial bad feeling within the party. When two members of the Revolutionary Policy Committee voted for the declaration, after protesting the steamroller tactics of the convention, Vladeck, his sense of humor still with him, replied: "I wish to tell the delegates that there is plenty of steam but no roller." Panken, exhausted by the debate, feared "we are face to face with a cleavage in the Socialist movement. . . ."

The vote endorsed the declaration: 10,822 votes cast by ninety-nine delegates in favor against 6,512 votes cast by forty-seven delegates opposed. The convention's decision was still not quite final, for the declaration was now sent to the membership to vote on in a referendum, and a committee of Socialist attorneys was asked to examine it for possibly illegal statements. They reported that the "declaration does not violate any law and is not illegal. . . ."

The convention's last act sealed the doom of the Old Guard. It elected a national executive committee composed of five Militants (Maynard Krueger, Franz Daniel, Albert Sprague Collidge, Dr. Michael Shadid, who founded and operated the cooperative hospital in Elk City, Oklahoma, and Powers Hapgood), four middle-of-the-road but anti–Old Guard Socialists (Thomas, Hoan, Hoopes, and James Graham), and a lone member of the Old Guard (James Oneal). Defeated for election were such Old Guard stalwarts as Louis Waldman, Mayor Jasper McLevy, John C. Packard, leader of the California Old Guard, and Lilith Wilson, a Socialist member of the Pennsylvania legislature. Oneal, citing the claims of victory by both factions on different issues, denied their validity: "What happened [at Detroit] is that the Socialist party suffered a defeat."[12]

Why did Thomas, who disapproved of the bombastic pseudo-revolutionary rhetoric of the Militants and the Revolutionary Policy Committee, support the Declaration of Principles which in great part parroted them? To some degree, his actions can be attributed to disaffection with the Old Guard leadership; they can also be attributed to his fear that Roosevelt and the New Deal were going to bring about the Socialist program of reforms and thus eliminate the party's reason for existence. But it was primarily Thomas's commitments to the young intellectuals, who he feared would abandon the party if the Socialists did not "revolutionize," which led him to support the declaration. Florence Bowers, a Socialist friend of Thomas and a book editor, explained the situation: "I thought Norman made the mistake of his life in Detroit. . . . But he had reasons. . . . All the young men follow him. . . . They thought we were getting too flabby. . . . they wanted to call a strong statement on party policy. . . . So they seized upon a lot of words which John Strachey thought up for them in *The Coming Struggle for Power* and settled down to 'profit' by the 'failures' of our comrades 'over there' [Germany]. . . . Norman saw all this and wanted to hold the younger crowd."[13] Yet by supporting the declaration, Thomas surrendered his actual leadership of the party in favor of the illusion of nominal leadership. In order to maintain their adulation, he had surrendered to those who favored what he opposed. Thomas did not understand that a leader's role is to win his followers to his point of view—not the other way around.

13

The struggle within the party became intensified during the referendum campaign. The Old Guard party members in New

York, who raised only $4.10 of a $4,050 quota in the national fund drive, were able to raise thousands of dollars for the campaign to defeat the declaration in the referendum. Julius Gerber, the Old Guard's chief strategist, who had never heard of Sir Stafford Cripps, a leader of the British Labor party's Socialist wing, pontificated in defense of the often disastrous actions taken by Social Democrats in Germany or by the Labor party in the United Kingdom. James F. Carey, a Socialist who served in the Massachusetts legislature before the turn of the century, was resurrected by the Old Guard to assail the declaration. Joseph Shaplen used his position as a reporter on the *New York Times* to threaten party leaders with dire consequences if the declaration were not defeated; he reported only a day after the convention adjourned that "more than 6,000 members represented by the opposition to the Thomas and the 'left wing' factions . . . have been placed under the necessity of seriously considering secession from the Socialist party." The decision on secession would depend on the outcome of the referendum, he reported. It was obvious to any serious observer that Shaplen's primary source was a leader of the extreme right wing of the party named Joseph Shaplen. Louis Waldman, who began to emerge as the most vocal opponent of the declaration, issued a statement to Shaplen repudiating "the essential features of the declaration of principles," which he termed "insurrectionary," "destructive," and "violent."

The efforts of the pro-declaration forces were no less strenuous. Most of those who favored the declaration assumed, with some justification, that Thomas's support was necessary to win the referendum, there being many middle-of-the-road Socialists who would automatically follow Thomas's advice. Moreover, Thomas favored modification of the declaration. The pro-declaration forces therefore began a drive to convince him that it was necessary to win the referendum. The leader of the drive was a young Militant named Paul Porter, whom Thomas considered a potential party leader. "If we lose in the referendum, I dread to think of the future of the party," Porter wrote Thomas. "It will, for one thing, mean a crushing defeat to your leadership." Porter was not to be disappointed by Thomas's reaction to his letter. Thomas saw the referendum as a virtual vote of confidence in his own leadership. Despite his opposition to much of the declaration and his attempts to modify it, he worked for it strenuously during the four-month-long referendum campaign. He called it an "aggressive and stirring statement of socialism" which answered "some questions which we . . . must answer if we are to get the support of thoughtful and eager spirits. . . ." He addressed party meetings to plead for the approval of the declaration; he denied that the statement was a call for violence, or that it was anti-democratic, and he repeated his faith in political democracy. He charged that the Old Guard was opposing the declaration primarily because of their "bitter disappointment at losing to a large degree its control over party machinery."

Despite talk of a party split should the referendum go one way or the other, some of the leaders on both sides worked for party unity. James Oneal, who belonged to the party's moderate right wing and was editor of the *New Leader,* assured national secretary Clarence Senior that he was more interested in party unity than in the outcome of the referendum. Thomas hoped to avert an outright split, but he did want to force the extreme right-wingers to leave the party. He doubted the schism would occur. "The right wing is very sore but very impotent," he wrote. Time, he assumed, was "on our side." No single party member worked harder to avert the party's collapse over the declaration than did Thomas's friend B. Charney Vladeck, the anti-Cahan business manager of the *Jewish Daily Forward.* Vladeck, a centrist who supported the Old Guard on the declaration, worked with Thomas in a futile effort to modify it in order to avert an open schism. Vladeck and Thomas suggested that the national executive committee issue a number of "supplementary statements very carefully drawn reiterating the Socialist position on several points, notably against physical force, anarchy, and terrorism whether in peace or war." The followers of Cahan and Shaplen, fearing that Thomas and Vladeck would succeed, organized a well-financed, misnamed Committee for the Preservation of the Socialist Party, and proceeded to use every form of personal attack and calumny against the supporters of the declaration, particularly Thomas. The personal attacks coupled with the Shaplen articles in the *New York Times* and a series of press statements by Waldman, acting in his role as New York state chairman, inferring that the state organization might withdraw from the national party, led Thomas to write Vladeck: "I am afraid that the action of the right wing has made it altogether too late to do what you suggest [modify the declaration]." The Militant extremists and members of the Revolutionary Policy Committee, who favored a split in the party in order to "cleanse" it of all those who opposed their position, were equally upset by the Vladeck-Thomas effort to modify the declaration. An attempt by Thomas to have Dr. Harry W. Laidler, executive director of the League for Industrial Democracy and a man respected by leaders of all factions within the party, work with Joseph Bearack, a Socialist attorney from Boston closely identified with the moderate Old Guard, to modify the declaration caused a major uproar on the left. Glenn Trimble, who went from theological seminary into the Revolutionary Policy Committee of the party, accused Thomas of betrayal.

Despite his misgivings about the extreme right and left wings, Thomas proposed that the national executive committee name a sub-committee composed of Maynard Krueger, for the left wing, and James Oneal, for the right, to draft a declaration "reiterating the historic party position against physical force, anarchy, and terrorism of individuals whether in time of war or peace." He also proposed that the declaration itself be modified so as to be acceptable to the moderate members of the Old Guard. Thomas conceded that the wording of the declaration was too blatant, and he wanted a special committee named to prepare a new declaration acceptable to both sides for the next national party convention. Delegates to the Massachusetts state party convention worked out proposed changes to the declaration which were approved unanimously, and which impressed Thomas. Samuel H. Friedman and Matthew Levy, who were independent of factional ties, tried to work out a revision of the declaration at the New York state party convention. Thomas was ready to accept the revision; but the extreme wing of the Old Guard refused to accept it. It was apparent at the New York convention, only a month after the national meeting at Detroit, that the two positions had become polarized, and that there could be no compromise. Thomas agreed that the declaration was less than perfect, but he saw it now as a "symbol for new life in the party." In urging a vote for the declaration, he admitted that neither its adoption or rejection "will of itself win America to socialism," but he feared the effect of its defeat on younger, more militant party members. He now proposed that the membership uphold the declaration unchanged and that the national executive committee propose modifications along the lines of the Friedman-Levy suggestions for action at the next national convention in 1936. Thomas's support was crucial; the declaration was supported in the referendum 5,995 to 4,872, with 10,087 members abstaining. There were indications, however, that it was to be a Pyrrhic victory for the declaration's supporters. Old Guard leaders in New York almost immediately began to insure themselves of control of affiliated organizations, such as the Workmen's Circle, the Rand School, and the *Jewish Daily Forward*, while ignoring the work of attempting to build the party. The Oregon state organization, with the largest per capita party membership in the United States, withdrew from the national organization for fear that the state's criminal syndicalism law would make all members liable for prosecution. Labor leaders, whose party affiliations were becoming more tenuous as they themselves moved closer to the Roosevelt–New Deal orbit, had a new excuse for refusing to support the party. Thomas began having doubts about the wisdom of his support of the declaration. But it was too late; he could not control the fight generated by a Declaration of Principles which he had opposed in principle but had supported in practice.[14]

14

Ideological disagreement was merely a façade, for the real struggle was over power within the party. Thomas perceived this fact early, but he believed that only the Old Guard was interested in personal advantage. He ignored the fact that there was also considerable interest in power—for its own sake—in the left-wing factions as well. "In general my objections to the Old Guard are not in the realm of theory," Thomas wrote Dan Hoan. Instead he feared the effect that "a curious combination of Waldman, Oneal, Lee, and Gerber, backed by the money of the *Jewish Daily Forward* and maintained in power by the blind bloc support of the Finnish [Socialist] Federation and the Jewish [Socialist] Verband" would have on the party. He feared the combination would drive away potential new party members, particularly among the young, because of the Old Guard's attitude "which paralyzes socialism." The cause of the schism was, to quote a Los Angeles Socialist intellectual, a "clash of personalities, which has its rise, I am convinced, not so much in ambition, as in differences of temperament and background." In essence, the party struggle was between the younger middle-class intellectuals, who came into the party since Thomas had assumed nominal leadership, and the older, union-oriented, more conservative members who had been in the party for many years. The younger element was employing revolutionary rhetoric in an effort to seize control of the party; the older members were unwilling to surrender control. Thomas supported the younger members, who were closer to him socially, if not chronologically.

Raphael Abramovitch, a leader of the Russian Social Democratic party in exile, then visiting the United States, observed that the Socialist party leaders were solely to blame for the disunity. "The overwhelming majority of your party has a will to unity," he wrote Clarence Senior, "but is there this will among the leaders? The great danger for your party lies in the idea many leaders have that a split will be useful for the Socialist movement in America." He perceived, correctly, that the Militants and the Revolutionary Policy Committee expected that they could merge with the various Communist sects into a united revolutionary party once the Old Guard was expelled. He deduced, again correctly, that the Old Guard wanted to oust the Militants and the Revolutionary Policy Committee in an effort to form a "semi-Socialist Labor party with [William] Green, [Robert] LaFollette [Jr.], etc." As later events were to prove, Abramovitch was an extremely astute observer.

The causes of the strife were far less important than the effect it was having on the party. Thomas, who believed there was room in the Socialist movement for "lots of difference of opinion," reported that he found it "pretty hard to carry on the work of the party with the extreme [right] and the extreme left both crazy." Despite Thomas's disdain for the extreme left, he did battle primarily against the Old Guard, and particularly against the *Jewish Daily Forward*. He accused Abraham Cahan, editor of the *Forward*, of using its great wealth to further aggravate the party feud. Thomas charged that Cahan was successfully advising trade-union leaders to cut off funds from the Socialist party. He also accused Cahan of sending an emissary to Milwaukee to warn the party there that he would cut off all financial support for the economically ailing *Milwaukee Leader* if the paper did not support the Old Guard in the party struggle. Thomas was convinced that if "it were not for *Forward* and its financial strength" the party dispute could be settled amicably. He was certain that the *Forward*-based extreme right wing was anxious for a split in order to form "its own little party" as an agency for job bargaining with LaGuardia and the trade unions.

After the tumult of the referendum had died down, a short-lived calm returned to the party. Thomas assumed that the danger of an open split had disappeared. He was sufficiently optimistic to appear at a meeting of the Forward Association, the organization which ran the Jewish daily, to explain his own position. His speech was received politely, but it was nonetheless a distressing experience. "I don't know what can be done with the ingrained notion of the Old Guard that what they do is right because they do it," he complained the next day. The *Forward* people, according to Thomas, acted as if "the party is their property."

Vladeck, who was growing continuously more discouraged with conditions inside the party, pleaded with Thomas to "take stock and make conclusions," and then act to salvage what he could of the organization. At Vladeck's suggestion, Thomas wrote a letter to David Dubinsky of the International Ladies Garment Workers Union, Joseph Baskin of the Workmen's Circle (a Jewish pro-Socialist fraternal order), and Adolph Held, president of the Amalgamated Bank, all of whom were closely aligned with the Old Guard, pleading with them for party unity. "I shall deeply appreciate further opinion from you as to any constructive action that I can take," he wrote. None of them replied. He appealed in vain to his old running mate James Maurer, in Reading, Pennsylvania, to use his influence to help heal party wounds. Thomas's actions brought cheer to some Socialists, but not by any means all. Sarah Limbach, an Old Guard leader in Pittsburgh, wrote Thomas in December 1934: "I doubt it is possible to mend the breach." The Forward Association, which since 1897 had required that its members also belong to the Socialist party, changed its bylaws to require only that its members belong to any labor or Socialist party which the Association itself might recognize.

At the beginning of 1935, Thomas attempted to divorce himself from the internal party feud, which was in great part of his own making. He refused to speak at meetings on the situation inside the party. "I belong to no faction," he wrote to a Brooklyn party member who upbraided him for refusing to speak on internal party matters, "and do my best to serve a party which is destroying day by day its chance of usefulness by absorption in internal struggles. . . ." But his effort at ignoring the factional struggle was doomed to failure; the only alternatives open to a party member in 1935 were either to become involved in the internal party disputes or to resign.

Still, there were some who hoped to salvage the party. They pleaded with Thomas to use his position to compromise the differences. William Feigenbaum, of the Old Guard, who felt "there will be nothing left in life for me to live for" should the party collapse, implored Thomas to "drop everything and become the agency for reconciliation." A member in Barberton, Ohio, reported to Thomas that the "membership of the party have, I believe, more confidence in your views than [those of] any other one man in the party." One of the oldest members of the New York party, Edward F. Cassidy, believed that "there are many [party members] who will take positions you take because they believe that in following you they can't go wrong." Despite pleas that he intervene and despite assurances that he alone could save the party, Thomas refused to move. His animosity toward the Old Guard had become more intense as the factional warfare became more heated. Although Thomas conceded that his animosity toward the right-wing leadership was more psychological than intellectual, by mid-1935 he was unwilling to attempt to avert the schism. He insisted that the Old Guard in New York was so inefficient that it "tends to become a kind of dead hand" upon Socialist energy and efficiency.

Although other areas were also affected by the factional strife, most of it was limited to New York. The Oregon party withdrew from the national organization, but this was due to that state's stringent criminal syndicalism laws and not to the internal party dispute. George E. Roewer, a leading Massachusetts Socialist sympathetic to the Old Guard, wrote to Thomas that he was pleased to be "here in Boston, removed from the scene of the bitterness." In Seattle, the Old Guard and the Militants united in inviting Thomas to be principal speaker at a major party rally.

In New York, Old Guard pressure prevented Thomas from being invited to address the 1935 convention of the Workmen's Circle, the Jewish pro-Socialist fraternal order. It was the first convention in six years to which he was not invited. Thomas was, however, a member of the organization and was seated as a fraternal delegate. Amid persistent cheering from the delegates, he was finally called upon to speak; his address brought a great ovation from the eighteen thousand delegates and friends at Madison Square Garden.

On June 16, 1935, the internal party feud finally reached its lowest level. Militants ransacked the office of the *New Leader* and scrawled obscenities on the desk of the journal's manager. Two young Thomas associates, John Herling and Sidney Hertzberg, were blamed for the raid; Herling denied he was involved.[15]

V
The disintegration of American socialism, 1934–1936

Norman Thomas's poor showing in the 1932 election, the inability of the Socialists to elect a single member to Congress, and the failure of labor and progressive forces to forge a new party in the United States caused many Socialists to rethink their position. Among those who decided that the way to socialism was through one of the major parties was Upton Sinclair, the famous veteran Socialist writer. Unlike most Socialists, Sinclair attempted to turn defeat for the Socialist party into a victory for socialism. He therefore announced that he would run for Governor of California in the 1934 Democratic primary on an End Poverty in California, or EPIC, program. Although the program was basically Socialist, it drew the wrath of the official party press and party spokesmen who prophesied—accurately, as it turned out—that the Sinclair candidacy would ruin the Socialist party in California.

Sinclair had discussed his program and his intention to resign from the Socialist party and run as a Democrat with Thomas, his friend for fifteen years. Thomas tried unsuccessfully to dissuade Sinclair from doing so. Sinclair, in a last effort to convince Thomas of the correctness of the move, sent him proofs of his book, *I, Governor of California*, in which he outlined his plan. Thomas was impressed with the plan, which was "Socialist in inspiration" and which made use of some Socialist platform planks, but he doubted that it was practical to try to implement it in a single state "in blissful disregard of other states." Thomas was unhappy with Sinclair primarily because he did not hold "aloft the banner of socialism." He castigated him, saying: "For you to haul that [Socialist banner] down is a loss to us not to be compensated by any of the dubious gains of your program even in the doubtful event of your being in a position to attempt it. Words are symbols. You alone, or with the help of a certain number of California voters, cannot make the word Democratic a symbol for Socialism." Recalling the efforts of the Non-Partisan League and other similar semi-Socialist movements which attempted to gain control of one of the major parties, Thomas asked Sinclair rhetorically: "Have they ever succeeded?"

Thomas warned Sinclair that his plan was doomed to failure. For it to succeed, he believed, would require sufficient power to destroy the capitalist system and replace it with socialism. Sinclair's candidacy, Thomas said, pointed up "a disquieting tendency on the part even of our friends to talk Left but to act Right; to praise Russia and be somewhat skeptical of socialism, as perhaps not radical enough, and then to rush off—as Upton Sinclair appears to be doing, to try to capture a Democratic nomination for governor on an ill-thought-out program of immediate Socialist demands."

The effect of Sinclair's candidacy on the Socialist party in California was in fact disastrous. Party activists, right and left, resigned to support Sinclair; among them were Jerry Voorhis, a youthful Socialist and future Democratic congressman; the pamphleteer Walter Thomas Mills; the left-wing organizer Kate Richards O'Hare; former Berkeley Mayor J. Stitt Wilson; and John Packard, a right-wing member of the state executive committee. Thomas's opposition to Sinclair's candidacy alienated many California Socialists, one of whom wrote to him: "Have you so thoroughly licked capitalism that you now have time to sail into a wing of the Socialist movement?" To most California Socialists, tired of fruitless campaigning, Sinclair's EPIC Plan offered the prospect of victory.

By September 1934, the California party was in a state of collapse. "Los Angeles has practically no movement left," a party leader wrote to Thomas. "In other parts of the state the same is true. Berkeley and Oakland have melted away. . . . We are short of cash, we are short of manpower, we are discouraged. . . ." Milen Dempster, the Socialist candidate for Governor, reported that "we have lost many who are really fine comrades." Unions which had previously helped Socialist candidates now threw all their resources into the Sinclair campaign. So did several wealthy pro-Socialists. Dempster was so discouraged that he wrote Thomas he was considering withdrawing from the race. Not only was the campaign impossible to conduct without funds, there were also serious charges that the Socialists were allied with the Republicans and conservative Democrats in an all-out effort to help defeat Sinclair. Thomas advised Dempster to stay in the race; if the Socialists dropped out of the gubernatorial contest in California, he remarked, "it would mean, in effect, that you sign your death warrant in California and that you set a precedent which will be used to the hurt of the Socialist party everywhere there is a more or less progressive candidate on an old-party ticket." Thomas was certain that, though it might be the unpopular thing to do in California in 1934, Socialists had to oppose "Sinclair's quack remedy" for "only by opposing it can Socialists be in a position to avoid blame for his failure."

The election sealed the doom of the Socialist party in California. Only 2,947 votes were cast for Dempster in all of California; Sinclair, who lost to Republican Frank F. Merriam, polled 879,537. As a direct result of the campaign, party membership in California declined from 1,238 in 1933 to 105 by 1935.[1]

2

The 1934 election campaign in New York, when Thomas ran for United States Senator, was the last in which he polled a significant vote. The Old Guard New York State party bureaucrats had wanted to nominate Charles Solomon for Governor, Oneal for the Senate, and Thomas for state comptroller. Some party members, hopeful of victory, had suggested that Thomas run for Congress, but Thomas feared the adverse effect a defeat in a local congressional election would have on party morale. He therefore informed City Secretary Julius Gerber that he would be willing to run only in a state-wide contest for Senator in which there could be no illusions of victory. Before allowing his name to be placed before the New York State convention, he inquired of Clarence Senior whether he thought he might be making a mistake by running for the office. Senior approved of Thomas's running, but for factional reasons. "There is no chance of trying to reorganize the New York City local from the outside," Senior said, "certainly not from outside the state itself." He believed that as candidate for Senator Thomas could build a stronger upstate party to counteract the Old Guard New York City local. Most of the members of the Old Guard understood the factional nature of Thomas's candidacy and opposed it; but some, like Gerber, were pleased that "with you on the state ticket it will insure an active campaign."

The nominating convention was dominated by the Old Guard. A moderate proposal to modify the declaration of principles was rejected in favor of a stronger one calling for outright repeal. Charles Solomon won the nomination for Governor overwhelmingly from the Militant candidate, Professor Coleman B. Cheney of Skidmore College, despite the fact that Solomon had done poorly the year before in the New York City mayoralty race. Waldman was re-elected state party chairman by better than a two-to-one margin. But Oneal, who recognized the dangers inherent in an open floor fight over the nomination for Senate between himself and Thomas, withdrew at the last moment before the Old Guard could find a substitute, and Thomas was nominated despite a chorus of "No" votes.

The campaign was one of the most slovenly in a long history of party incompetence. Its management was sloppy at best; there was no money to run the campaign, and internal disputes continued sapping the party's strength. Thomas blamed the poor campaign on "inefficiency, absorption in the intra-party fight, and the general New York provincialism rather than active sabotage" by the Old Guard. Despite the poorly run campaign and the internal feuding, Thomas received a respectable 194,952 votes out of 3,604,769 cast, while Solomon polled only 126,580. Some Militants cited the vote to disparage the Old Guard, but this was unfair. Thomas ran against a conservative Senator, Royal S. Copeland, who was less than popular even among most Democrats; Solomon opposed a liberal Jewish Governor, Herbert H. Lehman, who was extremely popular among the very voters whom the Socialists were trying to impress.[2]

3

In 1934, Norman Thomas was convinced that the one hope for American socialism lay in the formation of a farmer-labor party. He believed it would be a serious blunder for the Socialists to ignore any call for forming such a party. He was particularly impressed with the Canadian Cooperative Commonwealth Federation, which was showing unexpected strength only two years after its organization, particularly in the prairie provinces of Alberta, Saskatchewan, and Manitoba. He had Paul Porter investigate the CCF as a prelude to proposing an American equivalent. Thomas's hope was for a broadly based party; he even favored admitting Franklin D. Roosevelt or Senator Robert Wagner into such a party. He believed, however, that the new party would have to be more than a revamped 1924 Progressive party. "The times are quite too critical to water down Socialism into Progressivism," he wrote. Similarly, although Thomas believed the AFL would have to form the base for a new labor party, he insisted that such a party would have to demand "a great deal more than AFL leaders, of themselves, will demand or even, at first, desire." In 1935, Thomas was still optimistic that such a party could be organized.

Thomas's optimism was not completely illusory or self-deluding; there were significant signs that a new party was in the process of formation. Whether that party would contest the presidency in 1936 was questionable; even Thomas had serious doubts that the Socialists or a new labor party should enter the 1936 national election against Roosevelt. One of the most hopeful signs came from Wisconsin, where in 1935 the Socialists, under Mayor Hoan, were involved in forming the Farmer-Labor Progressive Federation of Wisconsin, in which they were to play a major role between 1936 and 1938. In Minnesota, the powerful Farmer-Labor party also raised Socialist hopes when it adopted a program calling for an end to capitalism. Although Thomas had some reason to suspect the politics of the Minnesota party, he told Farmer-Labor Governor Floyd B. Olson that he was delighted with the "outright Socialist platform adopted at your last convention."

The attempt to form a new national farmer-labor party reached its climax in late April 1935 when a conference of twenty leading progressive representatives, senators, and labor and political leaders met in Washington. The leading figure at the conference was Thomas R. Amlie of Elkhorn, Wisconsin, a pro-Socialist Progressive member of the House of Representatives. Although Thomas was invited, he did not attend. By this time, a new and, in Thomas's view, dangerous element had been added to the third-party situation: it was the rise of the demagogic spokesmen of the populist right, represented primarily by Senator Huey Long of Louisiana and Father Charles E. Coughlin of Michigan. "Frankly, I fear that any new party you may start now will be dominated by the spirit and attitude of Long and Coughlin," he told Amlie. Amlie agreed with Thomas that Long and Coughlin did present a serious danger to the new party, but he saw the alternatives to be that "we shall either enter this new mass movement and try to give it direction or it will be directed by the Longs and Coughlins and other essentially anti-democratic elements." The conference resulted in an attempt in early 1936 to revive the League for Independent Political Action which, despite such distinguished sponsors as Amlie, John Dewey, Governor Floyd Olson of Minnesota, Alfred M. Bingham, editor of *Common Sense*, Paul H. Douglas, Senator Ernest Lundeen, and Oswald Garrison Villard, along with Thomas as an interested bystander, proved to be a failure.

Thomas was now convinced that there was little hope for a new farmer-labor party. It was apparent that the labor unions were determined to support Roosevelt and all other Democratic candidates who favored the New Deal. The endorsement of Roosevelt by the United Mine Workers in February 1936 convinced Thomas "of the unwisdom of trying to act at this moment to bring about a farmer-labor party."[3]

The contradictory nature of Thomas's nominal leadership of the Socialist party during 1934–1936 was nowhere more evident than in the continuing dispute over the united front with the Communists. Since the early months of 1934, Thomas was convinced that there could be no united front because the Communists were not to be trusted. But he nevertheless allowed himself to become involved in joint negotiations with the Communists which were designed, among other things, to unite the two parties into a single electoral, if not organizational, entity. Along the way Thomas also alienated himself from the labor movement by joining with the Communists in a May Day celebration. All of Thomas's united front activities were undertaken, against his better judgment, because his young Socialist followers demanded it. No matter how ridiculous, Thomas was unwilling openly to oppose the desires of the young. It was yet another example of his failure to understand the role of leadership.

The Communists, who still considered the Socialists to be "Social-Fascists," denigrated the leftish swing of the 1934 Socialist convention. Earl Browder, the titular head of the Communist party, said after the new declaration of principles was adopted that "the course of the Thomas majority is distinctly to the right. . . . The Thomas group . . . in practice . . . carries out the line of the Old Guard. . . . This is not serious politics. This is the politics of surrender . . . [of] typical Social-Democratic opportunism— and is not improved because it is dressed in nice revolutionary-sounding phrases." Browder declared that there was no hope of winning over the Socialist leadership to the "true, revolutionary road." The Communists made no effort to hide their disdain. In July 1934, Powers Hapgood, who had flirted with the Communists during the 1920's in a fight for control of the United Mine Workers, Socialist party national Chairman Leo Krzycki, and Thomas suggested that the Socialists accept a Communist offer to negotiate if the latter agreed to end their vituperative attacks. The national executive committee disagreed and took no action on the proposal.

Before 1934 Thomas had favored the united front because he viewed the Soviet Union optimistically. To be sure, he recognized and deplored the lack of democracy in the USSR, but he believed that the Soviets were building a new socialist society, and that the dictatorship was only temporary. He assumed that it was necessary to make the socialist future of Soviet Russia secure, and thought a united front was the ideal way to do it. But in the latter part of 1934, Thomas developed doubts about the future of the Soviet Union. Several of his friends, who had been pro-Soviet, returned from Russia disillusioned. They cited the drive against the *Kulaks*, the successful Russian farmers, millions of whom were starved to death by Stalin in his drive to collectivize agriculture. By 1935, Thomas was shocked by the slaughter of millions of Russians, most of them Communists, on spurious charges of Trotskyism in the bloody reign of terror which followed the murder of S. Kirov, the leader of the Leningrad Communist party. To a Socialist who defended Stalin's purge, Thomas shot back: "As a Socialist, I see no excuse at this time for the kind of terrorism the Stalin government is applying. . . . As a Socialist, I want to emphasize regard for the individual. . . ."

Despite the Soviet purge, the demand for a united front with the Communists continued to grow within the Socialist party, especially among young Militants. Thomas received scores of letters during 1934 and 1935 from Socialists and sympathizers pleading that he announce his support for a united front. Thomas refused. "The Communists have repeatedly and continuously made it plain that the united front is for the purpose of destroying the Socialist party," he wrote to one correspondent. To another he cited developments in Russia—particularly the purge— as sufficient reason for refusing to consider the united front. Moreover, Thomas agreed with Hoan that as an issue the united front could only further divide the already feuding party. The demand became so strong, however, that toward the end of 1934 the national executive committee prohibited for eighteen months any negotiations aimed at a united front with the Communists, except in unique local situations, and then only with special permission. Thomas voted in favor of the prohibition; but since hope did not die easily in Thomas, he urged the committee to keep the door open for any possible future united front. Though he opposed joint action with the Communists in principle, he was ambivalent in practice because he again feared that the young Socialists would rebel against the prohibition and resign from the party. He was thus unable to prevent the most blatant violation of the national executive committee decision in 1935 when the Student League for Industrial Democracy, a Socialist organization of university and high school students, merged with the Communist National Students League. Thomas opposed the merger, saying: "I think we shall get along better if we do not have to fight within the same organization against Communist tactics." His advice came too late to be effective. It was ignored; within four years the American Students Union, the merged organization, fell completely under Communist control and finally dissolved under pressures engendered by the Nazi-Soviet Pact.

In late 1935, the Communists changed their international stance toward Socialists. They now worked hard at forming "people's (or popular) fronts" composed of Communists, Socialists, and any other non-fascists who were willing to cooperate. Thomas was unimpressed; he fathomed the reason for the new change: Soviet fear of a Nazi attack. He insisted that the Communist International, which ordered the new line, had not had a genuine change of heart. But many of the young Militants were impressed, temporarily at least. Despite his reservations about the genuineness of the Communists' newfound friendship for the Socialists, Thomas soon became involved in negotiations with them—the national executive committee ban to the contrary notwithstanding.

After the 1935 AFL convention, at which the Militant Socialist and Communist delegates worked together, Earl Browder and Jack Stachel, the "grey eminence" of American communism, conferred with Thomas and several of his supporters in an effort to organize a labor party in time for the 1936 election. The talks collapsed when the Communists, on orders from Stalin, tacitly supported Roosevelt in early 1936.

The only major united-front activity in which Thomas participated with the Communists was the 1936 May Day parade in New York. He was chairman of the committee which organized the parade of Militant Socialists and Communists. Almost half the New York Socialists, who supported the Old Guard, refused to march with the Communists. So did the pro-Socialist trade unions and fraternal organizations. To add insult to injury, the trade-union May Day rally at the Polo Grounds barred Thomas because he had participated in the parade with the Communists.[4] There were no further efforts at a united front.

Although Thomas's rhetoric changed considerably during 1934–1936, his overall position remained virtually the same: he was basically still a Social Democrat with strong pacifist tendencies. His socialism was so nonrevolutionary that even Father Charles E. Coughlin could say, "The kind of Socialism as predicated by Norman Thomas is not Socialism in its real sense and has more right than wrong in it." Whether Coughlin understood Thomas's socialism is debatable. But it is certain that Thomas's basic philosophy was no more revolutionary or radical than that of some of the New Dealers who feared Roosevelt was going neither far nor fast enough in economic and social reform.

There was something unique about America, Thomas maintained, and "an imported philosophy, program, vocabulary either of European fascism or European socialism will scarcely unite" American workers and farmers. What was needed, he believed, was "real fundamental Americanism" which "is devoted to making democracy, for which allegedly we stand, most genuine and effective." It was this "real fundamental Americanism" that was Thomas's ideal. Thomas believed this meant more "freedom of thought and expression" than existed in America in the mid-1930's as well as increased education "that depends for its validity upon an atmosphere of freedom." He wanted a reinterpretation of the Declaration of Independence in the light of changed conditions to "make democracy effective on the economic front." In effect, Thomas wanted this "fundamental Americanism" to be dynamic and "not a static acceptance of something that was once and for all established and never to be changed. It is rather a living spirit which seeks to meet the needs of the time." Thomas conceded there was a danger of regimentation inherent in socialism that would create a barrier against "fundamental Americanism." It was the job of Socialists to prevent the collective society which they sought from becoming stultified by regimentation. Socialism could actually increase man's individuality and creativity, Thomas insisted, because it would offer security against poverty, war, and unemployment, and would increase leisure, thus giving men "a great release of energy" that would "encourage rather than discourage the highest type of self-expression."

But if socialism and Marxism were coextensive, as many Socialists and all Communists believed in the 1930's, then Norman Thomas was no Socialist. "Metaphysically speaking," he said, "I am not a materialist. I do not think that modern science is consistent with the old-fashioned [Marxian] materialism." Moreover, Thomas rejected the deterministic element in Marxism; socialism, he insisted, was not inevitable. He maintained that "we have something to do with our own salvation." But he did not reject all Marxian precepts. He agreed with Marx's philosophy of history: "I believe that the conditions under which men make their living, the sort of tools they use, etc., are the principal factors in determining their social and political institutions." Thomas accepted, in other words, the Marxian postulate that the means of production established the relationships of society.

The depression also convinced Thomas that Marx's prophecy that the middle class would vanish as capitalism became more advanced was indeed coming true. But Thomas told a 1935 meeting of the League for Industrial Democracy that, although the middle class was disappearing as an economic entity, its social traditions—respect for private property, for example, and economic individualism—were persistent and permeated not only the middle class but the working class as well. He also believed that the American workers felt that they, or at worst their sons, would rise out of the working class. It was thus certain, he said, that no revolution could be made in the United States by a class-conscious urban proletariat alone. "The building of the cooperative commonwealth," he told a League for Industrial Democracy meeting, "is impossible of achievement, with or without great violence, except as large sections of a public which thinks in middle-class terms comes to think instead of what is possible under a cooperative commonwealth of the workers of hand and brain." Admittedly, the middle-class mentality prevalent in America placed the Socialists at a disadvantage.

Thomas's Social-Gospel Socialism remained basically pacifist. To a correspondent who asked what he would do should the United States be invaded, Thomas doubted he would bear arms; even in the case of invasion he hoped to be able to persuade other Americans that there were other, more effective methods—among them, strikes and nonviolent civil disobedience—of defending America. Although basically a pacifist, Thomas did occasionally indicate that he agreed with the Leninist position of turning "imperialist" war into civil war. In a symposium on "What Will I Do When America Goes to War" in the left-wing intellectual journal *Modern Monthly*, Thomas wrote: "If and when America enters a new war I shall keep out myself, do what I can to bring about prompt peace, and take whatever advantage I can of the situation in order to bring about the capture of power in government by the workers which is the basis of freedom, peace, and plenty." But what if the enemy were Hitler; would that alter the situation? Thomas said it would not. A war against Hitler or fascism by the capitalist powers would still be an imperialist war; the other powers would not be fighting against fascism but for their own national interest. Moreover, the "victory we want over fascism must be won by the workers themselves on other than a basis of nationalist war." There was still another problem to be met: suppose the war involved the fascist powers against the democratic-capitalist powers and the Soviet Union? The participation of Stalin's Russia, Thomas replied, would not change the nature of the war fundamentally. "It would still be a war of rival imperialisms."

It did not take Thomas long to prove his pacifism. At his insistence, the national executive committee voted to oppose sanctions against Mussolini's Italy for invading Ethiopia. The national executive committee resolution, which Thomas wrote, stated: "No more do we today trust war as a final solution for the safeguarding of democracy against fascism. Indeed, if there is anything of which we feel certain it is that fascism will be brought to the countries which thus far have escaped it, more definitely through war than any other means." When the secretary of the Labor and Socialist International, which had endorsed sanctions, protested the American party's action, Thomas replied that, even if only for expediency's sake, it would be necessary for the American party to oppose sanctions. He cited the American opposition to involvement and the position of the pacifist movement which, "despite weaknesses and superficialities, exercises great influence." To a considerable degree his statement was accurate; America was then basically isolationist. One of the great heroes of the day was Senator Gerald Nye, who had exposed the influence wielded by munitions makers on their governments. The 1930's was a period of innocent delusion that peace was secure—at least in America. Inside the American Socialist party the national executive committee resolution brought violent repercussions from both the right and the left. On the right, the *New Leader* was vehement in its protests; on the left, the Italian Socialist Federation, one of the few foreign-language federations to support the declaration of principles, objected bitterly. The Italian Socialist weekly newspaper *La Parola* ignored the official party stand and backed sanctions, as did the New York Italian Socialist daily *La Stampa Libera*.[5]

The Norman Thomas of 1935 was little changed from the Norman Thomas of 1918. Rhetoric apart, he was still a Social Democrat, still a pacifist. The more times changed, the more Norman Thomas remained the same.

4

Thomas's socialism was more Christian than Marxist, more pacifist than revolutionary, but it was neither servile nor passive. For Thomas lacked neither moral courage nor a willingness to fight for those things he considered worth the struggle. His dedication to the ideals of social equality never wavered; and nowhere was that dedication more vividly put into action than in his work with the sharecroppers of eastern Arkansas. Internal party feuds excepted, in the 1930's Thomas expended more energy and devotion to this activity than to any other.

The 1,250,000 sharecroppers in the United States were, in Thomas's words, "only a step removed from . . . slavery." Most lived in an area stretching from the Carolinas to Florida, from Missouri to Texas. They worked almost exclusively in the cotton fields. As the center of the sharecropper country, eastern Arkansas was one of the most impoverished areas in the country. Thomas had discussed the sharecropper situation many times with his friends, Dr. William R. Amberson, professor of physiology at the University of Tennessee at Memphis, and Dr. Alva Wilmot Taylor, a leading Social Gospeleer and a professor of theology at the Divinity School of Vanderbilt University in Nashville. But his active interest was first sparked by a letter late in 1933 from Mrs. Martha B. Johnson, an organizer for the Socialist party in the Southern states. From Tyronza, Arkansas, she wrote to Thomas: "Here you will find the true proletariat, here you will find inarticulate men moving irresistibly toward revolution. The question is: can the Socialist party formulate an effective enough program to hold these people until a concerted and . . . effective action can be undertaken? . . ." At the bottom of this letter, Thomas scrawled in pencil: "I consider this very important. . . ." He then arranged for the Reverend Howard Kester, a Southerner educated at Vanderbilt Divinity School under Taylor and a member of the party, to "run over to Memphis and probably eastern Arkansas for a few weeks' work."

Although Kester remained in the region, helping to organize the sharecroppers, the mantle of leadership fell on a young Tyronza tailor named H. L. Mitchell. Primarily self-educated, Mitchell was a brilliant organizer with close ties to most of the people in the region. He organized the Tyronza branch of the Socialist party, one of the most effective in the movement. Thomas arranged the first financing for the sharecroppers' union, obtaining the money from the American Fund for Public Service, of which he was a director. He also appealed for money from Socialists and made an impassioned plea for aid over the National Broadcasting Company's radio network.

Thomas's interest in the organization of the sharecroppers had a dual purpose. First, he wanted to win racial and economic equality, and here was the most blatant case of the denial of both. "It is impossible to treat Negroes as less than human without extending the same treatment to white men in the same economic status," he noted. "The deliberate exploitation of race prejudice by the planting [owner] class has been a favorite and hitherto successful means of preserving their power." Thomas was convinced that the organization of the sharecroppers into a single union of blacks and whites from the standpoint of race relations would be "about a hundred times more important" than the work of the National Association for the Advancement of Colored People. Secondly, there was a real threat that followers of Huey Long or some other demagogue might succeed in organizing the sharecroppers before the Socialists did so. The fears that Huey Long might capture the imaginations of the sharecroppers was genuine; Share-the-Wealth Clubs, the Huey Long organizations, were springing up all over Arkansas. Blytheville had three thousand members. As late as October 1934, Mitchell wrote Thomas that "the people [in Arkansas] will either go Socialist or Huey Long. . . ."

Thomas's interest in the organization of an agricultural proletariat was based on his hope for developing an agrarian socialism. He did not favor small farm holdings because they were unfeasible in a technologically developed society. Neither did he favor large private or state-owned farms; here the danger of exploitation was too great. Thomas wanted agricultural cooperatives to be organized along the lines of Jewish *kibbutzim* in Palestine, where farmers worked the large tracts and marketed the farm products cooperatively. But he wanted the cooperatives to be organized "without the heavy and premature pressure to collectivization which almost wrecked the Russian experiment and would be even more dangerous, I think, in America."

The Southern Tenants Farmers Union (STFU), which Kester and Mitchell organized, was an almost immediate success. Literally thousands of sharecroppers in eastern Arkansas, black and white, became members. No sooner had the STFU begun to show signs of life than the planters began to terrorize the sharecroppers and their friends. Night-riders shot up the homes of STFU members; organizers and active supporters of the union were beaten so severely that some of them had to be hospitalized in Memphis; union halls were destroyed, and union officials were arrested on frivolous charges. Roger Baldwin and Jennie Lee, a British Labour MP, were denied the right to enter the city of Marked Tree. The Reverend C. H. Smith, a volunteer organizer for the STFU, was arrested for "agitating labor"; and Simon Bass, a member of the union, was arrested and charged with "rioting" while walking peacefully down the street in Earle. While investigating conditions, Sherwood Eddy, an executive of the International Young Men's Christian Association, was arrested, questioned for three hours, and forced to leave Arkansas. "History is not up to date without saying there is slavery in Arkansas," he said upon his return to New York.

In the midst of the terror campaign, Thomas decided to challenge the deprivation of the rights of the sharecroppers. He scheduled a speech in Birdsong, a hamlet in the Arkansas cotton country. Outside the church where he was supposed to speak, Thomas was met by a mob of planters, and was knocked down and beaten. When he attempted to cite his rights under the law, he was told: "There ain't gonna be no speaking here. We are the citizens of this country and we run it to suit ourselves. We don't need no Gawd-Damned Yankee bastard to tell us what to do. . . ." Shortly after this attack, Thomas and Mitchell visited Governor J. Marion Futrell to ask for state protection against the nightriders. Futrell refused. "You can't go around preaching social equality in the state of Arkansas," he informed them, "nor economic equality either." Futrell believed that the "average sharecropper has the mentality of a twelve-year-old," that he was lazy and shiftless and that nothing could be done for him. But he named a commission, composed almost entirely of men hostile to the sharecroppers, to investigate the situation. Their report conceded that reform was necessary, but their proposals were minimal.

In late 1934 and throughout 1935, the STFU called major strikes. The effect of the walkouts startled even Mitchell. "They were not expecting as much as was won," he wrote Thomas. Cotton pickers won pay increases of from 25 to 50 per cent. But the planters were only yielding temporarily; they blacklisted all union members, evicted them and their families from their homes, and offered them jobs only if they repudiated the STFU. The men refused. Two sharecroppers were shot during a raid on a

union meeting near Earle; an attempt was made by vigilantes—
several law officers among them—to lynch a union official. Vigilantes also clubbed men, women, and children in a Methodist
Church near Earle. Attorneys attempting to defend arrested
STFU men were warned against entering the state. The union's
answer was a general strike which emptied the plantations—
more than five thousand east Arkansas sharecroppers walked
out. Strikers were beaten and arrested for vagrancy, assault, and
"interference with labor." The city marshal of Earle arrested
thirteen strikers and forced them to work on his farm. Despite
the persecution, the union won a decisive victory. In May 1936,
the salary of cotton field workers was increased almost 50 per
cent. A federal grand jury indicted the city marshal of Earle on
seven counts of slavery.[6]

During 1934 and 1935, Thomas made several futile attempts
to have the federal government intervene on the sharecroppers'
behalf. The Agricultural Adjustment Act, which paid planters
for reducing their crops, had the effect of forcing many sharecroppers off the land. Thomas tried to draw Secretary of Agriculture Henry A. Wallace into the situation. Wallace, whose
interest in the "common man" evidently did not include the
American peasantry, refused. Indeed, Wallace prevented the release of a report by Mrs. Mary Connors Myers of the Agriculture Department on the "shocking conditions she discovered in
the sharecropper country of Arkansas." In attempting to force
the release of the report, Thomas appealed to his friends Eleanor
Roosevelt and Felix Frankfurter, but neither could change Wallace's mind. Chester C. Davis, administrator of the Agricultural
Adjustment Administration, said he could not release the report
because it charged individuals with crimes. Thomas suggested
that those portions making such accusations be deleted. Davis did
not reply. Thomas charged that the Agriculture Department was
to blame for the reign of terror in Arkansas. He wrote to the
executive assistant to the administrator of the AAA: "By sup-
pressing the Myers report you have given these people [the
plantation owners] aid and comfort. They consider that the
Union has failed in its effort to get federal intervention, and that
they may now, with impunity, adopt any illegal methods which
they wish to employ." Wallace and Thomas carried on a battle
of letters during most of 1934 and 1935. Thomas accused the

Secretary of actively preventing "feeble efforts within his department to see that the most miserable of Americans—the sharecroppers, and farm laborers in the cotton country—got a little of the bounty the taxpayers poured into the lap of planters." Refusing even to meet with a delegation from the STFU, Wallace accused Thomas of demagogic appeals to city audiences. He ignored Thomas's proposals for guaranteeing the sharecropper a portion of the crop-reduction payments made to the plantation owner. While admitting to Thomas that Section 7 of the AAA meant that members of the STFU could be dispossessed at the whim of the planter, he still refused to do anything to protect the sharecroppers. Normally a forgiving man, Thomas never forgave Wallace for his disregard of the sharecroppers.

Thomas's efforts to aid the sharecroppers continued into 1936. He appealed to his old friend Rexford G. Tugwell, who could do little in view of Wallace's hostility. Thomas asked Senator Wagner to intervene; this also failed. Finally he turned to President Roosevelt. He recalled that Roosevelt had once suggested that Thomas could reach him directly, and that he would be pleased to hear from him at any time. On the issue of the sharecroppers, however, Roosevelt refused to meet with Thomas. FDR could not afford to be sympathetic with the sharecroppers so long as he needed the support of Arkansas' Senator Joseph T. Robinson, and Robinson needed the support of the Arkansas plantation owers. Roosevelt informed Thomas of this, and concluded by saying, "I'm a damned sight better politician than you are. . . ."

After the 1936 election, Roosevelt named a committee chaired by Wallace to look into the problems of farm tenancy and sharecropping. The committee's report supported all of Thomas's assertions, but it proposed a solution which would not have brought results in the forseeable future. Thomas was vindicated, in spirit if not in practice. By 1941, the sharecropper problem was almost completely eliminated by mechanization, which made human labor in the cotton fields uneconomical and thereby caused the sharecroppers and their families to migrate to the ghettos of New York and Chicago.

Even an unfriendly observer had to concede that the STFU, which Thomas was instrumental in founding, "focused the spotlight on the plight of the sharecropper in particular and on Southern agriculture in general. . . ." To quote one Southern friend of the sharecroppers: "The people of the South, without regard to race, color, or political affiliations, owe a profound debt to Norman Thomas."[7]

5

Although preoccupied with internal party strife and the sharecroppers, Thomas was also active in behalf of labor and Socialist organizations. Between 1932 and 1936, he spoke in every state except Mississippi, Nevada, South Carolina, and Wyoming, to audiences ranging from the Socialist party of Borough Park, Brooklyn, to the Methodist Church in Pocatello, Idaho. Between 1934 and 1936, he addressed the international conventions of the Brotherhood of Railway Trainmen and the United Auto Workers. He was active in the 1934 textile strike in Alabama, New York, New Jersey, and North Carolina; in the 1935 laundry strike in Birmingham, Alabama; in the strike of National Biscuit Company bakers in New York and Philadelphia. He addressed striking onion-field workers in Ohio, auto workers in Ohio, Michigan, and Missouri, zinc and lead miners in Oklahoma, shipyard workers in New Jersey, seamen in New York, and salesgirls at May's department store in Brooklyn. He also addressed central labor-union parades and meetings in, among other places, Phoenix, Toledo, and Rochester, New York.

Militantly organized labor, Thomas believed, was the key to avoiding fascism in the United States. Yet there were fewer than five million members in all American labor unions out of a work force ten times as large. The organization of industrial, rather than craft, unions won Thomas's support and aid. As early as 1933, he had been active in the strike against the Briggs Auto Plant in Detroit, where he addressed six thousand workers. This strike was in large measure responsible for the organization of the United Auto Workers. Thomas's repeated appeals to the AFL leadership against splitting the auto workers into craft organizations was ignored. After the Committee for Industrial Organizations was organized, Thomas was active in attempting to convince John Brophy, who was in charge of organizing the CIO, to press on with the auto drive.

In the 1934 textile strike, while in the midst of his New York

State campaign for the United States Senate, Thomas, in answer to an appeal from the union president, threw himself into the work of helping the strikers. He spoke in North Carolina as National Guardsmen patrolled the streets. He toured Alabama despite threats against his life. His popularity soared among the textile workers; the head of the Florence, Alabama, local of the United Textile Workers wired the state headquarters: "Please convey to Norman Thomas our plea for a visit with us here. The masses are hungry for his message."

Thomas's belief in labor organization and the right to strike created a dilemma for him, as it did for most Socialists. He favored strikes under capitalism, but what would he say to strikes under socialism? Thomas's answer was ambiguous. He said that the right to strike was the only recourse open to workers under capitalism—and this included even the right to strike against the government. Under capitalism, a strike was after all against the ruling class, as Thomas saw it, and hence a strike against a capitalist government was merely a strike against the ruling class's executive committee. A strike which would tend to paralyze government—as, for example, the police strike of 1919 in Boston —might be revolutionary, but it would also be justified. Under socialism, on the other hand, Thomas insisted that strikes could not be justified because they would not be against an owning and ruling class. Thomas was, however, enough of a pragmatist to realize that there might be conditions, even in Utopia, under which a strike might be necessary. He wanted therefore to leave open the option of striking under socialism, with the provision that the strike could not be used "to choke off" a Socialist government. Whether one was Social Gospel Christian or a doctrinaire Marxist, the question of the right to strike under socialism created an insoluble dilemma for the Socialist. Like every other Socialist, Thomas was faced with the stark reality that socialism, though it might possibly be politically democratic, had to limit democracy drastically in so far as labor's right to strike was concerned.[8]

6

In addition to raising theoretical questions for Socialists, the problem of strikes and trade unions also created internal disputes within the party. Thomas was vehement in his opposition to the willingness of many Old Guard Socialists to ignore union racketeering while fighting Communist or left-wing tendencies in unions. Thomas's animosity to labor racketeering was not an anti-labor stance, as some of the Old Guard maintained. "I believe that many of our labor unions must clean house," he declared, "but most emphatically I believe that there is hope in labor unions." Thomas's views of labor were based on moral premises; the Old Guard, many of whom were union officials or union attorneys, based their attitudes on practical, personal considerations. When the moral and the practical collided, Thomas sided with what he assumed to be the correct moral position, while Old Guard Socialists generally favored the position that best suited their practical position in the union involved.

Hyman Nemser was a case in point. In April 1935, the *New York World Telegram* and the *New York Post* accused Nemser, a member of the Socialist party, of racketeering in his position as counsel and manager of two clothing salesmen's locals of the AFL's Retail Clerks International Protective Association (RC IPA). Nemser had previously been fired from the Amalgamated Clothing Workers Union under questionable conditions. The *New York Post* reporter who unearthed the story against Nemser was Edward Levinson, himself a member of the Socialist party and a former associate editor of the *New Leader*. The Old Guard reacted violently to the story, but not against Nemser; instead they attacked Levinson. It was unconscionable, they claimed, for a Socialist to use the capitalist press to attack labor. The Old Guard position was of course ludicrous; Levinson was not attacking labor but a labor official accused of accepting bribes.

After the news stories appeared, the RCIPA suspended the charter of the two Nemser locals. Thomas then demanded that the New York party look into the charges against Nemser. "What I want to insist with renewed vigor," he wrote to I. Nussbaum, chairman of the Grievance Committee of the New York Socialist party, "is that the party owes it to itself, to its honor, to the labor movement—yes, and to Nemser—to initiate its own careful investigation. We suffer incalculably from the suspicion that we Socialists are either too indifferent or too impotent to get at the facts in this matter fearlessly. . . ." Nemser was finally

ousted by the RCIPA, but not by the party. The Old Guard Socialists were little interested in the ethics of the case; to them it
was now a struggle between themselves and the Militants and
their supporters. If it was necessary to ally themselves with an
accused racketeer, they were prepared to do so.

Other labor issues caused further serious irritations between
the Old Guard and the Militants. One involved an AFL decision
to bar Communists from membership. The action was hailed in
the daily press by Louis Waldman, the New York party's state
chairman, despite opposition by such labor stalwarts as David
Dubinsky, of the International Ladies Garment Workers Union,
and Sidney Hillman, of the Amalgamated Clothing Workers.
Thomas roundly condemned Waldman in print, calling his statement "contrary to the spirit of repeated Socialist declarations"
that "labor union representatives must be judged by acts and not
by political opinions."

The Old Guard believed it had the advantage over Thomas
and his followers on trade-union issues. Old Guard members
were almost all officials or activists in trade unions; they had almost all been active for years in the Socialist and labor movements; they were primarily workers or professionals whose liveli-
hoods depended on their contact with workers. Thomas and his
supporters, on the other hand, were generally middle-class intellectuals with little working-class contact. In any event, Oneal
challenged Thomas to a debate on labor policy as part of the factional party debate. Thomas, who knew the Old Guard advantage on the labor issue, suggested that they debate instead overall
Socialist policy. No debate was held, for it was too late—the
party was too near an open split.[9]

7

Disagreement over labor-union policy was only one of many
which contributed to the disintegration of the party after the
"radical" Declaration of Principles was adopted by the 1934 convention and confirmed by a party referendum. One shorter-lived
but equally contentious issue was the invitation to former Communists to join the Socialist party. This invitation, drawn up by
Thomas, played a major role in exacerbating the already serious
internal party situation.

Thomas's interest in uniting all radicals in a single "all-inclusive" Socialist party dated from his earliest days in the party. He had suggested to the 1919 convention of the Intercollegiate Socialist Society that the Socialist party reorganize to include all radical movements, from the anarcho-syndicalist Industrial Workers of the World on the left to the agrarian Non-Partisan League on the right. He still favored such an alignment in 1934 —and for three years thereafter—although he now preferred to exclude the Stalinite Communists. Thus, almost immediately after the Detroit convention, when Paul Porter, one of his protégés, proposed to Thomas that a committee of Militants and pro-Thomas Socialists approach the IWW, the Lovestoneite and Trotskyite Communists, and the American Workers party (the successor to A. J. Muste's Conference for Progressive Labor Action), and suggest that they enter the Socialist party *en masse*, Thomas was impressed. He even suggested that the national executive committee convene such a meeting, but a new development made it unnecessary. Ben Gitlow, a one-time Socialist assemblyman from the Bronx who turned Communist in 1919 and then joined Lovestone when the latter was dispossessed from the official Communist party in 1929, was interested in returning to the Socialist party. Gitlow had become genuinely disillusioned with the authoritarianism of Communist dogma, and he was impressed with the new militancy of the Socialist party, particularly since the declaration of principles had been enacted. There were more than a score of other former Communists, and deserters from other sects, who were now also interested in joining the Socialist party. Some were genuinely interested in returning to a democratic Socialist movement; others were interested primarily in sabotaging the party and enticing many of its younger members into their own versions of the one true faith. Thomas, who knew Gitlow and a few of the others, wanted them to be welcomed into the party. He wrote to six members of the national executive committee suggesting that it express its pleasure at "the coming to it of a number of representatives of radical groups." But Thomas's enthusiasm for welcoming the dissident Communists was not shared by the New York organization—to which most of these new members would belong. Mayor Hoan, who had no objection to the people concerned primarily because he knew none of them, was unwilling to compel any local organization to accept any new member against its will. He was convinced that the national executive committee had no authority to welcome them, and "certainly such action is bound to cause dissension."

Faced with an impasse, Thomas proposed to the national executive committee that it issue an invitation to all "who believe that the times require another American Revolution" to join together in building the Socialist party. It was an ambiguous statement which could as well have been an invitation to progressives, former members of the populist movement, or former Communists. Thomas made it ambiguous deliberately, because he knew that such a statement could not raise any serious opposition within the party. The key phrase, which highlighted the statement's ambiguity, read: "Some of you have been members of various parties which you have been compelled to leave because their tactics have been so badly adapted to the great end you seek." A Socialist could have found fault with the tactics of the Communists, the various splinter groups, the IWW, or any of the De Leonite parties on the left, and the Non-Partisan League, Progressive party of Wisconsin, or Farmer-Labor party on the right. Thomas understood this, but his primary interest was in making Gitlow and the other one-time Communists welcome in the Socialist party. Thomas, the moralist, was playing at Machiavellian politics.

The national executive committee, by a vote of 9 to 1, issued the invitation. Gitlow and seven other one-time Communist leaders accepted the invitation in a long and laborious statement issued to the press. Besides Gitlow, among those who accepted the invitation were Herbert Zam, former secretary of the Young Communist League; Lazar Becker, a founder of the Communist party and a former member of its ruling Control Commission; Harry Winitsky, another founder of the Communist party and the first secretary of its New York District; Jack Rubenstein, an organizer for the United Textile Workers; Harry Connor, one-time leader of the Communists in Fort Wayne, Indiana; and Emanuel Seidler, a leader of the Lovestoneites in Detroit. There were others who proposed to come in as well: Albert Weisbord, who left the Socialist for the Communist party eleven years earlier in 1924, and had led the 1926 Paterson textile strike only to be expelled from the Communist party because he opposed the "rule-or-ruin labor policies of William Z. Foster." In Chicago there was a portent of troubles to come: Albert Goldman resigned from the Trotskyite Workers party and, accepting Thomas's invitation, joined the Socialists—although his views on political theory or tactics remained unchanged.

The New York party, despite the national executive committee's invitation, adamantly refused to allow the ex-Communists into the local, and accused Thomas, with justification, of having been less than candid about his intentions. Thomas was undaunted. When the New York Socialists refused to admit Gitlow and his cohorts under any conditions, Thomas arranged for them to be admitted into the Militant New Jersey organization. Their sojourns in the Socialist party were generally short—some, like Gitlow, confessed the sins of their youth and turned against socialism with a vengeance; others simply dropped out of the radical movement, and a few eventually joined the Trotskyites.[10] Thomas's adventure in Machiavellianism was a failure. He was ill-suited for the role.

8

Conflicts within the party continued to worsen as one irritant was added to another. The bombastic ambiguity of the declaration of principles could be interpreted as a call to dictatorship by the Old Guard and as a call for parliamentary reformism by the Revolutionary Policy Committee. Gitlow and his cohorts were welcomed into the party with joy by Thomas and his followers, and rejected by the leaders of the Old Guard. Labor union racketeers, who were willing to fight the Communists and other left-wingers, were embraced by the Old Guard at the same time that they were despised by Thomas and the Militants. The Old Guard Socialists were unalterably opposed to any form of united front with the Communists, while Militants, members of the Revolutionary Policy Committee, and Thomas-supporters were, to varying degrees, sympathetic to the idea of a united front. All of these contradictory tendencies were ripping the party apart. Yet these disagreements might have been settled amicably—or, at least, without openly rupturing the party organization—had it not been for the disputes which threatened the power, position, and jobs of the leaders on both sides and made the split inevitable.

One such struggle involved the *New Leader*. Thomas, who might have acted as mediator, again allied himself with one faction, thus exacerbating a bad situation.

After the 1934 convention and the adoption of the declaration of principles, the *New Leader* became essentially a factional organ. In its pages nonparty members were privy to the most intimate details of party squabbling, always reported with a jaundiced eye. Appeals by Thomas that some of the more blatant attacks on the declaration be deleted were ignored. Moreover, immediately after the 1934 national convention, the board of the New Leader Association, which owned the paper, voted to turn it into the organ of the anti-declaration forces. Thomas, who had hoped to persuade the editor and managers of the weekly to use their positions in an effort to save the party, discovered almost immediately that his position on the *New Leader* had become untenable. In October 1934, he was not informed when the board decided to issue a special supplement on the declaration of principles, although as a columnist and hence technically a member of the editorial board, Thomas was supposed to have been advised. In February 1935, a Thomas column supporting a national executive committee action was deleted by Oneal, causing Thomas to announce that he would write no more columns for the weekly. The California party organization, or what was left of it, pleaded with Thomas to resume his column because "we beg of you not to take any steps that at this time will aggravate the situation." Thomas replied that the *New Leader* was plotting the secession of the New York organization and that he refused to have anything to do with it. The next month the New Leader Association, after urging "all who stand for democratic socialism to remain steadfast and loyal to their principles, to call a halt to the policies of the national executive committee which are threatening the party . . . ," repealed the long-standing bylaw which required all of its members also to be members of the Socialist party. Members of the association were now required to belong to any Social Democratic organization approved by the association. Thomas, his patience at an end, charged that the association's leaders had arrogated to themselves "final authority for deciding what is socialism and what constitutes the Socialist party," and resigned.

Thomas and his supporters now set about the task of organizing a new nonfactional Socialist publication. Thomas wanted the new organ to be located outside New York in the hope of avoiding possible further aggravation of the party strife. But most of the younger Militants demanded that it be published in the city. Thomas pleaded in vain with the New York Militants to allow the new organ to be published in Chicago or Milwaukee. But the New Yorkers insisted on an open break with the Old Guard. A drive was started to raise $5,000; the small New Jersey Socialist monthly, *New View*, was taken over; and on March 23, 1935, the Militant *Socialist Call* began weekly publication in New York. Mayor Hoan, who wanted the faltering *Wisconsin Leader* to replace the *New Leader*, was furious: "The starting of a new paper . . . is bound to be disastrous both from a business and tactical viewpoint," he wrote to Thomas. Although he had hoped the new Socialist weekly would be published outside New York, Thomas assured Hoan that the new journal would be a nonfactional "aggressive Socialist organ."

Thomas was to find almost immediately that the Militant editors of the *Socialist Call* were no more democratic than the Old Guard editor of the *New Leader*. In the first issue of the new newspaper, a paragraph in which Thomas lauded anti-Soviet books by Vladimir Tchernavin and his wife was deleted—the paragraph appeared in other Socialist newspapers which carried the column, but not in the *Socialist Call*.[11]

9

In a debate sponsored by the *Socialist Call*, Thomas took on Communist leader Earl Browder on November 28, 1935, before twenty thousand paying customers in Madison Square Garden in New York. It was obvious from the outset that the Thomas-Browder debate would only further aggravate party feuds. In the first place, the *Call* sponsorship was a direct challenge to the Old Guard, which considered the new Socialist weekly a dual organization whose primary aim was the destruction of the *New Leader*. In the second place, the Old Guard had developed a near-paranoid attitude toward the Communists, whom they wanted treated as lepers. Yet the protests of the Old Guard were at best based on questionable premises. Julius Gerber wrote to members of the national executive committee that debates with

Communists had been outlawed since 1931. He failed, conveniently, to recall that Thomas had debated Robert Minor, another Communist leader, in the Bronx only two years before, and that the Old Guard–dominated New York Socialist party office had sold tickets and accepted the commission. Moreover, there was no party rule prohibiting such a debate, though it had been frowned upon since the Madison Square Garden riot of February 1934. Gerber warned Thomas that he would be inviting expulsion if he debated Browder. But Thomas, citing precedent, defied him. The City Action Committee, which made decisions when other committees were not available, decided to deny Thomas permission to debate Browder. On the advice of his Militant friends, both in and out of New York, Thomas ignored the ruling because he could not recognize the authority of the city organization in prohibiting his "debating the vital issue of socialism under proper auspices." The sponsorship of the *Socialist Call*, he insisted, constituted proper auspices. He ridiculed the city organization's specious argument that the debate was an unauthorized united front. The city executive committee, for its part, decided it would expel him if he did not withdraw from the debate. Thomas told the city executive committee that it had no right to tell him whom or when to debate.

By a 10 to 1 vote, the pro-Thomas national executive committee ruled the debate was legal, and so informed the city organization, which promptly ignored the ruling. The national office staff hoped that the debate would replenish its treasury. Its finances had been hurt seriously by the factional fight; the national party organization had received almost no money from the New Yorkers since 1934. The debate, as Thomas pointed out, was to "be a source of sorely needed revenue for Socialist institutions—the *Call*, the Yipsels [Young People's Socialist League], the *American Socialist Quarterly*, and perhaps most important of all, the National office." All of the organizations he listed were closely linked to the Militant or pro-Thomas wings of the party. In fact, the debate did earn thousands of needed dollars for the party and its institutions. But it was a dull, intellectually vacuous affair. Browder, who wanted a united front, refused to debate the issues, and rambled in his usual pedantic manner. He limited his speeches to the one theme of a united front: "Why is the united front the central, all-dominating question today in the United

States and throughout the world? Because of the danger of fascism and war. . . . Time presses, comrades, fascism is coming to America if we do not unite to prevent its coming." It was apparent to anyone who attended the debate that Browder was not debating, but only politicking for a united front. The Communist claque, which made up fully half the audience, cheered Browder long and loud. Most Socialists were disappointed; they had learned nothing of Browder's (and his party's) real intentions. Nonradicals were mystified by the new Communist rhetoric of the "popular front."

Beginning on a friendly note, Thomas won a solid round of applause when he hailed the achievements of Soviet Russia. There was stony silence when he equated parliamentary democracy with freedom, and then declaimed: "I trust the democracy of a party more than I trust a rule from on top, a centralization so great that orders are handed down from Moscow, as in fact they have been since the formation of the Third International. . . ." The silence became almost sullen when Thomas rejected a formal united front because he was still not ready to trust the Communists and wanted to be sure that the united front they wanted was genuine, as they proclaimed in November 1935, and not a means to destroy the Socialists, as they had proclaimed in November 1933. Sullen silence turned to open hostility from the Communist side of the hall when Thomas went on to attack the Soviet Union for selling oil to Mussolini's Italy which was then invading Ethiopia. The Communists forgot their newfound manners; they hissed and booed.[12]

10

The *New Leader* battle could have been settled by moving the *Socialist Call* to another city. The Browder debate might have been canceled. But in the struggle for control of the New York organization there was no room for compromise, for several careers and whatever political bargaining power the Old Guard had left hinged on the outcome. Thomas might have salvaged a united party from the battle had he not himself been so deeply involved in it. His alliance with the Militants in this battle negated any usefulness he might have had to save the party.

Soon after the declaration of principles was enacted, Mary

Hunter, a Socialist moderate, predicted to Thomas in remarkable detail how the split would occur. First, she said, the Militants and their allies would within a year have a majority of the party members, and they would thus be in a position to gain control of the New York party's central committee. The Old Guard, she continued, would revoke charters of branches that might support the Militants, and expel those party members it suspected of favoring the Militants. The New York split would leave the two sides almost evenly divided, but she doubted there would be much of a schism outside the state. Her prophecy was not based completely on deduction; she was actually privy to some Old Guard conversations as early as October 1934 at which contingency plans were made for retaining control of the party in New York and for splitting the party if these plans failed.

That November the Militants showed unexpected strength in New York party elections. The city executive committee, which had been chosen by the old city central committee, therefore chartered "paper" branches which would give the Old Guard added representation, and dissolved ten branches which had been inclined toward the Militants. Thomas appealed to the city central committee to delay the reorganization and return to the *status quo ante* until a special committee, composed entirely of anti-Militants and headed by B. C. Vladeck, could work out details of a proposed compromise. The city central committee, which was still controlled by the Old Guard, upheld the city executive. The Militants attempted to prevent the seating of the city central committee delegates from "gerrymandered" or "colonized" branches. The Old Guard prevailed, but the vote was extremely close: Louis P. Goldberg, representing the least controversial of the new branches, won his seat by the slim margin of 63 to 57, despite the fact that some of the new branches were voting. In other instances the vote was even closer. Thomas was particularly upset by the situation; he sent a letter to all New York City party members proposing that the national executive committee take over the reorganization of the New York local. But Thomas's proposal was doomed from the start, for neither the Old Guard nor the Militants were prepared to compromise —and neither, in the end, was Thomas.

The national executive committee—and some Militants along with it—were alarmed. They tried to work out a settlement. But neither the New York Old Guard nor the New York Militants wanted it settled. The New York state executive committee refused to honor a summons from the national executive committee in March 1935 to present its side of the case. Algernon Lee, who as president of the Rand School had a personal stake in the Old Guard retaining control in New York, delivered a short, rude, and caustic statement to the national executive committee: "We do not recognize the authority of the [national executive committee] to declare itself prosecutor, judge, jury, and executioner," he declared. Darlington Hoopes asked, "Is it the position of the State Committee of New York that it can refuse to abide by provisions inserted into the national constitution by the national convention?" "I am not here to answer questions and lend to travesty," Lee replied. The Militants wanted the Old Guard leaders thrown out of the party. Thomas, who agreed with the Militants, feared that precipitous action might alienate some party members who were in none of the factions. He favored the appointment of a "strong committee" by the national executive committee to attempt to work out a solution. He was even interested in a proposal by Dr. Louis Sadoff, a Militant dentist from New York, that the party there be divided into Old Guard and Militant units, each with its own bureaucracies, which would run joint electoral tickets, but which would otherwise have no relation with each other. The Sadoff plan was never considered, however. Those few Socialists who treated the machinations of both the Old Guard and the Militants with equal disdain, the so-called Centrists, attempted to bring the warring Socialists together in peace. Their leader, Dr. Harry W. Laidler, executive director of the League for Industrial Democracy, who assumed that the issues of tactics and principle that were being raised were merely subterfuges, and that the real issue was power, told Thomas that the various Militant factions would war against each other with as much vigor as they now warred against the Old Guard as soon as the right wing was forced out of the party. Thomas, whose personal hatred of most members of the Old Guard blinded him to the correctness of Laidler's analysis, opposed any efforts by Laidler to heal the breach in the New York party. Although Thomas did not want an immediate split, he had decided that the Old Guard could not be trusted to carry on a campaign for socialism; the Old Guard's only interest, he maintained, was its own position. Daniel Hoan allied himself with Laidler and offered to arbitrate the New York dispute. He also suggested that Thomas withdraw publicly from the New York dispute and inform both sides that he would no longer listen "to details and tales of woe from either side." Thomas refused to heed Hoan's suggestion. August Claessens, whose job as New York City organizer made him a member of the Old Guard but whose sympathies were with the Centrists, appealed to Thomas to "devote ourselves to the larger aims and aspects of our movement and less to the vicious personal phase of this lamentable schism." But Thomas, recognizing that his having allowed himself to become enmeshed in the factional fight "terribly handicaps my usefulness," so despised the Old Guard that he could not extricate himself from the dispute.

In July 1935, after months of work by the mediation committee, a truce acceptable to a majority of moderate leaders on both sides was worked out by the national executive committee. Thomas voted for the compromise "with hesitation." Algernon Lee said, "I am well satisfied. . . ." But it was apparent that the compromise was not going to be effective. It had been supported by a bare majority of the national executive committee; such Militants as Powers Hapgood, Maynard Krueger, Franz Daniel, and the pacifist Devere Allen opposed it, and both staunch Militant and Old Guard Socialists made clear that they were not interested in avoiding an open conflict.

Within four months, the national executive committee, prodded by Thomas, removed James Oneal as its representative to the executive board of the Labor and Socialist International, because his reports contradicted Thomas's. The Old Guard, seeing this as a new threat to its position, resumed intramural warfare. In November, just before local party elections, the New York City executive committee voted to dissolve twelve pro-Militant branches and to expel all "troublemakers." The Centrists, appalled by the Old Guard's action, formed an alliance with the Militants which put the Old Guard in a minority. The city central committee meeting called to vote on the proposed reorganization was one of the most unruly in Socialist history. It was apparent from the outset that the Old Guard's hold was tenuous and that the coalition of Centrists and Militants was on the threshold of taking control of the party. After considerable maneuvering, the Old Guard chairman announced that the reorganization proposal had been approved, 48 to 44, though in fact it had actually been defeated 52 to 48. The Centrists and Militants stomped out, adjourning to a new meeting hall where they proclaimed themselves the official city central committee. Charles Garfinkel, a Centrist, was declared the official city chairman, and Jack Altman, a Militant, the official city secretary. Among those who appeared at the meeting of the Militant-Centrist city central committee was Norman Thomas. "The ruling faction in New York," he told the cheering meeting, "acted undemocratically, autocratically, in contravention to the bylaws of Local New York. . . ." He charged that the prime interest of the Old Guard was in "ousting the young, vigorous, and active elements of the party" in order to safeguard their own jobs.

Thomas was now so deeply engrossed in the internal dispute that he had to cancel a West Coast speaking tour. The Old Guard attacked him in near-hysterical terms, accusing him of being a neo-Communist, an armed insurrectionist, an anarcho-syndicalist. Thomas, for his part, hailed the split: "Already a new day for socialism has dawned in New York," he declared. "The loyal Socialists are coming together. It is utterly false that we want to make the party Communist or even that we are fighting Socialists in order that we have a general united front with the Communists. It is utterly false that we advocate armed insurrection. What we want is a clean, aggressive Socialist party. What we reject is the rule or ruin policy of Old Guard leaders."

The Old Guard bureaucrats had protected their positions. The Militant-Centrist coalition had won over a majority of the membership. But there were signs that they had both won Pyrrhic victories, for if these splits continued there would soon be no party left. The overall membership in New York was falling rapidly; the Socialist vote in the city showed a sharp decline. B. C. Vladeck, who stayed with the Old Guard, told Thomas: "If the present breach is not healed there will be no Socialist party to speak of in New York City. . . . And in spite of all differences of opinion and the accumulation of personal resentment and personal squabbles, I think there is still room in the party for all of us." Thomas rejected all talk of reconciliation; he insisted that Louis Waldman, Algernon Lee, Julius Gerber, and Abraham Cahan must "be out of the picture, which does not necessarily mean out of the party." Thomas accused the Old Guard of sabotaging socialism, of being in alliance with "capitalist and old party interests," and of docility in the face of trade-union corruption and dictatorship.

Instead of reconciliation, the Militant-Centrist coalition exacerbated the schism. A conference in Utica over the 1935 Christmas weekend, which had the tacit support of the national office, with delegates representing the major upstate party organizations —Buffalo, Nassau, Olean, Rochester, Schenectady, Syracuse, and Westchester—set up a new state organization. The national executive committee, after several futile attempts to avoid an open rupture, revoked the charter of the Old Guard organization and recognized the new Militant-Centrist state party.

Norman Thomas's personal popularity assured the Militant-Centrist coalition of majority support. When the city's Old Guard leaders refused to invite him to speak at branch meetings, members of the branches did. Invariably he outdrew Old Guard speakers at these branch meetings by ten and twelve to one. Jessie Wallace Hughan, a pacifist whose ideological opposition to the Militants was total, nevertheless supported the new state organization because Thomas was in it. "I, as one member of the rank and file," she wrote to him, "am declining to stand either for the Right or the Left, but I do stand unequivocally for Norman Thomas. . . ." Literally hundreds of other New York Socialists followed Thomas into the new organization.[13]

The Old Guard's one last hope was the primary election. Under New York State law the actual control of a party is decided by enrolled voters and not by dues-paying members. The decision of the national executive committee to reorganize New York State's dues-paying party organization did not affect the legal machinery of the party. Delegates to national conventions are similarly elected at primary elections open to all enrolled Socialist voters, though the choices of the dues-paying party organization had not been challenged since 1919. Thus the Old Guard, which retained legal control of the party, decided to settle the issue in the April primary election. The Old Guard launched an all-out campaign aimed at convincing the state's enrolled Socialist voters that it was the true democratic and Marxist party. It pictured the pro-Thomas group as a conglomeration of pro-Communists, quasi-Communists, and pure Communists. It was one of the most vituperative campaigns in the history of American socialism. The *Jewish Daily Forward* and the *New Leader* spared no invective; two other Socialist daily newspapers, the German *Volkszeitung* and the Finnish *Rajaava*, joined in the attack. The Old Guard had the money, the organs of mass communications, and the experience for such a campaign. All the pro-Thomas wing had was Norman Thomas. The Militant-Centrist coalition's press in New York State consisted of one small, poorly edited weekly; its funds were virtually nonexistent; and its leaders had little experience in administering an election campaign. On the surface, the campaign appeared to be weighted in the Old Guard's favor. Realizing that its one major impediment was Thomas, the Old Guard made him its chief target. Unable to reply in any but the weakest of Socialist organs, Thomas found an outlet in the pro-Democratic party Yiddish daily *Tog (The Day)*, for which he wrote a series of articles.

Thomas's articles in the *Tog* brought the wrath of the Old Guard down upon him. They insisted that the *Tog* was an organ of Tammany Hall. How could a supposed Socialist ally himself with such a newspaper, they asked? The Old Guard ignored the fact that the *Jewish Daily Forward*, with a circulation of more than 100,000, many of them enrolled Socialist voters, would publish nothing by Thomas. Thomas had no alternative but to use a non-Socialist organ if he was to reach his public during the primary battle. Thomas found the use of the *Tog* a distasteful necessity. "A great many of our enrolled voters read Jewish," he explained, "probably many of them read only Jewish. How are we to reach them and the Jewish public generally with a statement of our case unless we can have access to some medium now that the *Forward* is closed to us?"

The attacks on Thomas were almost all of a personal nature. He was accused of being ambitious, of using the party for his intrigues, and of tearing "the party to pieces." The *Forward* used invective against him of a kind rarely used against even the most corrupt of Tammany chieftains. It charged that Thomas was not intelligent enough to know what he was doing, that he followed blindly the policies of Professor Maynard Krueger. Thomas, the *Forward's* editor Abraham Cahan said, ". . . is only an agitator among college boys" who had "aligned with Krueger and followed his revolutionary policies of armed insurrection." *Ravaaja* remarked that Thomas owed his position to the party, and charged that he was using it for personal and financial gain. "This acclaim he has used for his own instead of the party's good. . . . Thomas traveled not as a party speaker but for the League for Industrial Democracy for which he received a good salary. The prestige which he received as the party's candidate for President made it possible for him also to find a market for his books."

Not all of the criticism of Thomas was as baseless as the editorial attacks in the *Forward* and in *Ravaaja*. Robert A. Hoffman, Old Guard leader of the Buffalo local, upbraided Samuel H. Friedman after the latter appealed for unity no matter who won the primary election. "YOU YOURSELF, COMRADE FRIEDMAN, ARE PERSONALLY responsible for one of the chief contributory causes of the present party crisis. You are the author of the ditty *Thomas is our leader—we shall not be moved*. The constant singing of that ditty by hero-worshiping Yipsels [young Socialists] turned the head of the man who once showed promise of being socialism's chief American asset—and made him the most despicable character in the history of the American Socialist party. . . ." In his anger, Hoffman overstated the case, but the adulation of the young Socialists had indeed been one of the chief factors which led Thomas into the factional strife—which he should have avoided as leader of the party. Hoffman blamed the party situation on the Social Gospel ministers. "I favor a membership clause BARRING CLERGYMEN OR FORMER CLERGYMEN," he told Friedman, "—since its inception the Socialist movement has been CURSED with its Thomases, its Lunns, its Hahns. With their peculiar dualism—they do not belong in any rational, working-class movement." (George R. Lunn, a minister, was elected as a Socialist mayor of Schenectady, turned Democrat, and served as a Democratic congressman and lieutenant governor; Hahn, another minister, was a member of Buffalo's Revolutionary Policy Committee.) Hoffman's argument had some merit; the Social Gospel Socialists had historically found themselves deeply immersed in factional disputes—but then so had most Marxian Socialists.

The primary underlined Thomas's hold on New York's Socialist voters. The Old Guard held more than twenty meetings of enrolled voters throughout the city; court suits were instituted to rule pro-Thomas candidates off the ballot on spurious grounds; labor leaders announced their support of the Old Guard slate. (Only one prominent trade-union official, Julius Hochman of the Dressmakers Joint Board, backed the Thomas wing.) Yet when the ballots were counted the Old Guard suffered a severe defeat. The Militant-Centrist coalition had polled 4,405 votes, or 56 per cent of the total; the Old Guard polled only 3,453, or 44 per cent. The Militant-Centrist slate elected thirty delegates to the national convention, the Old Guard only twelve. The Militant-Centrist coalition gained control of the official state committee and every major county committee. The Old Guard, in utter despair, demanded recounts; but the recounts confirmed the original results. It was apparent that New York's enrolled Socialists preferred Thomas to Cahan, or Oneal, or Waldman. It was a personal triumph, albeit a Pyrrhic one.[14]

11

The split in the Socialist party was formalized on May 24, 1936, when the national convention of the Socialist Party of the United States of America voted to seat the Militant-Centrist delegation from New York State. It was a hectic convention with four factions competing for control: the Old Guard, who were in command of the Jewish and Finnish federations and the party organizations in Pittsburgh, Baltimore, Philadelphia, Boston, and Bridgeport; the Centrists, composed of so-called practical politicians and centered in Reading and Milwaukee, whose primary interest was in salvaging what they could of the party; the ultra-leftists of the Revolutionary Policy Committee, who were noisy but had little support within the party; and the dominant Militants. Thomas was in no particular group, though his sympathies were divided between the Militants, whose youthful exuberance he admired, and the more practical Centrists, whose non-ideological approach to socialism he favored. Although the outcome of the fight over the seating of New York's delegates was never in doubt, it raged for more than ten hours over two days. Waldman, Lee, and Oneal of the Old Guard were pitted in the convention debate against Thomas, Jack Altman, and Frank Trager. Proposals to settle the New York struggle by compromise were all rejected. Then, after Waldman and Lee refused to rise for the singing of "The Internationale," the convention voted to formalize the schism by refusing to seat the New York Old Guard delegation. Thomas hailed the convention's action.

The effects of two years of "radicalization of the party" soon became apparent: membership dropped from 20,951 at the end of 1934, to 17,437 at the end of 1935, to 11,711 in mid-1936. Besides New York, where the split cost the party more than 40 per cent of its membership, there were major declines in Massachusetts, New Jersey, and Wisconsin. B. Charney Vladeck, disgusted with the continual feuding, left the party after blaming Thomas for the internal disputes. "[Your] active interest in party politics and party organizational leadership," he wrote to Thomas, "is detrimental to the movement. . . . real political leadership requires that at least one or two outstanding men in any situation be kept on the sidelines so that when an opportunity for peace comes, they are in a position to plan it and carry it out."

Disgusted with the continuing fratricidal confrontations, Theodore Debs, Eugene Victor Debs's brother and founder of the party almost forty years before, resigned. So, too, did John F. "Jack" Sullivan, a leader of the New York Centrists. "If it were not for my admiration of you," he wrote to Thomas, "I would have taken this step at least a year ago." Other party members, from all factions, resigned to support Roosevelt.

Probably the sharpest blow came when Leo Krzycki of Milwaukee, a Militant, national chairman of the party, and a vice-president of the Amalgamated Clothing Workers Union, decided to abandon the party to support Roosevelt. There were other Socialists—including such left-wing Militants as Franz Daniel and Powers Hapgood—who attempted to convince Thomas that the party ought not to run a presidential ticket against Roosevelt so as "not to cut ourselves off from the labor movement." Thomas was, in fact, less than enthusiastic about running against FDR in 1936. As early as 1935, he had made clear to Mayor Hoan that he was opposed to the Socialist party running a national campaign. He personally would have preferred to run for Congress in a New York district where he had some hope of being elected. He expected a Socialist debacle. Thomas doubted that the party could run a campaign; the defection to Roosevelt of almost all pro-Socialist labor leaders had deprived the party of its one major source of funds. Yet he feared a repetition of 1924 when, he claimed, the Socialists' failure to nominate a ticket had wrecked the party organizationally. "We do not have to repeat that gamble," he said. He therefore agreed to run, though without much enthusiasm.

From a Socialist point of view, the campaign itself was a disaster. Virtually no labor leader backed Thomas; what little support he had came from educators and ministers. The Vermont Socialist organization, which backed the party's Militant wing, decided against participating in the election campaign. Thomas was thus unable to appear on the ballot in that state. In Ohio the law, which required a petition with 300,000 signatures, made it impossible for the Socialists to be on the ballot; in North Carolina an impossible ten thousand signatures were required. All told, the party was effectively barred from the ballot by restrictive election laws in twelve states. From August until election day in November, Thomas campaigned in thirty-three states, and made 160 speeches—an average of almost two a day. But he was a less than enthusiastic candidate; in fact, he very much wanted Roosevelt to win.

The theme of Thomas's campaign in 1936 was socialism versus capitalism. "Nothing short of socialism will save us," he declaimed. Thomas did not belittle Roosevelt's accomplishments. "Roosevelt," he said, "has made the Democratic party profess nobler ideals and try certain reforms more or less favorable to the workers. . . ." He conceded that Roosevelt's administration was "probably as liberal as any capitalist administration in America is likely to be." Thomas suggested that if "reform is the way out, better stick to the Roosevelt administration." He claimed that Roosevelt had carried out the Socialist platform rather than his own during his first term. On specific New Deal legislation, Thomas was particularly impressed with the Tennessee Valley Authority and the National Labor Relations Act, though he wanted the latter to be revised in order to give "some protection to agricultural workers who are today the most exploited of all workers." Thomas held the New Deal in such esteem that he doubted the Republicans would dare reverse it. "Our failure to achieve that abundance which we can create is clearly the fault of the Old Deal; it is not the fault of the New Deal."

Despite these pro–New Deal sentiments, Thomas noted some serious weaknesses in the Roosevelt program. In Nashville, Tennessee, he assailed the failure of the Roosevelt administration to act against racial discrimination and for full racial equality. He charged that the plight of the sharecropper and tenant farmer had worsened under Henry Wallace's administration of the agricultural New Deal. "The beneficiaries of the agricultural program of the New Deal have been the landowners, the great planters," he claimed. "Thousands of the workers have simply been driven completely out of a job because of the reduction of acreage."

Thomas's campaign for socialism was only a façade. His real interest was not the 1936 election but the formation of an independent farmer-labor party. As labor leaders became more and more enamored of Roosevelt and the New Deal, however, that hope also faded. The Committee (later Congress) for Industrial Organization, which he hoped would be the nucleus around which the new party would be organized, disappointed him; its officials supported Roosevelt and showed no interest in forming such a party. Thomas even hoped that some of the populist sentiment for an immediate solution to the depression by some simplistic panacea would work to the Socialists' advantage. But early in the campaign Thomas reported that his crowds were smaller than expected because "Coughlin and Townsend draw off the curious masses who want an easy cure." (Coughlin, a Roman Catholic priest with a proclivity for anti-Semitic diatribes, had a huge following because of his nation-wide radio program. Dr. Francis B. Townsend, a sixty-nine-year-old California physician, prescribed a $200-a-month pension for every American over the age of sixty, to be financed by a 2 per cent federal sales tax.) Thomas suspected that Coughlin was a potential fascist; he believed that Townsend was deluding both himself and his followers. Thomas told the Townsend movement's convention in Cleveland in July 1936 that though Socialists, himself included, had long proposed old-age pensions more generous than those paid under the Social Security Act, they could not support Townsend's plan. "I don't think you can keep capitalism and make the capitalist system pay you twice as much for not working when you are sixty as you got on the average before you were sixty." He was roundly hissed when he assailed the proposed sales tax, and when he questioned that the pension would cure all of the ills of society. Even Townsend's plea for Thomas failed. The elderly in the crowd, their dreams of security challenged, continued to heckle Thomas. The Communists, as usual, intentionally misinterpreted Thomas's speech. Browder claimed that Thomas had offered the elderly "socialism *instead* of pensions." Father Coughlin had his own candidate in the race, Representative William Lemke, a North Dakota Non-Partisan Leaguer. Lemke appealed to the disaffected and the discontented, who were normally receptive to the Socialists. Marvin Halverson, Socialist state secretary in South Dakota, reported that farmers "supposedly friendly to us had become staunch Lemke supporters."

"I am frankly much more depressed about the outlook than I expected to be by last spring," Thomas wrote to Maynard Krueger before election day. Thomas had ample ground for despair. The crowds he drew were sparse, at best, and the situation within the party was as chaotic as before the Old Guard had departed. When the votes were counted, Thomas's worst fears appeared optimistic by comparison with the results. He polled only 187,572 votes of 45 million cast, or .4 per cent of the total vote. It was the lowest Socialist vote since 1900, and the smallest percentage of the total vote in party history. Roosevelt, who carried every state except Maine and Vermont, got 27,478,945 votes; Landon, who was badly beaten, received 16,674,665; and Lemke won 882,479. In Reading, Pennsylvania, a center of Socialist strength, where Thomas's vote declined from 16,000 in 1932 to less than 3,000 in 1936, every Socialist candidate was defeated for the first time in nine years. In Connecticut, the *Bridgeport Daily Telegram* noted in a headline: "Right Wing Socialists Cut Thomas for Roosevelt." The American Labor party, formed by ex-Socialist labor leaders to back Roosevelt, did so well in New York State that many Socialist party members, including Thomas, proposed to drop all future electoral activity and concentrate on working within the new party.

The 1936 campaign left Thomas so despondent he seriously considered resigning from the party. He had had his fill of its internal bickering and its inability to win even minor electoral victories. "Our campaign in 1936 frankly cost us dear in power and prestige," he wrote in a private memorandum to party members. "It did not even unite us internally. . . ."[15]

12

By the end of 1936, the Socialist party was in the final stages of disintegration. Its membership was declining rapidly; it was organizationally in a state of near-collapse; its financial sources were virtually cut off; it had reached the lowest point in its electoral history. The New York party, rent asunder by the 1934–1936 infighting, was beset with new factional struggles. The Bridgeport, Connecticut, organization followed Mayor Jasper McLevy's lead and withdrew from the Socialist party. In Reading, Pennsylvania, where the Socialists had been dominant in city politics, a struggle over patronage split the party. Thomas supported the young rebels; the regulars, led by Darlington Hoopes, who had supported Thomas in the New York feud, left the national party in disgust and joined the Old Guard–dominated Social Democratic Federation. In Milwaukee, the Socialist party gave up its electoral existence and became an integral part of the Farmer-Labor Progressive Federation (FLPF), a faction of the LaFollette-organized Progressive party of Wisconsin. After a short-lived show of strength, the FLPF disappeared and so did the vaunted political power of the Socialist party of Wisconsin.

How did the Socialist party come to reach so low an estate in 1936? Reflecting on the mid-thirties some twenty years later, Thomas blamed Roosevelt's popularity exclusively. He insisted that "our internal difficulties, unfortunate as they were, were never the major cause of our decline. . . ." But Thomas was wrong. Internal feuding was one of the key factors in the party's decline; it drove many active Socialists from the party between 1934 and 1936. Thomas, who was involved in the feuding throughout, was in great part to blame. Yet this should not detract from the obvious fact that the party was affected adversely by the popularity of Roosevelt among the very people to whom the Socialists hoped to appeal. In the national campaigns of 1928 and 1932, Norman Thomas had emphasized almost exclusively the ameliorative measures which Socialists had always advocated—minimum hours, public works, collective bargaining, social security for the elderly, and unemployment insurance. By 1936, the New Deal had enacted all of these measures. In 1936,

Thomas ran on the issue of socialism versus capitalism because he had no other issue left—Roosevelt had swept the ground out from under him. It was Roosevelt's enactment of the Socialists' program of reforms which made the party's position as an electoral force untenable. To an unemployed man, the question of socialism versus capitalism was insignificant; his primary interest was in receiving his weekly check so he could feed his family. The fact that the Socialists had proposed unemployment insurance almost thirty years before was of little consequence to the average workingman. What did matter was the fact that Roosevelt had instituted it. Once Roosevelt had enacted the Socialist-proposed reforms, the party and its leader, Norman Thomas, had little to offer the American worker in the mid-1930's. He wanted immediate relief from the vicissitudes of the depression, and in 1936 Norman Thomas could offer him little more than a pipe dream.

The effect of the split in the party was as deleterious organizationally as Roosevelt's popularity was electorally. The split was the result of many problems and innumerable irritations on both sides. One apologist for the Old Guard, J. R. Rich, writing in 1967, blamed the party schism on, first, the failure of Thomas and his followers in the party "to comprehend the nature of Communism," and, second, on their attempt to "maintain a vested interest in radicalism against the tremendous pull of the New Deal." Rich oversimplified to the point of inaccuracy. The split was the result of forces that antedated the New Deal, and the most pro-Soviet spokesman of the party, James Maurer of Pennsylvania, was in the Old Guard. The schism was in part the result of the Old Guard's predilection to support any labor leader, no matter how corrupt, so long as he opposed the pro-Communist wing of his union. This factor, exemplified by the Nemser case, more than any other led Thomas to fight the Old Guard so vehemently from 1932 onward. The party rupture was also in part the result of the young intellectuals' peculiar affection for revolutionary rhetoric; anyone reading the Militant manifestoes —and there were literally hundreds issued by the various "left-wing" factions during the two-year period—is struck by the repeated use of revolutionary jargon by young Socialists, many of whom were even then preparing to leave the Socialist party for the greater political horizons offered by the Democrats. There were other temporary factors in the party struggle: the shock of the German Social-Democratic collapse and the rise of Hitler; the temporary issue of the united front, an elusive and naive hope that could never have materialized; and the whole question of parochialism which infested the New York party.

Norman Thomas's role in the collapse of the party nonetheless cannot be ignored. He, more than any other individual, could have averted the schism. His friend, B. Charney Vladeck, appealed to him to save the party; his role as nominal party leader and his personal following made him the ideal party peacemaker. But Thomas refused to act responsibly in the face of party strife. Instead of serving as arbiter between the various factions, he sided with the Militants because of his personal distaste for the leaders of the Old Guard and his love of the adulation of his young followers. Instead of attempting to save the party from self-destruction, Thomas participated in the process. Thomas was responsible for the party's internal collapse in 1936 because since 1934 he had assumed that the role of the leader was to follow his young adherents in order to win their cheers. In sum, Thomas was miscast as a political leader. At heart he was an evangelist preaching the Social Gospel, a role which fitted his heritage and training; he was not a political leader, able to keep followers in line. That role was alien to his heritage and training.[16] From 1936 through 1942 Thomas worked untiringly for the Socialist party, with the result that it disintegrated completely.

VI
A leader
without followers,
1937–1940

B efore its 1936 national convention, the Socialist party was split into four factions. At the convention one faction, the Old Guard, was expelled—and then there were five. The Centrist-Militant coalition soon split into four warring factions, and within months a fifth was added. On the so-called right there was now an informal group of Centrists, headed by Norman Thomas, whose philosophical and political orientation was basically Social Democratic. The Centrists had opposed the Old Guard on purely tactical grounds. The second faction was composed of pacifists, who were divided among themselves on all issues except the abhorrence of violence. The third faction, the Militants, was essentially the old group of the same name, though now somewhat less bombastic in tone. The fourth faction, the far-left Clarity wing, proposed to remake the Socialist party into a "revolutionary" organization, far more radical than even the Communists. The fifth faction, the Trotskyites, was interested primarily in eliminating the Socialist party, which it considered a rival for revolutionary pre-eminence. Each of the factions played its part in further destroying the Socialist party—with Norman Thomas pitching in to help.

2

The Trotskyites came into the Socialist party for two reasons: to give Leon Trotsky a respectable base of operations against Stalin in the struggle for the soul of the world Marxist movement; and to complete the destruction of their main rival among Socialists in America. By 1928, Trotsky had lost his foothold in the international Communist movement. His followers inside

Russia were persecuted and murdered by Stalin's henchmen; in non-Russian Communist parties, Trotskyites were expelled and isolated from their erstwhile comrades. Followers of Trotsky were accused of all sorts of heinous crimes by their Stalinist enemies. Trotsky himself was in exile—first in Turkey, then in Norway, and finally in Mexico. His life was in constant danger from Stalin's minions. Still Trotsky dreamt of a counterattack against Stalin, and saw the Socialist movement as a base from which to launch his drive. As early as 1932 he had ordered his Czech followers to give up their independent existence and enter the Social Democratic party. In most other countries the Trotskyites were kept out of Social Democratic parties by Socialist leaders who did not trust them.

There were several impediments to the Trotskyites' admission to the Socialist party in America. A firm believer since 1919 in an all-inclusive Socialist party encompassing all radicals from the IWW to the Non-Partisan League (but excluding the Socialist Old Guard), Thomas was favorably inclined toward the Trotskyites. He assumed that in some areas, particularly Minneapolis where they were a major radical force, they "would strengthen us." The Old Guard effectively barred all Trotskyites and other quasi-Communists from the Socialist party before the 1934 convention. Even after the so-called left-wing Socialists gained control of the national organization at that convention, and the American Trotskyites made overtures to the national leadership, some of the pro-Militants were unwilling to have the party colonized by Trotsky's followers. In addition, there was the practical problem of absorbing the highly disciplined Trotskyites into a loosely organized party.

Anyone who was familiar with the activities of the Trotskyites during the period immediately following the 1934 Socialist convention would have doubted the advisability of admitting them. They had arrogated to themselves the job of advising and criticizing the Socialist party on principles and tactics in *The Militant*, their weekly newspaper. They made special efforts to contact personally some left-wing Socialist party members for the purpose of discussing internal party matters. Small groups of Trotskyites were sent into the Socialist party and Young People's Socialist League to organize a faction "in the interest of Bolshevik education of the left wing." Albert Goldman, the most significant

Trotskyite to enter the Socialist party during the early period, began almost immediately to publish *Socialist Appeal*, a "theoretical journal" which was in effect the organ of the Trotskyite faction in the Socialist party. Thomas was elated with Goldman's entry into the party in late 1934. He conceded that he and Goldman would "probably differ often and sharply," but he assumed such differences were healthy for the party.

Between 1934 and 1936, the internal party fights made it especially inadvisable for the Trotskyites to be admitted into the party. There were, however, continual negotiations between Norman Thomas and Trotskyite leaders, chief among them Sidney Hook, a professor of philosophy at New York University, Max Shachtman, and James P. Cannon. Hook acted as intermediary between Cannon and Thomas. Cannon, who like most Marxist-Leninists considered truth a bourgeois virtue, assured the Socialists that he and his followers had abandoned their insistence that a revolutionary party had to be monolithic. While in public Trotskyites called Thomas a great Socialist leader, in private they repeated Trotsky's quip about Thomas calling himself a Socialist as the result of a misunderstanding. It was not until early 1936 that Thomas and his followers reached agreement with the Trotskyites on the terms of the latter's admission into the Socialist party. The Trotskyites were to join as discrete individuals under the same conditions as any other applicants. They were to cease publication of *The Militant* and of their intellectual organ, the *New International*. "It was rather irritating," Cannon recalled, "but we were not deflected from our course by personal feelings. We had been too long in the Lenin school for that." Thus, as soon as the Cleveland convention of 1936 completed the task of ousting the Old Guard, Trotskyites from all over the country started joining the Socialist party. They came in ostensibly as individuals, but in fact they remained a cohesive group under the discipline of Cannon and Shachtman, who were themselves being directed by Leon Trotsky in Mexico City. They came in, to quote Cannon, "as we are, with our ideas." Oblivious to the apparent intent of the Trotskyites, Thomas believed they would add "valuable elements of strength" to the party.

The Trotskyite invasion proved almost immediately a catastrophe. Working "under the supervision of Comrade Trotsky," the Trotskyites made clear from the outset that they would either gain control of the party or wreck it. They conceived of themselves as the "cadres of the revolutionary movement destined to perform . . . [the revolutionary] historic mission and they will let nothing stand in the way of this task." Several female Trotskyites accepted voluntary (nonpaid) clerical assignments in the national office in order to act as spies. Lillian Symes, a perceptive life-wing Socialist, warned Thomas against using any national office stenographers for confidential communications. Other Trotskyites had themselves elected branch literature agents, a thankless post that most Socialists avoided, and then ordered only Trotskyite journals and pamphlets for the branches. Anyone who dared disagree with any Trotskyite dictum at a party meeting was labeled a Stalinist. Socialist party meetings became contests of endurance; 3 A.M. adjournments were commonplace; and where factional issues were concerned, "Trotskyites can stay awake longer and speak longer and more frequently than any other political types." In December 1936, less than six months after he had joined the party, Cannon, who had moved to California for "reasons of health," joined with Glenn Trimble, an ex-theologian with revolutionary pretentions, in an effort to seize control of what was left of the California party. Cannon convinced the state executive committee to publish a weekly newspaper, *Labor Action*, and appoint him editor. It was soon apparent that *Labor Action* was not a genuine Socialist party organ; Cannon has conceded that "if it was not a Trotskyist agitational paper, I will never be able to make one." The Trotskyites were succeeding beyond even their own expectations, particularly in the Young People's Socialist League. A majority of YPSL members had become, according to Thomas, "pure and simple Trotskyites."

The situation in the Socialist party had become so serious within six months after the Trotskyites were admitted that even Norman Thomas decided that there "is little time to lose." The party was in a state of near anarchy. In Minneapolis the state chairman and local secretary, both long-time Socialists, resigned from the party because the Trotskyites had created chaos in the local. The Wisconsin party threatened to withdraw from the national organization if the Trotskyites were not expelled. Thomas informed his friend Professor Hook that the party would "find a way, by agreement, I hope, by discipline, if necessary" to control the Trotskyites. When the Trotskyites ignored the warning, Thomas decided the time had come to act. He arranged for an emergency party convention for March 1937 to act against growing sectarianism in the party. He had to act swiftly; the Trotskyites would be eligible to be delegates by the time the next regularly scheduled convention was due in 1938 (they were still ineligible because they had joined the party too recently). Recognizing the threat posed by the convention, Cannon instructed his followers to stall for time. "We felt we hadn't yet had time enough to educate and win over the maximum number of Socialist workers and Socialist youth who were capable of becoming revolutionists," Cannon reported. "We needed about six months more time." In the election of delegates, Trotskyites and their supporters were defeated in virtually every state—even in their stronghold of California. The convention followed Thomas's advice by outlawing all factional organs, including the *Socialist Appeal*. The Trotskyites defied the convention and continued their factional journal. They also called a special "Appeal Conference" which was, in effect, a national convention of the Trotskyite faction in the Socialist party. The national executive committee therefore had little choice but to expel them. But it was too late, for Trotsky's followers, whom Thomas had welcomed into the party, had succeeded in further wrecking it. Many California, Indiana, Minnesota, and Ohio Socialists left the party with the Trotskyites, as did almost all of the members of the Young People's Socialist League. Cannon told Thomas after the expulsion: "We got what we wanted out of joining the party for a while, our aims are accomplished, and now goodbye. We're going to take with us a lot of your folks."

The experience with the Trotskyites led Thomas, who had been instrumental in allowing them into the Socialist party, to despair for the future of socialism. "I am feeling rather gloomy about the Socialist party, or perhaps I should say about myself," he wrote National Secretary Clarence Senior. "I think I am failing in doing what may be an impossible task for anybody; namely, building the kind of inclusive Socialist Party of America which . . . I had in mind."[1]

3

Stalin's murderous purges and a 1937 trip to the Soviet Union convinced Thomas that the so-called "Workers' Fatherland" was actually more of a fascist than a socialist state. "Nothing in my experience has been more of a blow to me," he wrote later, ". . . than the final evidence that the development of communism was not toward, but away from, democratic socialism, and that the Russian Revolution from which we hoped so much has produced the world's most totalitarian state." Nor was Thomas convinced that Stalin alone was to blame; it was the whole Leninist system which was at fault, he concluded. "I rather think that if Trotsky had won rather than Stalin we might have had much the same story with the positions reversed."

Some Socialists wanted Thomas to ignore the Moscow purge trials. They still dreamed of a united front with the official, Stalinist, Communist party, even though they were still smarting from their experience with the American Trotskyites. Alfred Baker Lewis, leader of the Massachusetts Socialist party, pleaded with Thomas to withhold any comment on the trials. Thomas rejected the plea. The purge "is too vital; it goes too deep; it plays too terrible a role now in dividing the working class and in discrediting socialist idealism to be ignored," he wrote Lewis. Nor did Thomas allow his antipathy toward the American Trotskyites to prevent him from working to assure Trotsky of asylum. When late in 1936 the Norwegian government decided, under Russian prodding, to expel Trotsky, Thomas protested. "For Norway to impair the historic right of asylum with all it implies in the case of Trotsky would be to make [the] world a prison house for all political exiles and give new tyrannical power to reactionary governments," he cabled *Arbeiderbladet*, the Norwegian Labor party's daily newspaper. After Norway expelled the Russian exile, Thomas joined with John Dewey and other civil libertarians in convincing President Lazaro Cárdenas of Mexico to offer Trotsky asylum.

Thomas assured Angelica Balabanoff, a self-exiled Russian revolutionary who had worked with Lenin and who knew all of the principals in the purge trials personally, that he agreed with her assessment that the trials were fraudulent. But he was not convinced, at the outset, that all of the defendants were innocent of plotting against Stalin. He assumed that Stalin's actions were based on considerations which were not "too creditable," but he suspected that some opponents of Stalin, particularly Gregory Zinoviev, had plotted against the Soviet dictator. "I do not think we can proceed to jump at conclusions that it's all lies in the face of the Zinoviev confession," he declared. "We can't stultify ourselves without further information by blank support of either Communist faction. We've got to urge the truth." What Thomas wanted primarily was an investigation by the Labor and Socialist International—an investigation that was barred by the Soviet government.

Although he was not convinced of the innocence of those on trial for their lives in Moscow, Thomas protested Stalin's methods and the timing of the trials. He was particularly upset with Stalin for dividing the working-class movements of the world at a time when they most needed to be united against the threat of fascism. "It is the basis for true liberty and true justice, as well as for the economic well-being of the workers," Thomas wrote in 1937, "that I must regard the Moscow trial and the temper it illustrates as a betrayal of Socialism. . . ."

Thomas's stance on the trials irritated the Stalin regime. In March 1937, the Soviet government refused for a month to grant Thomas a visa on the grounds that he had "supported the terrorists." A visa was finally, though reluctantly, granted. This visit reinforced Thomas's disillusion with the Soviets. He was particularly upset by the cruel treatment of political prisoners who worked at forced labor under horrible conditions. The Soviet Communist regime, he now insisted, was not moving toward the socialist dream of a classless society, but was, on the contrary, perpetuating and strengthening class divisions. The Soviet speed-up of production and the dehumanization of the worker that went with it, he reported, created perils "not only to individual well-being, but to Socialist ideals." Moreover, Thomas noted an "incalculable and poisonous weight of fear" in Russia which threatened any hope of socialism.

Thomas concluded in 1938 that Stalin was "the successor not of Lenin but of Ivan the Terrible." Now convinced that the defendants in the Moscow purge trials were innocent, he accused Stalin of murdering his opponents in a Machiavellian drive for power. "What has happened in Russia," Thomas declared, "represents the degeneration of socialism, the complete subversion of revolutionary idealism, an all but fatal wound to working-class integrity and confidence in its own destiny. There is no hope for socialism, which indeed deserves no support, unless it can divorce itself from everything that the Moscow trials stand for." Thomas charged that "Lenin, Trotsky, and above all, Stalin, pioneered in that contempt for pity and that Machiavellian ruthlessness in which Hitler has become so adept." By the end of the 1930's, Thomas had become as anti-Soviet as the most right-wing of the Old Guard.[2]

4

An onslaught by the fascist forces in Spain, under General Francisco Franco, against the moderate left-wing government there, and the civil war that resulted, led Thomas to abandon temporarily the pacifism which had led him into the Socialist party almost twenty years earlier. It also brought about a further split in the party. The civil war in Spain placed pacifists in a peculiar dilemma. Many of them were Socialists, all believed in democracy. A victory for the fascist forces would have spelled the doom of democracy in Spain. It would have made democratic socialism impossible in that country. The pacifists thus sympathized with the cause of the anti-fascist Loyalists. But as pacifists they could not recognize any war as justifiable. Moreover, peace, regardless of cost, was their most important objective. Thus Jessie Wallace Hughan, a leading Socialist-pacifist and executive secretary of the War Resisters League, proposed a negotiated peace in Spain. Thomas opposed her suggestion. Although Thomas's rejection of Miss Hughan's position was the negation of the pacifism he had espoused during and immediately after World War I, it came as no surprise to his fellow Socialists. In siding with the Militants during the internal party struggle, he had in effect supported the use of force to defend democracy or socialism. Thomas had come to believe that pacifism no longer offered a solution in the struggle against fascism. Mere abstention from war, he now reasoned, would eliminate neither war nor oppression. He considered it unrealistic, even mad, to assume that it did not matter who won in Spain. It mattered very much to Thomas that Franco and fascism should be defeated. It seemed to him necessary that the supporters of the Spanish republican government receive assistance.

The position of the anti-fascist Loyalists was weakened by an embargo imposed by America and other democratic governments against the supplying of arms to either side in the civil war. The fascist rebels were getting weapons from Italy and Germany, but the Loyalists were effectively cut off when their supposed allies, the democratic powers, declared an embargo. Thomas appealed to President Roosevelt for support for a democratic government under fascist attack. Roosevelt, after waiting for a year, finally answered his old friend "Dear Norman" by defending the embargo by assuming the position of a total isolationist. Only three years later Roosevelt was to be the opponent of isolationism while Thomas was to be its spokesman.

The disagreement over the Socialist party's stand on the Spanish civil war might not have had a deleterious effect on the party had not Norman Thomas and the New York organization undertaken, without endorsement from the national party organization, to organize a volunteer battalion of highly trained young Americans to fight in Spain. Taken after consultation with the Spanish government, the action was given wide publicity and received general support in the New York party. Outside of New York and among pacifists, however, there was strong opposition. Two nonpacifists, Mayor Daniel W. Hoan of Milwaukee and Max Raskin, his legal adviser, were the first to protest. Raskin called the decision to form the so-called Debs Column "impolitic" and "almost ridiculous." Hoan believed, correctly, that the move was little more than a sordid publicity stunt, and feared that it had done much damage to the party and would "forestall much work we could do for Spain." Despite the opposition of Raskin and Hoan, the party's national executive committee felt compelled by the publicity to support the New York organization officially while secretly castigating it for the action.

If the national executive committee felt constrained to lend formal support to the New York party in its adventure, the pacifists did not. Elizabeth Gilman, a Baltimore pacifist who helped support the party financially, called the decision "horrible," and complained that it was against "what I consider our basic Socialist philosophy." The Reverend John Haynes Holmes decried the "raising of an armed brigade and sending it to the battlefront to fight and kill," and protested that "to use the name of Gene Debs for this bloody business fills me with a horror which is indescribable." He refused to "stand by the party if this goes on." Thomas pleaded in vain with his pacifist friends to understand the conditions that led him to support the Debs Column. He told them he had not given up his lifetime search for methods other than war; but "there is no such method open as far as I can see in Spain. Certainly submission to Franco would merely make war for all the rest of us more likely." This was a far cry from Norman Thomas the conscientious objector of World War I, but Thomas maintained that there was a great difference between serving in the 1914–1918 war and fighting Franco in Spain. He insisted that the young men who would be fighting in Spain were, unlike those who fought in World War I, volunteers risking their own lives in a war against fascism. They were, he explained, involving no nation nor were they conscripting others. Thomas declared that they were merely living by Thomas Paine's slogan: "Where liberty is not, there is my fatherland." The argument failed to convince many pacifists, several of whom deserted the party. Whole locals, such as the one in Syracuse, New York, resigned *en masse* to protest the proposed organization of the Debs Column. Few of them returned to the party. The Debs Column was hardly worth the effort; it was, in fact, never organized.

Pacifist opposition was only one of the problems connected with the Spanish Civil War that plagued Thomas. Dissension within Spain, and the repression of the anti-Communists left there, also raised serious questions for American Socialists. During his voyage abroad, Thomas visited Spain and was upset by the Communists' rise to power as well as the measures they employed to decimate their left-wing opponents. "We American Socialists, who with all our hearts are on the side of the Loyalists," he informed James Middleton, secretary of the British Labour party, "are nevertheless sorely troubled by the strength of the Communist influence in Loyalist Spain toward making it a totalitarian state with no guarantees of civil liberty." The chief victims of the Communists were the members of the non-Communist Marxist *Partido Obrero Unificado Marxista* (POUM), who were violently suppressed on the spurious charge that they were Trotskyites—despite the fact that all Trotskyites had been expelled from the POUM before the outbreak of the civil war.

In August 1937, the Communists murdered Andres Nin, the leader of the POUM, in his jail cell in Barcelona. Thomas protested the "lynching," called it a "black mark against Loyalist Spain," and charged that it was part of the Communists' program for liquidating all Spanish radicals who refused to submit to their control. Thomas appealed to the Labor and Socialist International and the International Federation of Trade Unions to demand the release of all POUM members from jail in Loyalist Spain. The Communists, who controlled the Loyalist police force, retaliated by arresting Sam Baron, the American Socialist party representative in Barcelona. Only pressure from the British Labour party and the Labor and Socialist International forced the Spanish government to free Baron after a week in a Barcelona jail. After his release, he informed Thomas that "I have looked inside a chamber of horrors within the working class and I mean to expose it." He later broke with Thomas, resigned from the Socialist party, and testified against the Spanish Loyalists before the House Committee on Un-American Activities.

In 1938, Thomas still insisted that "victory for the Loyalists would be of overwhelming benefit to mankind." But he recognized that a simple victory over Franco would not be sufficient to win freedom for the Spanish people. Spain, he now believed, "would have to free herself of . . . Communist terrorism to be truly free."[3]

5

The strife within the Socialist party continued unabated. The members of the various factions had lost none of their enthusiasm for intra-party warfare. Paul Porter told Thomas: "This sectarian factionalism feeds on itself. It tends to bring to the fore in the branch meetings or in the party press the people who specialize in hair-splitting and intolerance. The comrades who are occupied with important mass work find themselves bewildered (or disgusted) by these trends, and drop more and more out of the party." Party members were, in fact, resigning by the thousands; by the end of 1936, the total national membership had fallen to approximately six thousand. Moreover, the party was almost completely without experienced or able administrators. But would-be Lenins, who relished internal disputations regarding obscure passages in Marx, were in their glory.

One of them was Gus Tyler, the new editor of the *Socialist Call*. Tyler had been the intellectual "boy wonder" of the party a few years before, but by 1937 it was apparent that his forte was revolutionary phrase-mongering and factional sniping. Under his editorship the *Call* degenerated into a poorly written organ of the "super-revolutionary" Clarity faction. A typical editorial declaimed that "America almost cries for a disciplined, centralized directing force with an ultimate Socialist aim and an immediate program and strategy of combat against the lowing forces of oppression." He wrote that "a huge electoral machine . . . is the direct anti-party of the revolutionary party we want." As if control of the *Call* was not enough, the Clarity caucus produced its own factional journal, *Socialist Clarity*. Its objective, like that of the *Call*, was the development of a "Marxist vanguard party of mass work."

The factional struggle was aggravated when Raymond Hofses wrote in *The Reading Labor Advocate*, the organ of the Reading Social Democratic Federation, that Thomas's position had by late 1937 become almost identical with that of the Social Democratic Federation. The statement would have gone unnoticed had it not served the purpose of the Clarity group, which was then attempting to seize control of the party. The caucus issued a broadside, "The Struggle for Revolutionary Socialism Must Go On!," which was little more than a violent attack on Thomas. It charged that Thomas was a "right-winger," and that he was threatening to resign from the party if his policies were not adopted. The attack brought speedy retaliation from Thomas, who declared war on the Clarity faction. He asked the national executive committee to fire Tyler as editor of the *Call* on the ground that the weekly had become more factional than Socialist. Tyler, Thomas charged, "seems to identify propaganda for socialism with propaganda for the point of view of one caucus. . . ." As a result, Thomas said, the *Call* was "not an adequate theoretical organ and neither is it the well-edited propaganda paper which we imperatively require." Agreeing with Thomas, the national executive committee voted seven to five to fire Tyler.

Meanwhile, the endless feuding continued to reduce further

the size of the party. By 1938 Arthur McDowell reported to the national executive committee that the "total dues-paying membership of the Socialist party, as of the calendar year of 1938, was 3,072."

As if things weren't bleak enough, at the 1938 national convention in Kenosha, Wisconsin, a new struggle developed over the seating of the New York delegates. Both the Clarity faction on the left and the Militant faction—which now found itself on the right—claimed the full twenty-four New York delegates. After a four-hour debate, the convention seated thirteen Militants and eleven Clarity delegates. Nationally, the Clarity caucus did far better, winning control of the national executive committee with a seven to six majority. Thomas refused to serve as national chairman unless "I am in accord with the attitude and plans of the majority" of the national executive committee. He soon learned that he could not work with the members of the Clarity group.

When Clarence Senior resigned as executive secretary of the party in 1937, the national executive committee named as his successor Roy E. Burt, a Social Gospel Methodist who had been secretary of the denomination's Board of Education since 1932. Burt had supported the pro-Thomas wing of the party, but he had not been actively engaged in factional infighting. Both he and his wife worked for the party for a single small salary. The Clarity caucus, which controlled the national executive committee, decided in 1938 to fire Burt, whom it could not control, and to replace him with Tyler. Moreover, the caucus leaders secretly moved the party's national office from Chicago to New York, despite opposition from both the New York and Wisconsin state committees. The Clarity "coup" roused Thomas's ire. Tyler, he declared, "has not in my judgment as yet shown the kind of responsibility nor the devotion to party apart from faction which would warrant his being made National Secretary." Thomas thus informed the national office he would be "utterly unwilling to accept" Tyler as national secretary, adding that Ben Fischer, who was the Clarity faction's alternate choice, would "in any place . . . be a calamity." Before Burt left his post in February 1939, Tyler had accepted a position with the International Ladies Garment Workers Union, which was considerably more prestigious than the Socialist party. Even the pro-

Clarity members of the national executive committee refused to consider Fischer for the post. A direct confrontation was thus averted.

The party plunged further in its rapid decline. In 1939, the *Call* was forced to reduce its size from eight to four pages and its publication schedule from weekly to biweekly. Party membership declined to 2,852 in late 1939, to 1,928 by late 1940, and to 1,801 by April 1941. The trend was now irreversible.[4]

6

Behind the theoretical façade of revolutionary rhetoric, genuine issues figured in the party disputes in which Thomas was involved. Much of the infighting of 1937–1941 admittedly served as little more than an outlet for the pseudo-intellectual pretensions of many of the participants, particularly the leaders of the Clarity faction. But there were serious points of difference within the party, particularly after the 1936 election made it clear that the Socialists had little future as an electoral organization.

By 1937, Thomas had decided that "it is not particularly good revolutionary Marxism to put so much stress on the imperativeness of running a Socialist candidate regardless of the external situation." He believed that the party should not run a candidate in 1938 against Michigan's Democratic Governor Frank Murphy once the CIO had endorsed him, particularly since party members who were also CIO officials would be forced to choose between their unions and the party. He told the Michigan Socialists: "I confess I can't see much use in the party's being right at the expense of losing one by one all the people who rise to leadership. It is an awfully easy way to save our Marxist souls to let him [Walter Reuther] resign, but is it a way to advance socialism?" The Michigan party, dominated by the Clarity faction, ignored Thomas and ran a candidate against Murphy. Reuther publicly supported Murphy and all other CIO-endorsed Democrats and resigned from the Socialist party. It was a blow from which the Michigan party never recovered.

In New York the issue involved the relation of the Socialist party with the new but powerful American Labor party. Almost immediately after the 1936 election, Thomas suggested that the Socialists begin negotiations with the American Labor party

(ALP) for the 1937 municipal election. He believed that the Socialists were in a "pretty good position to reach a satisfactory agreement" with the ALP on the 1937 city election slate. His assumption had some merit; it was considered unlikely that the Republicans would renominate LaGuardia, who would thus be the candidate solely of the American Labor party. There was even a possibility that LaGuardia might not seek re-election, in which case Thomas might himself be the candidate. He suggested to Clarence Senior, Jack Altman, and Harry W. Laidler that they approach the ALP and suggest that the two parties reach an agreement by which "we and the ALP nominate all, or most, of the same candidates on our two tickets." There were, however, three problems involved in the proposal. First, the founders of the ALP, fearful of a Communist invasion, had barred membership in the ALP to members of other political parties. This meant that Socialists were effectively barred so long as they remained members of a legally constituted party. Second, Alex Rose, the ALP's leading figure, was antipathetic to Thomas for personal reasons. Finally, there was strong opposition to the proposal within the party, particularly among the Clarity faction.

The die-hard Clarity faction insisted that the ALP was little more than a political prostitute whose nomination was available to the highest bidder among the major party candidates. Thomas disagreed: "The ALP with all its shortcomings is a mass labor party with a vote in New York City many times ours. . . . We are committed to a labor party. . . . The ALP does not yet meet our conditions for joining it, but we have seriously to consider whether it or any other mass labor party will ever meet these conditions. . . . If the ALP goes down the line for LaGuardia and we actively oppose him, we shall get a very small vote—I should be surprised if we got 30,000—but that might be enough to defeat LaGuardia. Fearing that result, the ALP will be very bitter against us. It will bring tremendous pressure on all labor union members. It may force Socialist office holders in unions to choose between the union offices and the SP. . . ." Thomas suggested that the party nominate candidates for minor offices only, and even in those cases he wanted the Socialists to run joint tickets with the ALP.

Opinion among the members of the New York party local was sufficiently divided for the city central committee to order a referendum of the full membership. Gus Tyler used his position as editor of the *Call* to prejudice the referendum and thus upset any negotiations with the ALP. In the midst of the debate within the party immediately before the referendum, Tyler charged, in a *Call* editorial, that the "reformists—the Communists, the ALP and Labor Non-Partisan League leadership—are placing the formation of a real labor party in danger." He insisted that the Socialist party run a campaign against the ALP. Thomas complained that Tyler's editorial attacks on the ALP had made "our general approval of the idea of a Labor party in New York State . . . academic, for we cannot work with those whose line of action we attack in the manner and spirit that the *Call* has shown." The party members supported Thomas in the referendum, and no Socialist ticket ran in 1937. Tyler appealed the local's decision to the national executive committee, but it backed Thomas, eight to seven. Thomas, who formally announced his neutrality in the 1937 campaign, supported LaGuardia, who ran as the candidate of both the Republicans and the ALP.

The 1937 election results were generally gratifying; not only was LaGuardia re-elected, but three independent ALP candidates endorsed by the Socialist party—Nathaniel Minkoff and Gerald Muccigroso in the Bronx, and Frank Monaco in Brooklyn—won seats in the State Assembly. When Thomas appeared at the Bronx headquarters of the ALP on election night, he was greeted with the singing of the *Internationale*. Among Socialists this taste of victory led to a growing demand that the party abandon its electoral activity in New York State and enter the ALP. Thomas agreed, but he recognized the problems this would create. Since the Socialist party was an official party under New York State law, it would have been possible for an unscrupulous political group—such as the Communist party or the Trotskyite organization—to capture the Socialist line on the ballot and trade on its name, if the Socialists were to abandon it. A difficulty would also arise regarding the national election of 1940—especially if the ALP supported the presidential candidate of one of the "capitalist" parties. After conceding these problems, Thomas noted that there was a significant drive within the ranks of labor for a new, independent national party; and he suggested that the Socialists could be more effective in such a drive from within the ALP than from without. Yet once again Thomas was deluding himself. B. Charney Vladeck, now a leader of the ALP, informed Thomas that he doubted the ALP would become an independent labor party in 1940. He forecast, correctly, that fascism would be the key issue in that election and that it would therefore "be foolish for the ALP to split the democratic front." Nevertheless, even if Vladeck was accurate, Thomas believed that the Socialists should enter the ALP in order to help steer it on an independent path.

There were, however, forces within the American Labor party opposed to admitting the Socialists as an organized unit. The Communists, who had by 1938 become a significant force in the ALP, feared the Socialists would pledge their support for Roosevelt should he decide to run again in 1940. Two significant forces within the ALP wanted the Socialists admitted as a unit: David Dubinsky, whose International Ladies Garment Workers Union supplied most of the finances and votes for the ALP; and the members of the Social Democratic Federation, who expected their old comrades to help them combat the Communist influence. Secret negotiations between the Socialists and Alex Rose had been going on for six months when, in June 1938, Paul Tobenkin, an enterprising young labor reporter for the *New York Herald-Tribune*, learned of them. He phoned Thomas for clarification of some of the details. His story reported, correctly, that the two parties were near agreement and that the Socialists would henceforth nominate no state or local candidates except those named by the ALP. The Socialists would be free in 1940 to support the ALP national ticket, or they could name their own if they found the ALP ticket unacceptable. Moreover, there was an implied assurance that the ALP would name independent candidates wherever possible. Tobenkin also made clear that the Socialists were being welcomed into the ALP because they were needed to fight the Communists who had infiltrated the party. Alex Rose was annoyed; he had wanted the privilege of announcing the outcome of the secret talks himself, and he considered the story too flattering to Thomas. Rose was so piqued that, despite appeals by Louis Waldman and Isadore Nagler, two ALP leaders, he refused to allow the Socialists into the party as a unit, but only as individuals.

Thomas was unhappy at the outcome of the negotiations:

"Socialists are unanimous in thinking that in the New York [state] campaign of 1938 they cannot make the ALP their electoral agency. . . . The ALP dragged out interminably negotiations with the Socialist party. . . . Meanwhile . . . the ALP made . . . old party deals. . . ." Thomas was nominated for Governor; and though he accepted the nomination, he did not campaign. The election results were disastrous for the Socialist party; Thomas polled only 24,890 votes. As a result, the Socialists lost their line on the ballot in New York State. The ALP gave Lehman the votes he needed to be re-elected; it polled 419,979 votes for him, giving him a margin of victory of a mere 64,004. After this electoral defeat, the Socialist party dropped its pretensions, and the state executive committee announced: "We consider the American Labor party as the electoral expression of the working class in New York." All Socialists in the state were advised to enroll in the American Labor party. One told Thomas that the "Socialist party has been murdered." His observation was accurate, albeit belated.

The Socialists' entry into the ALP as individuals proved to be almost immediately rewarding. In 1939, George Backer proposed that the Labor party nominate Harry W. Laidler for the City Council from Brooklyn. Laidler was nominated and elected. Thomas's charge that Michael Quill, city councilman and president of the Transport Workers Union, was a pro-Communist forced the Bronx County ALP to withhold its support from Quill, who was defeated in the election. But two years later, in 1941, the Communists had their revenge. They won control of the Brooklyn ALP in a primary election and denied Laidler renomination on the spurious grounds that he was an isolationist, despite the fact that he had by then broken with Thomas and supported massive aid to the Allies.

By late 1940, it was apparent that the Socialists' tenure in the ALP was to be a short one. The issue of whom to support in the presidential campaign created an insoluble dilemma for Socialists in the ALP. Thomas, who was running as the anti-war Socialist candidate, attempted unsuccessfully to win the endorsement of the ALP, which formally backed Roosevelt. Walter O'Hagen, a Socialist member of the ALP state committee from Auburn, asked Thomas: "What are we Socialists enrolled with the Labor party expected to do?" Thomas's answer was more pessimistic than informative. He now saw little hope for the ALP, and suggested that Socialists support their own national ticket. By 1944, the issue had become purely rhetorical when the Communists, in alliance with Sidney Hillman of the Amalgamated Clothing Workers and Representative Vito Marcantonio, had captured the American Labor party.[5]

7

Along with internal discord, foreign policy, and party politicking, Thomas was also involved during the latter half of the 1930's with the struggle for civil liberties. His contribution to the cause of civil liberties during that period was spectacular—but more spectacular than significant. The most visible of Thomas's assaults against authoritarianism in the United States involved Mayor Frank Hague of Jersey City, who was the Democratic national committeeman from New Jersey.

Although nominally a Democrat and a supporter of President Roosevelt, Hague was opposed to trade unions that were affiliated with the Congress of Industrial Organizations. Since Jersey City was a major industrial center, Hague's antipathy caused serious problems for CIO organizers. Owners of meeting halls, fearing Hague's displeasure, refused to rent them for CIO-union purposes. Permits for outdoor rallies by the CIO were denied by the commissioner of public safety on the basis of a city ordinance which provided that he had the right to refuse a permit "for the purpose of preventing riots, disturbances, or disorderly assemblages." Hague thus arranged with groups like the Chamber of Commerce, the Ladies of the Grand Army of the Republic, or some veterans' organizations for whom he had done a political favor, to protest against any proposed CIO meeting. If necessary, a veteran could be found who would allow himself to be quoted that "the veterans would take the matter into their own hands and see to it that the meeting would be broken up."

Because in 1937 the CIO was attempting to organize workers in major industrial plants, it found the Hague edict particularly difficult to live with. Appeals to President Roosevelt to use his influence with Hague brought no results. But a device was finally developed by which the legality of the Hague fiat could be tested. A number of speakers were sent into Jersey City to speak at Journal Square, Jersey City's chief intersection, in a test of the ordinance. The speakers included such diverse individuals as Roger Baldwin, of the American Civil Liberties Union, Senator William Borah, the Idaho Republican maverick, and W. M. Callahan, the editor of the *Catholic Worker*, who attempted to read a Papal encyclical. Hague averted a court test by refusing to arrest any of them; instead, they were seized by police and "deported" by ferry to New York. Thomas was scheduled to address a May Day rally in Journal Square. The police seized him as he approached the Square, pulled him into a squad car, and hustled him off to a New York–bound ferry. Undaunted, Thomas returned almost immediately to Jersey City, where he was greeted by a crowd of some two thousand sympathizers. The police grabbed him, jostled the crowd, and punched Mrs. Thomas, who had accompanied him, in the jaw. This time they took Thomas to the building of the *Jersey Observer*, a local daily newspaper, where he was kept a virtual prisoner. When the crowd discovered his whereabouts, they gathered in front of the building and cheered him heartily.

Thomas and the CIO now combined to attack Hague on three fronts. The CIO brought suit against Hague in Federal District Court, Thomas brought suit against him in the state courts, and both tried to force Hague to change his stance by attempting to put pressure on Roosevelt, the labor unions, and New Jersey industrialists. Thomas and the CIO were backed by some unexpected sources: Alfred M. Landon, the 1936 Republican presidential candidate, for example, wired his support to Thomas immediately after the Jersey City incident. Roosevelt informed Thomas that he would attempt to find an anti-Hague, or at least a non-Hague, Democrat to fill a judicial post that was open in New Jersey. The Montana State Federation of Labor voted at its 1938 convention to condemn Hague and to warn him "that we will be forced to place the products of New Jersey on the 'we do not patronize list' along with the products of Japan." Not all labor leaders supported the CIO or Thomas in their fight for civil liberties in New Jersey. William Green, the president of the American Federation of Labor, refused to intervene in the case, primarily because of the rivalry between the CIO and the AFL.

And two AFL officials helped organize a Hague-inspired mob which attacked Thomas when he attempted to speak in Newark in June 1938.

Thomas brought suit in New Jersey Superior Court in an effort to force Daniel Casey, the Jersey City Public Safety Director, to issue him a permit to hold an outdoor rally for a meeting in June 1938. The court did not act until October, when it ruled against Thomas on the grounds that he "has no more right to speak in public places in that city than he has to invade a citizen's home without invitation." The court cited the threats by veterans as endangering the tranquility of the city. Thomas appealed, but before the New Jersey Supreme Court could rule in October 1939 the issue was moot: the CIO had won its suit in federal court.

There were other cases in which Thomas worked for civil liberties during this period. In 1938 he pleaded for Fred Beal, an ex-Communist who had jumped bail in North Carolina where he was appealing a conviction for a murder during the Gastonia textile strike of some eleven years earlier. Beal fled to Russia, became disillusioned with the Soviet system, and returned to the United States. He was abandoned by his old Communist cohorts. Thomas organized the effort to have him freed. In 1940, Thomas appealed to President Roosevelt to set aside the four-year prison sentence meted out to the Communist leader Earl Browder for passport fraud.

Thomas's devotion to civil liberties was nowhere better demonstrated than by his protest against the "anti-subversive" Smith Act and its use against Minneapolis Trotskyites, who had only four years before wrecked the Socialist party in that city. Ironically, the Communists, who were later to be its victims, supported the Smith Act when it was used against Trotskyites.[6]

8

More than any other question, that of how Socialists should respond to the threat of Hitler kept the American Socialists divided after 1938. As the Nazi menace grew, so did the demand by some anti-fascists for a united political and military stance by the nonfascist states against incursions by the Nazis and their allies. By 1935, even the Communist International was calling for collective security; Thomas found this position "incredible." His incredulity at the cry for collective security indicated a return to his earlier pacifism. Although his rhetoric was now less Christian and more Marxian, it was, in fact, to a great extent Midwestern isolationist. His rationale was based on doubt that the nonfascist states intended to stop Hitler; otherwise, he reasoned, how could France have been so nonchalant about Germany's rearming?

Thomas maintained that each of the pro-collective-security groups had its own reason for favoring united action. Most obviously, he believed, were the Communists. He maintained that their change of heart was too blatant to deceive anyone. He found their old dogma that war was inevitable, and that it would be followed by civil war and revolution, to be both naive and dangerous. But Thomas maintained that their new position, in favor of collective security, was more dangerous than the old because it was based on their insistence that it was the chief duty of the working class to defend the Soviet Union. He accused the Communists of supporting collective security on the assumption that the United States would defeat Japan and Germany for Russia. In short, Thomas was accusing the Russians of being willing to fight until the last American.

Thomas conceded that the idea of collective security was emotionally appealing and, superficially at least, plausible. He warned, however, that it was "fundamentally unsound in the world in which we live." How could one draw hard and fast lines between democratic and anti-democratic powers? Could Russia be considered a democracy? Japan, he argued, was no fascist state, yet it was one of the three states collective security was supposed to oppose. He noted that the very methods the anti-democratic powers were employing had been used by their adversaries one hundred years earlier—and were still being used. He pointed out that Hitler's *Untermensch* was antedated by Britain's idea of the "lesser breed," Australia's exclusion act, or South Africa's *Apartheid*.

He questioned the assumption that there were two distinct camps, fascist and anti-fascist. Thomas saw no basic unifying principle among the nonfascist states; all that might unite them was a distaste for Hitler and Mussolini, and even this was not so strong as might appear on the surface. The "so-called democracies," Thomas claimed, had refused to do anything in Spain or Ethiopia, where fascism might have been nipped in the bud, because they feared that social revolution in Italy and Germany would follow the defeat of the fascists. He conceded that the nonfascist powers might unite because of a joint hate, fear, or common imperial interest, but never for an ideal. Democracy, Thomas said, would be what the young idealists would believe they were fighting for, but it would not be the guiding principle of the statesmen and generals. The real hope for overthrowing Hitler, Thomas declaimed, lay not with the British or French imperialists, nor with the totalitarian Stalin, but with the German workers. Thomas's hope for a revolution of the German workers against the Nazis was, at best, wishful thinking.

Thomas's disillusion with the Loyalists during the Spanish Civil War, his belated discovery that Russia was neither a utopia nor progressing toward a utopia, plus his innate Christian pacifism and Midwestern isolationism, combined to end his short-lived excursion into support of military action against fascism and in defense of democracy.[7]

9

There were in the Protestant Social Gospel movement several erstwhile allies of Norman Thomas who had by the latter part of the 1930's allied themselves with the Communist party. Although they did not favor civil liberty for their opponents, seven of the members of the national board of the American Civil Liberties Union were pro-Stalin. After his return from Europe, and his total disillusion with the Soviet Union, Thomas opened a frontal attack against them. His primary target was his one-time teacher at Union Theological Seminary Dr. Harry F. Ward, who was now closely allied with the Communists. Thomas opened his attack with an appeal to several fellow members of the ACLU board. He accused the pro-Communist members of the board, and particularly Dr. Ward, of favoring civil liberties for themselves but not for their opponents, and he accused them of giving blanket approval "for everything that happens in Russia." They were thus not genuinely interested in civil liberty, he asserted, since, despite their claims to the contrary, "there is as little civil liberty in Russia as there is in Germany or Italy."

Thomas did not imply that the civil liberties of the Communists should be impaired or denied, but he insisted that Communists had no right to be officials, or even members, of an organization which was dedicated to the preservation of the very liberties they would deny their opponents. "Communists belong on the board of the Civil Liberties Union as much or as little as fascists, who also want the protection of the Bill of Rights until they seize power," he wrote to his fellow members of ACLU. When Osmond K. Fraenkel, a leading ACLU attorney, upbraided Thomas for his "Red-baiting," Thomas shot back: "I think you and many liberals like you are doing very serious harm now to true liberalism in the United States by a kind of tolerance of intolerance." He warned that the Communists were only interested in a "wholly temporary, partial, and pragmatic defense of civil liberties," and he accused the Communists of being Machiavellians "destroying the soul of American labor" and thus hastening "the rise of an American fascism, Black or Red." No man, he said, could honestly defend civil liberties in the United States and at the same time condone the Communist denial of such liberties in Russia or, "when they get the chance, in America." He charged that pro-Communist members of the ACLU board had made public, in biased and inaccurate form, confidential information regarding the civil liberties organization. He also cited the Communist attacks on the 1934 Socialist anti-fascist rally at Madison Square Garden and the 1925 meeting for Menshevik leader Raphael Abramovitch. The Communists wrecked both by brute force. The Communists on the ACLU board, Thomas charged, had prevented it from condemning such assaults on civil liberties. "The Civil Liberties Union," he told Fraenkel, "impairs its own usefulness unnecessarily when it has to support not only the right of Communists to hold meetings and to enjoy benefits of the Bill of Rights, but also the right of a man to be chairman who was generally considered to have been for the last few years a principal apologist for Communism. . . ."

By 1940, Thomas had won considerable support for his drive to oust pro-Communists from the ACLU board. Conditions had changed, what with Stalin and Hitler now virtual allies. Sidney Hook, John Haynes, John Dos Passos, and Margaret de Silver supported Thomas—the latter two resigning from the ACLU to emphasize their point. Others, including the columnist Dorothy

Dunbar Bromley, the attorney Morris Ernst, and the playwright
Elmer Rice, were also prepared to resign; only a letter from
Thomas pleading that they continue their "aggressive and concerted" effort kept them in the organization. In February 1940,
faced with almost certain ouster, Ward resigned as chairman of
the Civil Liberties Union; he was replaced by John Haynes
Holmes. At the same time, the ACLU board voted twenty-three
to seven in favor of Thomas's motion to make membership in or
support of the Communist party ground for barring membership
on the ACLU board. All of the Communists and fellow travelers
were expelled.[8]

10

By the end of the 1930's, Norman Thomas had come full circle: from a Social Gospeleer to a democratic Socialist to a "revolutionary" Socialist to a democratic Socialist and back to a Social
Gospeleer. He could still call himself a "reasonably good Marxist," though he deplored the "tendency to make socialism a religion of the book," and he rejected dialectical materialism, a
cornerstone of Marx's philosophy, as inadequate metaphysics.
Thomas suggested it was necessary "to get more ethics into politics and life" than Marx's dialectic inferred. He also disagreed
with Marx on the demise of the middle class; he suggested, instead, that the mores and psychology of the middle class would
persist. Thomas now questioned the assumption of most Marxists
that at some stage in the development of capitalism the only
choice would be between fascism and socialism—a concept he
had himself expounded only two years earlier. His Marxism was
now non-Marxian, his socialism nonrevolutionary. He opposed
the use of the term "revolutionary socialism" as neither adequate
nor definable. He wrote one of his youthful admirers that the
"great battle of the future is not going to be between socialism
and private capitalism. . . . The outstanding struggle of the future
will be to determine how much collectivism is necessary for social well being." What troubled Thomas was his fear—especially
after his visit to Russia—that collectivism could lead to the totalitarian state. Given the choice between totalitarian socialism and
nontotalitarian capitalism, Thomas chose the latter. He had now

reversed his field completely from his stand during the 1934–1936 party controversy.

Bourgeois democracy, which Thomas ridiculed in 1934, he considered an important element of his program by 1938. "Socialism," he now said, "has to restudy its methods. It has to re-emphasize its essential democracy. Because of our tragic disappointment in Russia . . . we cannot possibly swing to the doctrine that democracy is tied up with a dying capitalist order." Political democracy, he still insisted, was of itself inadequate to assure the good life to all, but he considered it superior to any form of dictatorship as a means for ending social injustice and economic inequality. "At worst," he wrote, "there is always the possibility that voters in a democracy will learn something, a possibility reduced almost to a vanishing point in the case of the subjects or soldiers of a dictator." Thomas insisted that the rights of the minority had to be guaranteed against the "temporary caprice of a majority," lest democracy degenerate into mere majority rule which "might easily reduce government to the tyranny of the mob." This was a far cry from the rhetoric of revolution which he expounded several years before.

If Thomas's socialism was, by the end of the 1930's, barely revolutionary, his Social Gospel Christianity remained unsullied. He doubted he could return to the pulpit, but he still believed in the Christianity that proclaimed a social heaven on earth. He berated the organized Christian church for attempting to "make an impossible compromise between Christ and man," thus becoming the bulwark of a social order which he considered the antithesis of Christianity. "If the church is of any use," he wrote to a fellow Social Gospeleer in 1939, "it ought to be as a source of power and an inspiration for the application of high ethical standards."

Having abandoned his revolutionary stance for the Social Gospel, Thomas proposed that the Socialists abandon electoral politics generally. He suggested in late 1938 that the party cease electoral activity altogether and turn itself into an "educational and leavening force." He wanted the Socialist party to announce that there would be no further Socialist presidential candidates. He agreed that this would be a distasteful choice for many Socialists, but "there is no use forever batting one's head against a stone wall." He still favored a third party, preferably one based on labor and farm organizations, "but of that kind of party there is now no sign." He hoped that the Socialist party would be the nucleus of such a new party, though he admitted that this was not likely to develop in the near future. Other Socialists agreed with Thomas's analysis, and some drew the logical inferences from it: since there was almost no chance for a new party to be organized successfully, they suggested that the Socialists join the Democratic party. One Socialist wrote: "We have been calling spirits from the vasty deep for a long time, but so far none have come. The progressive and labor forces are definitely tied to the Democratic party. We will have to go to them." Thomas thought so, too, but a war in Europe and his pacifist isolationism prevented his proclaiming his agreement.

In May 1940, a tired Norman Thomas summed up the situation in the party twelve years after he had taken over the nominal leadership: "Socialism which we had hoped would triumph 'in our time' is today everywhere on the defensive. That is not because the capitalism and nationalism which socialism has fought are successful. . . . But socialism is on the defensive because under its social-democratic form it failed to achieve its ends in Germany and under its communist form it betrayed and corrupted those ends in Russia."[9] He forgot to mention that under its "revolutionary" form, socialism in America had committed political suicide.

VII
Keep America out of war

As Socialist talk of revolution subsided, it appeared for a time that the party might be able to regain some of its lost prestige. But the war in Europe intervened, and the Socialist party began its final decline into ultimate, irreversible disintegration. It was Norman Thomas's insistence that the Socialist party adopt a position of isolationism in the face of Hitler's near conquest of all Europe—including such Socialist bastions as Denmark and Norway—that led to the party's complete deterioration. The events of 1938–1942 eliminated any hope for a Socialist revival in the United States. The party was to emerge from the war as little more than Norman Thomas and a few personal followers.

2

Except for his support of the Loyalists in Spain, Thomas had been a pacifist since the earliest days of World War I. His pacifism had been one of the chief reasons for entering the Socialist party in 1918. Although he deviated from that pacifism in the case of Spain, it was apparent that he would oppose American participation in any war abroad. His tour of Europe in 1937 convinced Thomas that war between Hitler and the nonfascist powers in Europe was unavoidable—and that it was near. He was particularly distressed that most European Socialist leaders favored such a war and hoped American intervention would save European democracy. Fearful that the approaching European war would engulf the United States, Thomas proposed almost immediately upon his return from Europe that the Socialists' national executive committee authorize him to form a new, ostensibly nonpartisan but pro-Socialist organization whose sole aim would be to keep the United States out of the impending war. The national executive committee authorized Thomas to contact "leading elements among the anti-war forces in America" to organize a united effort aimed at keeping the United States isolated from the war that was expected to break out in Europe momentarily.

Thomas sent a letter to dozens of leaders of pacifist and isolationist organizations inviting them to a meeting in his New York City home in late January 1938 to form the new organization. About twenty pro-Socialist pacifists attended the meeting, where they formed the Keep America Out of War Congress (KAOW). Among the groups represented at the meeting were the American Friends Service Committee, the Fellowship of Reconciliation, Labor's Anti-War Council, the Methodist Episcopal World Peace Commission, the National Council for the Prevention of War, the War Resisters League, the Women's International League for Peace and Freedom, the Youth Committee Against War, and World Peaceways—a veritable roll call of American pacifist organizations. The founding members included Representative Jeanette Rankin, who voted against American participation in World War I and was to be the only member of either house of Congress to vote against American participation in World War II, Senator Robert M. LaFollette, Jr., of Wisconsin, and Norman Thomas. The organization's slogan, coined by Thomas at the first meeting, declared: "The maximum American cooperation for peace; the maximum isolation from war."

Typically, the new Keep America Out of War Congress began life with an internal feud which nearly led to its demise before it was fully organized. Among those invited accidentally by Thomas to the organizational meeting was Representative Hamilton Fish, Jr., an upstate New York Republican whose domestic record included opposition to almost all New Deal legislation. Although Fish did not attend the meeting, he did become a nominal sponsor of the Congress. Fish's name on the list of sponsors brought protests from many Socialists. The party's national executive committee was bombarded with demands from members that it withdraw from KAOW unless Fish's name was removed from the list of sponsors. The committee refused under any conditions to divorce itself from the organization it had founded; it issued instead, at Thomas's behest, a public statement decrying the listing of Fish as a sponsor of the Congress: "His record on domestic issues is such as to cast a serious reflection on his ability to sign a call to the Congress and accept [its] . . . program. His persistent Red-baiting constitutes a menace to civil liberties, without which there can be no sound foundation for the American system which he so highly lauds." The organizing committee of the KAOW refused to delete Fish's name from its list of sponsors, despite Socialist pleas, until Fish demanded that the United States intervene militarily to prevent Mexican nationalization of American-owned oil wells. He was then dropped as a sponsor.

In its first year the KAOW Congress showed unexpected virility. It was then the only national organization formed specifically to advocate American nonintervention in Europe. Its first major rally, in 1938, drew six thousand supporters to the New York Hippodrome to hear Norman Thomas, Senator LaFollette, the United Auto Workers president Homer Martin, and the liberal editor Oswald Garrison Villard. Most but not all of Thomas's party and nonparty supporters agreed with him on the war. Some, like Paul H. Douglas, warned that the peril posed by fascism could not be successfully met by isolation.[1]

3

Thomas's isolationism and pacifism came to the fore during the Sudetenland Crisis of 1938. Hitler had demanded that Czechoslovakia surrender to him all of the German-populated Sudetenland area; when the Czechs balked, the German Army moved to the Czech frontier. France, which had a defense pact with Czechoslovakia, began mobilizing its forces; Britain was digging trenches to be used as air-raid shelters, distributing gas masks to its civilian population, preparing to evacuate children from likely targets of the German *Luftwaffe*, and mobilizing its fleet. Except for a speech by Foreign Minister Maxim Litvinov before the League of Nations offering to join Britain and France in the defense of Czechoslovakia, Russia was too busy purging itself of old-line Bolsheviks to become involved in the crisis. War seemed days, possibly hours, away. Thomas professed sympathy for the Czechs, but he was dubious of the British and French motives; they were, he said, merely acting in their own self-interest. He compared the proposed Anglo-French defense of "bourgeois"

Czechoslovakia with their refusal to aid the left-of-center Spanish republic. Moreover, Thomas reasoned that Britain and France could stop Hitler without help from America. He also insisted that the crisis was of the Allies own making. If the peacemakers at Versailles had not placed so many Germans within Czechoslovakia's borders, Thomas asserted, the crisis could have been averted. Now, he argued, there was no service the United States could offer the Czechs that would be worth the loss of life involved. Thomas's prime interest during the crisis was to avert or postpone war. He doubted that delay would work to the benefit of Hitler. To believe that a delay would give Hitler more time to strengthen his war machine while it would not do the same for the nonfascist powers "is to believe that the inherent health of fascism is greater than that of democracy," he wrote as the crisis was worsening. If this were true, he argued, "the surgery of war can't cure the cancer of fascism."

As Europe was about to be plunged into war, British Prime Minister Chamberlain, French Premier Daladier, Mussolini, and Hitler reached an agreement at Munich which gave Hitler everything he sought and thus averted war temporarily. The reaction of the Socialist party in America to the appeasement at Munich emphasized the development of a new division within the party—a division that was to grow steadily more bitter. Some members, particularly those born in Italy, Spain, Germany, Poland, Yugoslavia, and Czechoslovakia, believed the Czech workers should have fought the Germans, and that the Socialists of France and Britain should have favored an immediate war against the Nazis. The larger group—headed by Thomas—considered the question of who ruled Czechoslovakia of far less importance than the problem of "imperialist war" between capitalist powers. The party's Anti-War Committee called the latter stance "a reiteration of the traditional position" of the party.

The Munich pact thus evoked a positive response from Thomas. He admitted it was a truce rather than a peace, but faced with the choice between war or appeasement Thomas chose the latter. The pact was, he conceded, unfair; it increased Hitler's power at Czechoslovakia's expense, and it placed new minorities under Hitler's oppressive rule. But, Thomas asked, would war have been a better alternative? Should there have been war, he contended, Czechoslovakia would have been pummeled by bombs and trampled over by opposing armies; it would have lost no matter who won the war. Aerial warfare, he feared, would have devastated Europe's cities; the social order would have crumbled; colonial peoples in Asia and Africa would have risen. Out of all this, Thomas forecast, would have come not socialism and democracy but totalitarianism which, by its very nature, would have been a defeat of everything Socialists believed in.

Within two months it was apparent to Thomas that the Munich pact had been a disaster. "It does not guarantee peace," he told the convention of the Youth Anti-War Committee. "It did give new prestige to Hitler's glorification of war. It put new minorities under his cruel and despotic power." New refugees, primarily German and Czech Jews, were fleeing the Sudetenland region and wandering through Europe. They were the victims of the appeasement Thomas had applauded only months before. Moved by reports of their suffering, Thomas asked his old friend B. Charney Vladeck to join him in a campaign to help these unfortunates. Vladeck advised against a public campaign for aid to refugees or for an easing of the immigration laws. Such a campaign, he warned, might backfire; public opinion was not prepared for it. Thomas then wrote a personal letter to President Roosevelt pleading for aid for those Jews and Christians who were fleeing from the Sudetenland. Roosevelt offered no help. Thomas despaired, but he did not cease his efforts to help the victims of the Munich pact. He now opposed even disarmament unless it was accompanied by "a positive guarantee by all nations of a cessation of the brutal persecution of the minorities which is today one of the chief emotional threats to the peace of the world."

At the beginning of 1939, Thomas was questioning his whole position on war. "It was framed before events had moved as far as they now have," he wrote the Reading Socialist editor Raymond Hofses. Within the party, pressure mounted for a change in position. Meyer Miller, a Jewish Socialist, pleaded: "This is 1939 not 1917! What was correct then must not necessarily be so today." The left-wing Jewish delegates at the Chicago Socialist city convention demanded that the party call for an immediate rupture of relations between the United States and the Nazi regime in Germany. Alfred Baker Lewis, the leader of the Massachusetts party, wrote a letter to the *Boston Post* in which he urged that the United States stop all trade with Hitler and announce that it would aid small nations—particularly in Scandinavia—if they were attacked by Hitler. Even Thomas's isolationist pacifism was fading. "I confess," he wrote to Lewis, "that I am not yet prepared in my mind to commit myself absolutely in advance on the question of whether, in the event of war in Europe, between any nations whatsoever, we should follow a policy of complete neutrality. . . ."[2]

But by now Thomas was too firmly committed to pacifism and isolationism to change his position more than superficially.

4

In August 1939, Hitler and Stalin signed their nonaggression pact. Within a matter of days, Hitler's armies moved into Poland and World War II was underway. Stalin's deal with Hitler shocked radicals throughout the world. Communists left the party in droves. Socialists saw their hopes shattered. But not Thomas. He felt revulsion, but not shock. Stalin was, after all, to his mind in no way a Socialist. "Socialism," Thomas wrote, "has been sorely wounded, but true socialism is not dead." He recognized that the agreement between the two dictators was basically an alliance against the nondictatorial powers; he called it a great contribution to Hitler's plans for expansion, charging that it represented brazen duplicity. He insisted that anti-war work continue unabated; he told his friend and fellow pacifist A. J. Muste that "it is immediately important to hold together that bloc which wants to keep America out of the war by keeping out the things that logically lead to war. . . ."

After Hitler invaded Poland, Thomas altered his view slightly. He conceded that Hitler, abetted by Stalin, was the aggressor in Poland—but only in Poland. He refused to concede that Hitler was also the aggressor against Britain or France. Thomas even had some doubts about Poland, which "only yesterday played jackal to Hitler's lion in the despoilment of Czechoslovakia." (Poland had seized the Teschen area of Czechoslovakia shortly after Hitler seized the Sudetenland.) Poland, he argued, was itself no democracy; its rulers from Pilsudski in 1918 to Smygly-Rydz in 1939 had been dictators. Thomas could not see how Poland could raise the cry of self-determination since it had denied that right to the people of the Free City of Danzig when they (foolishly, Thomas believed) had voted to return to Germany. Poland had also denied that right to its own Ukrainian minority, he argued. Nor did Thomas believe that the British and French could claim honestly that they were fighting for self-determination in view of their records in India and Morocco, where they had denied it to the native peoples. There was no ideology involved in the war, he insisted, not even the perverse ideology of Hitler, who had turned from an anti-Comintern front to a deal with the leader of the Comintern itself.

Alone among the countries involved in the early stages of World War II, Finland evoked Thomas's sympathy. He hailed Finland's resistance to the invading Russian armies, assailed the Stalin attack, and urged the United States to do all it could short of war to aid the Finns. He urged an embargo on arms to the Soviets, but he opposed breaking off formal relations. Formal recognition, he argued, did not mean approval of the Soviet regime; in critical times it was advisable to have diplomatic outposts wherever possible.

Thomas was now obsessed with keeping America out of the European war. He feared the United States would lose its democratic freedoms if it became involved, and he saw no compensatory gain for the world. In some European nations, he conceded, it was possible that Socialists would have no recourse but to fight. But even they, he argued, would have to admit that "no solution of anything" would come out of the war. He saw World War II as merely an extension of the 1914–1918 conflict. Its roots, he charged, were the same "age-old European power conflicts plus new imperialist struggles for oil, coal, spheres of influence and investment, and markets for exclusive trade." The ruling classes, Thomas said, were the same, and so were the power politics, the cliques, the spoils, and the men "on whose hands is the blood guilt of the last war." It was, he argued, the same old conflict being resumed after a short intermission. He called the war an attempt by the victors to hold onto their gains and by the vanquished to reverse "the harsh terms of Versailles." He conceded that the imperialism of the British and French was, in 1939, better than the German. But that, he held, was beside the point. What did matter was the fact that the "worse brand" of imperialism—

German fascism—was a progeny of the victory of the "better," or British and French, brand of imperialism. Any victory by any imperialist power would, Thomas said, merely sow the seeds for a new, aggressive form of fascism.

Thomas admitted that there were some things about this war that were new. Chief among these he considered the "more advanced stage of decay of the socio-political order out of which it springs." The more lethal weapons which extended the scope of the war to include old men, women, and children were also new, as were the speed with which men, machines, and the mass media were mobilized for the war. He even admitted that the brutal nature of the Nazi regime might be new—but basically Thomas maintained that it was the same old war between the same old imperialisms. Both sides—the British and French allies defending their empires and the "hungry, prowling and on-the-make" new German imperialism—were, he contended, bloody, brutal, and dictatorial aggressors against their subjects. The only difference he found was the color of the victims' skins—Hitler began his war against members of white minorities in his own country, while the British and French warred against black and brown subjects in Africa and Asia.

To keep America out of this extension of an old imperialist war, Thomas favored the enactment of more stringent neutrality laws in order to outlaw even minimal trade with the warring powers. He argued that "immense war trade" would result in direct American involvement. He wanted America to work instead for a negotiated peace. He feared that the "war profiteers and the international bankers," particularly J. Pierpont Morgan, wanted to drag the United States into the war in order to be able to dictate, rather than negotiate, a new "peace of vengeance" for Germany. The statement by Thomas played into the hands of the Nazi propagandists, who merely rephrased it. "Jewish bankers want to bring U.S. into the war," the Nazi organ *American Views* quoted Thomas as saying. The quote was a fraud, but it only pointed up the strange dilemma in which Thomas was placed for the next two years. Among the opponents of American involvement in the war were some who were also anti-Semitic. Thomas, who was not anti-Semitic, found himself allied with them, and thereby tainted. Yet Thomas was not without fault here. He was at no time willing to divorce himself from any but the most extreme anti-Semites so long as they joined him in opposing the war. Isolationism made strange bedfellows.

By early 1940, Thomas despaired of keeping the United States out of the war. "As I see the American scene," he wrote to pacifist friends, "things are going, not dramatically, but surely against our cause. At the moment the chief danger is probably the fact that the public shares with the President a kind of belief that we can play God to the world. . . ."

Beginning in March, Hitler's military might began its steady, seemingly irrepressible advance. Germany conquered Denmark and Norway, the Low Countries, and France. The French Army was destroyed. The sorely weakened British only escaped destruction by evacuation at Dunkerque. By late June it appeared that Hitler was on the road to victory. Even this threat of Nazi world domination did not change Thomas's view. He was still vehemently opposed to the war, which he continued to blame on Versailles. He agreed that "Hitler's victory creates new problems" and that it made the "application of our [anti-war] principles more difficult," but he insisted that his position was as sound or sounder than ever. He now proclaimed: "I hope with all my heart that Britain can beat off the Nazi invader decisively." But he did not, under any conditions, want the United States to help Britain defend herself. The Allied catastrophes only led Thomas to fight harder against the hysteria which he feared might lead the United States into the war. His rationale changed, becoming a good deal less logical. The United States, he now claimed, was not prepared for war and could thus not help stop Hitler. At the same time, however, he opposed increased preparedness by the United States lest it lead America into the war.

For all his Socialist rhetoric, Thomas was at heart a provincial American isolationist. Despite his façade of Socialist internationalism, his views were little removed from those of the most nationalistic defenders of the cause of American isolation. He even accepted their "Fortress America" concept without equivocation. The "United States," he told the Senate Military Affairs Committee, "thanks to geography and history, is not in the position of France and Great Britain. . . . Unless we are to go in for foreign military adventures, we are concerned for a relatively easy defense primarily to be entrusted to the Navy, the Air

Force, and highly trained operators of mechanized warfare." As for a Nazi invasion: "Nonsense! We still have two oceans to guard our ramparts." Thomas was certain that the Western Hemisphere was safe from Hitler's hordes.[3]

5

In 1938, before war broke out in Europe, Thomas was opposed to running a Socialist candidate for President. He wrote then: "There is no Socialist commandment: 'Yearly shalt thou nominate a full Socialist ticket.' The commandment is: 'Thou shalt at all times advance socialism; an understanding of it and an organization for it.' Socialists have no Marxist souls to save by always voting only for a true believer regardless of the effect upon the external situation and the psychology of the workers." As late as August 1939, Thomas was still ambivalent on the issues of the 1940 campaign. He feared that the party would lose more than it would gain if the campaign proved the party's growing weakness. But he was equally worried about the possible psychological effect of not running a Socialist candidate after forty years of doing so.

Thomas conceded that the New Deal "is in many respects very good; so good that no Republican will dare to advocate repeal of any of the major New Deal laws. . . ." He admitted that the New Deal had enacted Social Security and had "shown a concern for conservation both of natural resources and human values unprecedented in American political history." The New Deal was not Socialist, but Thomas agreed that it had put into effect much of what the Socialists had proposed. Moreover, Thomas recognized the legal and organizational problems that faced the Socialists if they attempted a national campaign in 1940. In some states, including such former Socialist strongholds as Ohio and Oklahoma, third parties were virtually barred from the ballot. In New York, California, and Wisconsin, the Socialist party was no longer a legal entity, and it was necessary to obtain petitions with thousands of signatures in order to run candidates. By late 1939, despite these impediments, Thomas had decided that the Socialists should run an all-out election campaign aimed at preventing American participation in the European war. "It is precisely because there is a war that I think we must run a candidate [for President]," he wrote his Auburn, New York, ally Walter O'Hagen. "There is not a single Republican who could be trusted to act much differently from Roosevelt if he were in office."

Not all Socialists agreed with Thomas about running a candidate. Even some Socialists who agreed with his assessment of the war were opposed to fielding a national ticket in 1940. For example, Coleman B. Cheney, a professor of economics at Skidmore College, feared a debacle which would have disastrous results for the party. There were other party members who had by 1940 begun to question seriously Thomas's position regarding the war; they were almost all opposed to a campaign. The national executive committee, however, supported Thomas, deciding at its January 1940 meeting that "our party can and must nominate its own national ticket in 1940 and wage a vigorous campaign against war and poverty." The party's national convention agreed, but not without acrimonious debate, in which Norman Thomas, Travers Clement, Aaron Levenstein, David H. H. Felix, and Frank Trager insisted that the party nominate a candidate, while Jack Altman pleaded against nominating one. In the course of the debate within the party, Altman told Thomas that he could have no electoral success so long as he insisted on running only as a Socialist. Altman inferred that Thomas could succeed politically if he would devote his efforts toward forming a farmer-labor party after the elections while supporting labor's choice—or, at least, not opposing him—in 1940. Labor's choice was Franklin Delano Roosevelt. An annoyed Thomas replied that "if I had been interested in what passes for political success, long ago I would have left the Socialist party and emulated, let us say, LaGuardia." Moreover, Thomas had considerable doubt about a labor party dominated by the leaders of the nation's trade unions. "The labor party we want," he wrote, "should, of course, have the support of the labor unions, but it would not be under the dictatorial control of their chiefs. . . . If it is to be a success for any truly Socialist end it cannot possibly be the property of John L. Lewis or William Green or even both of them in a miraculous alliance."

There was little hope of a large Socialist vote, even though Thomas was the only presidential candidate whose chief aim was keeping the United States out of war. "We may not get many votes this year," Thomas told a reporter for the *Washington Daily News*, ". . . but if we can make our fellow citizens stop and listen to our program for keeping America out of war . . . [we] shall not have failed." The campaign was closely tied to the Keep America Out of War Congress. The work of the party and the Congress were virtually merged during the campaign; Norman Thomas, Fay Bennet, Mary Hillyer, and Alice Dodge, the leaders of the KAOW, were also active Socialists. The Socialist-isolationists ran an active campaign; more than 3 million broadsides were distributed, buttons and stickers were produced, and Thomas spoke across the nation. A committee of intellectuals was organized, headed by John Dewey and including such figures as Van Wyck Brooks, V. F. Calverton, Henry Pratt Fairchild, Benjamin Huebsch, John Haynes Holmes, Sidney Hook, A. J. Muste, and John Sloan, which announced its support of Thomas in a statement whose chief plank called for American isolation from the war in Europe.

But the party had serious difficulties. In California it was unable to obtain a place on the ballot. Fortunately, the old Progressive party, which was still a legal political entity, decided to back Thomas and his running mate, Maynard Krueger. Even in Wisconsin, where the Socialists had in 1936 given up their place on the ballot to enter the short-lived Farmer-Labor Progressive Federation, they had difficulty in obtaining the thousand signatures needed to name a presidential candidate. Meanwhile, there was disaffection within the party. In New York, Socialists who left the party in order to back FDR formed their own organization, headed by Reinhold Niebuhr, which later evolved into Americans for Democratic Action. Thomas recognized that it was the war issue alone which separated him from his old comrades who had defected to Roosevelt. He pleaded with them in vain to collaborate with the party on domestic issues. Even such Socialist stalwarts as Albert Sprague Coolidge, professor of chemistry at Harvard and a recent member of the national executive committee, refused to support Thomas and sat out the 1940 campaign. Thomas's only new support came from the "unreconstructed" isolationists and the Lovestone Communists.

"This is the worst political campaign in all my political memory," Thomas told reporters as he left his New York City polling place, "and that goes for both old parties." Yet that same day he admitted that he "did not find the degree of apathy marked with occasional violence which I expected." But the Socialist vote was the smallest the party had ever polled—99,557 of 49,751,891. Roosevelt received 27,243,466 votes and Wendell Willkie 22,-304,755. The greatest Socialist losses were in New York, New Jersey, and Michigan. There were slight gains in California, Illinois, Minnesota, and Wisconsin—wherever isolationist sentiment was strong. In nineteen states, including such one-time Socialist centers as Ohio, there were no Socialist votes, since the party did not appear on the ballot.

In retrospect, Thomas told Senator Burton K. Wheeler, leader of the isolationist wing in the Senate, the vote was more disappointing than he had expected. "Nevertheless, I should have done the same thing over again."[4]

6

During the 1940 campaign, Thomas developed an animosity toward Roosevelt. He accused the President of abandoning the "traditional" American policy against alliances, and of acting without congressional or popular approval. He charged Roosevelt with abandoning the 1936 Democratic platform pledge of neutrality on which he was elected, and of trying to get the United States into the European war by subterfuge. Thomas charged in addition that Roosevelt was using an oblique approach because he was intent upon getting America into the war, though he knew that the people were opposed to involvement. Thomas accused Roosevelt, who had proposed emergency conscription, of favoring the draft as a means of increasing his personal power. Roosevelt was incensed: "I think that knowing me you will want to withdraw that grossly unfair suggestion," he answered. "You and I may disagree as to the danger to the United States—but we can at least give each other credit for the honesty that lies behind our opinions. . . ." Thomas admitted that he had overstated the case against FDR. He wrote the President that "neither in public nor in private do I mean to imply that you want power for power's sake. I do think that peacetime conscription . . . gives the executive excessive power, and while you might want that power only to use it for your conception of defense, there is no telling what another executive might desire." Thomas's answer pacified

Roosevelt, who after the election made one last valiant effort to reconcile his differences with Thomas. "Do come down here some day soon, I want to have a good talk with you. I am really worried about the trend of undemocratic forces in this country," Roosevelt wrote. Thomas was too busy attempting to isolate America from Europe to reply.[5]

The conscription issue convinced Thomas that his fears for American freedoms were well founded. "Conscription, whatever may be the hopes and intentions of its present supporters, in a nation potentially as powerful and aggressive as ours, is a road leading straight to militarism, imperialism, and ultimately to American fascism and war," he told the Senate Military Affairs Committee. Thomas warned labor that conscription would jeopardize its rights, because under it management would have the sole right to decide which employees were essential, and could thus arrange for the drafting of union activists no matter how vital their work. Conscription, as Thomas warned the House Committee on Military Affairs, was the "indispensable agency of totalitarianism." He called it the physical and psychological basis for war, and pointed out that conscription, which was almost universal on the Continent, was one of the prime factors in making possible World War I. Thomas decried the effect conscription would have on the individual. "For individuals," he testified, "military conscription is not freedom but serfdom; its equality is the equality of slaves." Why, then, did those most concerned with American security, particularly the military, insist that the draft was essential? Because, Thomas charged, the draft offered military officers "the hope of longer and more numerous careers." Unlike his other assumptions regarding the war, Thomas's position on conscription was accepted almost universally throughout the party. He himself explained the reason for that support when he noted, "Our Socialist party today is so much a young man's party that we could be pretty well broken up by the draft."[6]

7

The one positive aspect to Thomas's Socialist activity during his isolationist years of 1939–1942 was his attempt to influence high-level American officials—particularly Assistant Secretary of State Adolf A. Berle, Jr.—to save the lives of Socialists from the destruction of Hitler and Stalin. Most notable among these men was Francisco Largo Caballero, who had been prime minister of the Spanish Republic for a time during the civil war. Largo Caballero, a refugee in France when it fell to Hitler, faced deportation to Franco's Spain and certain execution. Thomas's appeals to Berle and Roosevelt brought speedy action after Largo Caballero's arrest by the Vichy government of Nazi-occupied France. The United States government asked for and received assurances that Largo Caballero and other Spanish refugees would not be deported to Spain.

Thomas was less successful at rescuing Jewish Socialists—in particular, members of the General Jewish Workers Bund of Poland—who were caught behind Russian lines. Two leading Bundists, Henryk Erlich and Viktor Alter, were already murdered by Stalin's Soviet government when Thomas asked Harry Hopkins to intervene in their behalf with Stalin when Hopkins visited Russia. Thomas did not then know, however, that they had already been slain. Hopkins inquired of Stalin about the pair, but the Soviet dictator "clearly does not appreciate American interest and advice about citizens of countries other than their own." When Thomas learned that the two Bundists had been murdered, he was incensed. He charged that the Soviet system was a complete negation of socialism; the Communists had merely purloined the name. Stalin's rule, he charged, was the most comprehensive and amoral dictatorship in the world. There were other Bundists, caught in Stalin's Russia, whom Thomas tried without success to rescue. He also failed in his efforts to save the lives of two German Social Democratic leaders, Rudolf Hilferding and Rudolf Breitscheid, who were caught in France after it was overrun by the Nazis. Although Thomas failed in these cases, he was successful in others. He did save from almost certain death the former Russian Communist Victor Serge, the former French Communist Marceau Pivert, and the former Spanish Communist Julian Gorkin. All three of these men had found refuge in Mexico, but Stalin wanted them murdered. The Russian dictator's followers in Mexico, therefore, demanded that Mexico deport them to their native lands, where each faced certain death. Thomas's plea led Berle to intervene with Mexico on their behalf, thus saving their lives.[7] His work for the refugees was one of the few bright spots in Thomas's career during these years.

8

The issue of what ought to be America's role in the war threatened what remained of the Socialist party with new splits and schisms. Party divisions now no longer followed left and right, Militant and Old Guard lines. Instead the party was split between internationalists, who favored some degree of American intervention in the European war to help defeat Hitler, and isolationists, who opposed any form of American involvement. The leading internationalists in the party included some of the former leaders of its most radical factions as well as some of those who were in the most moderate factions. Among the first to favor American intervention in the European war were Gus Tyler, a leader of the extreme—and extremely confused—Clarity faction and Jack Altman, of the now comparatively moderate Militant wing. The isolationists' chief spokesman was Norman Thomas.

The first issue on which the two factions disagreed was the embargo against shipping war materials to either side in the European war. Thomas favored making it more restrictive; Tyler and the other internationalists wanted it repealed outright so that the United States might supply arms to the anti-fascist allies. Thomas conceded that the internationalists were "good Socialists," and suggested that the position of each Socialist on the embargo ought to be made a matter of his own conscience; he opposed making it a matter of party discipline, "except, perhaps, in the case of extreme" public attacks on the party's stand. But it was soon apparent that the disagreement was too extreme to remain a matter of individual conscience. The Czech Federation was the first to demand that the party alter its stand on the embargo. The issue, the Czechs insisted, was Hitler's "*Ein Volk, Ein Reich, Ein Fuehrer*" versus the Allies' "*Liberté, Egalité et Fraternité.*" Almost as soon as war broke out, Alfred Baker Lewis, leader of the Massachusetts party, joined the Czech Socialists to demand that the party alter its position completely; he wanted it to back the allies. Lewis accused Thomas of being "completely isolationist and in effect pro-Hitler." He insisted that Thomas's isolationism was anti-Socialist and that the party should support the defeat of fascism—without which there could be no Socialist victory.

In early 1940, Garry Allard, editor of the *Socialist Call*, published over Thomas's opposition an editorial hailing the resistance of the Finnish Army to the Russian invasion. Allard called on the United States to offer military and economic aid to the Finns. The editorial set off a near revolt in the party. Bishop Paul Jones, an anti-Communist Social Gospeleer who supported Thomas, assailed the editorial as a plea for American participation in the war. Other isolationist Socialists agreed. But Alfred Baker Lewis, who became leader of the party's internationalist wing, applauded Allard and urged full economic aid to Finland and other victims of "totalitarian invasion." He called Finland more of a workers' government than Loyalist Spain, and thus more entitled to Socialist support. The editorial and the ruckus it created irritated Thomas. He forced Allard to resign as editor of the *Call* and had him replaced with Travers Clement, a confirmed isolationist. Allard retained control of the party in the southern Illinois coal area, however, and that organization was "active raising funds for the British" while Thomas was pleading for American neutrality and isolation. Allard and his southern Illinois Socialist followers—most of whom were Scots and Welsh—proclaimed that "as long as they shoot at Nazis we are for them."

La Parola, official organ of the party's Italian Socialist Federation, defied Thomas's leadership and became openly pro-Allied. It called for American intervention in the war. An annoyed Thomas chastized *La Parola*; it was, he insisted, a violently anti-fascist but not a Socialist journal. "To be anti-fascist," Thomas said, "is good, but it is not equivalent to being Socialist." When the Italians ignored Thomas's criticism, he pontificated: "If this sort of thing is the best that socialism has to offer, no wonder fascism wins. Strong ideas and strong loyalties must be opposed with better ideas and better loyalties, not merely with ferocious criticism based on placid acceptance of the old order out of which the new evils have sprung."

Jewish Socialists were even more adamant in rejecting Thomas's isolationism. "No more loyal comrades can be found anywhere in the party than in the Jewish section," the national secretary had reported in 1938. They had remained true to the party in defiance of the financially powerful *Jewish Daily Forward*, and at peril to their positions in such unions as the International Ladies Garment Workers and the Amalgamated Clothing Workers. But no ethnic group suffered more at the hands of Hitler than did the Jews, and no Jews had better access to information about the European catastrophe than did the Socialists, who maintained contact with the Polish underground, especially the organizations in the ghettos and the units connected with the Bund, the Polish Jewish Socialist party. A majority of the Jewish Socialists disagreed with the party's stand on aid to the Allies, favoring instead immediate military and economic assistance. The alternative, they warned, was a world ruled by Hitler and Stalin. "I can well understand how hard it is for some of you to agree with [me] . . . and I beg you to believe that you have my great respect and my deep appreciation," Thomas wrote to his "Jewish comrades." But he insisted that they were being emotional about the war, that the war would solve nothing. The Jewish Socialists rejected Thomas's reasoning. "I'd rather have no section at all than one run in the spirit" of intervention, Thomas wrote. The Jewish party section agreed; it dissolved.

The party fight over a Socialist war position reached its climax at the 1940 national convention. Two major resolutions on the war were placed before the convention. One, proposed by Thomas, declared that the "United States must be kept out of this conflict. The hope of the American people for peace is not the hope of victory for either imperialism, but for victory of the masses. . . . To keep America out of war is to aid the anti-war and anti-fascist forces of Europe as well as ourselves." This pro-isolationist resolution called for a constitutional amendment to require a referendum before war could be declared, a ban on conscription, and defeat of bills which would increase military preparedness. A second, opposing resolution, proposed by Alfred Baker Lewis and supported by the internationalists, called for support of the anti-fascist powers in the war, but not for actual American participation. The net result of the Lewis resolution would have been to turn the Socialist party from an isolationist-pacifist sect into an internationalist organization dedicated to the defeat of fascism. There was a third proposal, suggested by the Colorado party organization, which called for "a revolt against the exploiting class, including the imperial exploiters. . . ." But this third resolution was never debated, and its sponsors supported Thomas's proposal on the floor of the convention. Thomas's resolution was supported at the convention by Joseph Glass, a New York attorney, Albert Hamilton, former leader of the Methodist Epworth League turned Socialist executive, Phil Heller, New York union organizer, and Joseph Coldwell, who had been jailed for pacifism during World War I. Speaking for the Lewis resolution were Jack Altman, former secretary of the New York party and now a union organizer, Paul Porter, editor of *Kenosha Labor*, and Lazar Becker, a leader of the Jewish party members. Lewis argued that isolationism was a denial of what he insisted should have been the Socialists' primary cause: combating and eventually destroying Hitlerism. Thomas, on the contrary, called the war thoroughly imperialist, repeating that the best hope for the world lay in virtual stalemate. An America which stayed out of the war, Thomas reasoned, could affect a democratic peace. In the end, the Thomas position prevailed by a vote of 159 to 28.

The differences between the two wings made cooperation between them within the confines of a single party impossible. Barred from using the *Socialist Call* to advertise their position, the internationalist Socialists used other organs that were available to them. Jack Altman attempted to issue a statement to the *Call* explaining his resignation from the Keep America Out of War Congress. Travers Clement refused to publish it. Altman then sent the statement to the *New Leader*, which published it under the headline "Altman Joins in Repudiating Isolationists." He was quoted as telling the KAOW executives that "I cannot agree with your isolationist policy. I believe that a victory for Hitler would mean the death of civilization. I therefore take sides in the great conflict now raging and hope and trust and work for the victory of democracy." Altman also secured 2,500 labor and Socialist signatures on a petition to Congress urging repeal of the neutrality laws. Because of these "indiscretions" he was expelled from the party. Although personally friendly to Altman, Thomas agreed with the ouster. He now insisted that it was impossible for the party "in an emergency like this to face two ways at once." Thomas's position was meanwhile being weakened by opposition from unexpected sources.

The normally isolationist Wisconsin state organization called on the national executive committee to re-examine its war policy.

It wanted to end the party's isolationist stand after Mayor Daniel Hoan had been defeated for re-election by Carl Zeidler, a non-Socialist internationalist. There were resignations throughout the nation. One member called Thomas "one of America's greatest traveling fools." Another member, who had been a founder of the party in 1901, resigned because he was now convinced that Hitler could not be defeated except by military force. Opposition to Thomas's isolationism in the League for Industrial Democracy forced him to resign from that organization's board of directors. Few groups invited Thomas to speak; most of the democratic left was by now in favor of supporting the anti-Hitler forces in Europe; Thomas's total income for 1940 was less than $2,000.

The bloodletting within the party continued unabated. Ralph Harlow, a pro-pacifist Socialist and a friend of Thomas, agreed that it was necessary to keep America out of war, but he disagreed with Thomas's method. Whereas Thomas favored an economic embargo, Harlow favored aid to the anti-Hitler allies. He told Thomas that "the quickest and most certain road to military intervention . . . will be the dawning consciousness that Nazi Germany and Stalin are on the road to dictate a victorious peace." Thomas ignored Harlow's argument. If America were to get into the war, an annoyed Thomas warned, "it will be the good people, the intellectuals, the folks whose ethnical judgments are somehow bound up, subconsciously, with British or English-speaking supremacy" who would be to blame.

By the beginning of 1941, the internal dispute had become so serious that the New York organization found it necessary to call a special membership meeting to allow Thomas to explain his position. At the meeting he argued that "the great purpose of our party is to advance democratic socialism, and this means to fight fascism and all totalitarianism. The fight is a world-wide fight and we have world-wide interests, but we have peculiar responsibility as the world is organized today in and for this country. It is ridiculous to believe that we can win a fight against world-wide fascism if we lose it in this country." But the plea was in vain; a majority of those who belonged to the party in 1940 had already resigned; by early 1941 the total national membership of the Socialist Party was less than 1,200. By 1941, a majority of the members of the national executive committee elected at the 1940 convention opposed Thomas.

Thomas suggested that three of the national executive committee members who most vehemently opposed his position on the war—Professor Albert Sprague Coolidge of Harvard, David H. H. Felix of Philadelphia, and Frank Trager of New York—resign from the committee. He insisted that members of the national executive committee either agree with him or resign. Thomas in effect considered the Socialist party his personal preserve. Trager proposed that Felix and Coolidge resign because it was "Norman's party," and he would resign regardless. Coolidge objected. "What does somewhat disturb me," he wrote Trager, "is your suggestion that, since we cannot run the party without Norman, we had better let him run it his own way. . . . In general, nothing arouses my dislike faster than the attitude of people who threaten to resign or split unless they get what they want." The party fell apart completely, however, before Coolidge had an opportunity to challenge Thomas's threat.

In Chicago, four of the party's leaders, Kellam Foster, Arthur G. McDowell, John Mill, and Mordecai Shulman, issued a sharp attack on Thomas's war stance. Warning that "a fascist victory means enslavement of the workers" of Europe and thus of America, they called the slogan "keep America out of war" hopelessly inadequate. Moreover, they questioned Thomas's argument for a negotiated peace with Hitler, and concluded with a call for the party to change its stance and recognize that "fascism can only be defeated . . . by military defeat." McDowell then joined with Trager, Paul Porter, and United Auto Workers' leader Leonard Woodcock in resigning from the national executive committee because of its war position. "Our resignations are not to be construed as an effort to lead a split in Socialist ranks," they wrote. "That split has already occurred." They pointed out that nothing was left of the party except Thomas and "student pacifists." All four resigned from the party as well. Garry Allard refused to join the national executive committee as a replacement because "I am in sympathy with the four comrades who recently resigned. . . ." When Thomas appeared before the House Foreign Affairs Committee to oppose lend-lease as spokesman for the Socialist party, a group of prominent Socialists and former Socialists, including Reinhold Niebuhr, the Negro labor organizer Frank Crosswaithe, Alfred Baker Lewis, Jack Altman, Murray Gross (of the International Ladies Garment Workers Union), and Gus Tyler, issued a public statement accusing Thomas of "purely provincial selfishness." The pro-Socialist treasurer of the *New Republic* castigated Thomas: "Norman Thomas, exponent of the gospel of international solidarity of labor, has become . . . a proponent of the doctrine that the fate of the rest of humanity does not concern us if only we can continue to enjoy our safety and comfort—can save our money, our security, and our boys."[8] By March 1941, all of the internationalist Socialists were out of the party. There was, in fact, very little left of the party. Still worse was yet to come.

9

Apart from the pro-Socialist Keep America Out of War Congress, there were two major anti-war groups in the United States during the first two years of the European war: the Communist-front American Peace Mobilization and the conservative America First Committee. Thomas was a member of neither, though he was antagonistic to the former and cooperated with the latter.

The American Peace Mobilization came into existence when Hitler and Stalin signed their nonaggression pact and Communists the world over changed from support to all-out opposition to the anti-Hitler forces. The American Communists, like all other Stalinists, shifted their positions 180 degrees, their new slogan being "The Yanks Are Not Coming." The pro–collective security Communist-front American League for Peace and Democracy was dissolved, and the party organized the new American Peace Mobilization to replace it. Within the Socialist party there was an almost immediate demand, especially among pacifists, that the party work with the Communist group. The pro-Thomas Socialists rejected the suggestion: "We can no more cooperate with the Communists than we can with the Nazi [German-American] Bund or any other totalitarian group," the party's anti-war committee reported to the 1940 national convention. "The Nazis say 'keep America out of war' as a means to the end of helping Nazi Germany. The Communists say 'The Yanks are not coming' as a means to the end of helping Russia, now an ally of Germany."

Thomas went further than the party committee; he wanted the neutrality law extended to include Soviet Russia "because of its occupation by armed forces, without negotiation, of Polish territory." He considered Stalin as great a danger to the world as Hitler because of his potential for evil and his "subversion of the ideals of socialism." When Reverend John Howard Lathrop, a Brooklyn Social Gospeleer, suggested to Thomas that he should cooperate with the Peace Mobilization because the Communists now agreed with him on peace, Thomas replied that "the trouble is that you can never be sure Communists are for peace. . . . Very likely there will come a day when Hitler and Stalin fall out and, if that issue comes to war, the Communists would want us to do everything possible for Stalin." It was apparent that Thomas and the Communists could never cooperate on any issue, even opposing the war. Thomas may have been naive about the war, but he was no longer naive about the Communists.

The Communists during this period resumed the revolutionary rhetoric they had abandoned during the period when collective security served the needs of Stalin. One of the chief targets of their abuse, along with Britain, France, and Roosevelt, was Norman Thomas. True, he opposed the war, but he also opposed Stalin. One of the Communists' spokesmen charged that Norman Thomas "has actually enlisted in the imperialist fight of the Anglo-American bloc." He added that Thomas's anti-Stalin stance "exposes his 'anti-war' position as fake and fraud." During the 1940 election campaign, in which Thomas made the war the chief issue, the editors of the monthly party organ, *The Communist*, charged that he did not consider "the fight against the war and for keeping America out of it . . . a major issue." Even Earl Browder got into the act, insisting that Thomas was peddling a sugar-coated imperialism to the working class. V. J. Jerome, the intellectual *gauleiter* of the American Communist party, claimed that "Tartuffe Thomas always hedges his war incantations with qualifying loopholes—'ifs' and 'whens' and 'unless and untils.' "

The American Peace Mobilization was short-lived. On June 22, 1941, Hitler invaded Russia and, as Thomas had predicted, the Communists did a complete turnabout. But Thomas stood firm in his opposition to both Stalin and Hitler. On hearing of the Nazi invasion, he said, "Stalin, the man who made this war possible with his nonaggression pact with the Nazis, has now become its chief victim." He accused Stalin of attempting to make a deal with Hitler under which Western Europe would destroy itself in war, after which he would move in and assume control. Now Thomas hoped that the two dictators would be destroyed by a military stalemate. "A clear-cut victory on either side," he wrote, "would make Nazism or Stalin's Communism the master of the European continent and much of Asia. A stalemate might possibly give the people of both Russia and Germany a chance to settle accounts with the dictators who have so ruthlessly exploited them."[9]

10

The second organization which opposed American involvement in World War II was the conservative, isolationist America First Committee, whose chief luminaries were Senator Robert A. Taft, Charles A. Lindbergh, General Robert Wood, and Chester Bowles. Although Thomas was never a member of America First, he did speak under its auspices and was invited to serve on its board of directors. There were issues on which Thomas and a vast majority of the members of America First disagreed, especially peacetime conscription, which most America Firsters favored and Thomas opposed. Despite disagreements, Thomas favored cooperation between the America First Committee and the Keep America Out of War Congress, which he controlled. No formal coalition was organized, but the two groups did cooperate on rallies in specific areas.

In late 1940, America First's national office in Chicago invited Thomas to speak from its platform. Thomas at first declined the invitation because he was involved with a weekly radio series sponsored by the *Socialist Call*. But a series of events convinced him that it was imperative that he speak at these rallies. When local America First organizations learned that Thomas had been invited to speak, a small but noisy group of anti-Semites and pro-Nazis objected vehemently. Moreover, anti-Semites had been speaking before America First meetings. National leaders of America First were upset because of the anti-Jewish tone of their speeches. It was in order to counteract these anti-Semites that Thomas accepted invitations to address two major America First meetings, one in Brooklyn and one in Manhattan. His decision backfired, creating new and serious problems for Thomas and further tarnishing his reputation.

At the first of these meetings, Thomas spoke in Brooklyn with Senators Burton K. Wheeler and Gerald Nye, two of the leading isolationists in Congress, and with the editor John T. Flynn. In the audience was Joe McWilliams, leader of the Christian Front, America's version of Hitler's Storm Troopers. Also in the audience was Thomas's one-time friend, Dorothy Thompson, a columnist for the *New York Herald-Tribune*. Speaking from the platform, Thomas reproached McWilliams and assailed racial and religious bigotry. This did not phase McWilliams. He called Thomas "half right and therefore all right with me." The inference was clear: Thomas's views on race and religion might not meet with the approval of an American Nazi, but his opposition to American support of the anti-Hitler forces did. Miss Thompson addressed her column to Thomas, "who with the peculiar narrow vision characteristic of Social Democrats the world around insists on laying the faggots and hauling up the rope for the lynching of social democracy." She warned Thomas that "Joe McWilliams, who supports you today for your half-rightness, will kill you tomorrow for your other half-wrongness. Mr. McWilliams, with his primitive but not befuddled mind, sees things much more clearly than you do. This is a fight; he has chosen the winner; and, for the time being, you are his ally. Communism and fascism take their allies when and where they can find them. One can always stage a purge later." Thomas answered her—in pure Social Gospelese—but the *Herald-Tribune* refused to publish his reply. "I believe," he wrote in his unpublished epistle, "that my country with all its marvelous advantages and glorious traditions has not the power or wisdom to play the Lord God of Hosts to the world by the terrible means of total war."

The second meeting involved Colonel Lindbergh, and its consequences were more serious than those of the first. Lindbergh had been a Socialist folk-hero; his father, a congressman from Minnesota during World War I, had opposed the war on the floor of the House and defended the right of Socialists to oppose the war after it was declared. When the younger Lindbergh flew the Atlantic alone in a single-engine plane in 1927, Thomas wrote of him: "[What] a hero Charles A. Lindbergh is! His courage and skill are equalled by his modesty and tact. . . . Some of us are proud to remember that his father was our associate in the Progressive movement. Altogether the Lindbergh family makes us proud of our country and hopeful of the possibilities of character and achievement." By 1940, however, Lindbergh had begun to make isolationist speeches and had been accused of being pro-Nazi. Thomas wrote to Lindbergh to suggest that he make clear his opposition to Hitler's racial and political views. Lindbergh ignored Thomas's suggestion. Thomas then suggested to the leaders of America First that they prevail on Lindbergh to disavow Hitler publicly; but to no avail. When Harold L. Ickes, Roosevelt's Secretary of the Interior, called Lindbergh a fascist, several Socialists objected, most notably J. Clarke Waldron, a Socialist journalist from St. Louis, who insisted after a talk with the aviator that he was, in fact, a progressive isolationist. But Thomas knew better; he accused Lindbergh of "pigheadedness which makes him very slow to accept advice and unwilling to correct bad tactical errors in presenting his own cause." He accused Lindbergh of favoring cooperation with Nazi Germany—"we might have to get along with it," Thomas said, "but that is a different thing from cooperation"—and of being a white racist. "I would not want to see a close tieup between Lindbergh and the Socialist party," he wrote Waldron.

In May 1941, when Lindbergh was chief speaker at a mass meeting of America First in Madison Square Garden, Thomas was one of the other speakers. The fact that Thomas was scheduled to appear on the same platform with Lindbergh caused consternation among the few remaining Socialists. One anti-war Socialist wrote to warn that speaking on the same platform as the one-time hero "will destroy you and the party's reputation." Former Socialist Assemblyman Samuel Orr upbraided Thomas, accusing him of trying to "shine in the reflected glory of a Lindbergh or a Wheeler. What if you have gained their applause—you have lost your soul." The sharpest attack came from *Agrupacion Socialista Espanola*, the Spanish branch of the party. It accused him of "open collaboration with American reactionary forces and sympathizers of Nazi and fascist dictators," and of initiating "a corruption of the Socialist ideal which is parallel to the policy laid down by Mussolini before he rose to power and destroyed the labor and Socialist movement in Italy." After this statement, the Spanish branch withdrew from the party.

In September, Lindbergh delivered his most anti-Jewish speech at Des Moines, Iowa. He charged that the British, the Jews, and Roosevelt had formed an alliance to force the United States into the war. This statement finally roused Thomas. He still doubted the flier was an anti-Semite, but he called him "a great idiot" who had done considerable harm. The party's national executive committee quickly dissociated itself from Lindbergh. It condemned his speech and declared that "his act must bring upon him the condemnation of all believers in democracy and peace." Thomas joined in the condemnation. He urged America First to find a way to sever its connection with Lindbergh and to "clearly repudiate anti-Semitism or else the usefulness of America First will be terribly impaired. . . ." But, as usual, Thomas was too late. Anti-Semites already dominated many, if not most, America First branches. In Jersey City, William Philips, who replaced one of Thomas's sons as New Jersey organizer for the isolationist organization, delivered a vituperative anti-Semitic inaugural address. The *New York Daily News* published an America First statement which accused Jews of attempting to stampede America into the war. A protest by a "Jewish-American isolationist" brought a promise from Thomas that he would use his influence to prevent a recurrence of such an article. In Iowa, the leader of the isolationists was described by Thomas as "extraordinarily reactionary, bitter against Jews and Socialists, and inclined to use the Nazi formulation." Thomas condemned him, but again to no avail.

As 1941 drew to a close, Thomas charged that a "curious association of communism, finance capitalism," bureaucrats, labor leaders, and intellectuals wanted America to be drawn into the war for various selfish reasons: the Communists to protect Stalin's Russia; the bureaucrats and labor leaders "for the increase in power that war and armaments economics brings" to them, and the intellectuals to prove that their analysis of the situation was correct. Thomas insisted that he was "not now proposing that we make peace with Hitler," but was merely suggesting that "we do not make war." On December 6, 1941, one day before Pearl Harbor, Thomas wrote a letter to the *New York Times* opposing American involvement in the war. American entry, he feared, would prolong the war and make less likely the "constructive revolution of the people of Europe against . . . the system which makes for war." After Pearl Harbor, he withdrew the letter. But he still insisted: "I believe it [war] could honorably have been avoided and the world made better off by policies I have advocated."[10]

VIII
America
at war

On December 7, 1941, the last hope for keeping America out of the war disappeared when Japanese planes bombed Pearl Harbor. The declaration of war depressed Thomas: "I feel now that my whole world has pretty much come to an end, that what I have stood for has been defeated, and my usefulness made small." The alternative of opposition was no longer open to him, though, as he remarked, "God knows I'd love to be able to oppose this war." But once war came, he conceded that opposition to the Allied struggle would mean support for the aggressively imperialist and militarist fascists, and "however great are our faults, it is true that we and the British have made some gains worth keeping." Thomas still talked of absolute pacifism as the hope of the world, but he no longer had the religious faith that he considered a prerequisite for total pacifism. He now doubted that pacifism offered a practical political alternative to the war at that moment, and "until the day can come when I can offer a political alternative, I don't want to talk about political opposition or political non-support for the war."

But Thomas's newfound support for the war meant little, just as he himself had become unimportant by the end of 1941. For a political figure to have meaning he must have a constituency; for an evangelist to spread his Gospel, he must have a congregation. By the time America entered the war, Thomas had neither. Most Socialists had left the party before Pearl Harbor because of Thomas's obstinate isolationism—by January 1942, its membership was down to 1,141. The America First isolationists who had courted Thomas's support before the American involvement now avoided him; they were busily attempting to erase their anti-war pasts and, in many cases, they were antipathetic to Thomas's socialist reformism. Most Americans were too busy winning the war or reaping the economic harvest which war brought to be interested in hearing out an evangelist who preached a heaven on earth not unlike the earthly "paradise" that had been created in the past eight years by the New Deal. Except in a few specific instances, Thomas had little of consequence to offer after 1941. Politically speaking, he was a superfluous man.

2

In the small remains of the Socialist party there were still serious divisions on the war issue. Thomas proposed a five-point program which he suggested the national executive committee adopt as official party policy. His proposal called for the party to: (1) reiterate its contention that the war could have been avoided; (2) repeat its denial that the war was democratic in its origins, aims, or alliances; (3) admit that the only alternatives open by December 1941 were an Allied or an Axis victory— and that an Axis victory would be the greatest possible calamity; (4) refuse to become involved in a "peace offensive" at that time because such a movement could only help the Axis powers; and (5) devote itself primarily to working during the war for the expansion of civil liberties, racial justice, workers' rights, and rights for conscientious objectors. Thomas pleaded that "while this is not in the proper sense of the word a war for democracy, it is a war [against an enemy who] . . . glorifies things we hate, namely the doctrine of a master race, gross cruelty, torture, and duplicity as instruments of government." He labeled his position on the war after Pearl Harbor as one of "critical support." The Socialists were divided into factions ranging from pacifists to anti-war "revolutionary Marxists" to pro-war moderates to those who supported Thomas in "critically" supporting the war.

Most members of the national executive committee supported Thomas's five-point program, but many party members, still imbued with pacifism, accused him of betrayal. Thus, when the national executive committee, despite pleas to the contrary from the pacifist David Dellinger and the "revolutionary Socialist" Travers Clement, voted to support Thomas, there were mass resignations. Clement resigned as editor of the *Socialist Call* and threatened to leave the party as well. The defections created a threat to the very existence of the party that was so serious that the party's national action committee found it necessary to appeal to the members of the anti-war faction to remain in the party until its convention could decide its official position. The few remaining pro-war members, who had not left in the pre–Pearl Harbor exodus, were similarly unsatisfied with Thomas's position. The New York Cloakmakers branch, whose members favored all-out support of the war, withdrew *en bloc* from the party.

The 1942 Socialist national convention in Milwaukee found the party at its lowest ebb. Its membership was now less than one thousand, and even these few members could not agree on basic policy. At this shadow of a convention factional strife was at least as vituperative as it had been from 1934 to 1938. A group of Leninist-Socialists, headed by Dan Roberts of Los Angeles, issued an inflammatory broadside against Thomas, which was distributed in wholesale lots at the convention. The statement, which was long on revolutionary rhetoric but short on logic, read:

No Compromise with Thomas and the Whole Pro-War Group!
For Marxist Clarity on the War Question!
Against Pacifism!
For a Revolutionary Faction!
For a Revolutionary Socialist Party!
For World Socialism and World Peace!

At the convention itself there were four major factional blocs: Winston Dancis led the pacifist forces; Travers Clement led the anti-war Marxists; Norman Thomas led the "critical support" group; and Irving Barshop headed the pro-war faction. When, after three days of debate, the convention voted on the war resolution, Thomas's faction polled forty-six votes, Clement's group —allied with the pacifists—polled forty-nine, and Barshop only twelve. Under Socialist party convention procedures, a majority of voting members was necessary before any resolution was approved. With the Barshop resolution eliminated, Clement's anti-war position received fifty-two votes, Thomas's won fifty, and eight delegates—all of them pro-war—abstained. The party was thus faced with the dilemma of either ignoring the most momentous issue facing the people of the world, or taking a meaningless stand that a majority of its members refused to support. A special committee was named after it became apparent that the deadlock was insoluble, and it proposed a compromise which denounced war generally but avoided specific denunciation of the current conflict. Basically, it accepted Thomas's arguments while using Clement's rhetoric. Exhausted after three days of wrangling, the convention adopted the compromise by a vote of seventy-two to eleven, with seventeen delegates refusing to vote.[1]

3

Thomas's grudging support of the war won him few new friends. His old enemies, particularly the Communists, did not ease up their attacks against him. Because his anti-communism was to become an overriding feature of the last twenty-five years of his career, Thomas's relations with the Communists during the war take on special significance. While America was at war as Stalin's ally, the Communists became the most blatant American patriots; and as Thomas was less than dogmatically patriotic, as he was openly anti-Stalinist, their attacks on him became sharper than ever.

Thomas's fears that American civil liberties would be lost in the war proved groundless. Actually, Thomas was able to continue his activity unmolested by the government; his weekly radio program for the *Call* remained uncensored. Only the Don Lee Network in California and radio stations WOL in Washington and WISN in Milwaukee refused to broadcast his programs after America entered the war. About thirty other stations, including outlets in New York, Chicago, Boston, Detroit, and Madison, Wisconsin, continued to carry the program. In New York, Thomas had some difficulty with his outlet, WQXR, when that station refused to carry one of Thomas's talks because he charged that the "Third International is less an affiliation of free men than [it is] Stalin's other army, ready to justify and obey his every decree no matter what change of policy it may involve." American Communists, the most pro-war element in American society since Stalin's involvement against his erstwhile ally, brought pressure to bear on WQXR to deny Thomas use of its facilities.

The WQXR affair was part of an effort by the Communists

and their allies to silence Thomas—and all other critics—completely. They attempted to keep him from speaking in city after city, using even physical violence to prevent his being heard. In Seattle, Communist seamen used physical force to keep an audience from hearing Thomas and the ex-Communist writer Bertram Wolfe. In Minneapolis, the Communist-run CIO Council and Communist groups on the University of Minnesota campus demanded that the regents of the University bar Thomas from speaking there on the ground that he was an isolationist. The Communist efforts to silence him enraged Thomas, who charged that they were more dangerous to American democracy than any of the tiny domestic fascist groups. He warned the trade unions that the Communists were teaching "labor's enemies contempt for principle and fair play." He now equated communism with fascism. "For many years," he wrote, "I tried to . . . believe that, with all its faults, Russian communism represented revolution while fascism represented counterrevolution. Originally there was much truth in that distinction. There has been less and less truth in it, as power has become more and more the sole Communist goal, and the interest of Russia as interpreted by Stalin the guiding star of Communist intrigue."

The Communists, who labeled Thomas one of their chief enemies, refused to allow truth to be an impediment to their anti-Thomas polemics. Rex Stout, who headed the Communist-controlled War Writers Board, charged on the Columbia Broadcasting System's radio network that "during his America First career . . . doubtless his [Thomas's] fellow worker Laura Ingalls spoke to him, but she can't now because she is in jail as a Nazi agent. Probably, George Sylvester Viereck spoke to him, too, but Viereck is also in jail. Senator Wheeler and Charles Lindbergh apparently aren't speaking to anybody. As for Ham[ilton] Fish, he speaks only to people who may possibly be of help in his frantic endeavor to hang onto his job in Congress, and he certainly has no time to bother with Norman Thomas." In fact, Thomas had never been a member of America First, had never met Miss Ingalls, and had spoken to Viereck only once, shortly after World War I. A Communist party publication accused Thomas of saying he considered Soviet Russia a greater evil than Nazi Germany. Actually, Thomas had said that Soviet communism was the lesser of the two evils because it was not racist as was Nazism. The *Daily Worker* charged that Thomas, whom it now labeled an American quisling, had urged America to accept the "status of another Vichy," a wholly fabricated charge. Robert Minor, a pedestrian Communist cartoonist who erroneously considered himself a thinker, claimed that Thomas favored a Nazi victory over the Soviet Union. Israel Amter, a fine violinist with limited intellectual gifts who served as New York State Communist party secretary, accused Thomas, in a long and redundant diatribe in the *Communist*, of having served as a spearhead of American fascism. He charged that Thomas and the Socialist party were involved in "nothing but downright fifth-column activity." He insisted that the Socialists, and Thomas in particular, "must be stifled." Apparently unhappy that civil liberties were not denied to the Socialists, the Communists would have relished an American purge.

Behind Thomas's anti-communism and the Communists' anti-Thomas crusade was Thomas's opposition to the imposition of a Communist hegemony over the people of Eastern Europe, particularly in Poland. In 1944, he agreed that the Polish border of 1939 should have been altered; but he wanted the alteration to be made on the basis of a plebiscite held under international control. He warned that unless Stalin's imperialism was challenged there was a grave danger that the "President may be committing us and our sons after us not only to the prolongation of this war but to the certainty of the next." So sharp were Thomas's attacks on Soviet imperialism that *PM*, the pro-Soviet New York newspaper, published a cartoon showing Thomas passing the ammunition for a war against Soviet Russia to Russophobes Clare Booth Luce, William Randolph Hearst, Elizabeth Dilling, and Gerald L. K. Smith.

True, the Communists were not alone in assailing Thomas's position. The former Socialist *Jewish Daily Forward* virtually accused him of fearing that Hitler might lose the war. In 1944, it charged him, incorrectly, with urging an immediate armistice that would benefit Hitler, "his ne'er-do-well partner Mussolini," and Tojo. The charge was of course untrue. During the 1944 Presidential election campaign, Daniel Tobin, of the International Brotherhood of Teamsters, accused Thomas of being pro-Hitler, a charge Tobin was forced to retract in the face of a court suit.[2]

4

During the war Thomas was involved in several civil rights and civil liberties cases. Among the more significant were the cases involving the anarchist editor Carlo Tresca and the Socialist activist Alton Levy, both New Yorkers. Tresca, an old Wobbly who edited the Italian-language anarcho-syndicalist weekly *Il Martello*, was murdered by an unknown gunman on a New York City street in January 1943. Thomas, who had known Tresca from his East Harlem days, became involved with the case almost as soon as it developed. It was Thomas's pressure which forced a reluctant police department and district attorney to continue at least the pretense of hunting for the slayer. (Even now, twenty-seven years later, the murder remains unsolved.) Thomas believed from the beginning that Tresca was murdered either by the Communists, whose control of the Italian-American Victory Council he had fought, or by a pro-fascist publisher with strong Mafia connections. The Levy case involved a young Socialist draftee who had led a fight against segregation in the Army, for which he was arrested and faced a court martial. Thomas led a successful fight to have him freed.

Nor was Thomas's fight for civil liberties limited to defending the rights of those on the left. When thirty pro-fascists were arrested and tried for sedition and conspiracy, Thomas defended their right to equal justice under the law—just as he was to defend the same right for Communists more than a decade later. If the government were allowed to convict thirty pro-fascists "without proving any overt act, it will be in an exceedingly strong position to clamp down on any discussion of terms of peace, or of the time of peace," he warned. "It will allege that such discussion may give aid or comfort to the enemy or provoke dissatisfaction in the armed forces." The case ended in a mistrial, and the thirty pro-fascists were freed.

Thomas also pleaded the cause of conscientious objectors, though he no longer considered himself one. He still called them the "prophets and pioneers of the future," but he now questioned that they had a practical political program to offer. He was particularly interested in the rights of nonreligious objectors. Members of pacifist denominations, such as the Mennonites and the Friends, had little difficulty in obtaining exemption from military service as conscientious objectors. But young men who objected to military service on philosophical, political, or moral grounds were almost invariably imprisoned. Thomas tried in vain to persuade Social Gospel churchmen that "the church ought not to be satisfied to accept exemption as a kind of special ecclesiastical privilege." He attempted, again unsuccessfully, to convince Brigadier General Lewis B. Hershey, director of Selective Service, that a man could be as honest a conscientious objector on philosophical, political, or moral grounds as on religious.[3] As with most causes that Thomas championed, it was a long time before his position gained legal credence. It was not until 1969 that a federal judge agreed with Thomas's 1942 position that denomination and conscience were not synonymous.

5

No action by the United States government during the war so incensed Thomas as the forcible evacuation of Japanese-Americans from the West Coast. He called it another case of greed and panic, likening it to the Nazi persecution of the Jews; and he warned that it could have included "any of us." His attempt to win justice for Japanese-Americans on the West Coast began almost immediately after the first signs of anti-Japanese activity in California. Informed in January 1942 that alien Japanese were being seized in San Luis Obispo and Guadalupe, California, he appealed to the American Civil Liberties Union, which he had helped to found during World War I and of which he was a national board member. "It is a pretty terrible situation," he said, "and one which ought not to be accepted without protest. . . ." The Civil Liberties Union national board refused to intervene. Thomas told his old friend Roger Baldwin, executive director of the ACLU, that "what the Civil Liberties Union is now doing amounts objectively to betrayal of a cause." He condemned the ACLU in a public statement. The Northern California Civil Liberties Union joined Thomas in assailing the national organization's stand, and only an appeal by Thomas that "you people can be more useful by staying in the organization" averted its withdrawal from the ACLU.

After the national Civil Liberties Union refused to act, Thomas made direct appeals to Attorney General Francis Biddle,

Assistant Secretary of War John McCloy, and President Roosevelt. He told Biddle that "our hope in war and peace depends upon decent cooperation with men of other races." Such cooperation, he warned, would be more difficult if the United States allowed itself the luxury of expulsion from California of Japanese-Americans because of their race or ethnic origin. To the argument that Japanese-Americans might be disloyal because of their attachment to their ancestral homes, Thomas replied: "Why not intern all German-Americans? Or Italo-Americans? Couldn't they, too, be spies?" For his efforts, Thomas won the friendship of many Japanese-Americans. But he was assailed by the *Los Angeles Times* and by the Communists.[4] The expulsion of the Japanese-Americans was eventually upheld legally, much to the Supreme Court's shame.

Thomas cited Hitler's slaughter of the Jews and the ferocity with which America fought Japan as proof that the war was exacerbating racial and ethnic feelings. Americans, he claimed, considered the Japanese an inferior race which had to be "kept down"; and this attitude, he charged, had turned the war in the Pacific into a virtual race riot. The net effect of this attitude would be to turn other Asians against the United States. This aspect of the war, he feared, would undo the slow progress he believed was being made toward the acceptance of Christian standards of mercy and kindness. The thesis that any cruelty was justified against the "Japanese rats" was, he warned, immoral and could easily be extended beyond the Japanese.[5]

At home Thomas found that Negroes were still excluded from the prevalent economic affluence and increasing liberalization of American society. Thomas saw this as one of the great tragedies of American life, there being no excuse for racial discrimination in so affluent a country as America. Discrimination could be ended only in a society which had conquered poverty and was "harnessing our machinery" for the creation of a utopian society in which poverty would no longer exist. Until such a society had been achieved, he proposed that "we do what we can by law" to end racial discrimination. Such legislation would require treating Negroes as humans, "not as some special subsection of the human race." He proposed laws against lynching, against discrimination in employment and housing, and for abolition of the poll tax which made it economically impossible for

Negroes to vote in many Southern states. He upbraided Princeton, his alma mater, for not admitting more than a handful of Negroes. Princeton's refusal to open its enrollment for Negroes meant, he charged, that it was "not a true university, but a glorified country club with intellectual features." He called for an end to segregation in schools because it impaired the building of a "common citizenship in a democratic country." He wanted the Southern states' delegations to Congress reduced because Southern Negroes had no right to vote, "a right open to barely literate white men."

Although staunchly against racial injustice, Thomas opposed militant tactics. Shortly after a bloody race riot in Detroit in 1943, he advised his friend James Farmer that the time was not yet ripe for civil disobedience. The Negroes, he said, were themselves not prepared for it, nor did they understand its implications. "You might merely produce irritation," Thomas warned. "I still think that there are other methods [which if] properly pushed would be more effective. I do not believe that Negroes should give weight to civil disobedience until they are willing to use more effectively the ballot and other methods of action which in many parts of the country they are in a position to use." Instead of civil disobedience, Thomas suggested that the Negroes join those labor unions that would admit them—and he proposed, further, that labor unions be required by law to end racial discrimination "now that membership in labor unions is so often a necessity for a job or a voice in collective bargaining."[6]

6

During the war, Thomas's attitude toward labor changed from that of a defender to that of a sharp critic. It was one of the most complete changes in Thomas's career. True, he opposed the wage freeze and the forced arbitration of labor disputes suggested by the wartime Roosevelt administration. He also fought the Roosevelt-proposed draft of labor, which he charged was born of Roosevelt's "love for power and his pique at labor." Moreover, he insisted that strikes—coal mine walkouts were then receiving widespread unfriendly publicity, and the United Mineworkers president John L. Lewis was one of America's wartime bogeymen—"rank far down in the list of factors retarding production for defense or war." Of far greater significance, he believed, were sickness, accidents, unemployment, "and haggling [by employers] about contracts for the sake of larger profits." But Thomas no longer considered the labor movement as the chief defender of the working man. It had lost that claim, in Thomas's view, because unions had proved themselves undemocratic. As early as 1935, Thomas had insisted that labor unions could not accept the protection of the Wagner Labor Relations Act without admitting that labor tactics were "the public's business." He therefore came to question the concept of the closed shop, under which membership in a specific union is a prerequisite for employment. "I believe that if the unions are going to ask for a closed or union shop," he wrote Monroe Sweetland, a young Socialist on his way to becoming Democratic state chairman of Oregon, "they must let whoever work in jobs in those industries join the union on reasonable terms. . . . I see no other alternative except to reject the whole concept of the closed shop." In 1945, Thomas even supported Cecil B. De Mille when the Hollywood producer refused to pay a union assessment aimed at defeating the "right-to-work" law proposed in California.

Thomas agreed that the increased power of labor unions had been beneficial to society in general. "We all owe far more than history makes us aware to the unknown soldiers of labor who by relatively peaceful means of labor organization have so greatly served in emancipating workers from the horrors of earlier days of the industrial revolution and in raising the whole level of human dignity and well-being." Unfortunately, Thomas noted, labor unions and labor union leaders were becoming increasingly unpopular even among union members. So serious was the dislike for the unions and their officials that Thomas feared that a skillful political leader could, in time of economic distress, "acquire great strength on the basis of a program which proposed to deliver the people generally and the workers themselves from the tyranny of labor unions and the labor bureaucracy." This, Thomas contended, was due to three trade union evils: (1) labor racketeering, "a heinous evil which unions have been too slow to seek aggressively to remedy"; (2) the trade unions' insistence on practices that "make employment for their members but greatly retard production"—such as the prohibition on the use of paintsprayers, or ready-mixed concrete, or prefabricated houses; and,

(3) most fundamental of all, the lack of democracy in labor unions. "Indeed, to some degree," he wrote, "strike abuses, racketeering, and even practices restrictive of production, are symptoms of an underlying lack of democracy in the labor union setup."

To cure these evils, Thomas said it would be necessary to compel unions to lower their initiation fees (some of which were thousands of dollars) and to admit all workers in a given trade or industry regardless of race, color, or creed. "It is especially disquieting," he said, "that so progressive an organization as the Brotherhood of Railroad Trainmen will not admit a Negro." He also wanted special labor courts established which would hear appeals from union members who claimed arbitrary expulsion which denied them the right to earn a living. This particular proposal was aimed primarily at the Amalgamated Clothing Workers Union, "which has accomplished much to benefit workers in what used to be a sweated industry," but which Thomas now considered "one of the bad unions in respect to arbitrary discipline and other denials of democracy." Ideally, he conceded, the unions should set their own house in order. Nothing would have pleased him more than "to have unions take action to correct abuses without any action by government." But he had no hope that this would happen. He therefore proposed that unions be required to meet "minimum standards of democracy" before they could be certified as legitimate trade unions by the National Labor Relations Board. Unions that did not meet Thomas's standards would thus be unable to avail themselves of the facilities of the national or state labor relations boards. "I do not think," Thomas wrote, "[that] our economic order can stand the strain of continual struggle between an increasingly monopolized private control of business and increasingly self-centered unions at public expense."[7]

7

Thomas had qualms about running for President in 1944, and rightly so, for the outlook was less than hopeful. What was left of the Socialist party was almost totally alienated from the labor-union movement; there were few people on the liberal left who any longer looked to Thomas and his party for direction and leadership. As early as 1940, Thomas had pleaded with his followers not to nominate him again. There were, he insisted, personal and party reasons which mitigated against his being the party candidate for President in 1944. But events between 1942 and 1944 convinced Thomas that he would have to run. The first of these was what he considered FDR's vindictiveness. One of the prime examples of this, Thomas maintained, was the drafting into the army of Coleman B. Cheney, a middle-aged professor of economics at Skidmore College in Saratoga Springs, New York. Considerably older than most draftees, Cheney was also the Socialist candidate for Governor of New York State in 1942. Thomas insisted that Cheney was conscripted to prevent his campaigning against Governor Herbert H. Lehman, Roosevelt's ally. As though to lend credence to Thomas's charge, the Army prohibited Cheney's direct involvement in the election drive.

Pressures existed within the party as well as on its periphery to run a presidential candidate. In Connecticut, Mayor Jasper McLevy, who had left the Socialist party in 1936, pleaded with Thomas to run. "We owe it to our boys and girls in the armed forces," McLevy told Thomas, "to work for a peace which will make future wars impossible." McLevy insisted that the achievement of such a peace would require a Socialist America. In Reading, Pennsylvania, where the Socialist J. Henry Stump had just been elected Mayor, there was also a strong demand for a Socialist presidential campaign. The Reading Socialists, still basically pacifist-isolationists, refused to forgive Roosevelt for having involved the United States in the war.

Besides party pressures and his distaste for Roosevelt, there was one other substantive reason for Thomas's favoring a Socialist national campaign in 1944: he was convinced that such a campaign was necessary to help form a new mass party. (This same delusion was also to lead Thomas into the disastrous 1948 campaign.) By 1944, he admitted that the two-party system was more effective than a three- or four-party system would be in the United States, but he continued to claim that there was no significant difference between the two major parties. "The cement which holds the two parties together," he said, " is compounded of tradition, inertia, lust for office, and sometimes love of a strong individual leader. . . ." Thomas believed that parties ought to differ on matters of policy. The Socialist party was therefore in the campaign, he said, to "keep the ballot open to a new party which someday will do what the Republican party did in 1856 and 1860."

On the other hand, there were salient arguments against a national campaign. The Socialist party was in desperate straits—in New York City, for example, there were only three branches left: one each in Manhattan, Brooklyn, and the Bronx. Total party membership nationally was less than one thousand. Within the party there was opposition, particularly from members with trade-union connections, to running a presidential candidate. Even a left-wing Socialist like Powers Hapgood refused to support the party in a national campaign; he believed he had to support labor, which backed Roosevelt almost universally, though he believed it was mistaken in doing so.

The Socialist convention in Reading ignored the arguments against a national campaign and nominated Thomas for President and Darlington Hoopes for Vice-President. Thomas set the tone of the campaign, which was almost completely aimed at Roosevelt's policies. "My case against Roosevelt," he declared, "is that the foreign policy or lack of foreign policy is unnecessarily prolonging this war and inviting the next; that his endorsement of a draft for labor showed a very dangerous attitude; that, on the whole, the government's wartime policies have aided big business; that by the President's own admission there is no more New Deal and that since 1937 the President has not powerfully backed any important progressive legislation." Thomas was particularly distressed by Roosevelt's talk of total victory in the war. He warned that the "absolute power of total victory will corrupt the victors." He doubted that the rulers of the Allied powers could be trusted to put moral limits on the power they would achieve through total victory. In place of total victory, or unconditional surrender, Thomas wanted a peace based on self-determination, organized cooperation among nations, and an international form of mediation and arbitration to prevent future wars. He wanted Germany and Japan to be offered places in the new system, providing they would forgo future aggression and withdraw their forces from occupied countries. Thomas also campaigned for a United States of Europe and an end to imperialism and colonialism. He still spoke of socialism—but it was much modified from the socialism he had espoused ten years earlier. His new socialist society would have a mixed economy with public corporations in control of the "commanding heights of industry"; consumer cooperatives would operate most retail outlets, and private enterprise would remain in control of nonessential industries, though under strict control. Domestically, Thomas's emphasis was on planning.

The campaign was, as Thomas admitted nineteen years later, a lackluster affair, though it did make a contribution to civil liberty. In August, Roosevelt spoke in Bremerton, Washington, in what was labeled a nonpolitical address. The speech was carried on the Armed Forces Radio Network. Thomas challenged the nonpolitical label. The Army agreed, at first, that the other candidates were entitled to equal time for reply on the military network. But Assistant Secretary of War John McCloy, a Roosevelt appointee, reversed that decision on the ground that the President spoke as commander-in-chief and not as a presidential candidate. Thomas raised a public clamor which forced McCloy to agree to give all candidates equal time, though he never admitted that the Roosevelt speech was political. Thomas gained little political advantage with his demand for equal time, but he set the precedent that during an election campaign even a President must allow his opponents equal time for reply on government-operated facilities.

Support for Thomas's campaign was almost nonexistent. A committee composed of fifty-six ministers and the conservative Negro journalist George Schuyler supported him. There were no major labor figures in his camp. In California, Illinois, and Ohio, normally states with significant Socialist votes, stringent election laws kept Thomas's and Hoopes's names off the ballot. Almost all newspapers, particularly such voices of official liberalism as the *New York Post* and *PM*, which were committed to Roosevelt, ignored Thomas completely. Only at Yale Divinity School, where he led the poll 59 to 58 for FDR and 46 for the Republican Thomas E. Dewey, did Thomas show any strength.

Faced with almost certain electoral disaster, Thomas decided to shame the former Militant Socialists into supporting him. He wrote an open letter to Reinhold Niebuhr, who had resigned from the party in 1940 to support Roosevelt and intervention, and who had since formed the Union for Democratic Action as a political home for ex-Socialists turned New Dealers. In the letter Thomas claimed that FDR had introduced no progressive legislation in seven years, that he had failed to solve the unemployment problem, and that he had "no program adequate to the conquest of poverty." Moreover, Thomas charged that Roosevelt was "underwriting white supremacy in the Far East and Balkanization of Europe between Moscow and London." He further claimed that the Democratic vice-presidential candidate, Harry S. Truman, was one of "Convict Boss [Thomas J.] Pendergast's protégés, whose record is not adequately redeemed by the fact that he has been chairman of a useful senatorial committee." Thomas added that "Roosevelt told us that Dr. New Deal died. The [Democratic national] convention proceeded to jump on its grave."

Niebuhr's reply was devastating—it is one of the most effective and accurate critiques of Norman Thomas ever written:

"One of the more interesting ironies of this time has been the spectacle of American Socialists talking of 'winning the peace'; if America and the democratic world had listened to those Socialists who before Pearl Harbor were telling us that our capitalist society was not pure enough in heart to take up arms against fascist aggression, Hitler would be making [his] peace today.

"You suggest that because the Administration no longer manifests its earlier New Deal militancy, American progressives should abandon their efforts to make the Democratic party the liberal party and should cast in their lot with the Socialists. But we believe . . . that the New Deal must be revived and strengthened.

"[Your political] irresponsibility, which led to the folly of your pre–Pearl Harbor isolationism, stems from your inability to conceive of politics as the art of choosing among possible alternatives. This blindness makes it impossible for you correctly to gauge the political climate of the country.

"America, in the years immediately ahead, may be the scene of basic political realignments. But America will not in the foreseeable future be called on to make a choice between socialism and reaction. A sizeable Socialist vote in November will prove nothing and influence no one. The realistic actual choice before Americans is that of reverting to the period of Hoover-Coolidge normalcy . . . or of moving militantly forward in the determination to make the last four years of the Roosevelt era a period of social reconstruction and reform. . . .

"I remind you once again that the battles ahead will not be simple contests between unmitigated evil and absolute good, and that a true perspective cannot be had from the Olympian heights of Socialist dogma."

The results of the 1944 election were the worst in Socialist party history. Of 47,976,263 votes cast, Norman Thomas and Darlington Hoopes polled only 80,426, or less than .17 per cent of the total. Roosevelt won 25,602,504 and Republican Thomas E. Dewey won 22,006,285 votes. In New York State only 10,553 voters supported Thomas.[8]

8

Besides Thomas's battles for civil liberties and civil rights, and his changed position on labor, he pleaded for a program to avert the new economic crisis he feared would follow the war. He assumed that most civilians favored the war because they feared the economic consequences of peace. He fought against the proposal that Germany and Japan pay the total cost of the war; and he was particularly annoyed by the Morgenthau plan, which would have turned industrial Germany into a pastoral state. He charged that the Big Three—the United States, Britain, and Russia—were merely playing the old imperialist game, each for its own gain. The net result of the Big Three conferences at Yalta, Teheran, and Cairo, he warned, would be either chaos or Stalinite hegemony of the world, because he expected that there would be native revolts which would win the cynical support of the Soviet dictator.

Thomas's revulsion at the war reached its height in August 1945 when the United States dropped atomic bombs on Hiroshima and Nagasaki. Thomas was horrified, viewing the bombings as immoral atrocities which called for national penitence. They could have been avoided, he told an audience at New York's Christ Church. Japan had made earlier peace overtures, one of which had been transmitted to the White House. Thomas saw no reason for an atomic bomb to be dropped on a nation prepared to surrender. Even if it was necessary to demonstrate to Japan the awesome power in American hands, he asked, why was the bomb not dropped on an unpopulated area? Why was it necessary to drop it on a city like Hiroshima with women and children? What possible excuse could there be for dropping a second bomb on Nagasaki without waiting for the results of the first?

The atomic bombings were, Thomas insisted, inexcusable. He appealed to America's conscience never to use the bomb again.[9]

Almost immediately after the bombs fell on Hiroshima and Nagasaki, the war came to an end with Japan's surrender. (Germany had capitulated three months earlier.) Thomas feared that the real victor in the war had been Stalin; no power on earth was now capable of defeating both the Soviet military machine and internal Communist conspiracies. Behind Stalin's power he saw the huge land area and the large and resilient population of the Soviet Union. He saw the large Communist parties in Europe as another base for Stalin's power, and he accurately forecast that postwar tensions would develop between the West and the Soviet Union in the Middle East, the Balkans, and in Asia. Postwar events in Korea, Vietnam, Greece, Israel, the Formosa Straits, and Laos have borne out his analysis. Despite his animosity toward Stalin and his objections to appeasing the Soviet dictator, Thomas still opposed war, preventive or otherwise, as a means for containing Russia.[10] But Thomas's anti-communist obsession and his quasi-pacifism created a dilemma which he was never able to resolve.

9

Thomas's role during World War II, both before and after Pearl Harbor, was more a symptom than a cause of his failure. His politics from 1939 to 1945 were as consistent as they were naive. Before American involvement, Thomas believed that the United States could best serve the purposes of freedom by remaining aloof. This was an assumption that merely emphasized his long-standing pacifist leanings. Given this premise, plus his beliefs that Europe faced almost total destruction in the war, that Britain and France were interested primarily in preserving their imperial positions, and that the United States would be the sole nation capable of saving Europe's economy only if it stayed out of the war, there does not appear to have been any alternative open to Thomas except his isolationism. His assumptions were erroneous, his rationale faulty, and his conclusions ludicrous. True, Europe was being destroyed in the war, but the alternative was total subjugation under Hitler. Perhaps Britain and France were interested primarily in safeguarding their imperial positions, but

Thomas ignored the obvious fact that the alternative to an Allied victory was a return to the Dark Ages under Hitler. Perhaps the United States could have done more to revive Europe if it had not become directly involved in the fighting; yet it is probable that the Europe left to have been revived would have been a continent of slaves working for Hitler. After Stalin became involved in the war, Thomas hoped that the two dictators would eliminate each other, and thus obviate the necessity for the West to battle Hitler. But this assumption was as naive as his others. For the two dictators would have been capable, even after the June 1941 invasion of Russia by Hitler, of reaching a *modus vivendi* and turning against the West if it served their interests. Hitler and Stalin proved in 1939 that they had a remarkable ability to ignore such trivial issues as ideology in the interests of *Machtpolitik*.

Thomas's fatal weakness was his inability to recognize that politics was in effect the art of the possible, and this doomed him to failure. The years 1939 to 1941 merely emphasized the fact that he could not understand that absolutes belonged in a church or a revivalist's tent, but not in politics. To assume the posture of an ecclesiastic on the stage of politics is to invite failure; and this is precisely what Thomas did. His inability to recognize that politics is not a struggle between ultimate good and ultimate evil was nowhere so obvious as in his rhetoric during the days before Pearl Harbor. Yet this same fatal weakness existed in his arguments within the party during the Militant–Old Guard struggle, and in his insistence that Socialists had to run a candidate in 1933 in New York against LaGuardia, in 1934 in California against Sinclair, and in 1936, 1940, and 1944 against Roosevelt.

True, after Pearl Harbor Thomas acknowledged that he had to choose between evils: war or fascism—there was no other alternative. He could oppose the war, and thus tacitly aid Hitler, or he could support the war, apart from the fact that the Allies were less than absolutely good. Despite his remarkable capacity for self-delusion, Thomas had to accept that only defeat in the war could topple Hitler. Under these conditions, Thomas had no alternative but to admit, however reluctantly, that the war had to be won. Yet his decision came too late to salvage either Thomas or the Socialist party. By 1941, Thomas had ceased to be a political factor; since 1936, the party had been little more than a hollow shell. After the war, neither was relevant.

IX
Love
your enemies

America did not become a totalitarian state during the war as Thomas had feared in his isolationist days. By 1947, he admitted that he had been mistaken in assuming that civil liberties would be endangered should the United States get into the conflict. ". . . The record stands that we and we alone of the major powers got through the Second World War without the conscription of labor or any major infringement on the rights of free speech, free press, and assemblage," he wrote. That America retained its civil liberties he attributed less to "our virtue" than to the lack of organized political opposition. In retrospect, he found only two wartime occurrences which disturbed him: the harsh treatment of the Japanese-Americans and the drift toward total conscription.

As late as 1963, Thomas still insisted that the United States could have served the cause of freedom better had it remained aloof from the war. But he admitted, "I failed to realize that vigorous action by France and Britain, with definite encouragement from America, would rather easily have checked the rearmament of Germany."

Thomas was elated when British voters chose the Labour party in the 1945 general election. Perhaps he saw in this the hope that the people of the world might choose democratic socialism over all other systems, if given the opportunity. But he was not certain that the opportunity would be made available; he feared that it was more likely Stalin would impose his own version of socialism on the rest of the world. He doubted that the world in 1945 was ready for the federation of cooperative commonwealths that would comprise the utopia he envisioned. Nor did he expect it to come about in the foreseeable future. In the meanwhile, the job of Socialists, Thomas said, was to prepare the world, "in which both peace and democracy are empty dreams for socialism and democracy."[1]

2

Thomas opposed drastic measures to punish the people of Germany and Japan. Such proposals were legion during the period immediately following the Japanese surrender. He believed vengeance against a whole people both immoral and impractical. The Germans and Japanese had, he said, suffered enough during the war, having been bombed into submission.

The basis for a peace settlement, Thomas believed, should be a general plan for cooperation under which the disarmed, de-empired Axis powers, purged of their fascist and militarist rulers, would participate in drawing up the terms. He wanted the vanquished Axis powers disarmed—but only as a first step toward liquidation of all competitive armaments. He wanted their empires dismantled as the first step in a general, rapid, and progressive liquidation of all imperialism. He conceded that the Axis powers were the principal culprits in the war, but denied that they were solely to blame for it. The United States, the Western powers, and especially the Soviet Union were also at fault.[2]

As early as 1942, Thomas had favored punishment of Nazi leaders "because of [their] cruelty going even beyond the bounds of accepted cruelties of war." He suggested that they be tried by an international tribunal in order that the punishment meted out would be more than "blind satisfaction of hate by victors." But when the surviving Nazi leaders were tried by an international tribunal at Nuremberg, Thomas had qualms. In the first place, he charged, "there exists no proper codification of law" to deal with excessive war cruelty. Secondly, he believed that no court "containing a representative of the Soviet government, which collaborated with Hitler in aggression," was competent to pass on the "guilt of aggression." He also doubted that the trials had won universal respect, which he considered essential if they were to be instrumental in diminishing the likelihood of further aggressive war. Moreover, the Nazis were not alone in committing war crimes; "how about those responsible for the atomic bomb, especially over Nagasaki?" he asked.

The peace terms, especially the division of Germany in 1945

under which Berlin was left an island in a Communist sea, roused Thomas's ire. This "act of madness," he charged, was based on a desire for vengeance against the Germans, plus the failure of the Allies to recognize Stalinism for what Thomas insisted it was: a power-mad form of imperialism which outdid even Hitler. Thus when in 1948 the Russians clamped a blockade on Berlin, Thomas, while hailing the American airlift which got supplies to the city, charged that it had come too late to save Europe; an earlier, more resolute stand, instead of Roosevelt and Churchill agreeing with Stalin to divide Germany, could have saved Europe from the threat of Communist aggression.[3]

3

Thomas's position on world organization differed considerably at the end of World War II from what it had been at the end of World War I. In the early 1920's, he had opposed American membership in the League of Nations because he considered it an alliance of imperialist powers interested only in protecting their possessions. In 1945, he urged the United States Senate to ratify the United Nations Charter, though his testimony in favor of ratification read almost as an indictment of the UN.

"There is nothing in this charter to guarantee peace," he told the Senators. "It perpetuates the myth of nationalism." The UN was, he said, little more than "a glorified and uneasy alliance which in its fundamental principles defeats its declared aims of the establishment of peace." He considered the UN to be primarily a forum where nations could discuss matters of mutual interest and little more. Thomas conceded that there were some useful organs in the UN, particularly the Economic and Social Council, but he charged that the chief organ of the UN, the General Assembly, was based on "the dangerous and amoral fallacy of equal rights of 'sovereign nations.'" He also questioned the UN's ability to prevent a war involving the United States and the Soviet Union, though he insisted that no great war could develop except between these two great powers. Thomas was, in effect, urging ratification of an ineffective, amoral, almost totally useless UN because the alternative might be worse.[4]

Despite his belief that the UN was ineffective, Thomas opposed strengthening it or using it as the basis for some form of world state. He conceded that there might be merit in the idea of world government, but he claimed that the time was not propitious. Thomas agreed that the right form of world government might prevent war, but added the wrong type of world government would likely lead to war. He saw no hope for a world state unless the Communists abandoned their authoritarianism, and he saw no possibility of this coming to pass. He was convinced that Stalin would never accept democratic rule. Under these conditions, the only type of world state possible would be one controlled by the Communists, and such a state would be the worst possible political abomination because it would mean universal tyranny. "The creation of one world under one government might conceivably deprive lovers of liberty of any asylum from tyranny."[5]

4

On the domestic scene, Thomas still hoped to see the formation of a new semi-Socialist Farmer-Labor or Progressive party. "If democracy is to be intelligent and effective," he said, "political parties should present meaningful platforms . . . and in office they should seek to carry out their platforms." He considered a new political party a necessity, and in 1946 appealed to labor and progressive leaders to help in its organization. Labor's Political Action Committee, which supported friendly New Deal candidates, was, he argued, little more than a pressure group which could get an occasional law passed but which could not "carry through a program for peace, plenty, and freedom." What was needed was a new third party, which would eventually become one of the two major parties. There was considerable support within labor and progressive circles for Thomas's view.

In the spring of 1946, a large group of Socialist, labor, and farm organization leaders met to discuss the formation of such a party. Thomas acknowledged that there were three basic problems confronting a third party: (1) fear that such a party would lead to the atomization of the political system "which proved so hurtful in Germany and France"; (2) the fact that the primary system of nominations, coupled with "the American love of riding the bandwagon, and the American fear of being in a small minority, all tend excessively to handicap third parties"; and (3)

the enactment since 1912 of state laws which made it more difficult for third parties to get on the ballot in key states. But he still
believed the task possible. By mid-1946, however, when David
Dubinsky, leader of the powerful and progressive International
Ladies Garment Workers Union, announced his opposition to
the proposal, the movement died.

It was thus apparent to Thomas that the third party he desired
would not come into existence in 1948. He assumed, however,
that the Republican candidate, Governor Thomas E. Dewey,
would be elected President and that Dewey's election would
convince labor and progressive leaders that their sole hope was
to be found in the formation of a new party which they themselves controlled. He believed that the election of Dewey would
give labor leaders pause to reflect on the fact that their support
of the Democratic party had won "an end to progressive legislation since early in 1937; and a tragic mishandling of the problem
of proper peace settlements."

Apart from the collapse of the third-party movement, the Socialist party situation in 1948 was more optimistic than it had
been in almost ten years. Frank Zeidler, a Socialist party leader,
had been elected Mayor of Milwaukee in a nonpartisan election in which his Socialist affiliation was an issue. There were
now three Socialist mayors in middle-sized to large cities—Irving
Freese in Norwalk, Connecticut, Jasper McLevy in Bridgeport,
and Zeidler. In Reading, a united opposition defeated J. Henry
Stump for Mayor by a mere seventy-two votes out of 23,012
cast. The Socialists therefore assumed, with some justification,
that they were regaining some of their political strength. Moreover, McLevy and the Connecticut Socialist party had rejoined
the national organization, and though the Social Democratic
Federation refused to reunite with the Socialist party, locals of
the SDF and its affiliate, the Jewish Socialist Verband, had voted
to support the Socialist party should it run national candidates.
Even the *Jewish Daily Forward*, which had spearheaded the
anti-Thomas drive twelve years earlier, announced that "Social-
ist-inclined citizens . . . could permit themselves the luxury of
voting for the candidate of the Socialist party."

Thomas wanted the party to run a candidate for President in
1948. But he was reluctant to be that candidate. Violet Thomas,
his wife of thirty-seven years, had died in 1947. He was tired,

and believed that at sixty-four he had earned a rest. He agreed with Mulford Q. Sibley, a leading Socialist intellectual, that it was bad for the party not to develop new leaders. Thomas wanted the party to nominate Professor Maynard Krueger of the University of Chicago for President, but the latter preferred to run for Congress as a non-Socialist independent in Chicago. It was only after Krueger refused to run that Thomas agreed to accept the nomination.[6]

If Thomas had any qualms about a Socialist campaign in 1948, they were soon dissipated by the formation of the Progressive party to support Henry A. Wallace for President. Wallace's candidacy was supported by a strange assortment of pacifists, left-wing New Dealers, and Communists, with the Communists in actual control of the Progressive party national organization. A former New Deal Secretary of Agriculture, Vice-President, and Secretary of Commerce, Wallace resigned from his cabinet post in protest against the hardening anti-Soviet foreign policy of the Truman administration—a policy which Thomas supported with reservations. Since Wallace's foreign policy line agreed with Stalin's, the Communists and their camp-followers worked tirelessly in his behalf. Detesting both the Communists and Wallace personally, Thomas feared that unless the Socialists ran a major campaign Wallace and his Communist allies would capture the third-party movement.

"If Henry Wallace had been the kind of man that thousands of good people who support him believe him to be," Thomas said, "if the control of his new party had not been so largely in the hands of the expert Communist minority, most Socialists—emphatically I—would have supported him." He conceded that Socialists and Wallace would agree on some issues of domestic policy, but Thomas rejected "any bid for leadership in democracy by the apologist for the slave state of Russia, and the preacher of peace by appeasement." He warned Wallace that anyone who had ever worked with the Communists—including himself—had lived to regret it. He noted that Wallace opposed the Marshall Plan for rehabilitation of Europe, which "puts you in the company of the Communist *Daily Worker* and Colonel [Robert] McCormick [reactionary, isolationist publisher of the *Chicago Tribune*]." Thomas tried to draw Wallace into a debate, but failed. He tried to get Wallace to explain his relations with the Communists, but Wallace refused to answer.

There were other reasons for Thomas's dislike for Wallace. He complained of Wallace's "ruthless handling of complaints by sharecroppers and field hands against the cruel working of his agricultural plan in Roosevelt's first term." Thomas accused Wallace of being hostile to all efforts at revising the Agricultural Adjustment Act to benefit the sharecroppers, adding that he had suppressed reports indicating the poor condition of the sharecroppers and had fired Jerome Frank as Agriculture Department solicitor because the latter attempted to aid the sharecroppers.[7]

Nor was Thomas satisfied with the three other candidates. Dixiecrat Strom Thurmond, he said, represented a "racism that disgraces America." Governor Thomas E. Dewey's "political character is synthetic, deliberately made up by himself on the basis of a shrewd calculation of factors making for success." Although Thomas considered Dewey's record as Governor of New York State commendably liberal, he insisted that Republican party members were generally "ardent believers in capitalism and the automatic working of markets." He doubted that a Republican victory would mean repeal of welfare legislation, though he believed it might mean more restraints on organized labor. The Republicans, Thomas felt, had learned "by bitter experience" that if they wanted to win elections they had "to appease the masses."

He thus saw little difference between the Republicans and the Democrats. Truman was a genuine liberal, Thomas conceded, but his progressivism was superficial, and "it still remains true that he is so inept, so in bondage to his Pendergast past, so enamored of brass hats and Wall Street operators in high office, that he cannot give effective liberal leadership in the extraordinarily unlikely event of his election." He doubted that the Democratic party, containing as it did such disparate individuals as the progressive Secretary of Labor Lewis B. Schwellenbach and the white supremacist Congressman John E. Rankin of Mississippi, could ever become the vehicle for progressive government.

Most labor leaders supported Truman; few, notably Louis Nelson of the Knitgood Workers Union and Joseph Schlossberg of the Amalgamated Clothing Workers, supported Thomas. Thomas was also endorsed by Dorothy Thompson, who had disagreed with him so vehemently only seven years before, and by John Dewey, John Haynes Holmes, James T. Farrell, Van

Wyck Brooks, Paul Blanshard, Erich Fromm, Sidney Hook, C. Wright Mills, Richard Rovere, Edmund Wilson, and Morton Wishengrad.

Although Thomas and his running mate, Tucker P. Smith, campaigned vigorously on a limited $60,000 budget, it was apparent when the election returns were in that the Socialist party had again failed politically: Thomas polled only 139,009 votes of 48,538,998 cast. Truman, the surprise victor, received 24,105,695, Dewey 21,969,170, Thurmond 1,169,021 (all in the deep South), and Wallace 1,156,103.[8]

Clearly the labor unions had delivered the votes that carried the election for Truman. Labor's ability to deliver the vote for a Democrat convinced Thomas that Socialists would have to abandon plans for building a new major farmer-labor progressive party. The election also revealed how deep-rooted the two-party system was in America. Thomas therefore concluded that it was imperative for the Socialist party to cease all electoral activity. He admitted that after fifty years it was less than pleasant for Socialists to concede that they had, in effect, wasted their energies by running electoral campaigns. But, he argued, most of the Socialists' important electoral issues had in fact since become law. Thomas claimed that "the workers have made a great mistake in their failure to make the Socialist party a mass vehicle of social change." In view of the party's electoral failure, he suggested that "we should no longer spend our energy on political campaigns which gave us only a handful of votes. . . . My position is, simply, that we can do a better job of educating the labor, liberal, and farm forces that we need to win socialism" by dropping electoral activity. Political parties, he argued, "do not exist to save our Socialist souls or to lessen the guilt complex of voters who still refuse to vote according to their Socialist inclinations. A Socialist political party exists to advance the cause of socialism. We do not advance the cause of socialism when, by default or sheer lack of resources, we become less and less able to put Socialist tickets in the field." After citing the difficulties facing Socialists attempting to get on the ballot, and the continually declining vote, he announced: "I shall not run again. . . ."

The 1949 elections reinforced Thomas's view. Joseph P. Glass, Socialist mayoral candidate in New York, polled fewer than 9,000 votes; in New Haven, the Socialist candidate polled only 3,400 votes whereas only two years earlier he had polled more than 11,000; and in Reading, two years before a Socialist bastion, the party's vote fell to 5,300 of more than 30,000 votes cast. In light of the low estate of Socialist fortunes, the national executive committee accepted Thomas's proposal to end all electoral activity. But the 1950 national convention rejected the decision and decided to continue to run candidates. This resolution, devised by a coalition of Samuel H. Friedman, Darlington Hoopes, and Jasper McLevy, declared that a national ticket was necessary "for our political survival as an entity which attracts some measure of journalistic and popular attention, and for the educational opportunities it brings." Thomas was incensed; his personal choice for national secretary of the party, Harry Fleishman, resigned. When the 1952 party convention nominated a ticket over his opposition, Thomas arranged a trip to Asia, thus absenting himself from his first national campaign in twenty-four years. He made no secret of his personal support for Adlai E. Stevenson for President. Of the Republican candidate, Dwight D. Eisenhower, he said: ". . . It is a little short of shocking that a man should seek the high office of President without taking more trouble to inform himself of the issues." He charged that "the public doesn't know" Eisenhower's position "on great issues (except for his advocacy of universal military training and racial segregation)." On election day the Socialist vote convinced most party members that Thomas had, finally, analyzed the situation accurately. Darlington Hoopes and Samuel H. Friedman, the party's 1952 ticket, polled only 18,322 votes nationally—fewer votes than had been polled by the Socialist Labor party sixty years before.

Although Thomas proved correct in his assessment of Socialist electoral opportunities, he had lost control of what was left of the party machinery. He therefore organized a new Socialist group called the Union of Democratic Socialists (UDS), an American equivalent of the British Fabian Society. It "ought not to be thought of as a political party," he wrote Hugh Gaitskell, the leader of the British Labour party, "but as [an organization] which I hope can hold together little *s* socialists who feel they must work within the old parties, but who nevertheless believe in socialism and are willing to do some new thinking on the whole subject." Thomas noted that, though conditions had changed, Socialists and non-Socialists alike "still use a language which no longer conforms strictly to the facts." It was against this doctrinaire spirit that he hoped the UDS could succeed. But, as with most other such groups, within five years the Union of Democratic Socialists withered and disappeared.[9]

On the question of third parties, Thomas now believed that they had served a useful purpose, had often been gadflies, had raised significant issues, but that they no longer served any significant end. He was still not satisfied with the two major parties, saying that "the differences within each party are greater than the average differences between them." But he doubted a new third party would alter the situation; the change would have to come from within each of the parties. By 1956, Thomas had succeeded in prodding his party into giving up electoral activity, though Hoopes and Friedman ran a write-in campaign that year.[10]

5

Thomas's anti-communism became more pronounced as the relations between the United States and the Soviet Union worsened after the war. He charged in 1948 that the Soviet leadership had "pioneered in the worst forms of repression of civil liberties," adding that the Nazis and fascists had followed Lenin's and Stalin's lead. Far from being the farthest left of political movements, he argued that it was the farthest right, a totalitarian state capitalism and a form of fascism. Despite his strong animus for communism and the Soviet Union, Thomas's record during the late 1940's and 1950's—a period of repressive anti-communism in the United States—was ambivalent, but biased in favor of civil liberties, even for the Communists. Most of the ostensible opponents of communism had "little understanding of, or concern for, democracy," he noted, and many of the sharpest and most vocal "anti-Communists" of the postwar period had been complacent about the Soviet threat only a few years before. He was worried that the "high degree of rather hysterical anti-communism, which is being exploited by reactionaries," would endanger civil liberties and possibly boomerang to the benefit of the Communists.

The chief political beneficiary of the anti-Communist hysteria of the period was Senator Joseph McCarthy, whom Thomas loathed. Despite this antipathy, it was Thomas who inadvertently turned McCarthy into a professional anti-Communist. When during the 1946 senatorial campaign in Wisconsin, McCarthy's opponent, Howard J. McMurray, a liberal non-Communist Democrat, was endorsed by the *Daily Worker*, Thomas, speaking at a Socialist picnic near Milwaukee, suggested that McMurray repudiate this Communist endorsement. McMurray ignored him. Several Wisconsin daily newspapers picked up the cry and reiterated Thomas's plea that McMurray openly reject the Communist support. Again McMurray remained silent. McCarthy quickly picked up the cry originally raised by Thomas, and assailed his opponent for not denouncing the Communists. The charge breathed life into an otherwise listless campaign; because of it, McCarthy began more and more to exploit the anti-Communist theme until it became the overriding issue of his career.

Although Thomas was in this sense responsible for McCarthy's "anti-communism," it should be noted that Thomas opposed his irresponsibility and the hysteria he engendered. He accused McCarthy of causing "Communist schemers deep satisfaction by the harm you are doing our American democracy by your methods of investigation. . . ." He charged McCarthy with serving the Kremlin "by discrediting our government to the puzzled and scornful mirth of our allies."[11]

Thomas's objections to McCarthy and other self-appointed anti-Communists did not, however, keep him from agreeing with them that Communists should be removed from places of responsibility on the mere finding that they were Communists, because "membership in the Communist party or implicit acceptance of its leadership is *per se* an act which puts unhesitating loyalty to a party controlled by the Soviet dictatorship ahead of all other loyalties." Thomas insisted that Communists had no right to teach in public schools. That right, he said, "is not a necessary or logical deduction from the Bill of Rights or the right to free speech." After citing the role played by public school teachers in molding the social outlook of the young, Thomas declared that "the first basic principle in America is faith in democracy. . . . There is absolutely no case for allowing Communists any more than Ku Klux Klanners or fascists to teach in the public schools; not unless one is to believe that the imparting of ideals in school is an impossibility, or that growing children are capable of guarding against the unfortunate influence of teachers, or that our democracy has no standards worth imparting."

But if Communists did not belong in sensitive positions, neither, Thomas believed, did they belong in jail. Only those convicted of such overt acts as espionage or conspiracy should be imprisoned, he argued. Nor did Thomas believe that there was need for the loyalty investigations and subversive hunts which were then endemic in America. In the first place, he wanted to protect loyal citizens from "a kind of witch hunt." In the second place, he did not believe that investigations were necessary to prove the subversive nature of the Communist movement; the actions of the party leaders, their official statements, and the whole history of the party and its affiliates were sufficient, in Thomas's view, to establish the subversion of the Communist movement. Moreover, he did not trust the investigators and assumed that "a Republican fight on communism will be mostly a fight for reactionary capitalism and nationalism. . . . There is a danger that everything liberal or progressive will be called Communist. . . ."[12]

Despite his loathing for the Communists, and his assumption that they were involved in a conspiracy against the United States, Thomas defended their right to be heard and their right to fair trials, and he decried all attempts to imprison Communist leaders. He actively opposed the execution in 1953 of Julius and Ethel Rosenberg, the convicted atom-bomb spies, though he was convinced of their guilt. Similarly, he used his considerable influence with Princeton University to assure Alger Hiss, who was convicted of perjury for denying his role in Communist espionage, the right to speak before students.

Although convinced that prosecution and persecution of the Communists would not solve the problem they posed to American security, Thomas recognized the need to protect the United States from what he considered the real danger of Communist treason. He suggested to Matthew Connelly, President Truman's secretary, that the federal government organize a bipartisan commission—similar to the Royal Commission in Canada which had a short time earlier exposed a spy ring in that country operating through the Communist party—to "review the situation and . . . make specific recommendations concerning changes in the law and possible prosecutions." Congress preferred to enact a series of laws of questionable constitutionality which would, in effect, outlaw the Communist party. Thomas pleaded in vain that these laws "would do more harm than good . . . [and] would make martyrs of the Communists, win them sympathy, and intensify their dangerous underground activity." He was confident that communism would be rejected by the American people "through the competition of ideas in the market," and that overt espionage and treason could be handled by existing laws. He testified against the Mundt-Nixon Bill which would have forced the Communists to register (". . . although communism is a disease, the remedy is not to bleed civil liberties") and against the McCarran Act, which virtually outlawed the Communist party ("It will instill fear into reasonable debate").[13]

The arrests of Communist leaders and some rank-and-file members under the Smith Act were, in Thomas's view, "an error in policy likely to make them martyrs and otherwise to impair America's standing as a land of liberty." So opposed was Thomas to these prosecutions that he became one of the most active defenders of the Communists, whom he hated and who in turn hated him. George Charney, one of the defendants, recalled how in 1953:

"We were so bold as to visit Norman Thomas to solicit his intervention in our case. Bold is the word, for he represented in our official eyes the spokesman for social democracy. No adjective could describe the cumulative contempt expressed by some of our leading colleagues who had never forsaken the idea that Thomas and his ilk were social fascists. We had a remarkably pleasant and extensive interview and found him, though old and somewhat ill, sympathetic, keen, and eager to help. Only once in a wry, humorous fashion did he refer to the past, never, in all our extensive dealings with him to mention it again. He wrote letters, contacted Roger Baldwin of the American Civil Liberties Union and countless other people, solicited funds, spoke at gatherings, and was available at all times for conferences. I still remember the shocked silence that greeted my first reference to him at a mass meeting, though in time even our comrades sloughed off their ingrained prejudices in appreciation of his role. . . . He was magnificent and I could only wince when recalling our past attitudes. . . ."[14]

Among those for whom Thomas pleaded was his one-time close friend Alexander Trachtenberg, whom he described as "essentially a good man—distorted by the creed to which he gave his allegiance," and Junius Scales, former leader of the Communist party of North Carolina, who was imprisoned five years after he resigned from the party in disgust after the Khrushchev revelations of the Stalinite purges and the suppression of the Hungarian revolution. Thomas's statement in defense of Scales summed up much of his philosophy:

"In this perilous time, the fate of a single man may not seem to be sufficient cause for sustained effort. Yet if this nation loses its complete sense of compassion and equity and keeps Junius Scales in prison, it also surrenders a part of that moral force which it needs in order to face the huge issues."[15]

Thomas's anti-communism put him in an awkward position after World War II. He had himself, in effect, inadvertently led a demagogue down the path of anti-communism and was then appalled by what he had reaped. For Thomas was opposed to the Communists as a group—he wanted the party as an entity to suffer—but true Christian that he was, he bore no individual ill, and wanted no individual hurt. Thomas politicized the biblical injunction: "Ye have heard that it hath been said, Thou shalt love thy neighbor and hate thine enemy. But I say unto you, Love your enemy" (*Matthew* 5:43–44).

Thomas's commitment to civil liberties did not extend beyond the political realm. A social Puritan, he opposed extending freedom to literature or art, when they impinged on his moral standards. He favored stringent laws against pornography, which he defined rather broadly. Called in as an expert in civil liberties before a Senate committee investigating pornography in 1955, he denied that obscenity was protected by the First Amendment—or that it should be. "It is an outrage to freedom," Thomas declared, "to say there is any guarantee of freedom for this kind of thing." But Thomas did not favor outright censorship, which he feared could be extended beyond pornography, nor did he trust voluntary censorship by publishers. He suggested instead "outright prohibition of the circulation, by any device whatever, of the kind of pornography stuff you have been discussing. . . ." In 1955, he was, in essence, proposing that the Post Office use the same techniques against publications which did not meet his standards of morality that had been used successfully against Socialist periodicals thirty-five years earlier.[16]

6

In 1950, the Communist rulers of North Korea invaded the pro-American Republic of South Korea. Thomas saw no alternative but to support armed intervention; any other course, he feared, would convince Stalin that men would yield indefinitely to Communist aggression. Peace and freedom would have been the victims, Thomas maintained, had President Truman not intervened militarily. Some of his former followers who still clung to their pacifism pleaded with Thomas to change his stance, but he rejected their pleas because they presented no practical solution "to the terrible alternative that was adopted on June 25, 1950, in Korea." Gandhi's method of passive resistance, which had been successful against the British in India, would, he was convinced, have failed in Korea. In the same circumstances, Thomas assumed that the Communists would have drugged or tortured Gandhi into making a weird confession. Pacifism in 1950, he warned, would result in surrender to totalitarian might and the defeat of peace and justice.

The war in Korea ended for a time Thomas's hope that disarmament was possible. He saw no practical alternative to an intensified arms buildup. He even believed now that it might be necessary to use the fear of atomic war to keep the peace. Even when rearmament was necessary, as he conceded was the case in 1950, Thomas warned that the nation had to be on guard lest the psychological and economic effects of such mobilization hasten total war.

The Korean War also temporarily ended Thomas's opposition to conscription. His first major political action had been in January 1917, when he led a group of pacifist clergymen who had petitioned against the draft law. He had fought against conscription during World War I, before World War II, and continued to fight against it immediately after the war. Now, in 1951, he testified before the Senate Armed Services Committee in favor of retaining the draft. Thomas argued that Stalin's drive for universal power left no alternative open to the United States except to build a larger army, and this required conscription. Despite his formal support of conscription, Thomas continued to oppose it in principle. He wanted selective service continued as an emergency measure for the duration of the war only; immediately thereafter, he wanted it repealed.[17]

7

By the end of the Korean War, Thomas had abandoned his assumption that socialism offered the alternative to war. He no longer considered capitalism the cause of war nor socialism the panacea. He still believed war had economic roots, and that in a capitalist economy capitalism would perforce be a root cause of war. But he now reasoned that under another economic system that system would be the cause. He considered nationalism, similarly, to be a cause of war, but he no longer considered nationalism itself a product of the capitalist order. The Soviet Union under Stalin, Thomas argued in 1953, was not a capitalist nation in the accepted meaning of the term, yet it was a nationalist, imperialist power.

It would be dangerous, Thomas argued, to insist that peace be made dependent on a "fairly rigid politico-economic system." There was little prospect that any such system would develop in the foreseeable future, and men had to live at peace despite differences in ideals and interests. Religious leaders had too often caused wars with their insistence that only they knew the true road to salvation; and Thomas warned Socialists that they had to avoid this pitfall. He now held that Socialists ought to work for peace within the framework of democratic institutions and free of dogma.

Despite misgivings about the United Nations, by the mid-1950's Thomas suggested that it be given additional power. He believed that it might eventually be able to enforce the concept of the rule of law in international affairs. He also favored a permanent UN police force capable of "putting out" small wars. But he remained opposed to world government because "there is in our time not even the minimum common denominator of culture, economic development, and traditional loyalties which would make possible anything like what mankind associates with the word 'government' on a world-wide scale."[18]

8

Thomas's search for a disarmed world and his anti-communism created a dilemma for him which he could never wholly resolve. He recognized that there could be no disarmament without agreement between capitalist and Communist nations—primarily, that is, between the United States and the Soviet Union. At the same time, he rejected any assumption that there could be an accommodation between the two power blocs. He thus rejected suggestions that he and his few remaining fellow Socialists remain neutral in the East-West power struggle. He claimed that there could be no middle ground in the power struggle between totalitarianism and democracy, thus rejecting his pre–World War II insistence that there were no right and wrong sides in "imperialist" wars, a position which helped lead him into isolationism. He now maintained that Cold War tensions were the responsibility of Stalin. He cited the Soviet record of broken treaties, Stalin's alliance with Hitler, the seizure of "free nations" by the Soviet Union during and after the war, the Berlin blockade, the aggression in Korea, and Stalin's persistent rejection of "all workable plans for disarmament."

Soon after Stalin's death and the thaw that followed, Thomas was hopeful about the possibility of a major change in international relations, but the forcible repression of the 1956 uprising in Hungary killed that hope. "As for Hungary," he wrote his friend Hugh Gaitskell, leader of the British Labour party, "our hopes had been so high. Now they have literally been drowned in innocent blood. The world . . . should know that communism has not shaken off those terrible errors concerning the road to socialism which began with Lenin not Stalin." Nikita Khrushchev had denounced Stalin, Thomas said, but he had not renounced Stalin's methods or philosophy. What he had changed were tactics not objectives. Thomas saw no possibility of converting the Soviet rulers to the "spirit of Christmas" as did some pacifists. The most that he hoped for from the rulers of the Soviet Union was the realization that their own lives and positions were endangered in a new war.

A. J. Muste was among those pacifists who believed that the spirit of Christian charity would prevail among the rulers of the

Soviet Union if only the United States would set the proper example by disarming unilaterally. Thomas disagreed: "I think, to talk unilateral disarmament is to hurt not improve our chances for the only thing that will save us [from destruction]: universal disarmament. If the United States . . . had merely completely disarmed immediately after World War II . . . I think that communism would have covered Europe and probably made greater advances in Asia. And it would not have been a peaceful communism, for the Communist struggles for power under those circumstances *under* Stalin would have assumed desperate proportions." Had not Lenin called war between capitalist and Communist nations inevitable? All that stood between Khrushchev and military conquest of the world, Thomas argued, was his realization that the development of nuclear weapons had made military adventures too costly, with no victor possible. Thomas argued that communism could not be strangled militarily. His proposed alternative was thus a competition of ideas in place of a competition of might.

Thomas's rejection of Muste's pacifist proposal of unilateral disarmament was balanced by his refusal to go along with Sidney Hook's argument that nuclear war would be preferable to surrender to the USSR. He suggested that Hook presented the alternatives in "too clear-cut form." Hook, he said, made an erroneous assumption that freedom could survive an atomic war, which Thomas doubted even "in the dubious event that men in considerable numbers should survive the vast physical, social, and moral devastation of nuclear war." At any rate, there were, he claimed, alternatives to nuclear war in the struggle against communism; these included "democracy's zeal for peace and disarmament . . . , development of the will and capacity to resist a conqueror by Gandhian methods, or by the cultivation of guerrilla techniques." Hook and others, he argued, oversimplified the alternatives; the choice was not between communism and war. Thomas denied that Russia's expansion was accomplished by force of arms alone; the Soviet domain grew, he insisted, by exploiting the social misery and injustice prevalent throughout the world. He noted that the expansion of communism was aided by the work of native communists; Russia had never conquered a nation without that nation having a strong Communist party. (This argument was, at best, questionable: Poland, for example, which the Soviets turned into a Communist state in 1944, had no Communist party after 1938 when Stalin killed most of that country's Communist leaders and then dissolved the party.) The danger of a Communist takeover of the United States or the United Kingdom was thus, Thomas argued, nonexistent.[19]

9

A forty-seven-page pamphlet Thomas wrote in 1953 emphasized his changed view of the world and of human nature. Entitled *Democratic Socialism: A New Appraisal*, it outsold any other Thomas book or pamphlet and was quoted widely as proof that Thomas had abandoned socialism, a charge that he denied. Despite his denial, the pamphlet leaves little doubt that Thomas had in fact abandoned socialism. The man who had as late as 1938 insisted that he was a "pretty good Marxianist" was fifteen years later proclaiming that "it is . . . untenable to hold a rigid view of the materialistic conception of history which Marx advanced." He now asserted that history had made many Marxian concepts, including the class struggle, anachronisms. In the ultimate heresy against Marx, Thomas declared: "The groups into which men divide are not exclusively determined by economics. Consider the importance of nationalism and religion, neither of which is adequately explained by economic determination, in drawing men together. . . . [There] is no such tight fusion of all different economic groups into two and only two contending classes of owners and workers, as Marxism postulated." Moreover, the fellowship of free men, which Thomas and his fellow democratic Socialists sought, could not be the "automatic consequence of the victory of 'the workers' in a class struggle."

Actually, Thomas's views almost coincided with those of the Russian anarchist Peter Kropotkin, after conceding that many of Kropotkin's postulates were "subject to revision in the light of our increased knowledge of the evolutionary process." Thomas declared Kropotkin's theory of mutual aid—which held that there was a biologically ordained symbiotic relationship between all men, which required a system of society based on voluntary cooperation rather than competition—"indispensable to the great achievements of humanity." Mutual aid was, in Thomas's opinion, ethical and moral rather than moral and "scientific." It was man's disregard for this principle, he maintained, which had led to innumerable wars. Since "the great ends" of peace, plenty, and brotherhood, which Thomas assumed man desired, required "a social goal and an ethical approach to unite and inspire men," he suggested that it could be found in mutual aid. The so-called revolutionary Socialists and Communists as well as the defenders of laissez-faire capitalism talked of society as though it were an amoral fact, but Thomas maintained that "every attempt to construct an amoral politico-economic system . . . independent of ethics, has been fraught with disaster."

There was a distinct difference between the views of Thomas and Kropotkin, despite the former's acceptance of the creed of mutual aid. Kropotkin, who accepted science as his god, based his social theory on biological evolution as propounded by Charles Darwin; Thomas, the nonprofessing social-Christian evangelist, accepted the social theory of mutual aid on the basis of the ethics of Jesus, modified, perhaps, by Walter Rauschenbusch, William D. P. Bliss, and George D. Herron.

Although Thomas's newfound philosophy was anarchist and Christian, he still called himself a democratic Socialist. But now he denied that democratic socialism had an encompassing or complete philosophy of life and the universe. The man who twenty years earlier had insisted that a political party required an overall philosophy now argued that religions "may be formed on an absolute and inclusive philosophy, but not a democratic political party. Part of the genius of democracy must lie in its capacity to progress through compromise." This was an almost complete negation of the Socialist myth that there was an irrepressible struggle between the forces of capitalism and the forces of socialism which could not possibly be compromised—a myth Thomas helped propagate. Thomas now rejected the assumption that social ownership was, invariably, a desirable end. He now suggested that private ownership might be preferable to "statism" under many conditions, especially since social controls, such as labor legislation and taxation, on privately owned enterprises had proven compatible with social planning for social needs. To the old Socialist argument that social ownership would eliminate the conflict between labor and capital, Thomas replied: "Under any conceivable economic order, all workers will always want higher pay for their work and lower prices for commodities which they must buy." Thomas was obviously no longer a Socialist, except in his own redefinition of the term.

But Thomas refused to admit that he was outside the Socialist pale. Socialism, he argued, "like other great words, such as Christianity, has come to mean many and rather different things to different men." To Thomas socialism meant, in order of importance, the democratic process in all government controls and operations; cooperation—or mutual aid—as a dominant principle; and government control which "does not always and necessarily mean government ownership."

Thomas's changed position on social ownership did not indicate any lessening of his antipathy to the morality of American capitalism. "We have an acquisitive society," Thomas wrote, "in which we tend to measure the worth of a man by his wealth. The wastelands of our own lives and of our culture are in no small part the consequence of false standards of value inherent in the grim struggle for profit which encourages escape through vulgar sensationalism." The result of this capitalist ethic was, according to Thomas, corruption, fraud, and graft which were inherent in the system.

Norman Thomas's socialism was modified, but his Social Gospel was not.[20]

X
Blessed
are the
peacemakers

After Korea, Thomas resumed his anti-militarist campaign, thus exacerbating the dilemma caused by his opposition to the use of military force and his anti-communism. But a problem that had been latent became manifest in 1960 in connection with his work for the Committee for a Sane Nuclear Policy, which Thomas had helped found in 1957.

Sane, as the committee came to be known, was originally organized at the behest of A. J. Muste at an informal meeting of the representatives of the Fellowship of Reconciliation, the Women's International League for Peace and Freedom, the War Resisters League, and the Religious Society of Friends. Muste was delegated to bring together a group of prominent Americans to head a new organization to oppose the continuation of nuclear testing and to fight against the nuclear arms race. The first two men he sought out were Thomas and Norman Cousins, editor of the *Saturday Review*. They were the nucleus around which Sane developed.

The response to Sane was unexpected; it grew, to quote Thomas, "rather like Topsy." Within three years of its establishment, the loosely organized group filled the eighteen-thousand-seat Madison Square Garden in New York, and Thomas led a parade of five thousand to the United Nations to plead for peace. As often happened in such organizations, the well-organized Communists infiltrated Sane and attempted to dominate it. Especially in New York was Sane heavily laden with Communists and Communist fellow-travelers. In 1960, Senator Thomas Dodd charged that the Communists were gaining control of the organization—a charge not wholly without merit. The Senate Internal Security Committee subpoenaed Henry

Abrams, one of the organizers of the Madison Square Garden meeting and a former member of the American Labor party when it was under Communist control. Abrams refused to testify, citing the Fifth Amendment. The national board of Sane asked Abrams whether he was a Communist; he again refused to answer "on principle." Thomas then insisted that Sane "take reasonable precautions that men and women elected to official positions in national and local organizations" shall not be Communists or fellow-travelers. The alternative, he warned, would be the dissolution of the organization. He denied that his action was an infringement on anyone's civil liberties, since Communists and their followers, who opposed American but not Soviet atomic saber-rattling, "have no more right to positions of power [in Sane] . . . than [do] Roman Catholics to become officers of the Methodist Church or vice versa."

Sane's national board issued a policy statement barring Communists from membership. The statement, which merely reaffirmed an already established Sane policy, set off a massive struggle within the organization. Robert Gilmore, who represented the American Friends Service Committee and whom Thomas had called Sane's "guiding hand and brain," resigned in protest. The New York City Sane chapter openly opposed the national policy. Thirty-seven members of the New York organization were subpoenaed by Senate investigators; the national board, at Thomas's insistence, refused to come to their defense. When the New York organization protested, the national board revoked its charter. The *Nation*, among others, assailed Thomas's action, but he prevailed and remained active in Sane until his forced retirement, seven years later.[1]

Despite his experience with Sane, Thomas was not disheartened in his search for an effective anti-war peace group which would be politically sophisticated enough to bar Communists and their fellow-travelers. As late as 1962, the indefatigable Thomas was instrumental in forming the Turn Toward Peace, which the *New York Times* described as the largest single force in the peace movement. Composed of twenty organizations, ranging from the militantly pacifist Committee for Nonviolent Action to the American Veterans Committee to the Church of the Brethren to several trade unions, its aim was to devise an alternative to the threat of war as the primary means for implementing United States foreign policy. All of the groups involved agreed that such an alternative would require the preclusion of any surrender of democratic values. Significantly, the seventy-eight-year-old Thomas was able to coalesce such disparate organizations. But by 1962 he was too old and tired to carry the burden of organization, and the Turn Toward Peace never achieved its potential.[2]

2

The crises of the later 1950's and 1960's, and Thomas's reactions to them, pointed up his inability to recognize that there could be no absolute victory for absolute justice.

Thomas had long felt that the "entire gentile world bears a burden of guilt for anti-Semitism . . . ," and for many years Thomas shared "the guilt complex of the Christian world because of anti-Semitism." But he could not bring himself to accept Zionism or Israel as the answers to the Jewish problem. He opposed "political Zionism, as a matter of principle." He believed the Zionist movement was retrogressive, in that it led the Jews from liberal internationalism to narrow nationalism. He feared that the Jews could have their homeland only at the expense of the Moslem Arabs. He assumed that the Christian world would thus be able to escape the onus of its own anti-Semitism by making the innocent Arabs the vicarious sufferers for the Christians' crimes. Essentially, Thomas favored the binational state concept of Rabbi Judah Magnes, which foresaw an Arab-Jewish Palestine with its capital in Jerusalem. Although he recognized that both Arabs and Jews rejected the Magnes proposal, he was primarily annoyed at Jewish intransigence.

Although the *kibbutz* movement and the democratic socialist orientation of the Zionist leaders had impressed him for many years, Thomas remained highly critical of the State of Israel after its establishment. "I am . . . very skeptical of the success of political Zionism," he wrote Rabbi Elmer Berger, leader of the violently anti-Zionist American Council for Judaism. "I think that, if I were a Jew, I would join your organization." But Thomas's anti-Zionism was by no means anti-Semitic, for he favored asylum in the United States for Jews from Europe, and had worked for such asylum since the 1920's. With good reason, he accused some American Christian pro-Zionists of favoring the establishment of the Jewish state in the Middle East in order to keep more Jews out of this country. He challenged the ethical right of the English or the Americans to give away any part of Palestine to the Jews because "they were giving away what was not theirs." Yet when the Jewish state was established in 1948, Thomas proposed that the United States offer it immediate and full recognition, called on the United Nations to seat Israel as a full member, and urged that it be given sufficient control of enough territory to assure its economic viability. Thomas vehemently opposed the proposal by Count Folke Bernadotte, the UN representative in Palestine, that the Negev region be given to the Arabs. But by 1956 Thomas was upset by three developments which became apparent during the decade: the rise of Jewish and Israeli nationalism, the fear of a religious state there, and his impression that the Arabs were denied their rights. Jewish nationalism was nowhere more apparent than in New York State with its large Jewish population. During the 1956 senatorial campaign in which Jacob Javits defeated Robert Wagner, Thomas was "worried that both of you thought you were running for mayor of Tel Aviv because of the prominence given discussion of the question of how to help Israel." He agreed that Jews had "a special reason to be interested in the prosperity of Israel. But Israel is one nation and the United States is another. . . ." Moreover, he feared that the ultra-Orthodox Jews were working toward making Israel into a "narrow Jewish state and society." This religious nationalism, Thomas opposed, for in his version of the Social Gospel nationalism was equated with Satan.

Not all Social Gospeleers agreed with Thomas on Israel. Many saw in the Israelis' high level of social consciousness much of what they themselves equated with Judeo-Christianity. The pro-Israeli Social Gospel movement was organized into the American Christian Palestine Committee, one of whose leaders was Thomas's old colleague, Reinhold Niebuhr. Thomas called the committee members *Shabbos Goyim.** "What troubles me," he wrote to Niebuhr, "is the extraordinary partisanship for Israel which some liberals, especially liberal churchmen, yourself included,

---

* Yiddish for Sabbath Gentiles. Because pious Orthodox Jews are prohibited from lighting fires or doing any work on the Sabbath, non-Jews are employed to do household chores on the Sabbath. Thomas, it might be noted, had in his long association with Jewish Socialists become quite proficient in the Yiddish language.

have shown. [It] doesn't help in the education of Jew or Arab to a necessary reconciliation. . . . Hope that Israel will be a blessing certainly depends on beginning the slow process of reconciliation."

The hope for Arab-Israeli reconciliation diminished almost immediately after the establishment of the Jewish state. By 1956 it vanished completely in the short war in the Sinai Peninsula. Thomas agreed that the Arab nations were, at least in part, to blame for the hostilities. "They should have accepted the armistice and worked for a settlement. Egypt ought to have kept the Canal open to Israeli shipping." But, he insisted, "Israel as well as Egypt had flouted the UN armistice commission" and the Arab guerrillas, the *fedayeen,* were recruited primarily from among homeless Arabs "whose lands [the] Israeli now enjoy." He deplored Israel's invasion of the Sinai peninsula because he feared that it would increase Arab hatred and thus darken Israel's future. Thomas therefore supported President Eisenhower's call for the United Nations action against Israel and its allies in the Suez adventure, France and Great Britain.

In late 1957, Thomas spent six weeks touring the Middle East with Don Peretz, one of the few American experts in that area of the world. After visiting Egypt, Iraq, Lebanon, Syria, Jordan, and Israel, Thomas returned favorably impressed with Israel, particularly its attempts to integrate the various strains of Jews from different cultures into the social and economic life of the country. He was also convinced that Israel was moving rapidly in the direction of raising its Arab minority to a position of equality. But he was still disturbed by the hostility between Israel and the Arab states. He wanted Israel to take the lead in solving the problems of the area by convincingly presenting "positive proposals containing some sort of pledges and proof that she . . . is eager to find practicable ways to do justice to the refugees as human beings—not pawns in politics." He insisted that America was morally obligated to aid in this endeavor and that the Arab states, on whom he placed much of the blame for the refugee problem, had to cooperate as well. They had, after all, been responsible for the exodus by inferring that the Arabs would return to their lands in triumph.

After ten years of life as a nation, it would be impossible for Israel or the Arabs to turn back the clock of history. Thomas maintained in 1958 that the Arab fears of Israeli expansion, and the ambivalence of Israeli leaders on the issue, worsened the situation, but the Arabs had to recognize that Israel was a permanent fixture on the map of the Middle East. His views received favorable notice among Israelis, both inside the government and out. But in the United States, the once-Socialist *Jewish Daily Forward* attacked him as an enemy of the Jewish state because he insisted on raising pertinent questions on Israeli policy.[3] The constant skirmishing between Israelis and Arabs culminating in the 1967 Six-Day War caused him anguish. Although he opposed the Israeli action, he recognized that it had been caused by Soviet-Arab provocations, and he supported the official Socialist party statement which was sympathetic to the Israelis.

3

Since his days at Princeton, Thomas had rejected his father's religious creed and moral code. In 1963, he wondered whether his father's philosophy, apart from its strict Calvinism, its narrow Sabbatarianism, and its overly enthusiastic belief in heaven and hell, was without advantage, and admitted that he preferred the morality of his youth—when his father's creed was dominant—to the new morality.

Having rejected his father's faith in an omnipotent, omniscient, and anthropomorphic God, Thomas did not follow in the footsteps of many of his fellow Social Gospeleers, who redefined God to fit their own non-theistic social code. Instead he became a self-professed agnostic unaffiliated with any religious body or movement. He called religion basically escapist. And "the current return to religion" he found to be "a reaction from the failure of man to solve his problems by his own reason." With the development of the atomic bomb, he said, "science . . . the hope of the turn of the century, has revealed its potentialities for the destruction of the race." Faced with the demise of science as man's hope, Thomas maintained, people were turning to religion. One of man's new religions, he said, was the secular faith of communism. Like believers in the "divine" religions, Communists assumed the dogmatic posture of intolerance on the assumption that "they have a hold on truth, of all the truth, a truth which for the salvation of mankind they have a right to enforce, no matter how." Thomas agreed there was a difference: Communist intolerance ended on this earth, it did not follow the victim after his death; orthodox religion's intolerance was, on the contrary, infinite and eternal and could not be erased by mere death.

The heritage of orthodox Christianity, Thomas declared, was a heightening of man's inhumanity to man. Citing the doctrine of hell, Thomas asked: "Why should we be kinder than God to his enemies?" The eternal torture of hell as a punishment for mistaken belief or wrong conduct had fortified—or perhaps even suggested—the cruelties of the twentieth-century world. "If God can carry on eternal concentration camps in the interest of his truth or his power or his divine ability to choose the elect; if God can do that, why can't a Hitler or a Stalin use concentration camps and cruelty to enforce his particular religion?"

Thomas was convinced that religion as organized in the mid-twentieth century offered no salvation for humanity or civilization. It could only offer salvation to individual believers—and even that was "out of the world." He argued that its value to its followers did not rest on its contributions to better racial or economic relations, or to the problem of war. And these for Thomas were the "challenges which must be met if our civilization is to endure." Unless humanity recognized that social problems must be met, it would fail in the twentieth century "as badly as did Catholic medievalism, the Protestant reformation, or yesterday's humanistic rationalism to save an unfraternal civilization from the disintegration of social injustice and the destruction of war."[4]

Whatever the appearances to the contrary, Thomas had not abandoned the Social Gospel. He accepted its basic assumptions; he still accepted the values of the Social Gospel—temporal rather than divine salvation, economic equality, and Puritan morality. But he no longer accepted some of the rhetoric of Social Christianity, considering it hypocrisy to pledge obeisance to a God and a religion which had laid the groundwork for the travail of humanity.

4

The 1960's were a period of great pessimism for Thomas. True, he had lived to see many of the proposals he supported against what was once almost universal opposition accepted by most Americans, even the very conservative. No one seriously opposed Social Security any more, nor was there any serious effort made to abolish collective bargaining, or any of the other New Deal innovations which Socialists had originally proposed and against which Republicans and many Democrats had railed. But the outlook for peace and democracy was still bleak. Thomas still believed that in pacifism "lies our hope," but he feared that the evil of authoritarianism had made the pacifist "attempt to conquer evil with good" a failure. The radical movement which he had known and led was disintegrating. The Socialist party and the Social Democratic Federation did reunite in 1957; Max Shachtman, the former Trotskyite turned moderate Social Democrat, had returned to the Socialist fold, but even with the added strength there were barely a thousand members in the party. There was now a new radical movement, the New Left, whose followers "don't really know whether they are Trotskyites or pacifists," as Thomas complained. Their irrationality disturbed him, as did their refusal to abide by Thomas's puritanical standards of dress, behavior, and language.

There were other reasons for Thomas's pessimism. By the 1960's, it was apparent that the military-industrial complex was gaining an increasing hold on the colleges and universities of the nation. Thomas warned the 1963 graduating class at Haverford College that higher education was in peril because government contracts have become "virtually a substitute for intellectual curiosity."[5]

By 1960, Thomas was seventy-six and, by his own admission, an old man. But he was still articulate and politically active— first as a moderate supporter of the liberal wing of the Democratic party and, for the last three years of his life, a severe though somewhat tarnished critic of American policy. In 1960, he supported Adlai Stevenson and, when the Democrats nominated John F. Kennedy, complained that he was "not at all happy" because he feared "most of the issues will be terribly blurred." A small group of Stevenson supporters in California agreed, and attempted to nominate Thomas and A. Philip Randolph, the Negro labor leader, for President and Vice-President. But Thomas refused because "neither of us . . . can afford to do what is obviously futile." In the end, Thomas supported Kennedy and Johnson, though reluctantly.[6]

Race relations and the problems raised by automation were the two domestic problems that absorbed most of Thomas's interest during the early 1960's. Thomas had pleaded for racial equality as early as 1919, and in the 1930's had been singularly active in organizing sharecroppers, many of whom were Negro, in an effort to help them win racial and economic equality. For most of his political life, Thomas demanded an end to the poll tax which prevented Negroes from voting, urged federal intervention to assure the right of Negroes to vote in the South, and pleaded for fair employment practices laws, a nonsegregated military establishment, federal aid to education with anti-discrimination provisions, total desegregation, and an end to all legal disabilities facing Negroes. His 1956 proposal for a bipartisan commission on race relations won the support of Maxwell M. Rabb, President Eisenhower's chief personal aide, but Eisenhower refused to support it. By 1963, Thomas maintained that all civil rights legislation would be futile unless the economy were healthy and there was full employment. No one could find freedom or human dignity in "equality of joblessness." He feared that the increasing automation of industry posed a serious threat to the Negro's ability to share in prosperity. Most Negroes were unskilled, and it was the unskilled who would lose their jobs as machines took over the "backbreaking, monotonous, dull, repetitive tasks" for which unskilled workmen were normally employed. As a solution, Thomas proposed planning and large-scale education in job skills.[7]

During the 1964 presidential campaign, Thomas said of Lyndon B. Johnson: "We all have reason to be grateful for him, in the way he is handling civil rights and poverty. I ought to rejoice and I do. I rub my eyes in amazement and surprise." If Thomas was enthusiastic about Johnson, he was almost ecstatic about his running mate, Hubert H. Humphrey, whom he called "the type of Democrat I like and who would be a Socialist if he got to England." The Republican candidate, Barry Goldwater, was, in Thomas's opinion, "the greatest evil" in American politics, and he called Governor George A. Wallace, who entered Democratic primaries against Johnson, a disgrace. Thomas campaigned actively for Johnson.[8]

5

Because of his commitment to the anti-Communist left, Thomas was to find his reputation tarnished by his relations with the Central Intelligence Agency. Thomas's involvement with the CIA dated back to the 1950's, when he knowingly obtained funds for the Congress for Cultural Freedom through the CIA. But this went unnoticed during the era of violent anti-communism. His second involvement with the CIA in the 1960's left an undeserved blemish on Thomas's reputation.

In 1957, Thomas and Sacha Volman, a Rumanian refugee who had been in Nazi and Soviet concentration camps, organized the Institute for International Labor Research which trained pro-democratic Latin-American political and labor leaders. Among those affiliated with the organization were José Figueros, the American-educated, democratic Socialist ex-president of Costa Rica, and Juan Bosch, the pro-Socialist Dominican leader. The Institute was in almost constant financial trouble until 1960, when an appeal from Thomas brought it financial aid from the J. M. Kaplan Foundation. This help allowed the Institute to expand its work against both the Communists, who had by then become dominant in Cuba, and the military dictatorships, which were endemic in Latin America.

In 1963, after the ouster of Dominican dictator Rafael Trujillo, the Institute moved to Santo Domingo, where it produced films to teach illiterate Latin peasants how to read and write. It helped Bosch to become president of the Dominican Republic. When a military coup overthrew the Bosch regime in 1964, Thomas and the Institute left the Dominican Republic. A few months later Dominican sources allied with the military dictatorship charged that Thomas and Bosch had both been aided by CIA money funneled through the Kaplan Foundation to the Institute; Thomas denied knowledge of any CIA aid. In 1965, the Institute condemned the United States for its intervention on the side of the anti-Bosch forces. Kaplan Foundation funds were also used by Thomas to publish a strong attack on American actions during the civil war—especially the dispatch of troops to support the anti-Bosch forces.

During the 1966 Dominican election, Bosch threatened to withdraw as a candidate because the military prevented him from campaigning effectively and because his life and the lives of his associates were threatened. Thomas pleaded with Bosch not to withdraw, offering to send in hundreds of observers to assure that the election would be fair. On the basis of this assurance,

Bosch remained in the race. Thomas, Bayard Rustin, and some seventy other Socialists acted as observers in the election. Bosch was defeated by Joaquim Balaguer, a moderate conservative who had been linked to the Trujillo dictatorship. Thomas and his colleagues, however, called the election fair and honest.

Then in early 1967 a check revealed that the 1964 charge that Thomas's Institute had received considerable aid from the CIA was true. Thomas denied that he knew the source of the money. "I am ashamed that we swallowed this CIA business," he said. But "what we did was good work and no one tried to tell us what to do." He agreed that "if I had a choice I would never have accepted CIA support." J. M. Kaplan, the man who acted as the funnel for CIA gifts to the Institute, agreed that Thomas "never knew where we got the money for the substantial grants."[9]

6

American involvement in the Vietnam War was to bring Thomas full circle back to his pacifism of 1918. He had as early as 1947 appealed to his friend Léon Blum, the French Socialist leader and premier, to find a nonimperialist solution to the Vietnamese war for independence. He conceded that Ho Chi Minh and his followers were Communists, but he warned that "communism and a latent fascism will be the direct or indirect gainers from the effort of the French government under any pretext to maintain by force its very dubious dominion over Indo-China. . . ." He did not consider French colonialism to be the proper alternative to the threat of communism in Southeast Asia.

When the French were driven out of Vietnam in 1954, Thomas had some second thoughts about the danger of communism. In 1956, he signed a letter that read: "It seems clear, then, that no moral obligation remains to insist upon fulfillment of the 1954 Geneva pronouncement. What commitments there might have been have been negated by the consistent armistice violation of the [Communist] Viet Minh." Thomas supported the supposedly nationalist but admittedly corrupt and authoritarian Diem regime in South Vietnam on the assumption that it could both retard the advance of communism and end colonialism in Indo-China. But by 1963, Thomas began to have second thoughts about the threat which communism posed: the Communist monolith, he postulated, had now become a polycentric force, with centers in Peking and Belgrade struggling for power with the center at Moscow. Thomas also recognized the grave danger which the growing power of the military posed for the United States as a democracy. Thus in 1963 he suggested that the United States seek a peaceful alternative to military involvement. But he considered Vietnam to be a minor issue; in a 280-page book written in 1963, in which more than one hundred pages were devoted to international affairs, there was only one passing reference to Vietnam.

It was not until January 1965 that Thomas actively assailed American intervention in Southeast Asia. In a lengthy letter to the *New York Times,* he called for immediate withdrawal from Vietnam. A victory for the pro-Communist Viet Cong, he wrote, would result, "at worst, in a Yugoslav type of communism" which he considered "infinitely preferable" to the alternative of Asian or world war. "In a bad situation the worst thing possible is American participation in Vietnam's civil war, and the time for extrication is now." Two months later, Thomas threw all of his energy into the movement to withdraw from Vietnam. At the age of eighty-one, in a ten-hour debate on the war with his former colleague, Frank Trager, he warned that "this is a war you do not win." In June, he told seventeen thousand listeners at a Sane rally in Madison Square Garden that an American effort to police the world would only unite "a divided communism." He allied himself with Dr. Benjamin Spock in working to extricate America from an "immoral" and "stupid" war which "I think we had no right getting into." He engaged in a private heated debate with Dean Rusk on the war in the Secretary of State's office. Thomas reported: "I went. We talked, and perhaps we understand each other better now. But we made no converts."

When President Johnson offered to talk to "any government, any place, any time," Thomas ridiculed his posture, because Johnson did not consider the National Liberation Front, the political organ of the pro-Communist forces in South Vietnam, a government. Thomas insisted that Johnson had to offer unconditional negotiations. "The President, who has knocked on many doors, must now knock on the Viet Cong's door, insistently and clearly." Accused of being inconsistent in supporting the American intervention in Korea and opposing it in Vietnam, Thomas answered that Korea was a defense against aggression, Vietnam an assault against indigenous rebels.[10]

The failure of Johnson to extricate the United States from the war in Vietnam embittered Thomas against him within a year after the 1964 election. An early supporter of Eugene McCarthy, the anti-war candidate for the Democratic nomination, Thomas refused in 1968 to support his old friend Vice President Humphrey for the nomination, or for election, until the last week of the campaign. "No memory of personal friendship should make me endorse a politician who has been so opportunistic about the terrible war in Vietnam," he wrote in August 1968. After the election, he admitted that he was not unhappy at Humphrey's defeat, though "I think very little of Nixon." Thomas accused Humphrey of being so equivocal in the campaign that he "could contradict himself and then deny doing it."[11]

7

In May 1966, Thomas's raincoat caught in a taxicab door as he was leaving the cab, and he was dragged along Nineteenth Street in New York. After a week in the hospital, he resumed his activities, which at this point meant speaking throughout the country four or five times a week. He spoke out against the war in Vietnam, against conscription ("the chief denial of civil liberty of which the state is capable"), and against racial and economic injustice. At the age of eighty-one he mused: "I like human beings. I'm glad I'm one of them. But I think we're crazy. . . . We're irrational. Look at our race prejudice, look at our inability to get out of war, look at the crazy things we do in our personal lives. . . . If only we used our brains, we might just come out well." He was worried that in his old age he was accepted, tolerated, and admired. That, he bemoaned, was bad—a dissenter must never be tolerated.

In October 1967, "blind, crippled by arthritis and an automobile accident, his face chalky white from heart trouble . . . [Thomas] reached a podium at the Sheraton-Atlantic Hotel [in New York] with the help of two persons" to make what was billed as his farewell address to 109 students. He delivered a strong speech at the rate of two hundred words per minute, his age and infirmities undetectable as he spoke. He announced that on January 1, 1968, he would close his office of forty-six years and withdraw "from all committees I've worked with—how many? I don't know, lots." This, he said, was to be his last speech. But Thomas could not keep his promise; he had to deliver one more speech. Two weeks later he addressed four hundred anti-war labor leaders in Chicago, and on his way home from the rally suffered a stroke. He was hospitalized, then moved into a nursing home, where he dictated *Choices,* his last book. A month before his death, a reporter found him to be "vigorous in mind and ebullient in mood, but gloomy about the state of the nation."

On December 19, 1968, Norman Thomas died in his sleep in a nursing home in Huntington, Long Island, at the age of eighty-four.[12]

XI
Full circle

The Socialist party Norman Thomas left behind at his death in 1968 was a shell of the party over which he had assumed leadership in 1928. Its membership had declined to less than one thousand, it no longer entered election campaigns—not a single Socialist held elective office—and it was almost totally ignored as a political force, even among radicals. Perhaps time had passed the party by, perhaps it was no longer a relevant entity. But there were indications in 1968 and 1969 that democratic socialism still had relevance—in Sweden, the Socialists had won their first clear parliamentary majority in twenty-eight years; in Canada, the democratic Socialists had won control of Manitoba and were threatening to become a major party nationally; Labour and Social Democratic parties were showing signs of resurgence in Australia, in Germany, in New Zealand; and in the United Kingdom the ruling Labour party was again talking about its commitment to democratic socialism. The fact was, under the leadership of Norman Thomas the Socialist party of the United States had disintegrated and was on the verge of total extinction because it had lost its reason for existence. Part of the reason for the Socialist decline was Thomas's style of leadership.

Thomas was a popular figure, respected by Socialists and non-Socialists during all of his career as a Socialist leader. A Republican state legislator once said that "if socialism were synonymous with Norman Thomas, I should have no misgivings [about socialism]. . . ." There was little reason why even the most socially conservative Americans should have any misgivings about a man who looked "like a cultivated aristocrat," and who "would fit naturally into the atmosphere of an English manor house party with Balfour and Asquith," as one conservative observer noted. Thomas's speeches depended more upon what Claude Moore Fuess described as "logic than upon emotions," and his manner was "faintly academic." Yet, as Thomas himself admitted, "it has been my fate to be able to do little to influence American public opinion." He was, in fact, respected and admired because he had so little influence. Unable to put his own programs into effect, Thomas could be, "in the way of Isaiah and Micah, a prophet among us to chide us when we do wrong."[1] But he could do little more. He was a moral reformer, in the sense that Wendell Phillips once used the term. It was as a politician, not as a reformer, that he failed. He could not surrender half his ideals to achieve the other half. And to succeed, as Thomas's hero Wendell Phillips realized, a politician had to be prepared to make such compromises.

Thomas won the hearts, if not the votes, of many Americans because he served a distinct function for them. He was "a great denouncer, aroused to indignation by one injustice or another and so skillful with words and so sharp and witty that he carried almost every audience with him, often to a standing ovation." In essence, Thomas acted as the conscience of the American people, and as such he served a useful purpose. But he was not a true Socialist politician with the primary aim necessarily of gaining political power in order to remake the society he criticized. As his closest friend Roger Baldwin pointed out, Thomas was "a dissenter from the system and values of American society . . . an opponent of any society, whatever its label, marked by oppression of the human spirit or denial of equality and justice." It was because his audience could share his indignation at the injustices of the world that it could respect and admire him.[2] He articulated much of their own feeling—but he could not convince enough of them that he could bring about a change in these conditions, and this made him an unsuccessful politician and an unsuccessful leader of the American Socialist party.

In denouncing evil in the world, and in portraying a heaven on earth, Thomas was performing his chosen role of evangelist. The greatest part of an evangelist's job is the denunciation of evil and the promise of reward, and this Thomas did with fervor. Like the great evangelist he was, Thomas was an eloquent speaker who loved to face an audience. "He could rise from a chair, when he looked near exhaustion . . . and put such passion and wit into a speech as to win a standing ovation." Like the other great evangelists who preceded him, Thomas was always debating opponents—"seen and unseen." Baldwin recalled that Thomas wrote his notes as though they were an answer to an argument for an opposing position; he was essentially playing the role of a latter-day Jonathan Edwards debating with the devil, except that his diabolical opponent was the social order, and the salvation he offered was social rather than celestial.

Yet Thomas's only church was an amorphous organization called the Socialist movement. It included the party and peripheral organizations (primarily the League for Industrial Democracy), and this movement claimed to be political, not ecclesiastic. It was in great part because he treated the movement as his church that it disintegrated. To argue, as Thomas and his political supporters have done, that the Rooseveltian reforms alone destroyed the Socialist party is to admit the failure of his leadership. For it was the failure of the American Socialist movement under Norman Thomas to move on after one of the "capitalist" politicians adopted its immediate programs that caused the party's demise. In true ecclesiastical fashion, the Socialists refused to permit anyone but a "true believer" to map out the path to the "promised land."

It should have been apparent to anyone who studied the party's decline and fall after 1932 that more was involved in its collapse than simply Roosevelt, though it is true that the New Deal exacerbated its problems. The party's internal squabbling, which Thomas refused to mediate, and in which, on the contrary, he played a significant role, and Thomas's isolationism during the pre–Pearl Harbor period were significant factors in the party's fall. In both instances, Thomas's unwillingness to accept the need for political compromise—the need to choose between possible rather than ideal alternatives—was responsible for the party's failure.

It was only natural that Norman Thomas was more ideologue than practical politician. His background was Calvinist, and based on a dogmatic acceptance of the idea that invariably there were only two choices: good and evil. No room for compromise was allowed. Thomas's own training as a Presbyterian minister reinforced this early environment, and even his departure from the church, and his eventual rejection of it as an institution, did not eliminate the Calvinist influence. In fact, Thomas left the active ministry because church leaders, faced with a condition for which there were no ideal solutions, chose what they considered to be the best possible alternative under the circumstances and supported World War I. Thomas's entry into the Socialist party and abandonment of his parish ministry was merely a political reiteration of his Calvinism. He was appalled by the "inhumanity of Christian institutions" precisely because these institutions had to acclimate themselves to political reality—which he, as an unattached evangelist of the Social Gospel, could avoid doing.[3]

The erroneous assumption that the Socialist party and Norman Thomas's political future were destroyed by the success of the New Deal is based on two facts: Thomas's future had seemed bright from 1929 to 1934; and he had been the choice of independent progressives to be the leader of a new crusade for an American welfare state. But the truth is that Thomas could never have achieved political success; he did not understand that politics must, by definition, be the art of the possible, not the search for absolute ideals. He failed as a politician precisely because he succeeded as an evangelist. *America*, the Jesuit weekly, put it well shortly after his death: "Mr. Thomas grew in public esteem not because he moderated his 'radical' proposals as the years went by, but because so much of what he advocated became the law of the land. So it was with minimum wages, jobless compensation, old-age pensions, health insurance, and a half-dozen other key reforms. Decades before the civil rights crusade and the poverty war, Norman Thomas had mounted the barricades." The truth was that Thomas and the other Social Gospeleers had evangelized so well that much of what they and their Socialist allies preached was adopted by defenders of capitalism. Thomas was not the first evangelist to preach that gospel, nor was he the first to propose those parts of it which were adopted—Socialists had urged a graduated income tax, old-age pensions, unemployment insurance, workmen's compensation, and the abolition of the use of injunctions in labor disputes from 1908 onward.[4] None of the Socialist leaders who preceded Thomas succeeded in winning political power or in having his program enacted by another party. It was Thomas's political misfortune that the program he had been propagating—as had his predecessors—was adopted by a capitalist President while he was the leader of his party. Perhaps the Socialist party would have collapsed as completely had Debs or Berger or Hillquit been at the helm when Roosevelt enacted the New Deal's modified Socialist platform of a quarter-century earlier. More likely, however, these men would have accepted the reality of the situation and worked out a compromise which would have saved the party and its political existence—even if only as a wing of a labor-progressive coalition in the Democratic party. But it was under Thomas's leadership that the party faced the New Deal, and it was his inability to effect a compromise by which the party could have accepted the new realities that helped lead to its demise.

The split of 1936 was more a symptom than a cause of the party's decline. It merely pointed up the social differences within the party: between the stolid, working-class, so-called Marxist Old Guard, the younger, middle-class, intellectual Militants, and the party's pro-Thomas wings. Debs despised the petty bureaucrats in the party as much as did Thomas; certainly he was more militant than Thomas. Yet Debs was able to abide the party functionaries who made up the Old Guard, while Thomas's personal antipathy toward the Old Guard prevented him from reaching an accommodation with them. Debs was a labor leader turned Socialist; despite his animosity for the party hacks, he could understand and work with those members of the working class who by sheer dint of partisan loyalty became the bureaucratic apparatus that is so necessary for the administration of a political or labor organization. Neither Thomas nor his young followers— the intellectuals, ministers, publicists, and university professors —could cooperate with them; the petty bureaucrats' personal aspirations, along with their inherent conservatism on party matters, made them an anathema to the bright young middle-class intellectuals. The unfortunate fact was that Thomas could not understand the working man and his aspirations. While Thomas and his intellectual followers spoke in terms of grandiose utopias where freedom abounded, the worker wanted only an assurance of plenty in a world where tranquility reigned. Writing in 1961 in the Yiddish daily newspaper *Der Tog*, Herman Morgenstern placed Thomas nicely:

"Norman Thomas is the symbol of American socialism and at the same time he is American socialism's greatest liability. . . . On the one hand, he is the only one who popularizes socialism in America; one might say he is socialism's 'prophet.' At the same time he is, unintentionally, doing everything possible to repel the broad masses of workers organized in trade unions from socialism to which he has dedicated his life.

"After all the years that Norman Thomas has been in the movement and close to the trade unions, he still does not understand them. . . .

"Here, in the actuality of the market place . . . the worker and the employer . . . bargain over each penny. . . . The union membership consists of a cross-section of the broad mass of the general public. Some are upright, some are not; yet, above all, the members want to earn a living, for that is the reason for their belonging to unions.

"It is not possible for a man such as Norman Thomas to fit into this situation. On the market place, where the union is active, the cry is 'bread! bread!'; 'another penny! another penny!' [This is] the shrill cry of stark necessity—and this is alien to Norman Thomas. He approaches the labor movement with a conscience, a sympathy, and with abstract justice. In the 'pell mell' of the union . . . on those few occasions where the abstract concept of democracy is violated, Norman Thomas falls into an ecstasy of righteous indignation, and is ready to condemn [the entire labor movement] because of it. He never sees the whole picture—but only just the corner where the injustice was committed. He confuses the cause of the war with the soldier's wounds. Abstract democracy is more important to him than a bigger piece of bread, which is the reverse of what the union offers the worker.

". . . Thomas stands always . . . above right and left, above the practical considerations. . . . He ignores the practical implications of his interventions. . . ."[5]

Granting Morgenstern's overstatement of the case, Thomas's inability to understand the interests of the working class because of his own origins and training made it impossible for him to relate to the petty trade union and Socialist party functionaries who ran the organization, even though his philosophy of gradualism and theirs were almost identical. But he could relate to the Militants, whose ideological position of rhetorical revolution was the opposite of his, because they were both middle-class intellectuals more interested in abstractions than in the practical day-to-day work of a labor or political organization. Thomas's fatal political weakness was apparent to Mayor Daniel W. Hoan of Milwaukee as early as 1933, when he wrote James Oneal that Thomas "leans too heavily on the college groups" and that he was impulsive in union matters. It was this failure to understand the working class, this reliance on the intellectual, that made it impossible for Thomas to devote his energies to salvaging the Socialist party while it rent itself in dubious internal battles from 1934 to 1936. I have earlier noted other of Thomas's traits which helped destroy the party at the time of its multiple schisms: chief among them, his need for the adulation of the young and his refusal to accept the responsibilities of leadership. These, combined with his inability to compromise and unwillingness to reach an agreement with the more working-class-oriented Old Guard, because he neither understood nor appreciated the aspirations of the working class, proved fatal to his political aspirations and American socialism in general. As the *Christian Century* declared in its eulogy of him, "Nobody has manifested more than Norman Thomas the dignity and decency which can be the marks of democratic socialism."[6] Yet these very virtues spelled the doom of Thomas as a politician; dignity and decency are not the chief attributes of the successful political actor.

Five years before his death, Norman Thomas told me that the Socialist party would have disintegrated even if there had been no Roosevelt, no New Deal, and no split in the party. He was, I believe, correct in this assumption. The war issue alone would have caused the party to fall apart. From 1938 onward, no issue so rent the party as did the question of World War II. Party divisions were then no longer along Militant–Old Guard lines; Militant members of the extreme left wing, Old Guard members of the far right wing, and even some normally pro-Thomas intellectuals, broke sharply with him on the war. They recognized that the choice had been narrowed to Hitler or war, however unappealing the alternatives. Thomas and his few remaining followers could not accept this, and instead persisted in demanding the impossible—peace and freedom, when in fact the only choices were peace *or* freedom. Only after the war, when there was no longer a viable Socialist party, did Thomas recognize, grudgingly and with reservations, the real choices. In choosing freedom, Thomas alienated many of his remaining followers; for some, like Travers Clement, still refused to recognize the obvious, and others, like David Dellinger, chose peace over freedom.[7]

Thomas's failure as a politician was merely a reflection of his success as a human being. He came to socialism not because of what it could gain for him personally (he had nothing to gain); he came to socialism because he was an ethical Christian, impressed by the religious and ethical approach to the solution of man's problems. As a true Social Gospeleer, Thomas was convinced that the common good was "no by-product of self-seeking." He became involved in a political movement only because he was convinced that "It's by politics that we'll have peace or war in the end, no matter how much good will is diffused." By 1947, Thomas recognized that he had failed as a political leader. "I have always been aware that a critic might list various factors that qualified my usefulness as a political leader, one of them being my dislike of some of the means that a given situation seems to impose upon a political leader." He conceded that a ruler might do more harm than good if he attempted to rule on a purely moral basis. By 1956, he could write his old friend and one-time vice-presidential running-mate, Tucker P. Smith, that "final moral and political generalizations have to be judged very often in terms of attainable goals. . . ." Yet, even as he wrote those lines, he declared: "I still believe that we fallible men, very imperfectly rational, can make progress toward the only Utopia I can imagine—a fellowship of free men utilizing their marvelous technical skills for life and not for universal destruction."[8] Thomas could never fully accept politics for the halfway house it is—he always required a final goal, a utopia, a heaven on earth.

Fifty-one years after Norman Thomas, the Christian pacifist, spoke to the Quaker youth of Philadelphia in the *Christian Patriot*, the dying Socialist spoke to the youth of the nation in *Choices*. The message was little changed: "As I approach the end of my life, my deepest concern involves the end of war, all war. . . . Will there be interracial fraternity, or war? Will there be economic justice? Can this country help to build a world without war? I believe these goals can be achieved. . . . I continue to say that this world can be motivated and structured in such a way as to achieve a world without war—a world to end the madness which continues to condemn children everywhere to hatred, starvation, disease."[9]

Norman Thomas had returned to the beginning he never left.

Notes

All but four of the periodicals cited in the Notes may be found at the New York Public Library. The exceptions are *Hammer and Tongs*, available at Perkins Memorial Library, Duke University, and at the Tamiment Institute Library, New York University, though neither collection is complete; *World Tomorrow*, available at Princeton University Library and at Union Theological Seminary; *Intercollegiate Socialist*, available at the New York State Library, Albany; and the *Milwaukee Daily Leader*, available at the Milwaukee Public Library.

Introduction

1 Morris Hillquit, *History of Socialism in the United States* (New York, Funk and Wagnalls, 1910), especially pp. 194–357; Daniel Bell, "The Background and Development of Marxian Socialism in the United States," in Donald Drew Egbert and Stow Persons, eds., *Socialism and American Life* (Princeton, Princeton University Press, 1952), especially pp. 242–320; David A. Shannon, *The Socialist Party of America* (Chicago, Quadrangle, 1967), pp. 72–78.

2 Hillquit, *History of Socialism in the United States*, pp. 369–377; Morris Hillquit, *Socialism in Theory and Practice* (New York, Macmillan, 1909).

3 James Dombrowski, *The Early Days of Christian Socialism in America* (New York, Columbia University Press, 1936), especially pp. 17, 19–20, 21, 26–27, 29–30; C. Howard Hopkins, *The Rise of the Social Gospel in American Protestantism, 1865–1915* (New Haven, Yale University Press, 1940); Albert T. Mollegen, "The Religious Basis of Western Socialism," in Egbert and Persons, *Socialism and American Life*, pp. 97–123.

4 Quoted in Irving H. Bartlett, *Wendell Phillips: Brahmin Radical* (Boston, Beacon Press, 1961), pp. 129–130; see also Norman Thomas, *Great Dissenters* (New York, Norton, 1961), pp. 129–168.

5 Roger Baldwin, "Norman Thomas: A Memoir," *Saturday Review*, LII (April 12, 1969), 41–42.

1 The making of a socialist

1 Biographical sketch of Norman Thomas (undated) in files of *Marion Daily Star*; United States Census Office, *12th Census, 1900*, Part I (Washington, D.C., United States Census Office, 1901), p. 469; *World Almanac, 1893* ([New York], Press Publishing Company, 1893), p. 366; *World Almanac, 1897* ([New York], Press Publishing Company, 1897), p. 457; *American Almanac, Yearbook, Cyclopaedia, and Atlas for 1904*

(New York, W. R. Hearst, 1903), p. 787; interview with Norman Thomas, Oneonta, New York, October 1963; interview with Homer Waddell, Marion, Ohio, June 1968; interview with Charlton Myers, Marion, Ohio, June 1968. Norman Thomas, *As I See It* (New York, Macmillan, 1932), pp. 155–159; *Portrait and Biographical Record of Marion and Hardin Counties, Ohio* (Chicago, Chapman Publishing Company, 1895), pp. 515–516; *Marion Daily Star*, June 4, 1901; *New Leader*, August 18, 1928; George Arthur Johnson, *A History of the Marion Presbytery, 1836–1952* (Marion, Marion Presbytery, 1952), pp. 48–50; *Our Hundredth Anniversary* (Marion, First Presbyterian Church, 1928), p. 11.

2 Interview with Homer Waddell, June 1968; interview with Norman Thomas, October 1963; *Commencement Program*, Marion High School, Grand Opera House, Marion, Ohio, May 31, 1901 (in personal holdings of Homer Waddell); Raymond Warren Young, "American Socialism Under the Leadership of Norman Thomas" (unpublished Ph.D. dissertation, Johns Hopkins University, 1949), p. 48; *New Leader*, August 25 and September 1, 1928; Norman Thomas to Professor Sinclair W. Armstrong, November 12, 1956, in Norman Thomas Collection, New York Public Library (hereafter cited as NT Papers); for data on Winthrop M. Daniels, see *New York Times*, January 4, 1944, p. 17; for data on Walter Augustus Wyckoff, see *New York Times*, May 16, 1908, p. 1, and *New York Tribune*, May 16, 1908, p. 7.

3 *New Leader*, September 1, 1928; interview with Norman Thomas, October 1963.

4 Norman Thomas to D. R. Sharpe, March 26, 1941; Norman Thomas to H. M. Applegate, November 27, 1935; Norman Thomas to Franklin D. Stone, June 22, 1942; in NT Papers. Devere Allen, "Norman Thomas," in *A Plan for America: Official 1932 Campaign Handbook of the Socialist Party* (Chicago, Socialist Party of America, 1932), p. 19; *New Leader*, September 1, 1928; interview with Norman Thomas, October 1963.

5 Norman Thomas to _____ (first page missing) [1916]; A. R. Williams to Norman Thomas, September 28, 1909; Norman Thomas to Paul A. Hill, December 22, 1933; in NT Papers. [Norman Thomas] *The Church and the City* (New York, New York Presbytery, 1917), pp. 73–74, 76–77, 85, 88–89. "A Statement from the Home Missions Committee" [1917?]; Norman Thomas to "Dear Harold," December 6, 1915; Norman Thomas to "Dear Ralph," March 22, 1916; Norman Thomas to James M. Speers, September 28, 1916; Norman Thomas to Mrs. Lois Yergin Zeek, May 14, 1941; "Some Residents in 116th Street" to Norman Thomas [1915?]; in NT Papers.

6 *The Church and the City*, pp. vi, 100–111; "Memoranda from Conference on Christian Industrial Work, 156 5th Avenue, January 28, 1916" (NT Papers).

7 "My Forty Years in Politics," Leipziger lecture by Norman Thomas, Town Hall, New York City, May 29, 1956, pp. 4–5 (typescript in NT Papers); interview with Norman Thomas, October 1963; State of New York, Assembly Committee on the Judiciary, *Hearings*, 1920, pp. 1672–

1673; Norman Thomas to "Dear Harold," December 6, 1915 (NT Papers).

8 *The Church and the City*, pp. 7, 9–11.

9 *Ibid.*, pp. 11, 94; Norman Thomas, *The Christian Patriot* [William Penn Lecture] (Philadelphia, Young Friends Movement, May 13, 1917), pp. 10, 13–14.

10 Louis Waldman, *Labor Lawyer* (New York, Dutton, 1944), pp. 177–178; *New World*, I (February 1918), 30; Norman Thomas to Henry Wadsworth Longfellow Dana, May 11, 1917, in Henry Wadsworth Longfellow Dana papers, Swarthmore Peace Collection, Swarthmore College Library, Swarthmore, Pennsylvania (hereafter cited as Dana Papers); Norman Thomas, *Conscientious Objector in America* (New York, Huebsch, 1923), pp. 54–55; Norman Thomas to Reverend Howard A. Walter, January 31, 1917 (NT Papers); Norman Thomas to "Dr. Pennington," April 19, 1917 (NT Papers); Henry T. Hodgkins to Miss Emily G. Balch, October 20, 1915, in Fellowship of Reconciliation Papers, Swarthmore Peace Collection (hereafter cited as FOR Papers); Minutes of Fellowship of Reconciliation Council, December 3, 1916, in Fellowship of Reconciliation Minutes, Swarthmore Peace Collection; petition to the House Committee on Military Affairs, January 16, 1917 (FOR Papers); Gilbert A. Beaver and Edward W. Evans to "Members and Friends of the Fellowship of Reconciliation" (FOR Papers); Norman Thomas to Archibald McClure, March 9, 1917 (NT Papers); Minutes of Business Committee meeting, February 22, 1918 (FOR Papers); Leroy Arthur Sheetz to Norman Thomas, January 13, 1917 (NT Papers); "My Forty Years in Politics," p. 1.

11 Norman Thomas, *A Socialist's Faith* (New York, Norton, 1951), p. 308; Norman Thomas to H. W. L. Dana, January 9, 1918 (Dana Papers); Norman Thomas, "A Defense of Dissenters," *Princeton Alumni Weekly*, XVI (March 15, 1916), 527; *The Christian Patriot*, pp. 6, 12–13, 21, 26–27, 36–37, 46.

12 *Conscientious Objector in America*, p. 273; Norman Thomas, "What of the Church?," *New World*, I (February 1918), 45; Norman Thomas, W. Fearon Holliday, F. W. Armstrong, and Richard Roberts, *The Conquest of War* (New York, Association Press, 1917), p. 52; Norman Thomas, "Conscience and the Church," *Nation*, CV (August 23, 1917), 199; Norman Thomas to Ralph Harlow, September 7, 1917 (NT Papers).

13 Norman Thomas, *War's Heretics* (New York, Civil Liberties Bureau of the American Union Against Militarism, 1917), pp. 9–10; *Conscientious Objector in America*, pp. 2–3, 9, 126, 143–164, 182–202, 258; Norman Thomas to H. W. L. Dana, January 9, 1918 (Dana Papers); H. C. Peterson and Gilbert C. Fite, *Opponents of War* (Madison, University of Wisconsin Press, 1957), pp. 260–261. Although one of Norman Thomas's brothers, Evan, was a conscientious objector, two other brothers, Ralph and Arthur, served in the Army as volunteers. *War's Heretics*, pp. 9–10; "Conscience and the Church," p. 199. *The Conquest of War*, p. vii.

14 *Conscientious Objector in America*, pp. 3, 6, 8–9, 284–285, 287.

15 Max Beer, *Social Struggles and Modern Socialism* (Boston, Small, Maynard, 1926), pp. 163, 165, 170, 175, 186, 187; *Opponents of War, 1917–1918*, pp. 43–48, 157–166; Morris Hillquit, *Loose Leaves from a Busy Life* (New York, Macmillan, 1934), p. 167; Leslie Marcy, "The Emergency National Convention," *International Socialist Review,* XVII (May 1917), 665–669; "Resolution on War and Militarism," *ibid.,* 670–671; *New York Times,* April 7, 1918, sec. I, p. 10. Norman Thomas to Lillian Wald, March 1, 1918 (NT Papers); David Karsner, "The Passing of the Socialist Party," *Current History,* XX (June 1924), 404–405.

16 Robert William Iverson, "Morris Hillquit: American Social Democrat" (unpublished Ph.D. dissertation, State University of Iowa, 1951), p. 397; Norman Thomas to Morris Hillquit, October 2, 1917 (NT Papers); *New Leader,* November 28, 1925; *New York Call,* October 10 and November 1, 1917; Mary Ware Dennett to "Dear Member," November 15, 1917 (NT Papers).

17 Norman Thomas to Dr. Patrick McCarton, March 10, 1919 (NT Papers). *The Christian Patriot,* p. 57.

18 Norman Thomas to "Mrs. Douglas," September 20, 1917 (NT Papers); "Notes on 10th Annual Convention, I.S.S.," *Intercollegiate Socialist,* VII (February–March 1919), 25; Norman Thomas to Mrs. Anne G. Brush, September 24, 1918 (NT Papers).

19 Norman Thomas to Alexander Trachtenberg, October 18, 1918 (NT Papers); Alexander Trachtenberg to Norman Thomas, October 25, 1918 (NT Papers).

20 Young, "American Socialism Under the Leadership of Norman Thomas," p. 28; Norman Thomas to Professor Sinclair W. Armstrong, November 12, 1956 (NT Papers); John Nevin Sayre to Norman Thomas, October 15, 1918 (NT Papers).

21 Walter Fletcher to Norman Thomas, September 29, 1917 (NT Papers); Norman Thomas to Walter Fletcher, October 2, 1917 (NT Papers); *War's Heretics,* pp. 4–5; *The Conquest of War,* pp. 8–9.

22 *Ibid.,* pp. 9–15; "What of the Church?," p. 46; Norman Thomas, "Reflections on Russia and Revolution," *World Tomorrow,* III (September 1920), 261.

II Road to leadership

1 Nathan Fine, *Labor and Farmer Parties in the United States,* 1828–1928 (New York, Rand School Press, 1928), p. 214; *American Labor Year Book,* VI (New York, Rand School Press, 1925), 141; James Oneal and G. A. Warner, *American Communism* (New York, Dutton, 1947), p. 180; James Oneal, "Changing Fortunes of American Socialism," *Current History,* XX (April 1924), 95; Hillquit, *Loose Leaves from a Busy Life,* p. 300; David Karsner, "The Passing of the Socialist Party," *Current History,* XX (June 1924), 402–407; *New York Times,* May 20, 1923, sec. II, pp. 1–2.

2 Interview with Norman Thomas, October 1963; [Norman Thomas] "The Socialist Schism," *World Tomorrow,* II (October 1919), 270;

New Leader, December 5, 1925; *Socialist Review,* IX (January 1921), 16.

3 *New York Times,* January 25, 1919, pp. 1, 4, and November 10, 1919, pp. 1–3. Amnesty Conference, Washington, D.C., April 13–14, 1921, list of delegates, in Socialist Party of America Collection, Perkins Memorial Library, Duke University, Durham, North Carolina (hereafter cited as Duke); Thomas represented the Fellowship of Reconciliation. *New Leader,* October 29, 1927; Nat Hentoff, *Peace Agitator: The Story of A. J. Muste* (New York, Macmillan, 1963), p. 57; Norman Thomas to Miss Beverly Acquilino, February 16, 1953 (NT Papers).

4 Norman Thomas to Charles W. McAlpin, January 6, 1919 (NT Papers); Norman Thomas, "The Return to Religion," sermon delivered at the Unitarian Church of Germantown (Philadelphia), Pennsylvania, June 7, 1953, p. 5 (Tamiment Institute Library, New York University, New York).

5 Norman Thomas to Board of Managers, Colonial Club, Princeton University, November 14, 1918 (NT Papers).

6 Norman Thomas, "Can Pacifism Act Against Injustice?," *World Tomorrow,* VII (July 1924), 210–211; "War, Politics and Economics," *World Tomorrow,* V (January 1922), 11; "Democracy and the Unions," *World Tomorrow,* VII (June 1924), 191.

7 Norman Thomas, "What Is Bolshevism?," *World Tomorrow,* II (February 1919), 37–39; Norman Thomas, "Religion and Civilization," *Atlantic Monthly,* CLXXV (August 1947), 34.

8 "Verbatim Report of Mass Meeting Called by Committee of Justice to the Negro at the Harlem Casino, New York City, November 13, 1919," pp. 32–34 (Lusk Committee Files, New York State Library, Albany, New York).

9 "Notes on 10th Annual Convention, I.S.S.," *Intercollegiate Socialist,* VII (February–March 1919), 24–25; "My Forty Years in Politics," p. 5; *New York Times,* July 10, 1921; Mina Weisenberg, *The L.I.D.: Fifty Years of Democratic Education, 1905–1955* (New York, League for Industrial Democracy, 1955), pp. 5–6, 9–10, 11, 13–14.

10 Norman Thomas, "Labor and the Press," *Forum,* LXXI (May 1924), 591–596; *New York Leader,* October 1, 1923; *New Leader,* July 20, 1929.

11 James Oneal, "The Changing Fortunes of American Socialism," pp. 92, 96–97; *New Leader,* July 12, 1924; "The American Labor and Socialist Parties," *Intercollegiate Socialist,* VII (April–May 1919), 12–13; Norman Thomas, "What Can We Expect from a Third Party?," *World Tomorrow,* VII (June 1924), 178.

12 *New Leader,* February 16 and March 8, 1924; Harold Lord Varney, "An American Labor Party in the Making," *Current History,* XX (April 1924), 91.

13 Norman Thomas, "Progressivism at St. Louis," *Nation,* CXVIII (February 27, 1924), 225; "What Can We Expect from a Third Party?," p. 180; *New Leader,* February 23 and March 8, 1924; Hugh L. Keenleyside, "The American Political Revolution of 1924," *Current History,* XXI (March 1925), 833.

14 *New Leader*, February 16, May 16, June 28, July 5, and July 12, 1924.

15 *New Leader*, July 12 and July 26, 1924; Kenneth C. MacKay, *The Progressive Movement of 1924* (New York, Columbia University Press, 1947), p. 149.

16 *New Leader*, June 28 and July 26, 1924.

17 MacKay, *The Progressive Movement*, p. 199.

18 *New Leader*, August 2, August 9, and October 18, 1924; Bruce Rogers to Frank Walsh [no date, but apparently October 1924], quoted in MacKay, *The Progressive Movement*, pp. 202–203.

19 Norman Thomas to Kenneth C. MacKay, May 21, 1943 (NT Papers); *New Leader*, October 25, 1924; *New York Herald Tribune*, August 17, 1924.

20 See, for example, *New Leader*, August 23, September 6, September 20, October 4, and October 18, 1924; *New York Times*, September 19, 1924.

21 *New Leader*, November 8, 1924, December 13, 1924; Albert Bushnell Hart, "Events in the United States," *Current History*, XXI (February 1925), 754–755.

22 *New Leader*, November 29 and December 6, 1924, February 28, 1925; *New York Herald Tribune*, February 21 and February 22, 1925.

23 "Verbatim Report of the 1928 National Convention of the Socialist Party of America" (typescript at Duke), pp. 34e–35e; Clarence Senior, "Growth of the Socialist Party in the Last Decade" [1933] (typescript at Duke). "Radio Speech of Norman Thomas, Socialist Candidate for President, over Radio WCFL, Chicago, 7:45 p.m., October 16, 1936" (typescript at Duke); Norman Thomas, *How Can the Socialist Party Best Serve Socialism?* (New York, Norman Thomas, 1949), p. 6.

24 *New Leader*, March 27, April 17, April 24, and October 2, 1926.

III Emergence of the leader

1 "Membership Report" [no date, but apparently May 1928], Socialist Party of America Collection, Duke University, Durham, North Carolina, hereafter cited as SP of A Papers, Duke; *New Leader*, January 7, 1928, May 28, 1927.

2 "Verbatim Report of 1928 National Convention of Socialist Party of America" (SP of A Papers, Duke), pp. 23e–24e.

3 *American Labor Year Book*, X (1929) (New York, Rand School of Social Science, 1929), p. 147.

4 For Thomas's earlier view of Soviet Russia, see *New Leader*, December 5, 1925, March 12, 1927; for Hillquit's earlier view, see *New Leader*, January 2, 1926. The symposium is fully reported in *New Leader*, February 4, 1928.

5 Norman Thomas to Robert J. Alexander, November 11, 1953 (NT Papers).

6 *New Leader*, March 31, 1928; interview with Norman Thomas, October 1963; "Verbatim Report of 1928 National Convention," pp. D55, D79.

7 Franklin Folsom, "More Campaign Oratory," *Quarterly Journal of*

Speech, XV (April 1929), 252–254; "The Socialists Nominate an Intellectual," *Christian Century* XLV (May 23, 1928), 560–561; *New Leader,* May 19, June 2, June 9, September 1, September 29, and October 6, 1928.

8 Reinhold Niebuhr, "Governor Smith's Liberalism," *Christian Century,* XLV (September 13, 1928), 1107–1108; *An Open Letter to Progressives* (New York, Socialist National Campaign Committee, 1928); *New Leader,* January 7, February 11, June 9, and July 7, 1928; Norman Thomas, "Socialism and the Tariff" (typescript in SP of A Papers, Duke); "Verbatim Report of 1928 National Convention," pp. A14, D68–71.

9 Eugene H. Roseboom, *A History of Presidential Elections* (New York, Macmillan, 1964), pp. 425, 428; Norman Thomas to Mayor Daniel W. Hoan, November 12, 1928, Daniel W. Hoan Collection, Milwaukee County Historical Society (hereafter cited as Hoan Papers); Daniel W. Hoan to Norman Thomas, November 14, 1928 (Hoan Papers); *New Leader,* September 1, November 10, November 17, and December 22, 1928, February 23, 1929.

10 "Membership Report" [1928–1932] (SP of A Papers, Duke); *New York Times,* November 26, 1928, p. 10, December 29, 1928, p. 2; *New Leader,* November 10, 17, 1928.

11 For an example of Henry's anti-Semitism, see William H. Henry to Daniel W. Hoan, November 3, 1932 (Hoan Papers); Norman Thomas to Mayor Daniel W. Hoan, November 17, 1928 (Hoan Papers); "Confidential Memorandum from Norman Thomas on the Future of the Socialist Party" [December 1928] (typescript in Hoan Papers); Shannon, *The Socialist Party of America,* pp. 199–202. The prudery of the American Socialist movement has never been fully explored; yet it was a prevalent force. Prudery was only natural, in fact, because the Social Gospel, a segment of the Christian Church, played a large role in the Socialist party. For some examples of Socialist prudery, see Max Eastman's article, "Editorial Policy," *Masses,* December 1913 (in William L. O'Neill, ed., *Echoes of Revolt* [Chicago, Quadrangle, 1966], pp. 29–32), particularly the letter by Vida Scudder reprinted therein. Other letters in the same article emphasize the point. A letter by the future Senator Paul H. Douglas in *Masses,* November 1916, pp. 32–33, reinforces Professor Scudder's position. Puritanism is also evident in the municipal campaign literature of the Socialist party, particularly in Ohio, Wisconsin, and New York during the decade 1910–1920 (SP of A Papers, Duke; Social Democratic party Papers, Milwaukee County Historical Society; and Socialist party of New York City materials, Tamiment). For Thomas's prudery see Chapter 10 of this book.

12 "Confidential Memorandum from Norman Thomas"; *New Leader,* January 12, January 19, and July 6, 1929.

13 "Confidential Memorandum from Norman Thomas"; "Supplemental Memorandum to Confidential Memorandum from Norman Thomas on the Future of the Socialist Party [December 1928] (Hoan Papers); Norman Thomas to James Oneal, January 30, 1929 (SP of A Papers,

Duke); "Supplemental Memorandum"; *New Leader,* December 1, 1928, July 12, 1930.

14 *New Leader,* February 25, May 5, and November 17, 1928, May 4 and June 22, 1929.

15 For a full description of the Seabury investigations, see Herbert Mitgang, *The Man Who Rode the Tiger: The Life and Times of Judge Samuel Seabury* (Philadelphia, Lippincott, 1963), pp. 159–310; Norman Thomas and Paul Blanshard, *What's the Matter with New York?* (New York, Macmillan, 1932), pp. 128–167, 218, 314–315; "The Mayoralty Circus," *Nation,* CXXIX (October 23, 1929), 455; Carl Hermann Voss, *Rabbi and Minister* (New York, World, 1964), p. 271; Devere Allen, "Norman Thomas," in *A Plan for America: Official 1932 Campaign Handbook of the Socialist Party* (Chicago, Socialist Party of America, 1932), p. 21; *New Leader,* September 14, October 12, October 19, and November 2, 1929; Norman Thomas, *As I See It* (New York, Macmillan, 1932), p. 132. Norman Thomas, *The City for the People* (New York, Socialist Campaign Committee, 1929) [broadside] (Tamiment).

16 *New Leader,* November 9, 1929, January 11, 1930.

17 *New York Times,* November 17, 1929, p. 1; December 9, 1929, p. 3; *New Leader,* November 23, 1929, January 4, 1930; Norman Thomas, "Twisting Tammany's Tail," *Forum,* LXXXV (June 1931), 339; *As I See It,* p. 139.

18 Memorandum [from Norman Thomas] to Rosner, White, and Maslow, December 3, 1933 (NT Papers). Voss, *Rabbi and Minister,* pp. 272–280, gives the date of founding as 1930; contemporary records indicate the date was 1929. Thomas and Blanshard, *What's the Matter with New York?,* pp. 183–185.

19 A. J. Muste, "To Militant Socialists," January 11, 1932 (SP of A Collection, Duke); Press Release, Socialist Party [of New York City], October 29, 1931 (SP of A Papers, Duke); *New Leader,* November 7, 1931.

20 *New Leader,* May 11 and November 2, 1929, May 17, 1930; Norman Thomas, "Issues of the Day," in *A Plan for America: Official 1932 Campaign Handbook of the Socialist Party,* p. 27; Norman Thomas, "A Program for Unemployment," *World Tomorrow,* XIII (May 1930), 216; *New York Times,* February 27, 1933, p. 3.

21 "A Program for Unemployment," p. 216.

22 Karl Denis Bicha, "Liberalism Frustrated: The League for Independent Political Action, 1928–1933," *Mid-America,* XLVIII (January 1966), 19–28; *New Leader,* December 22, 1928, November 16, 1929, May 10, 1930; *New York World,* August 12, 1930; *The American Labor Year Book,* XII (1931) (New York, Rand School of Social Science, 1931), 143; Edward J. Flynn, ed., *Manual for Use of the Legislature of the State of New York* (Albany, J. B. Lyon, 1931), p. 893.

23 Sidney Hertzberg, "Political Dissent in 1932," *Current History,* XXVII (November 1932), 166; *The American Labor Year Book,* XII (1931), 157–158. *New Leader,* November 23, 1929, January 3 and January 24, 1931, February 20, 1932, March 12, 1937; Daniel W. Hoan to John Dewey, February 13, 1932 (Hoan Papers); Morris Hillquit to Howard

Y. Williams [February 12, 1932] (in private collection made available to author; quoted in *The American Labor Year Book*, XIII [New York, Rand School of Social Science, 1932], 100–112; also in SP of A Collection, Duke).

24 Paul H. Douglas, *The Coming of a New Party* (New York, Whittlesey House, 1932), Dedication, pp. 202–203; *The American Labor Year Book*, XIII, 100–101.

25 Howard Y. Williams, "The L.I.P.A. Replies" (letter), *World Tomorrow*, XV (June 1932), 191; Paul H. Douglas, "State Farmer-Labor Parties," *World Tomorrow*, XVI (September 28, 1933), 544; "Minutes of the Meeting of the National Executive Committee Held in Reading, Pennsylvania, July 2-3-4, 1933" (Hoan Papers); *New Leader*, September 5, 1931, July 9, July 23, October 1, and December 10, 1932, September 2, 1933.

26 Hentoff, *Peace Agitator: The Story of A. J. Muste*, pp. 76–77; John Dewey, "Labor Politics and Labor Education," *New Republic*, LVII (January 9, 1929), 211–213. *The American Labor Year Book*, XI (1931), 124; *New Leader*, January 26, February 2, June 1, and July 20, 1929; *New York Times*, June 13, 1929, p. 28.

27 *New Leader*, February 8 and March 8, 1930, October 10, 1931.

28 *New Leader*, November 14, 1931.

29 Almost complete records of the early internal Militant–Old Guard strife are published in the *New Leader* from April 19, 1930, to June 1932. Of particular interest are the issues for April 19, 1930, January 3, February 7, May 9, September 5, September 19, and October 24, 1931, January 23, January 30, and February 6, 1932. See also Paul Blanshard to Clarence Senior, January 23, 1931 (SP of A Collection, Duke).

30 Iverson, "Morris Hillquit: American Social Democrat," pp. 393–395, 406–408; James Oneal to Algernon Lee, June 26, 1935, Oneal Collection, Tamiment Institute Library, New York University (hereafter cited as Oneal Papers); "Statement by Morris Hillquit," July 11, 1931 (Oneal Papers); *New Leader*, June 27 and July 4, 1931.

31 "Statement by Morris Hillquit," July 11, 1931; James Oneal to Algernon Lee, June 26, 1931; James Oneal to Frederick Umhey, July 5, 1931; Morris Hillquit to James Oneal, July 10, 1931; Charles R. Hill to James Oneal, July 21, 1931; "Statement by James Oneal to the Board of Management of the *New Leader*," July 1, 1931; cablegram from James Oneal to Morris Hillquit [July 29, 1931]; James Oneal to "Jack," July 21, 1931; in Oneal Papers. *New Leader*, August 8, 1931.

32 James Oneal to Algernon Lee, July 17, 1931 (Oneal Papers); "Confidential Memorandum from Norman Thomas"; Norman Thomas, "Why I Am a Socialist," *Princeton Alumni Weekly*, XXVII (April 6, 1928), 747; Norman Thomas, "Conclusion," in Harry W. Laidler and Norman Thomas, eds., *Socialism of Our Times* (New York, Vanguard, 1929), p. 375; *New Leader*, March 16, 1929.

33 "Why I Am a Socialist," pp. 747–748; K[irby] P[age], "Socialism According to Thomas," *World Tomorrow*, XIV (April 1931), 119. Norman Thomas, "Is Marxian Socialism Abreast with the Times?," speech

at Socialist discussion group, New York, May 1929 (in private collection). A transcript of the speech also appeared in the *New Leader*, June 15, 1929, and there are some minor differences between the manuscript copy and the *New Leader* transcript. Because Thomas rarely read a speech, it is probable that the *New Leader* version is the more accurate. Norman Thomas, "Socialism Upheld," *World Tomorrow*, XIII (February 1930), 70; "Norman Thomas on the Class Struggle," *World Tomorrow*, XV (August 1932), 239; "Why I Am a Socialist," pp. 748–749; "Conclusion," in *Socialism of Our Times*, pp. 374—375; *New Leader*, April 27, 1929.

iv Socialism in our time, 1932–1934

1 "N.E.C. Memo #1" [1932] (Duke); "N.E.C. Memo #7" [1932] (Duke); Jack Kaye, "The Socialist Convention," *Labor Age*, July 1932, p. 17; Clarence Senior, "Our Organization Forges Ahead," in *The March of Socialism: Journal of Seventeenth National Convention, Socialist Party* (Chicago, Socialist Party of America, 1932), p. 4.

2 "Draft of Report of James Oneal to LSI, 1935" (Oneal Papers); Leonard Bright, "The Socialist Party," *Labor Age*, July 1931, pp. 14–16; Theodore Shapiro, "The Militant Point of View," *American Socialist Quarterly*, I (April 1932), 29–32; [Anna Bercowitz] "Is This Militancy?," *American Socialist Quarterly*, I (April 1932), 39–41; Sidney Hertzberg, "Political Dissent in 1932," *Current History*, XXVII (November 1932), 162–163; MacCalister Coleman, "Who Are the Socialists?," *World Tomorrow*, XV (October 12, 1932), 347–349; MacCalister Coleman, "Socialism's Bed-Rock," *World Tomorrow*, XV (November 30, 1932), 517; Edward Levinson, "Labor Turns to Politics," *Nation*, CXXXIV (June 8, 1932), 648; "Socialist Militants and the C.P.L.A.," *Labor Age*, February 1932, p. 3; *New Leader*, April 12, April 19, and May 14, 1932.

3 Algernon Lee to Daniel W. Hoan, February 1, 1934 (Hoan Papers); Daniel W. Hoan to Harold W. Houston, January 9, 1932 (Hoan Papers); Daniel W. Hoan to Julius Gerber, October 26, 1932 (Hoan Papers); Daniel W. Hoan to William M. Feigenbaum, February 26, 1935 (Hoan Papers); "A Resolution by the Tompkins County, N.Y., Local" (Duke); Iverson, "Morris Hillquit: American Social Democrat," p. 414; interview with Norman Thomas, October 1963; Jack Kaye, "The Socialist Convention," pp. 16–17; Levinson, "Labor Turns to Politics," pp. 649–650; Anna Bercowitz, "The Milwaukee Convention," *American Socialist Quarterly*, I (Summer 1932), 49–53; *New York Herald Tribune*, May 23, 1932, p. 8, May 24, 1932, p. 13, May 25, 1932, p. 11; *Milwaukee Leader*, May 21, May 23, and May 24, 1932; *Jewish Daily Forward*, May 24, 1932; *New Leader*, January 2, May 28, June 18, and July 9, 1932. Material relating to the 1932 convention must be used with great care. The transcript is available in fragments only. Although newspaper coverage is thorough, the reporter for the *New York Times*, Joseph Shaplen, actively supported Hillquit; the reporter

for the *Herald Tribune*, Edward Levinson, was involved in the anti-Hillquit movement; and the Socialist press attempted to minimize the struggle. The *Milwaukee Leader*, the host city's Socialist organ, virtually ignored the struggle over the chairmanship, as did the *New Leader*. The *Jewish Daily Forward*, despite its pro-Hillquit bias, covered the fight thoroughly. Except for three letters in the Hoan collection, there are few data available to explain Hoan's antipathy for Hillquit, a vital factor in the struggle. Thomas's position cannot be explained on the basis of letters in his collection or in the SP of A collection at Duke.

4 Most studies of the 1932 Socialist campaign erroneously report that harmony reigned after the convention had adjourned. See, for example, Shannon, *The Socialist Party of America*, p. 218, or Iverson, "Morris Hillquit: American Social Democrat," p. 218. Unfortunately, documentation of party feuding during the campaign was not generally available to the authors of these studies. Now that materials in the Hoan Collection are accessible to researchers, the following documents (all in Hoan Papers) reveal a decided lack of harmony in the party: "National Campaign Notes, 1932"; Herbert M. Merrill to National Campaign Committee, August 1, 1932; Julius Gerber to Daniel Hoan, September 2, 1932; Daniel W. Hoan to William H. Henry, November 12, 1932; Julius Gerber to Daniel Hoan, November 12, 1932; Daniel Hoan to Editor, the *Nation*, November 15, 1932; William H. Henry to Daniel W. Hoan, November 22, 1932. See also William M. Feigenbaum to Meta Berger, Daniel W. Hoan, Leo M. Krzycki, William A. Cunnea, June 23, 1932; Norman Thomas to Bertha E. Winslow, July 13, 1932; "What Socialism Is and Is Not," Broadcast by Norman Thomas over Blue Network, National Broadcasting Company, Saturday, June 18, 1932, 7:30 P.M."; "Radio Speech by Norman Thomas over Columbia Network, July 13, 1932"; "Socialism and the Fulfillment of Americanism, Speech delivered by Norman Thomas at Bennington, Vermont [1932]"; at Duke. "Statement by Norman Thomas to the *Literary Digest*" (typescript in NT Papers); "Election Statement of Norman Thomas," November 9, 1932 (typescript in NT Papers); *Labor and Socialist Press Service*, September 16, October 28, and November 12, 1932 (mimeographed copies at Duke and Tamiment); Eugene H. Roseboom, *A History of Presidential Elections*, p. 441; Norman Thomas, "Socialist Opportunities," in *The March of Socialism, 1928–1932: Journal of the Seventeenth National Convention, Socialist Party*, p. 5; Norman Thomas, "A Note on the American Political Scene," *American Socialist Quarterly*, I (Summer 1932), 3; Claude Moore Fuess, "Norman Thomas: Socialist Crusader," *Current History*, XXXVII (November 1932), 162; Paul H. Douglas, "Pairing Votes for Thomas," *Nation*, CXXV (November 2, 1932), 430; Daniel W. Hoan, "Pairing Votes," *Nation*, CXXV (December 7, 1932), 560; *Jewish Daily Forward*, November 5, 1932; *New Leader*, August 20, September 3, September 17, November 5, November 12, and December 3, 1932, April 8, 1933.

5 Clarence Senior, "Growth of the Socialist Party in the Last Decade"

(typescript at Duke); "Membership Report by States, 1928–1932" (Duke); Norman Thomas to Editor, *New York World-Telegram*, April 22, 1932 (typescript in NT Papers); Norman Thomas, "Is Peaceful Revolution Possible?," *World Tomorrow*, XV (September 14, 1932), 252; Gabriel Heatter, "The Future of the Socialist Party: Open Letter to Norman Thomas," *Nation*, CXXXV (December 14, 1932), 584; *As I See It*, pp. 15–20, 140–144, 147, 152; Norman Thomas, "The Challenge of Peaceful Revolution," in Harry W. Laidler, ed., *Socialist Planning and a Socialist Program* (New York, Falcon Press, 1932), pp. 226, 229, 234; *New Leader*, November 28, 1928, January 16, 1932.

6 Norman Thomas to Edward A. Filene, November 23, 1933 (NT Papers); [Press Statement by Socialist Party] March 13, 1933 (original at Duke); Norman Thomas, "What Has Roosevelt Accomplished?," *Nation*, CXXXVI (April 12, 1933), 399–400; Norman Thomas, "New Deal or New Day," *World Tomorrow*, XVI (August 3, 1933), 488–489; Norman Thomas, "Our Immediate Task," *World Tomorrow*, XVII (February 15, 1934), 83; Norman Thomas, "On Our Way, But Where Are We Going?," *Saturday Review of Literature*, X (April 14, 1934), 625–626; Norman Thomas, *The Choice Before Us* (New York, Macmillan, 1934), pp. 7, 88, 92–93, 124, 132; Norman Thomas, *The New Deal: A Socialist Analysis* (Chicago, Socialist Party of America [1933]), pp. 7–12, 16–17; *New York Herald Tribune*, October 5, 1933, p. 8; *New York Times*, February 7, 1933, p. 5, June 12, 1933, p. 11, August 8, 1933, p. 18, October 5, 1933, p. 7; *New Leader*, April 22, September 9, November 18, and November 25, 1933. Interview with Norman Thomas, October 1963. In January 1934 Thomas suggested that the Socialist party discard plans for a 1936 presidential campaign and concentrate its energies in 1934 on opposing only anti–New Deal Democrats. He concurred with Cahan's basic premises but disagreed with his formal declaration of his position at that time for reasons of internal party policy. A letter from Cahan in a private collection, which Thomas agreed was accurate, claimed that Thomas and Cahan had discussed the matter immediately before the ILGWU meeting and that Cahan had made the statement with Thomas's knowledge.

7 Norman Thomas to George Steinhardt, July 21, 1933; Norman Thomas to "The Editor," September 14, 1933; Norman Thomas to John Haynes Holmes, September 14, 1933; John Haynes Holmes to Norman Thomas, October 11, 1933; Norman Thomas to Clarence O. Senior, November 14, 1933; "Memorandum to Rosner, White, and Maslow, December 19, 1933; Norman Thomas to Senator John J. Dunnigan (telegram), January 1, 1934; Norman Thomas to W. J. Kitchen, June 8, 1934; Norman Thomas to City Affairs Committee, June 8, 1934; Norman Thomas to Clarence Senior, August 16, 1934; Norman Thomas to Joseph Schlossberg, December 18, 1935; in NT Papers. Paul Blanshard to Coleman B. Cheney, November 21, 1933 (Duke); interview with Norman Thomas, October 1963; "Paul Blanshard, Ex-Socialist," *World Tomorrow*, XVI (September 28, 1933), 531; Norman Thomas, "Along the Class Struggle Front," *World Tomorrow*, XVI (September 28, 1933), 538; Norman Thomas, "The Present Shape of Things," *World Tomorrow*, XVI

(November 23, 1933), 633; *New York Times*, February 11, 1933, p. 3, October 5, 1933, p. 2; *New Leader*, July 22, September 9, and November 11, 1933, June 9 and December 15, 1934; *Socialist Call,* December 21, 1935.

8 Samuel Shore to Norman Thomas, June 5, 1933; William Feigenbaum to Norman Thomas, June 5, 1933; Julius Gerber to Norman Thomas, June 5, 1933; William Feinberg to Norman Thomas, June 5, 1933; Norman Thomas to William Feinberg, June 15, 1933; Norman Thomas to Samuel Shore, June 6, 1933; N. Chanin to Norman Thomas, June 8, 1933; Norman Thomas to N. Chanin, June 12, 1933; [Norman Thomas], "Memorandum on the Situation in the Fur Industry as It Affects Socialist Party," June 14, 1933; Norman Thomas to Secretaries of Branches, September 7, 1933; Norman Thomas to Meeting of Waiters, September 18, 1933; Norman Thomas to David Kaplan, September 21, 1933; "Statement by Fur Workers Union [A.F. of L.]," November 1933; Norman Thomas to Samuel Perlmutter, November 28, 1933; Louis P. Goldberg to Norman Thomas, December 30, 1933; Norman Thomas to "Dear Louis" [P. Goldberg], January 3, 1934; Louis Hendin to Norman Thomas, January 3, 1934; Norman Thomas to Julius Gerber, January 4, 1934; Norman Thomas to Leo Krzycki, January 16, 1934; Norman Thomas to Clarence O. Senior, January 16, 1934; Norman Thomas, "Memorandum on Taxi Strikers' Situation," April 15, 1934; in NT Papers. *New Leader*, February 4, July 15, July 22, and September 9, 1933.

9 "Central Committee, Communist Party, U.S.A., to the Toiling Masses of the United States; the National Executive Council of the American Federation of Labor; the National Committee of the Socialist Party; the National Committee of the Conference for Progressive Labor Action; the National Committee of the Trade Union Unity League; All Other Trade Unions and Working Class Organizations, National and Local, Negro and White," March 29, 1933; Communist Party, New York District, to All Socialist Party Branches [March 1933]; "Minutes of the National Executive Committee Meeting, May 5–6–7, 1933; Julius Gerber and Edward Levinson, for the National Executive Committee, Socialist Party, to "The Workers of the United States and All Opponents of War" [1933]; in Hoan Papers. Norman Thomas to Roger Baldwin, July 26, 1934 (NT Papers); Norman Thomas to Milton Harvey, April 12, 1934 (NT Papers); Earl Browder to National Executive Committee of the Socialist Party, June 19, 1934 (NT Papers); Albert Sprague Coolidge to Clarence Senior, June 24, 1934 (Duke); *Labor and Socialist Press Service*, July 23, 1932 (mimeographed, Duke); Sidney Hertzberg, "Political Dissent in 1932," p. 163; "If I Were a Politician: The Story of Norman Thomas," *World Tomorrow*, XIII (June 1930), 261; Norman Thomas, "Proposals for Action at Detroit," *World Tomorrow*, XVII (April 26, 1934), 206; Earl Browder, "The Revolutionary Way Out: Report of the Central Committee to the Eighth Convention of the Communist Party, Held in Cleveland, Ohio, April 2–8, 1934," in Earl Browder, *Communism in the United States* (New York, International Publishers, 1935), pp. 34–35, 61, 63; *The Choice Before Us*, p. 151.

10 "Report of the American Delegation to the Special Conference, Labor

and Socialist International" [September 1933] (Duke); Manakkal Sabhessan Venakataramani, "Norman Thomas and the Socialist Party of America, 1932–1936" (unpublished Ph.D. dissertation, University of Oregon, 1955), pp. 195–203. See also Bernard K. Johnpoll, *The Politics of Futility: The General Jewish Workers Bund of Poland, 1917–1943* (Ithaca, Cornell University Press, 1967), pp. 198–201.

11 Norman Thomas to Andrew J. Biemiller, September 14, 1933; Norman Thomas to Dr. William Bohn, September 26, 1933; Norman Thomas to Amicus Most, October 5, 1933; Norman Thomas to Nathan Chanin, December 16, 1933; Robert J. Alexander to Norman Thomas, April 2, 1934; Clarence Senior to Norman Thomas, August 15, 1934; Norman Thomas to Franz Daniels, December 5, 1934; in NT Papers. Earl Browder, "New Developments and New Tasks in the United States" [November 1934 report to the Executive Committee of the Communist International], in *Communism in the United States*, pp. 191, 200–201; Earl Browder, "The United Front Against War and Fascism" [address at the opening of the Second U.S. Congress Against War and Fascism, Chicago, September 28, 1934], *ibid.*, pp. 244–245; Jacob Panken, *Socialism for America* (New York, Rand School of Social Science, 1933), pp. 11, 14–15; Norman Thomas, *The New Deal: A Socialist Analysis* (Chicago, Socialist Party of America [1933]); "An Appeal to the Socialist Party from 47 Members," *World Tomorrow*, XVII (April 12, 1934), 183–188; "The Program of the New York Militant Socialists," *World Tomorrow*, XVII (June 14, 1934), 306–308; Francis Henson, "Must We Have Revolution?," *Christian Century*, XLIX (November 30, 1932), 1472–1473; Norman Thomas, "Our Immediate Task," *World Tomorrow*, XVII (February 15, 1934), 83–84; Norman Thomas, "Proposals for Action at Detroit," *World Tomorrow*, XVII (April 26, 1934), 206–208; interview with Norman Thomas, October 1963.

12 Daniel W. Hoan to "Dear Comrade," February 4, 1935 (Hoan Papers). "Membership Report by States, 1928–1933"; "Membership Report as of May 31, 1934"; "Membership Report as of December 1934"; "Membership Report, 1903–1933"; Paul Porter to Norman Thomas, November 24, 1933; Andrew J. Biemiller to Norman Thomas, January 2, 1934; Norman Thomas to Leo Krzycki, January 16, 1934; Norman Thomas to Ralph Harlow, January 17, 1934; Jacob Panken to Norman Thomas, January 23, 1934; Jacob Panken to Norman Thomas, January 26, 1934; Paul [Porter] to Norman Thomas, January 28, 1934; Norman Thomas to Paul Porter, January 30, 1934; Clarence Senior to Norman Thomas, March 22, 1934; Norman Thomas to Clarence Senior, March 26, 1934; Clarence Senior to Norman Thomas, March 28, 1934; Norman Thomas to Clarence Senior, March 30, 1934; Clarence Senior to Norman Thomas, April 2, 1934; Georgeanna H. Findley to Norman Thomas, February 20, 1934; Norman Thomas to Georgeanna H. Findlay, April 12, 1934; Norman Thomas to Clarence Senior, April 10, 1934; Norman Thomas to Members of National Executive Committee, [November 1934]; in NT Papers. *The Choice Before Us*, pp. 206–207; "Stenographic Report of the Debate on the Declaration of Principles," *Ameri-

can Socialist Quarterly, III (Special Supplement, July 1934), 2, 5–9, 11–17, 21, 23, 27, 29–32, 35, 41–42, 46–47, 49–51, 56–58; "Fight Fascism," in *Socialist Advance* ([Eighteenth National Convention, S.P. of A.] Socialist Party of America, 1934), pp. 4–49; Norman Thomas, "What Happened at Detroit," *World Tomorrow*, XVII (June 28, 1934), 322; *New Leader*, January 27, April 14, June 9, and June 23, 1934.

13 [Florence Bowers] to Edward J. Meeman, August 8, 1934 (NT Papers); Edward J. Meeman to "Dear Florence" [Bowers], August 6, 1934 (NT Papers).

14 B. C. Vladeck to Norman Thomas, August 14, 1934, Vladeck Collection, Tamiment Institute Library, New York University (hereafter cited as Vladeck Papers); "Suggestions for a Substitute Declaration of Principles Proposed by Platform and Resolutions Committee of New York State Socialist Party Convention, June 30–July 1, 1934" (Duke). Clarence Senior to Norman Thomas, March 15, 1934; Glenn Trimble to Norman Thomas, June 12, 1934; Norman Thomas to Glenn Trimble, June 13, 1934; B. Charney Vladeck to Norman Thomas, June 14, 1934; Norman Thomas to Samuel H. Friedman, June 15, 1934; Paul Porter to Norman Thomas, June 17, 1934; Norman Thomas to B. Charney Vladeck, June 19, 1934; Clarence Senior to Norman Thomas, June 19, 1934; James Oneal to Clarence Senior, June 23, 1934; Norman Thomas to Clarence O. Senior, June 25, 1934; James H. Maurer to Norman Thomas, June 26, 1934; Samuel S. White to Norman Thomas, July 4, 1934; Herbert M. Merrill to National Executive Committee [July 1934]; Norman Thomas to Clarence Senior, Maynard Krueger, Andrew J. Biemiller, July 5, 1934; Norman Thomas to Members of the National Executive Committee, July 18, 1934; Norman Thomas to Samuel S. White, July 19, 1934; Harold Kelso to National Executive Committee, July 22, 1934; Clarence Senior to Members of the N.E.C., August 8, 1934; Clarence Senior to Members of the National Executive Committee, August 9, 1934; George R. Brickerwood to Clarence Senior, September 1, 1934; Clarence Senior to Monroe Sweetland, September 6, 1934; Norman Thomas to "the Meeting in Support of the Declaration of Principles," September 6, 1934; William H. Amberson to Norman Thomas, September 14, 1934; Darlington Hoopes to Norman Thomas, September 19, 1934; Clarence Senior to National Executive Committee, October 17, 1934; Alfred Baker Lewis to Norman Thomas (telegram), October 19, 1934; Norman Thomas to Clarence O. Senior, October 23, 1934; Norman Thomas to Members of the New York State Committee, November 7, 1934; Norman Thomas to the *Jewish Daily Forward*, December 7, 1934; Norman Thomas to William Feigenbaum, February 26, 1935; Alfred Baker Lewis to Norman Thomas, June 11, 1935; Norman Thomas to Alfred Baker Lewis, June 13, 1935; in NT Papers. "What Happened at Detroit," pp. 321–322; *New Leader*, June 16, June 30, July 14, and September 20, 1934.

15 "Minutes of the National Executive Committee, SPUSA, Boston, Massachusetts, November 30, December 1, 2, 1934," p. 2; Jarvis B. Albro to Clarence Senior, March 24, 1935; A. Sumner Thompson to Clarence

Senior, April 6, 1935; Lylith M. Brown to Clarence Senior, April 5, 1935; Clarence Senior to Lylith M. Brown, April 9, 1934; Clarence Senior to Jack Altman, May 3, 1935; Jack Altman to Clarence Senior (telegram), May 7, 1935; "Report of Executive Secretary to 19th National Convention [1936], Memo #25," pp. 1–2; at Duke. Daniel Hoan to William M. Feigenbaum, February 26, 1935 (Hoan); Norman Thomas to "Dear Dan," October 30, 1935 (Hoan); Norman Thomas to B. Charney Vladeck, July 24, 1934 (Vladeck Papers); Friedrich Adler to Norman Thomas and James Oneal, July 16, 1935 (Oneal Papers); James Oneal, "Draft of a Report to Labor and Socialist International [November 1935]" (Oneal Papers). Norman Thomas to Seward Collins, March 13, 1934; Norman Thomas to Horace J. Jaquith, April 12, 1934; Norman Thomas to "Dear Comrades" [June 1934]; Doris Preisler to National Executive Committee, June 6, 1934; Norman Thomas to Paul Porter, June 7, 1934; Memorandum of Norman Thomas to Biemiller, Krueger, Krzycki, Senior, June 8, 1934; Norman Thomas to Clarence O. Senior, June 8, 1934; Phillip P. Greer to Norman Thomas, June 11, 1934; Norman Thomas to Alfred Baker Lewis, June 12, 1934; Norman Thomas to Siegfried Ameringer, June 13, 1934; Norman Thomas to Clarence Senior, Daniel Hoan, Leo Krzycki, Al Benson, and Andrew Biemiller, June 14, 1934; Norman Thomas to Dr. Friedrich Adler, June 15, 1934; Norman Thomas to Members of the National Executive Committee, June 19, 1934; Norman Thomas to Clarence Senior, June 25, 1934; J. F. Higgins to Norman Thomas, July 2, 1934; Joseph M. Coldwell to Norman Thomas, July 12, 1934; Edward F. Cassidy to Norman Thomas, July 26, 1934; George E. Roewer to Norman Thomas, July 26, 1934; B. Charney Vladeck to Norman Thomas, August 1, 1934; Norman Thomas to J. L. Adler, August 10, 1934; William M. Feigenbaum to Norman Thomas, October 19, 1934; Norman Thomas to William Feigenbaum, October 27, 1934; William Feigenbaum to Norman Thomas, October 29, 1934; B. Charney Vladeck to Norman Thomas, October 30, 1934; Norman Thomas to Members of the National Executive Committee [November 1934]; Norman Thomas to James H. Maurer, November 5, 1934; "Memorandum on the R.P.C." [November 1934]; Norman Thomas to Clarence Senior, December 3, 1934; Norman Thomas to State Committee, Socialist Party, December 5, 1934; Norman Thomas to D. Dubinsky, J. Baskin, A. Held, A. Miller, B. C. Vladeck, December 5, 1934; Frank Crosswaithe to Norman Thomas, December 18, 1934; S. Wolos to Norman Thomas, December 18, 1934; Norman Thomas to Alice S. Eddy, December 27, 1934; Norman Thomas to Clarence Senior, January 12, 1934; Louis Schaeffer to Norman Thomas, January 16, 1935; Norman Thomas to Samuel Smidlowitz, January 31, 1935; Samuel S. White to Norman Thomas, March 2, 1935; James D. Graham to Norman Thomas, March 31, 1935; Norman Thomas to Paul Porter, Max Delson, Murray Baron, April 3, 1935; R. Abramowitz [Abramowich] to Clarence Senior [April 1935]; Samuel A. De Witt to Norman Thomas, May 31, 1935; Ben Josephson to Norman Thomas, June 17, 1935; Norman Thomas to Al

Hamilton, November 16, 1935; S. Gordon to Norman Thomas, December 13, 1935; in NT Papers. Haim Kantorovich, *The Socialist Party at the Cross Roads* (New York, Max Delson, 1935), pp. 6–7; Alfred Baker Lewis, *The Truth About the Declaration* (Boston, Alfred Baker Lewis, 1934), p. 4; *New Leader*, October 19, 1935.

v The disintegration of American socialism, 1934–1936

1 "Stamp Report as of November 30, 1935" (Duke). "Membership Report as of December 1934"; Norman Thomas to Upton Sinclair, September 4, 1933; Jerry Voorhis to Norman Thomas, September 18, 1933; Norman Thomas to Upton Sinclair, September 27, 1933; Jerry Voorhis to Norman Thomas, April 2, 1934; Upton Sinclair to Norman Thomas, April 25, 1934; Norman Thomas to Upton Sinclair, May 1, 1934; Milen Dempster to Norman Thomas, September 4, 1934; Mrs. Fred W. Jackson to Norman Thomas, September 5, 1934; E. Backus to Norman Thomas, September 7, 1934; Norman Thomas to Milen Dempster and the State Executive Committee of the Socialist Party of California, September 11, 1934; Samuel F. White to Clarence Senior, September 17, 1934; Milen Dempster to Norman Thomas, September 17, 1934; Clarence Senior to Norman Thomas, October 17, 1934; Samuel S. White to Norman Thomas, March 2, 1935; in NT Papers. Norman Thomas, "Along the Class Struggle Front," *World Tomorrow*, XVI (September 28, 1933), 537–538; *New Leader*, October 7 and December 16, 1933, July 14 and November 17, 1934.

2 Norman Thomas to Clarence O. Senior, March 30, 1934; Clarence Senior to Norman Thomas, April 2, 1934; Norman Thomas to Julius Gerber, May 9, 1934; Julius Gerber to Norman Thomas, May 25, 1934; Norman Thomas to Charles Solomon, July 2, 1934; Norman Thomas to Maynard Krueger, October 13, 1934; in NT Papers. Edward Flynn, ed., *Manual for Use of the Legislature of the State of New York* (Albany, Lyons, 1935), p. 978.

3 Norman Thomas to B. C. Vladeck, April 17, 1934 (Vladeck Papers); Norman Thomas to B. C. Vladeck, Joseph Schlossberg, David Dubinsky, *et al.*, November 1, 1934 (Vladeck Papers). B. C. Vladeck to Daniel W. Hoan, December 28, 1933; Norman Thomas to B. C. Vladeck, December 29, 1933; Norman Thomas to Ray S. Kellogg, January 12, 1934; Norman Thomas to Siegfried Ameringer, January 21, 1934; Norman Thomas to Floyd Olson, April 10, 1934; Daniel W. Hoan, George Hampel, Al Benson, and Andrew Biemiller to Norman Thomas, April 10, 1934; Norman Thomas to Philip Nemoff, April 10, 1934; Howard Y. Williams to Norman Thomas, April 18, 1934; Norman Thomas to James H. Dailey, August 9, 1934; Daniel W. Hoan to James Oneal, November 13, 1934; Norman Thomas to B. Charney Vladeck, January 10, 1935; Thomas R. Amlie to Norman Thomas, March 30, 1935; Norman Thomas to Thomas R. Amlie, April 1, 1935; George J. Schneider,

Ernest Lundeen, Vito Marcantonio, Thomas R. Amlie to Norman Thomas, April 23, 1935; Norman Thomas to Alfred Baker Lewis, December 14, 1935; Norman Thomas to Daniel W. Hoan, December 24, 1935; Howard Y. Williams to Norman Thomas, January 7, 1936; Norman Thomas to "Dear Howard" [Y. Williams], January 13, 1936; in NT Papers. *Socialist Call*, September 14, 1935, February 29, 1936.

4 "ALL OUT TO ANTI-FASCIST DEMONSTRATION," November 18, 1934 [handbill]; "Minutes of National Executive Committee, Socialist Party, U.S.A., Boston, Massachusetts, November 30, December 1–2, 1934"; N.E.C. Memo #1, July 13, 1935, pp. 6–7; "Minutes of Action Committee, January 23, 1936"; "Minutes of the Action Committee, February 7, 1936"; "Action Committee Minutes, February 12, 1936"; "National Call by the Interstate Conference, May 10, 1936"; "Minutes of the State Convention of Socialist Party [Session of June 28], 1936"; Charles Krumbein to New York State Convention, Socialist Party, June 23, 1936; "Convention Memo #25" [1936]; at Duke. Norman Thomas to Ralph Harlow, January 17, 1934; Norman Thomas to Clarence O. Senior, July 3, 1934; Powers Hapgood to Maynard Krueger, July 3, 1934; Daniel Hoan to Clarence Senior [July 3, 1934]; Daniel Hoan to Harold Kelso, July 9, 1934; Harold Kelso to National Executive Committee, July 26, 1934; Clarence Senior to Members of the National Executive Committee, August 8, 1934; Norman Thomas to Clarence Senior, August 16, 1934; Norman Thomas to Earl Browder, August 21, 1934; Norman Thomas to Norman Lewis, October 8, 1934; Daniel W. Hoan to Clarence Senior, October 19, 1934; Clarence Senior to National Executive Committee, October 29, 1934; Norman Thomas to Members of the National Executive Committee, October 22, 1934; Norman Thomas to William Sherman, December 3, 1934; Clarence Senior to National Executive Committee, December 18, 1934; Norman Thomas to Monroe Sweetland, December 26, 1934; Clarence Senior to the N.E.C., January 4, 1935; Norman Thomas to Marion S. Alderton, January 6, 1936; in NT Papers. Browder, "The Situation in the Socialist Party," pp. 279–282; Browder, "The United Front Against War and Fascism," p. 264; *Syracuse Herald*, December 19, 1934; *New York Times*, February 19, 1939, p. 21; *New Leader*, December 8, 1934; *Socialist Call*, August 3, September 21, and September 28, 1935, April 18, 1936.

5 Norman Thomas and Devere Allen to Friedrich Adler, November 3, 1935 (Oneal Papers). Norman Thomas to William Krebs, February 5, 1935; Norman Thomas to Donald F. Caswell, June 11, 1934; Norman Thomas to O. Sewell Palmer, September 7, 1934; Norman Thomas to Bob Thompson, September 22, 1934; Norman Thomas to Miss Mabel E. Bontz, October 29, 1934; Reverend Charles E. Coughlin to Steward Woods Taylor [November 1934]; in NT Papers. *The Choice Before Us*, pp. 159, 201, 203; Norman Thomas, "What Will I Do When America Goes to War?," *Modern Monthly*, IX (September 1935), 264–265; *New Leader*, December 14, 1935; *Socialist Call*, July 6, 1935.

6 Martha B. Johnson to Norman Thomas, November 7, 1933; William R.

Amberson to Norman Thomas, March 4, 1934; Norman Thomas to Mrs. Martha B. Johnson, March 6, 1934; H. L. Mitchell to Norman Thomas, March 25, 1934; Norman Thomas to H. L. Mitchell, March 26, 1934; Norman Thomas to H. L. Mitchell, March 28, 1934; H. L. Mitchell to Norman Thomas, June 14, 1934; H. L. Mitchell to Norman Thomas, June 26, 1934; Norman Thomas to the American Fund for Public Service, June 26, 1934; H. L. Mitchell to Norman Thomas, July 4, 1934; H. L. Mitchell to Norman Thomas, August 14, 1934; H. L. Mitchell to Norman Thomas, September 5, 1934; H. L. Mitchell to Norman Thomas, October 4, 1934; H. L. Mitchell to Norman Thomas, October 12, 1934; Ward Rodgers to Norman Thomas, January 24, 1935 [1934 date on letter is obvious error]; "Norman Thomas Visits the Cotton Fields" [mimeographed release, undated but March 1935]; Norman Thomas to American Fund for Public Service, March 21, 1935; "Telegrams Received from Arkansas [mimeographed, March 23–27, 1935]; Norman Thomas to H. L. Mitchell, March 29, 1935; Norman Thomas to Mary Hillyer, March 30, 1935; H. L. Mitchell to Jack [John] Herling, April 1, 1935; Howard Kester to Norman Thomas and John Herling, April 19, 1935; C. T. Carpenter to Norman Thomas, April 27, 1935; Norman Thomas to Editor, *New York Times,* April 30, 1935; H. L. Mitchell to Frank Morrison, October 4, 1935; H. L. Mitchell to Howard Kester (telegram), January 16, 1936; H. L. Mitchell to Norman Thomas (telegram), January 17, 1936; Howard Kester to Norman Thomas, January 18, 1936; "Press Release of Southern Tenant Farmers Union," January 18, 1936; "Press Release of Southern Tenant Farmers Union," May 28, 1936; in NT Papers. *The Choice Before Us,* p. 99; John Herling, "Field Notes from Arkansas," *Nation,* CXL (April 10, 1935), 419; Oren Stephens, "Revolt in the Delta," *Harper's Magazine,* CLXXXIII (November 1941), 656, 659, 660; M. S. Venkataramini, "Norman Thomas, Arkansas Sharecroppers, and Roosevelt's Agricultural Policies, 1933–1937," *Mississippi Valley Historical Review,* XLVII (September 1960), 225–226, 233–234.

7 Norman Thomas to Henry A. Wallace, February 22, 1934; Norman Thomas to Heber Blankenhorn, March 1, 1935; Norman Thomas to Felix Frankfurter, March 2, 1935; Chester C. Davis to Roger N. Baldwin, March 2, 1935; Norman Thomas to Chester C. Davis, March 7, 1935; Norman Thomas to Paul Porter, April 4, 1935; Henry A. Wallace to Norman Thomas, May 14, 1934; Henry A. Wallace to Norman Thomas, December 19, 1934; Norman Thomas to Henry Wallace, December 21, 1934; Norman Thomas to Rexford G. Tugwell, March 28, 1935; Norman Thomas to Senator Robert F. Wagner, April 4, 1935; Norman Thomas to Franklin D. Roosevelt, April 9, 1935; Franklin D. Roosevelt to Norman Thomas, April 22, 1935; Norman Thomas to the Senate Committee on Agriculture, May 1, 1935; C. T. Carpenter to Ward Rodgers, May 18, 1935; William R. Amberson to Norman Thomas, December 17, 1935; H. L. Mitchell to Norman Thomas, December 16, 1935; Norman Thomas to Senator Joseph T. Robinson [July 1936] (telegram); in NT Papers interview with Norman Thomas,

October 1963. Stephens, "Revolt in the Delta," pp. 659, 664; Norman Thomas, "Republicans and Democrats Are Stealing from My Socialist Platform," reprinted from *Look*, August 17, 1948 (copy at Tamiment), p. 2; Venkataramini, "Norman Thomas, Arkansas Sharecroppers, and Roosevelt's Agricultural Policies, 1933–1937," pp. 235–236, 240–245.

8 Norman Thomas to Editor and Officers, Progressive Miners of America, November 20, 1933; Norman Thomas to Warren D. Mullin, April 3, 1934; Norman Thomas to William Green, April 6, 1934; Norman Thomas to Max Danish, April 7, 1934; Norman Thomas to Raimondo Fazio, August 22, 1934; Norman Thomas to Frank Gorman, September 13, 1934; Norman Thomas to Hugh Johnson, September 19, 1934; Roger N. Baldwin to Prof. Lawrence M. Sears (telegram), September 17, 1934; Norman Thomas to E. E. Ledford, September 17, 1934; J. C. B. Ehringhaus to Norman Thomas, September 19, 1934 (telegram); A. L. Wirin to Prof. Lawrence Sears, September 20, 1934; John B. Goins to Clarence Senior, September 21, 1934; Norman Thomas to Edward Keating, December 18, 1934; Norman Thomas to John Brophy, December 12, 1935; Norman Thomas to Marcy W. Rosebraugh, October 24, 1936; Norman Thomas to Heywood Broun, November 12, 1936; "Memorandum to H. W. L[aidler], and [Aaron] Levenstein, [May 1936]; *Otis Cox v. Paul V. McNutt, Elmer F. Strand, Earl E. Weimer, William Becker, James Mitchell, Phillip Lutz, Raymond J. Kearns:* In the District Court of the United States for the Southern District of Indiana, Terre Haute Division, amended bill of Otis Cox [no date]; in NT Papers. See also *New York Times*, February 2, 1933, p. 6, February 7, 1933, p. 5.

9 Norman Thomas to I. Nussbaum, September 24, 1935; Murray Baron to Clarence Senior, September 25, 1935; Clarence Senior to National Executive Committee, September 26, 1935; James Oneal to Norman Thomas, October 6, 1935; Norman Thomas to James Oneal, October 8, 1935; in NT Papers. *New York Times*, January 2, 1933, p. 22; *New Leader*, April 13 and April 20, 1935; *Socialist Call*, August 17 and October 26, 1935.

10 Clarence Senior to National Executive Committee, September 24, 1934; News Release, October 29, 1934; James Oneal to "My Dear Dan" [Hoan], November 2, 1934; in Hoan Papers. Paul Porter to Norman Thomas, July 29, 1934; Norman Thomas to [Franz] Daniel, [Powers] Hapgood, [Daniel W.] Hoan, [Darlington] Hoopes, [Maynard] Krueger, [Leo] Krzycki, August 17, 1934; Daniel W. Hoan to Norman Thomas, August 21, 1934; Clarence Senior to Norman Thomas, October 2, 1934; Clarence Senior to National Executive Committee, October 8, 1934; in NT Papers. "Notes on the 10th Annual Convention, I.S.S.," *Intercollegiate Socialist*, VII (February–March 1919), 24–25; *New Leader*, November 10, 1934.

11 N[orman] T[homas] to Dan Hoan, Maynard Krueger, Clarence Senior [March 1935] (Hoan Papers); Statement of Local Buffalo [April 1934] (Duke); Herman Wolf to Maynard Krueger, Clarence Senior, and

Andy [Andrew] Biemiller, January 29, 1935 (Duke); "Convention Memo #25" [1936] (Duke). Norman Thomas to the Board of the *New Leader*, June 6, 1934; National Headquarters to the National Executive Committee, June 27, 1934; Norman Thomas to Members of the N.E.C., July 18, 1934; Norman Thomas to Andrew J. Biemiller, September 17, 1934; Norman Thomas to Jack Herling, [November 1934]; Clarence Senior to Norman Thomas, January 29, 1935; Norman Thomas to Clarence O. Senior, February 1, 1935; Norman Thomas to Daniel W. Hoan, February 2, 1935; Max Delson to Andrew Biemiller, February 5, 1935; Norman Thomas to the New Leader Association, February 25, 1935; Samuel S. White to Norman Thomas, March 2, 1935; William Feigenbaum to "Dear Norman" [Thomas], March 4, 1935; Norman Thomas to Samuel S. White, March 7, 1935; Daniel W. Hoan to Norman Thomas, March 7, 1935; in NT Papers. *New Leader*, February 16, March 9, and May 25, 1935; *Socialist Call*, March 23, 1935.

12 [Julius Gerber] to Daniel Hoan, Darlington Hoopes, Albert S. Coolidge, Leo Krzycki, October 5, 1935 (Duke). Norman Thomas to Alfred Baker Lewis, March 2, 1934; Julius Gerber to Norman Thomas, October 4, 1935; Paul Porter to Norman Thomas, October 6, 1935; Norman Thomas to Julius Gerber, October 8, 1935; Matthew M. Levy to Norman Thomas, October 9, 1935; [Norman Thomas] to "Dear Comrade [Henry] Fruchter," October 14, 1935; Norman Thomas to Andrew J. Biemiller and Paul Porter, November 2, 1935; Norman Thomas to Alfred Baker Lewis, November 18, 1935; [Norman Thomas], "Statement on the Thomas-Browder Debate," November 28, 1935; Norman Thomas to Irwin Nussbaum, December 2, 1935; Alfred Baker Lewis to Norman Thomas, December 5, 1935; in NT Papers. Norman Thomas v. Earl Browder, *Which Road for American Workers, Socialist or Communist?* (New York, Socialist Call, 1936), pp. 6–9, 18–19, 45–46; *New York Times,* November 28, 1935, p. 18; *New Leader*, December 16, 1933; *Socialist Call*, October 19, 1935.

13 "Draft of Report by James Oneal to L.S.I." [no date, but 1935] (Oneal Papers); Norman Thomas to Dan Hoan, Maynard Krueger, Clarence Senior [March 1935] (Hoan Papers). Norman Thomas to the "Membership of New York City" [March 1935]; "Minutes of Regular Meeting of City Central Committee, New York, March 6, 1935"; "Statement on the Party Situation in New York" [March 12, 1935]; "Minutes of Regular Meeting of City Executive Committee," March 13, 1935; Herbert Merrill to the State and Local Organizations and the Members of the Socialist Party of the U.S.A., March 22, 1935; Norman Thomas "To Upstate Comrades" [March 1935]; "RESOLUTION introduced and passed by Central Committee at its meeting on November 13, 1935, on reorganization of branches in Local New York so as to put an end to factional organizations and disruptive activities"; Minutes of Local New York Executive Committee, November 27, 1935; Norman Thomas to B. Charney Vladeck in Minutes of New York City Action Committee, December 12, 1935; "Memorandum Submitted to the National Executive Committee of the Socialist Party at Its Meet-

ing January 4–5, 1936, Philadelphia, Pa., by State Committee, Socialist Party of New York, Max Delson, State Chairman [Militant Committee]"; S. A. Moore to Clarence Senior, January 5, 1936; "Convention Memo #25" [1936]; "Convention Memo #29," [1936]; at Duke. Mary Hunter to Norman Thomas, October 17, 1934; Amicus Most to Norman Thomas [November 1934]; Norman Thomas to the Central Committee of the Socialist Party, January 2, 1935; Norman Thomas to Clarence Senior, January 12, 1935; [Max Delson] to Andrew Biemiller, February 5, 1935; Norman Thomas to Jasper McLevy, Devere Allen, Irving Freese, Darlington Hoopes, Daniel Hoan, M. Benson, Andrew Biemiller [February 1935]; Maynard C. Krueger to Norman Thomas, March 4, 1935; Daniel Hoan to Norman Thomas, March 7, 1935; Jack Altman to Norman Thomas, March 15, 1935; Norman Thomas to Harry Laidler, March 30, 1935; Daniel Hoan to Norman Thomas, May 10, 1935; Harry W. Laidler to Norman Thomas, May 13, 1935; Max Delson to Norman Thomas, May 29, 1935; August Claessens to Norman Thomas, June 8, 1935; Norman Thomas to Darlington Hoopes, July 8, 1935; "N.E.C. Memo #17," July 13, 1935; Clarence Senior to Friedrich Adler, July 25, 1935; Julius Gerber to Members of the National Executive Committee, July 26, 1935; Herbert M. Merrill to National Executive Committee, October 7, 1935; James Oneal to "Dear Comrade," October 17, 1935; Daniel W. Hoan to Norman Thomas, October 18, 1935; Daniel W. Hoan to Executive Committee of the Socialist Party of New York City, October 18, 1935; James Oneal to Clarence Senior, October 25, 1935; Jack Sullivan to Devere Allen, Arnold Freese, Darlington Hoopes, Maynard Krueger, Paul Porter, November 18, 1935; Herbert Merrill to Coleman B. Cheney, December 2, 1935; Arthur G. McDowell to Norman Thomas, December 2, 1935; Devere Allen to Norman Thomas, December 3, 1935; Clarence Senior to the N.E.C., December 4, 1935; Stafford Cripps to Norman Thomas, December 6, 1935; Jacob Bernstein to Norman Thomas, December 9, 1935; Norman Thomas to Clarence Senior, December 11, 1935; Clarence Senior to "Dear Comrade," December 12, 1935; B. C. Vladeck to Norman Thomas, December 13, 1935; Norman Thomas to Alfred Baker Lewis, December 14, 1935; Leonard Bright to Norman Thomas, December 14, 1935; James Oneal to Clarence Senior, December 14, 1935; Norman Thomas to B. C. Vladeck, December 20, 1935; Jessie Wallace Hughan to Norman Thomas, December 22, 1935; "Minutes of New York State Conference, Utica, December 28 and 29, 1935"; Herbert Merrill to National Executive Committee, December 29, 1935; "Release of Socialist Party of America, January 8, 1936"; William E. Bohn to Norman Thomas, January 8, 1936; Norman Thomas to Miss Helen Phelps Stokes, January 9, 1936; Norman Thomas to George Dimmock, January 15, 1936; "Resolution Adopted at Interstate Conference, New York City, January 19, 1936"; Winston Dancis to Norman Thomas, January 20, 1936; in NT Papers. *New York Herald Tribune*, January 5, 1935, p. 10; *New Leader*, March 16, July 20, November 9, and November 16, 1935; *Ravaaja*, December 7, 1935 (translation in NT Papers); *Socialist Call*, July 20 and December 14, 1935.

14 Norman Thomas to Alfred Baker Lewis, March 2, 1936 (Vladeck Papers). James Oneal to E. R. Carnes, January 27, 1936; "Minutes of City Executive Committee, March 11, 1936"; Herbert M. Merrill to Locals and Members, April 20, 1936; Minutes of City Executive Committee, April 21, 1936; Herbert M. Merrill to "Locals and Members," May 6, 1936; Robert A. Hoffman to Samuel H. Friedman, May 14, 1936; "Convention Memo #25" [1936]; "Trench Warfare in New York" [Old Guard statement], 1936; at Duke. Norman Thomas to Daniel Hoan, December 18, 1934 (NT Papers); Resolution of the Massachusetts State Committee to the National Executive Committee Meeting at Buffalo, New York, March 22, 1935 (NT Papers). Abraham Cahan, "Vote at the Primaries for the Unity of the Socialist Party," *Jewish Daily Forward*, March 28, 1936; since the translation in the NT Papers is inaccurate, the translation used here is my own. *Ravaaja*, January 15, 1936 (translation in NT Papers); *New Leader*, April 11, 1936; *Socialist Call*, March 14, March 28, and April 18, 1936.

15 Norman Thomas to Daniel Hoan, October 30, 1935 (Hoan Papers). Clarence Senior to National Executive Committee, "Memo #6," January 4, 1936; "Comparative Membership Gain or Loss for First Ten Months of 1932–1936"; "Excerpts from speeches Norman Thomas is delivering on his western tour, April 10 to May 1 [1936]"; "Minutes of the National Convention—May 23–26, 1936"; "Summary of Address by Norman Thomas, Socialist Candidate for President, at the National Education Association Convention, Portland, Oregon, July 2nd, 1936"; "Speech of the Hon. Norman Thomas Before Second Townsend National Convention, Cleveland, Ohio, July 18, 1936"; "Radio Speech by Norman Thomas, Socialist Candidate for President over Station WCFL, Chicago, 7:45 P.M., October 16, 1936"; "Acceptance Speech [of Norman Thomas], 1936"; Norman Thomas, "You Can't Cure Tuberculosis with Cough Drops," [handbill, 1936]; [Norman Thomas, "The Split of 1936"] 1957; at Duke. B. Charney Vladeck to Norman Thomas, June 14, 1934; Norman Thomas to Maynard Krueger, May 4, 1936; Norman Thomas to Leo Krzycki, May 4, 1936; Norman Thomas to Andrew J. Biemiller, May 8, 1936; "News Release of National Affairs Committee, Socialist Party, May 8, 1936"; Leo Krzycki to Norman Thomas, May 13, 1936; Norman Thomas to Leo Krzycki, May 18, 1936; B. Charney Vladeck to Norman Thomas, May 20, 1936; Clarence Senior to Norman Thomas, June 4, 1936; John F. Sullivan to Norman Thomas, July 2, 1936; Clarence Senior to National Executive Committee, July 7 and July 22, 1936; "Report to National Executive Committee on Thomas and Nelson Independent Committee, Mary W. Hillyer, Director," July 17, 1936; James D. Graham to Norman Thomas, August 14, 1936; Norman Thomas to Clarence Senior, August 18, 1936; "Summary of Address by Norman Thomas, Thursday, August 20, 1936, at Chautauqua, New York"; Francis A. Henson to Norman Thomas, September 11, 1936; Norman Thomas to Maynard C. Krueger, November 1, 1936; Marvin [Halverson] to Norman Thomas, November 12, 1936; Norman Thomas to Franklin Delano Roosevelt, November 12, 1936; "N.E.C. Memo #6," November 15, 1936; "Report to the Special

National Convention, Chicago, March 26–29, 1937," p. 3; in NT Papers. Roseboom, *A History of Presidential Elections*, p. 457; interview with Norman Thomas, October 1963; Earl Browder, "Democracy or Fascism?," in *The People's Front* (New York, International Publishers, 1938), p. 34; Norman Thomas, "The Election of 1936 and the Prospects of a Farmer-Labor Party," *American Socialist Monthly*, V (December 1936), 8; Norman Thomas, "Roosevelt Faces Re-election," *American Socialist Monthly*, V (April 1936), 7; Norman Thomas, "Why Labor Should Support the Socialist Party," *American Socialist Monthly*, V (July 1936), 3–4; *New Leader*, May 1, June 13, and October 24, 1936; *Socialist Call*, April 18, May 9, and June 6, 1936, March 11, 1939, August 11, 1944.

16 [Norman Thomas, "The Split of 1936"] 1957, p. 3 (Duke). Clarence Senior to "Dear Comrades," March 16, 1936; Daniel W. Hoan to the Members of the N.E.C., Socialist Party, March 18, 1936; Darlington Hoopes to Norman Thomas, April 8, 1936; "Referendum B, 1936, Local Berks County, Socialist Party," James H. Maurer to "My Comrades in Berks County," June 25, 1936; Norman Thomas to Darlington Hoopes and George Rhodes, August 19, 1936; Darlington Hoopes to Norman Thomas, August 26, 1936; Norman Thomas to Jesse Holmes, September 1, 1936; Norman Thomas to Mayor Daniel W. Hoan, September 23, 1936; Devere Allen to the "Members of the N.E.C.," November 6, 1936; Norman Thomas to Clarence [Senior], [Jack] Altman, and [Harry W.] Laidler, November 6, 1936; Norman Thomas, "The New York Municipal Campaign," 1937 (mimeographed); in NT Papers. Paul Porter, *Which Way for the Socialist Party?* (Milwaukee, State Executive Board, Socialist Party of Wisconsin, 1937), pp. 14–15; J. C. Rich, *The Jewish Daily Forward* (New York, The Forward Association, 1967), pp. 45–47; Norman Thomas, *Socialism on the Defensive* (New York, Harper, 1938), p. 287; *Reading Eagle*, July 7, 1936; *Reading Times*, October 27, 1936; *Socialist Call*, November 14, 1936, May 28, July 16, August 6, and November 12, 1938, April 13 and September 21, 1940, September 27, 1941, January 3, 1942.

vi A leader without followers, 1937–1940

1 "Report to the National Convention, April 21–23, 1938, Kenosha, Wisconsin," pp. 3–5, 20 (Hoan Papers). Minutes, National Committee, Workers Party, June 1935; "Circular on WP Factional Situation and SYL," August 1935; "Circular Letter on Opponents' Work [mimeographed handbill], August 29, 1935; "Report of New York District, Spartacus Youth League, August 10–11, 1935"; "Minutes of the Action Committee, January 23, February 7, and February 12, 1936"; "Minutes of the Steering Committee" [February 1936]; "Why We Are Joining the Socialist Party" [Workers Party Handbill, no date]; "Report of the Subcommittee on Question of Appeal Association and Publication of 'Socialist Appeal' and Related Matters" [September 1–4, 1937]; at Duke. Norman Thomas to Maynard Krueger, October 13, 1934; Nor-

man Thomas to Arthur G. McDowell, February 11, 1936; Norman Thomas to Maynard Krueger, May 4, 1936; Norman Thomas to "My Comrades in Pennsylvania," June 1936; L. Kruhe to Clarence Senior, July 28, 1936; Norman Thomas to Max Delson, Murray Gross, Murray Baron, Hal Siegel, and Jack Altman, August 7, 1936; Glenn Trimble to "Dear Friend," November 7, 1936; J. P. Cannon to "Dear Comrade," November 7, 1936; Norman Thomas to Jack Altman, December 5, 1936; Frank [Trager] to Norman Thomas, December 15, 1936; Norman Thomas to Clarence Senior, January 4, 1937; Norman Thomas to Mrs. Horace A. Eaton, January 21, 1937; Robert G. Spivack to Norman Thomas, January 28, 1937; Devere Allen to Norman Thomas, February 2, 1937; Paul Porter to Norman Thomas, February 3, 1937; Norman Thomas to Paul Porter, February 4, 1937; Lillian Symes to "Dear Norman," February 16, 1937; Ward Rodgers to Hal Siegel, February 18, 1937; Mrs. O. F. Hawkins to Members of the National Executive Committee, March 18, 1937; Roy E. Burt to Members of the National Executive Committee, September 15, 1937; Norman Thomas to Devere Allen, Jack Altman, Gus Tyler, October 6, 1937; in NT Papers. James P. Cannon, *The History of American Trotskyism* (New York, Pioneer Publishers, 1944), pp. 195, 210–211, 213, 225–227, 231–233, 241, 243–245, 247–253; *Labor and Socialist Press Service*, December 31, 1932; *Socialist Call*, August 21 and October 9, 1937.

2 Norman Thomas to Leon Despres, August 28, 1936; Norman Thomas to Aaron Levenstein, September 1, 1936; Norman Thomas to "Inquiring Comrades," September 3, 1936; Angelica Balabanoff to Norman Thomas, September 9, 1936; Norman Thomas to Miss Hildegard Smith, September 23, 1936; Norman Thomas to Angelica Balabanoff, September 26, 1936; George Novack to "Dear Comrade Thomas," December 2, 1936; Alfred Baker Lewis to Norman Thomas, January 27, 1937; Norman Thomas to Alfred Baker Lewis, January 29, 1936; Norman Thomas to Devere Allen, Roy Burt, Maynard Krueger, and Clarence Senior, January 29, 1937; Norman Thomas to Paul Porter, February 4, 1937; Norman Thomas to Editor, *New York World-Telegram*, February 8, 1937; Norman Thomas to Ambassador Alexander Troyanovsky, March 17, 1937; in NT Papers. Norman Thomas, "Preface," in Friedrich Adler, *The Witchcraft Trials in Moscow* (New York, Pioneer Publishers, 1937), no pagination; *Socialist Call*, December 26, 1936, April 3, June 3, June 19, and September 25, 1937, March 12, 1938, September 7, 1940.

3 [Norman Thomas], "Memorandum on the Socialist Party and the Debs Column" [December 24, 1936]; Norman Thomas to Devere Allen, Roy Burt, and Staff, December 24, 1936; "Statement of National Executive Committee, Socialist Party, U.S.A., on Present Confusion on the Spanish Question," January 11, 1937; at Duke. Norman Thomas to Devere Allen and Max Delson [November 1936]; Norman Thomas, "Memorandum on the Spanish Situation in the Socialist Party" [December 1936]; "Statement of the Fellowship of Reconciliation on Socialist Party Recruiting for Spanish War" [December 1936]; Elizabeth Gilman to

Norman Thomas, December 24, 1936; Norman Thomas to John Haynes Holmes, December 24, 1936; John Haynes Holmes to "Dear Norman," December 28, 1936; Roy Burt to Norman Thomas, December 30, 1936; Norman Thomas to John Nevin Sayre, December 30, 1936; Norman Thomas to Jessie Wallace Hughan, December 30, 1936; Roy E. Burt to National Executive Committee, January 6, 1937; Norman Thomas to Joseph Colt Bloodgood, January 18, 1937; Louis Mann to Norman Thomas, January 21, 1937; Fenner Brockway to Norman Thomas, September 27, 1937; Norman Thomas to the "St. Louis Local" [October 1937]; Norman Thomas to Fernando de los Rios, November 8, 1937; Fenner Brockway to Norman Thomas, November 11, 1937; Norman Thomas to "Dear Comrade Middleton," November 27, 1937; Franklin D. Roosevelt to Norman Thomas, December 25, 1937; Sam Baron to Socialist Party of the U.S., November 19, 1938; in NT Papers. Norman Thomas, *Socialism on the Defensive* (New York, Harper, 1938), p. 142; Jessie Wallace Hughan, "Pacifists Face Dilemma," *Nation*, CXLV (July 17, 1937), 82–84; Norman Thomas, "Pacifists' Dilemma," *Nation*, CXLIV (June 19, 1937), 698–700; *Socialist Call*, June 5, June 19, June 26, July 3, August 14, and November 18, 1937.

4 "Report to the National Convention, April 21–23, 1938," pp. 3–4 (Hoan Papers). "Norman Thomas to Members of the National Executive Committee," November 22, 1937; "Minutes, National Executive Committee, Socialist Party, U.S.A., December 10–12, 1937," pp. 9–10; Arthur G. McDowell, "A Memorandum to the Members of the National Executive Committee and the National Action Committee," March 13, 1939; "Apportionment of Delegates, National Convention, 1940"; "Report of Executive Secretary to N.E.C. Meeting, December 10–12, 1937"; Dues Stamp Report as of December 31, 1940; at Duke. Paul Porter to Norman Thomas, January 27, 1937; Norman Thomas to Maynard Krueger, February 8, 1939; Norman Thomas to Harry W. Laidler, February 17, 1939; Paul Porter to Norman Thomas, February 20, 1939; Norman Thomas to Roy Burt, February 20, 1939; Norman Thomas to "Messrs. Burt, Porter, and Allen," February 21, 1939; Norman Thomas to Alfred Baker Lewis, February 23, 1939; "Report of the Acting Executive Secretary to the City and State Convention, Socialist Party, New York, February 11–13, 1939"; in NT Papers. "The Struggle for Revolutionary Socialism Must Go On" (broadside published by Clarity Group, 1937, copy in NT Papers); *World Tomorrow*, XV (October 12, 1932), 352; *Socialist Clarity*, I (March 1, 1937), cover; Gus Tyler, "For a United Party of Revolutionary Struggle," *ibid.*, p. 10; *Socialist Call*, November 21, 1936, March 11, 1939, September 30, 1939.

5 Norman Thomas to B. C. Vladeck, July 13, 1937 (Vladeck Papers); Norman Thomas to B. C. Vladeck, September 8, 1937 (Vladeck Papers); "ALP Report by Alfred G. McDowell," July 21, 1938 (Duke); "Comment by Thomas on New York Municipal Situation, August 3, 1937" (Duke); Minutes, National Action Committee, August 3, 1938 (Duke). Norman Thomas to "Clarence, Altman and Laidler," November 6, 1936; Julia Loewe to Norman Thomas, January 7, 1937;

Norman Thomas, "The Municipal Campaign" [May 1937]; Norman Thomas, "Memorandum for Laidler, Altman and Lipsig," September 3, 1937; Murray Gross to Norman Thomas, November 27, 1937; Norman Thomas to Alan Strachan, January 3, 1938; Norman Thomas to Leonard Woodcock, January 5, 1938; Norman Thomas to Paul Porter, June 17, 1938; Norman Thomas to "Dear Ben and Tucker," August 19, 1938; Arthur McDowell to Ben Fischer, December 7, 1938; Release by Socialist Party of New York, December 25, 1938; M. L. Severn to Norman Thomas, February 7, 1939; Norman Thomas to Michael Quill, September 18, 1939; Press Release by Norman Thomas, "The Labor Party Purge of Communists Is No Denial of Civil Liberty" [October 1939]; Walter O'Hagen to Norman Thomas, February 11, 1940; Norman Thomas to Walter O'Hagen, February 13, 1940; Norman Thomas to Coleman B. Cheney, August 14, 1940; Norman Thomas to Editor, *New York World-Telegram,* October 20, 1941; in NT Papers. *Socialism on the Defensive,* p. 291; *New York Herald Tribune,* June 3, 1938, pp. 1, 37; *New York Times,* August 28, 1938, p. 4, December 8, 1938, p. 5, September 12, 1941, p. 4; *Socialist Call,* December 12, 1936, July 17, August 7, August 28, September 11, October 9, and November 6, 1937, February 5, March 19, and August 6, 1938, January 14, 1939, April 14, 1944.

6 James D. Graham to Norman Thomas, July 3, 1938; Franklin D. Roosevelt to "Dear Norman," November 28, 1938; Norman Thomas to Franklin D. Roosevelt, November 26, 1941; *Thomas* v. *Casey* (121 N.J.L. 185 [1938]; 123 N.J.L. 447 [1939]); in NT Papers. Zachariah Chafee Jr., *Free Speech in the United States* (Cambridge, Harvard University Press, 1942), pp. 410–412; Norman Thomas, "The Menace of Fascism," *Socialist Review,* VI (July–August 1938), 2; *Socialist Call,* February 5, February 26, and June 11, 1938, June 24, 1939, February 10 and July 6, 1940.

7 Bernard K. Johnpoll, "Norman Thomas's Position on War, 1917–1962" (unpublished M.A. thesis, Rutgers University, 1963), pp. 52–56.

8 Norman Thomas to Elmer Rice, February 22, 1939; Norman Thomas to Osmond K. Fraenkel, December 19, 1939; Norman Thomas to Dorothy Dunbar Bromley, Morris Ernst, John Haynes Holmes, Roger Riis, Elmer Rice, and James Finnerty, January 9, 1940; in NT Papers. *Socialist Call,* December 16, 1939, February 17 and February 24, 1940.

9 Norman Thomas to the Reverend Joe H. Carter, October 22, 1936; Norman Thomas to Paul Porter, February 4, 1937; Norman Thomas to Llewelyn Jones, November 11, 1938; Norman Thomas to Raymond Hofses, November 9, 1938; Norman Thomas to Roy Burt, November 9, 1938; Norman Thomas to Simon Bass, November 14, 1938; Norman Thomas to Frank Knight, December 1, 1938; Norman Thomas to the Reverend Lee A. Howe, Jr., January 9, 1939; Norman Thomas to Nina Bull, March 17, 1939; Norman Thomas to Henry Sloane Coffin, July 14, 1939; Norman Thomas to Morris Milgrim, January 2, 1940; Norman Thomas to the Reverend P. Minwegen, OMI, January 23, 1941; Norman Thomas to Mrs. G. M. Brill, October 1, 1941; in NT Papers.

Norman Thomas, *Democracy versus Dictatorship* (New York, League for Industrial Democracy, 1938), pp. 6–7, 9, 24–26; *Socialism on the Defensive*, pp. 148–149; Clarence E. Rust, "Into the Democratic Party," *Hammer and Tongs*, I (February 1940), unpaged; *Socialist Call*, March 9 and May 4, 1940.

VII Keep America out of war

1 "Report to the National Convention, Kenosha, Wisconsin, April 21–23, 1938," p. 9 (Hoan Papers); Minutes, National Executive Committee, April 24, 1938 (Duke); Norman Thomas to "Dear Friend," January 21, 1938 (NT Papers); Norman Thomas to Ellen Starr Brinton, December 15, 1950 (NT Papers); interview with Norman Thomas, October 1963; *Socialist Call*, March 5, March 12, May 7, and July 30, 1938.

2 Norman Thomas to B. C. Vladeck, October 8, 1938 (Vladeck Papers); Minutes of National Anti-War Committee of [Socialist] Party, September 30, 1938 (Duke). Norman Thomas to Ralph Oscar Robinson, October 14, 1938; Franklin D. Roosevelt to Norman Thomas, October 29, 1938; Arthur G. McDowell to Frank N. Trager, December 6, 1938; Norman Thomas to Columbus Convention of the Youth Anti-War Committee, December 22, 1938; Norman Thomas to Murray Baron, December 24, 1938; Meyer Miller to Norman Thomas, February 15, 1939; Norman Thomas to Meyer Miller, February 17, 1939; Norman Thomas to Raymond Hofses, February 18, 1939; Norman Thomas to Alfred Baker Lewis, February 20, 1939; in NT Papers.

3 Socialist Campaign Publicity Bureau Release, July 9 [1940] (Duke); "Statement of Norman Thomas Before Senate Military Affairs Committee on Burke-Wadsworth Bill—July 11, 1940" (Duke). Norman Thomas to Alfred Baker Lewis, August 29, 1939; Norman Thomas to A. J. Muste, August 22, 1939; Norman Thomas to Mrs. Mary H. Blanshard, July 18, 1939; Norman Thomas to E. Worth Higgins, September 8, 1939; Norman Thomas to Mrs. John Randall, March 7, 1940; Norman Thomas to H. R. Hoffmann, December 30, 1939; Norman Thomas to Dorothy Detzer and Frederick Libby, February 9, 1940; Norman Thomas to "Dear Mr. Green," August 8, 1940; Norman Thomas, "Stop the Draft!," Speech at Anti-Conscription Mobilization, August 1, 1940; Norman Thomas to Charles E. Nixhorff, August 28, 1941; in NT Papers. *Socialist Call*, June 29, 1940.

4 Norman Thomas to Burton K. Wheeler, December 5, 1940 (NT Papers); Norman Thomas to Morris Liebman, July 17, 1941 (NT Papers); *World Almanac, 1942* (New York, New York World-Telegram, 1942), pp. 771, 776, 783–784, 790–792, 811, 813; *New York Times*, November 6, 1940, pp. 2, 9; *Washington Daily News*, April 9, 1940. See also *Socialist Call*, April 20–November 9, 1940.

5 Franklin D. Roosevelt to Norman Thomas, July 31, 1940; Franklin D. Roosevelt to Norman Thomas, August 12, 1940; Norman Thomas to Franklin D. Roosevelt, August 15, 1940; Franklin D. Roosevelt to "Dear Norman," November 9, 1940; in NT Papers.

6 Norman Thomas to the Members of the House Military Affairs Committee, July 30, 1940 (NT Papers); *New York Times,* July 12, 1940, p. 9, July 27, 1940, p. 5; *Socialist Call,* August 10, 1940.

7 Adolf A. Berle, Jr., to Norman Thomas, January 7, 1941; Franklin D. Roosevelt to "Dear Norman," January 9, 1941; Asher J. Finkel to Norman Thomas, February 3, 1941; Norman Thomas to Asher Finkel, February 5, 1941; Norman Thomas to Adolf A. Berle, Jr., February 5, 1941; Norman Thomas to the Ambassador of France, February 13, 1941; Cordell Hull to Norman Thomas, February 13, 1941; Norman Thomas to Victor Serge, February 21, 1942; Adolf A. Berle, Jr., to Norman Thomas, February 23, 1942; Norman Thomas to Harry Hopkins, September 4, 1942; Norman Thomas to David Meyer, September 10, 1942; Harry L. Hopkins to Norman Thomas, October 1, 1942; in NT Papers. See also Emanuel Nowogrodsky to Norman Thomas, October 23, 1939, and Mrs. S. S. Rosen to "Dear Comrade Thomas," June 7, 1942, which indicate the extent of Thomas's work for Socialist refugees; in NT Papers. *Socialist Call,* September 27, 1941.

8 "Report to the National Convention, April 21–23, 1938, Kenosha, Wisconsin," p. 6 (Hoan Papers). Kellam Foster, Arthur G. McDowell, John Mill, Mordecai Shulman, "An Address to the National Executive Committee of the Socialist Party," January 15, 1941; "Comment by Trager on Motion #8," February 24, 1941; [Paul Porter, Arthur McDowell, Frank Trager], "A Statement Accompanying Resignation from N.E.C.," February 1941; "Minority Report on Peace Resolution Submitted by Alfred Baker Lewis of Massachusetts," April 7, 1940; at Duke. Myrtle Vacirca to Aaron Levenstein, May 6, 1939; Norman Thomas to "The Jewish Comrades," September 26, 1939; Alfred Baker Lewis to Norman Thomas, September 30, 1939; Norman Thomas to Travers Clement, September 21, 1939; Norman Thomas to Harry W. Laidler, January 26, 1940; Norman Thomas to the Members of the N.E.C., March 1, 1941; Daniel Mebane to Norman Thomas, March 7, 1941; Ralph [Harlow] to Norman Thomas, March 21, 1940; Norman Thomas to Ralph Harlow, March 22, 1940; Norman Thomas to Meyer Motlin, May 10, 1940; Norman Thomas to Harry W. Laidler, June 3, 1940; Alfred Baker Lewis to Frank Trager, July 19, 1940; Norman Thomas to Alfred Baker Lewis, July 20, 1940; Norman Thomas to Alfred Baker Lewis, July 23, 1940; Norman Thomas to Travers Clement, July 30, 1940; Norman Thomas to Travers Clement, August 1, 1940; Irving Barshop to Norman Thomas, August 6, 1940; Norman Thomas to Irving Barshop, August 7, 1940; Norman Thomas to Edward C. M. Richards, October 3, 1940; Harry T. Smith to Socialist Party, Local New York, January 15, 1941; Arthur G. McDowell to "Dear Fellow Workers," January 17, 1941; Norman Thomas to Socialist Membership Meeting, February 17, 1941; Albert Sprague Coolidge to Frank Trager, March 1, 1941; Norman Thomas to Albert Sprague Coolidge, March 3, 1941; S. Gottlieb to Norman Thomas, March 5, 1941; Gerry Allard to "Dear Judah" [Drob], March 19, 1941; Norman Thomas to L. A. McGillivray, May 12, 1941; Norman Thomas to General Robert E.

Wood, June 10, 1941; in NT Papers. State Action Committee of Colorado, "Looking Forward: A Statement of Colorado's Position," *Hammer and Tongs*, I (February 1940), 9; "Minutes of Socialist Party National Convention," *Hammer and Tongs*, I (May 1940), 3–5, 31; *New York Times*, January 23, 1941, pp. 1, 8, April 29, 1941, p. 9; *Socialist Call*, October 28 and November 4, 1939, January 6, June 22, and August 3, 1940, February 8, 1941, March 22, 1941; *Jewish Daily Forward*, February 21, 1941.

9 Al Hamilton, "Anti-War Committee," *Report to the National Convention, Washington, D.C., April 6–8, 1940*, p. 45 (mimeographed copy at Duke). Norman Thomas to Members of the Governing Board [Keep America Out of War Committee] [September 19, 1939]; Norman Thomas to John Howard Lathrop, July 10, 1940; Norman Thomas to Corliss Lamont, February 3, 1941; Norman Thomas to Morris R. Cohen, November 4, 1941; in NT Papers. V. J. Jerome, *Social Democracy and the War* (New York, Workers Library Publishers, 1940), pp. 35–39; "Review of the Month," *Communist*, XIV (June 1940), 494; Earl Browder, "The Domestic Reactionary Counterpart of the Bourgeoisie," *Communist*, XIV (July 1940), 608–609; "Social-Democracy Exposes Itself Further," *Communist*, XV (May 1941), p. 399; *New York Times*, June 23, 1941; *Socialist Call*, July 5, 1941.

10 "America First Committee, Madison Square Garden Rally, May 23, 1941" (handbill at Duke); "Socialists and America First; Statement of Executive Committee, Local New York" [May 1941] (Duke). Press Release of *Agrupación Socialista Española* (Spanish Socialist Group), June 19, 1941; the author of the statement was Antonio Reina, editor of *Justicia* and a member of the pro–Largo Caballero left wing of the Spanish party, which Thomas also supported (Duke). Norman Thomas to Senator Burton K. Wheeler, John Flynn, Sidney Hertzberg, and J. F. Libby, January 11, 1940; Norman Thomas to Charles A. Lindbergh, August 9, 1940; R. Douglas Stuart, Jr., to Norman Thomas, November 15, 1940; Norman Thomas to R. Douglas Stuart, November 19, 1940; J. Clarke Waldron to Norman Thomas, November 26, 1940; Norman Thomas to J. Clarke Waldron, November 29, 1940; Willard Johnson to Norman Thomas, January 6, 1941; Norman Thomas to Willard Johnson, January 9, 1941; Norman Thomas to Ken Cuthbertson, January 27, 1941; Norman Thomas to Dorothy Thompson [February 28, 1941] (the letter was written under such stress that Thomas forgot to date it); Norman Thomas to R. Douglas Stuart, May 1, 1941; R. E. Wood to Norman Thomas, May 2, 1941; Norman Thomas to General Robert E. Wood, May 12, 1941; Grace Milgrim to Norman Thomas, May 21, 1941; Samuel Orr to Norman Thomas, May 24, 1941; Norman Thomas to Morris Milgrim, June 4, 1941; Arthur Sturcke to Robert L. Bliss, July 11, 1941; Miriam and Emanuel Muravchik to John T. Flynn, September 9, 1941; Emanuel Muravchik to Norman Thomas, September 9, 1941; Norman Thomas to Emanuel Muravchik, September 16, 1941; Norman Thomas to R. Douglas Stuart, September 16, 1941; Norman Thomas to Emanuel Muravchik, September 19, 1941; Norman Thomas to Morris R. Cohen, November 4, 1941; Norman

Thomas to Editor, *New York Times*, December 6, 1941; Norman Thomas to Edward A. Lyman, December 12, 1941; in NT Papers. Dorothy Thompson, "On the Record," *New York Herald-Tribune*, February 24, 1941, p. 13; *New York Times*, September 12, 1941, p. 2, September 23, 1941, p. 6; *New Leader*, May 28, 1927; *Socialist Call*, March 29, May 31, and September 27, 1941.

VIII America at war

1 "N.E.C. Statement on War," December 21, 1941; "Minutes, National Action Committee, January 22, 1942"; "Report of the Administrative Secretary to the National Executive Committee Meeting, April 10–12, 1942"; "Statement of Dan Roberts," May 23, 1942; "Minutes of the National Convention, Socialist Party of U.S.A., May 31, 1942" [Sunday morning session, p. 2], Minutes, National Labor Committee, August 2, 1942; Norman Thomas, "Statement Against the Symes Amendment" [1942]; at Duke. Norman Thomas to the National Executive Committee [December 9, 1941]; Norman Thomas to Devere Allen, December 11, 1941; Norman Thomas to Maynard Krueger, December 11, 1941; Norman Thomas to Frank McCallister, December 23, 1941; Norman Thomas, "A Short Personal Statement on the War" [January 1942] (typescript); in NT Papers. *Socialist Call*, February 7, June 12, and June 26, 1942.

2 Harry Fleischman, "Report on Third Thomas Radio Show," in "Report of the Administrative Secretary to N.E.C. Meeting, Chicago, Illinois, April 10–12, 1942," p. 2; Norman Thomas to William Paley, May 14, 1942; Norman Thomas to Editor, *New York Teachers News*, May 2, 1943; Norman Thomas to Mrs. R. F. Gardner, May 4, 1943; in NT Papers. Robert Minor, "Lenin and the Globe War," *Communist*, XXI (January 1942), 20; Israel Amter, "Norman Thomas, a Spearhead of Fascism," *Communist*, XXI (June 1942), 451–452; *Daily Worker*, January 20, 1942; *Jewish Daily Forward*, June 13, 1944; *PM*, June 8, 1945; *Socialist Call*, January 3, May 8, May 22, and June 5, 1942, January 14, April 28, and July 7, 1944, December 16, 1946.

3 Norman Thomas to Walter Uphoff, December 18, 1941; Norman Thomas to Brigadier General Lewis B. Hershey, February 11, 1942; Norman Thomas to Reverend A. K. Chalmers, February 17, 1942; Norman Thomas to Elmer Davis, January 19, 1943; Alton Levy to Norman Thomas, December 30, 1943; Norman Thomas to [Laurence] Dennis, January 6, 1944; in NT Papers. *Socialist Call*, January 22, 1943, January 14, 1944.

4 "Memorandum of an Interview by Norman Thomas with Mr. McCloy, Assistant Secretary of War, on the Subject of the Right of the Army to Evacuate Persons from Their Homes" [September 1942] (typescript at Duke). Ann Ray to Norman Thomas, January 14, 1942; Hugh E. Macbeth to Norman Thomas, March 9, 1942; Norman Thomas to Hugh E. Macbeth, "March 9, 1942" (obviously an error on Thomas' part, since the correct date would be about March 19, 1942); Norman Thomas to Paul Hutchinson, June 23, 1942; Norman Thomas to Roger

Baldwin, September 1, 1942; Clarence E. Rust to Norman Thomas, May 22, 1943; Norman Thomas to Clarence E. Rust, June 2, 1943; Norman Thomas to Francis Biddle, February 13, 1942; in NT Papers. *Los Angeles Times,* May 19, 1942. See also Johnpoll, "Norman Thomas's Position on War," pp. 91–92.

5 Norman Thomas, "Our War with Japan," *Commonweal,* XLII (April 20, 1945), 7–8.

6 Norman Thomas to Alfred T. Carton, November 21, 1942; Norman Thomas to Mrs. Betty Bryant, February 26, 1943; Norman Thomas to "Dear Mr. [James] Farmer," March 15, 1943; Norman Thomas to Dr. R. N. Douglas, November 2, 1945; in NT Papers. *Socialist Call,* August 11 and September 15, 1944.

7 Norman Thomas to Monroe Sweetland, May 2, 1942; Norman Thomas to William Green, August 28, 1942; Norman Thomas to Robert M. LaFollette, Jr., January 12, 1944; Norman Thomas to Roger Baldwin, January 24, 1945; Norman Thomas to Merlyn S. Pitsele, January 7, 194[7]; in NT Papers. Norman Thomas, "How Democratic Are Labor Unions?," *Harper's Magazine,* CLXXXIV (May 1942), 655–662; *Socialist Call,* May 29, 1942, December 10, 1945.

8 "Release of Socialist Party, New York State," November 2, 1942 (Duke); Norman Thomas to Daniel Bell, November 10, 1947 (Daniel Bell Papers, Tamiment); Norman Thomas, "Suggested Draft of a Platform," 1944 (typescript at Tamiment). Norman Thomas to Irving Barshop, January 18, 1943; Norman Thomas to Maynard Krueger, February 1, 1943; Norman Thomas to Robin Myers, September 22, 1943; Elizabeth Bowman to Norman Thomas, December 26, 1943; Norman Thomas to Louis Burkhardt, April 20, 1944; in NT Papers. Roseboom, *A History of Presidential Elections,* p. 490; *Socialist Call,* November 12 and December 10, 1943, February 11, February 25, May 26, June 16, July 28, August 18, August 25, September 8, October 6, October 27, November 3, November 17, December 1, and December 22, 1944.

9 Norman Thomas to Ernest Lehman, March 17, 1942 (NT Papers); *Socialist Call,* May 26 and June 10, 1944, March 12, 1945.

10 Norman Thomas, *What Is Our Destiny?* (Garden City, Doubleday, 1944), pp. 74–75, 113–119; Norman Thomas, "On Bates on Russia," *Nation,* CLIV (January 31, 1942), 124; Norman Thomas, "What Next for the Post War World Council?," *Post War World Council Bulletin,* IV (August 1945), 1; United States House of Representatives, Committee on Post War Military Policy, *Hearings on Universal Military Training,* July 1945, p. 245; *New York Times,* February 26, 1941, p. 5, March 4, 1941, p. 3, February 22, 1945, p. 18, September 28, 1945, p. 19.

ix Love your enemies

1 Norman Thomas, "What's Right with America," *Harper's,* CXCIV (March 1947), 238–239; *Socialist Call,* August 6 and October 15, 1945.

2 Norman Thomas to Elliott Cohen, May 21, 1947 (NT Papers); Johnpoll, "Norman Thomas's Position on War, 1917–1962," p. 103.

3 Norman Thomas to Gertrude Helena Urban, May 17, 1946 (NT Papers); Norman Thomas, "What Are We Going to Do About the Germans?," 1942 (typescript in NT Papers); *Socialist Call*, September 24, 1945, March 4, 1946.

4 United States Senate, Committee on Foreign Relations, *Hearings on Ratification of the Charter of the United Nations* (Washington, D.C., Government Printing Office, 1945), pp. 584–587; Norman Thomas, *Appeal to the Nations* (New York, Holt, 1947), pp. 23–24; *A Socialist's Faith*, p. 278; *Socialist Call*, July 16, 1945.

5 *Appeal to the Nations*, p. 65; *A Socialist's Faith*, p. 281; *What Is Our Destiny?*, pp. 108–109.

6 "Press Release, Socialist Party Campaign Headquarters, September 19–20, 1948" (original at Duke); Norman Thomas to Frank Zeidler, February 3, 1947 (NT Papers); Norman Thomas to Jesse T. Overholt, June 18, 1948 (NT Papers); Norman Thomas, *How Can the Socialist Party Best Serve Socialism?* (New York, Norman Thomas, 1949), p. 7; Norman Thomas, "Do Left-Wing Parties Belong in Our System?," *Annals of the American Academy of Political and Social Science*, CCLIX (July 1948), 25–29; *Jewish Daily Forward*, May 30, 1948; *Socialist Call*, March 4, April 8, April 15, June 10, June 24, and July 15, 1946, August 6, August 13, November 7, and November 14, 1947, February 27, March 19, March 26, April 9, April 16, June 4, June 11, June 25, and October 1, 1948.

7 Norman Thomas, "The Progressive Party," August 19, 1948 (typescript at Duke); "By Norman Thomas," June 1948 (typescript in NT Papers); Norman Thomas to Henry A. Wallace, December 20, 1947 (NT Papers); Norman Thomas to Jesse D. Overholt, June 18, 1948 (NT Papers); Norman Thomas to Alfred Baker Lewis, September 13, 1948 (NT Papers); Norman Thomas, "Why I Am a Candidate" [acceptance speech, May 9, 1948, Reading, Pennsylvania] (Tamiment); "Do Left-Wing Parties Belong in Our System?," pp. 27–28; *Socialist Call*, January 9, 1948.

8 "Press Release, Socialist Party Campaign Headquarters, September 19–20, 1948 (Duke); Norman Thomas, "The Republican Party," August 19, 1948 (typescript at Duke); Norman Thomas, "The Democratic Party," August 19, 1948 (typescript at Duke); Roseboom, *A History of Presidential Elections*, p. 504; *Socialist Call*, April 9, 1947, September 3–October 29, November 11, and December 17, 1948.

9 Norman Thomas to Harry Fleischman, November 15, 1951; Norman Thomas to Mrs. Yvonne Ferrari, September 10, 1952; Norman Thomas to Hugh Gaitskell, June 14, 1956; in NT Papers. *How Can the Socialist Party Best Serve Socialism?*, pp. 2–5, 7–8, 13; Roseboom, *A History of Presidential Elections*, p. 522; Norman Thomas, "How I See the Democrats," *New Republic*, CXXXIII (August 22, 1955), 8; *Socialist Call*, April 16 and November 11, 1948, November 18, 1949, June 9, 1950, February 23, April 27, and October 26, 1951, January 4, July 25, August 18, October 17, and December 12, 1952, April 10, 1953.

10 Norman Thomas to C. Michael Darcey, April 13, 1956; Norman Thomas to Rosamond Clark, June 11, 1956; Norman Thomas to Henry

Luce, June 20, 1956; Norman Thomas to Carroll Chouinard, June 21, 1956; in NT Papers.

11 Norman Thomas, "Draft Survey for N.E.C.," April 22, 1947 (typescript in NT Papers); "Memorandum from Norman Thomas to Directors of the American Civil Liberties Union, November 15, 1948" (NT Papers); Norman Thomas to Roger Baldwin, December 22, 1948 (NT Papers); "Do Left-Wing Parties Belong in Our System?," p. 29; Norman Thomas, "In Vigorous Defense of Democracy," *Saturday Review*, XLII (September 5, 1959), 18; *Socialist Call*, May 15, 1953. Data regarding Norman Thomas's influence on the McCarthy "anti-Communist" crusade come from conversations in February 1948 in Milwaukee with John Work and, over a long period of time, with Frank Zeidler. The information is also based on privately held documents which were made available to the author by several Socialists, ex-Socialists, and ex-Communists in Milwaukee. The gist of the speech, made on August 25, 1946, can be found in Norman Thomas's column in the *Socialist Call*, September 9, 1946. The first newspaper to pick up Thomas's cry was the *Green Bay Press-Gazette*. See also Ronald Radosh, "Norman Thomas and Cold War Socialism," *Liberation*, XIII (February 1969), 6.

12 Norman Thomas to Colonel Bonner Fellers, May 7, 1946; Norman Thomas to Roger Baldwin, September 12, 1947; Norman Thomas to American Civil Liberties Union, October 20, 1947; Norman Thomas to American Civil Liberties Union "in support of my motion with regard to Communist teachers in public schools," November 18, 1948; in NT Papers. "My Forty Years in Politics"; *Socialist Call*, June 6, 1947, April 8, 1949.

13 Norman Thomas to Matthew J. Connally, November 26, 1948; Norman Thomas to Royal W. France, December 16, 1952; Norman Thomas to Herbert Brownell, January 22, 1953; Norman Thomas to Harold Dodds, April 13, 1956; Norman Thomas to Hugh Gaitskell, June 14, 1956; in NT Papers. "Do Left-Wing Parties Belong in Our System?," p. 29; *Socialist Call*, March 26, 1947, June 4 and July 30, 1948, May 12 and September 29, 1950.

14 George Charney, *A Long Journey* (Chicago, Quadrangle, 1968), pp. 230–231.

15 A. J. Muste and Norman Thomas to Dwight D. Eisenhower, January 1, 1956 (NT Papers); Norman Thomas to Alexander Bicks, August 10, 1958 (NT Papers); Norman Thomas to "Dear Friend," December 6, 1961 (Duke).

16 United States Senate, Committee on the Judiciary, *Hearings Before the Subcommittee to Investigate Juvenile Delinquency* (Washington, Government Printing Office, 1955), pp. 217–221.

17 Norman Thomas to R. I. Lovell, February 6, 1951; Norman Thomas to M. J. Hildreth, January 23, 1952; Norman Thomas to Royal W. France, December 16, 1952; in NT Papers. *Socialist Call*, July 7, 1950. See also Johnpoll, "Norman Thomas's Position on War, 1917–1962," pp. 119–123.

18 Norman Thomas, *Democratic Socialism: A New Appraisal* (New York, League for Industrial Democracy, 1953), pp. 14–15; Norman Thomas,

The Prerequisites for Peace (New York, Norton, 1959), pp. 87, 155–156; Norman Thomas, "Disarmament: A New Beginning," *Socialist Call*, XXV (July 1957), 94; the *Socialist Call* became a magazine in 1953. *New America*, July 28, 1961.

19 Norman Thomas to A. J. Muste, June 18, 1956 (NT Papers); Norman Thomas to Hugh Gaitskell, November 5, 1956 (NT Papers); *The Prerequisites for Peace*, pp. 32–33, 39, 42–43; Norman Thomas, "Norman Thomas's Position," *Nation*, CXLII (April 8, 1961), 292; Norman Thomas, "In Vigorous Defense of Democracy," *Saturday Review*, XLII (September 9, 1959), 18.

20 Norman Thomas, *Democratic Socialism: A New Appraisal*, 2d ed. (New York, Post War World Council, 1963), pp. 7–11, 13–14, 17–18, 24–26, 29, 31, 35, 37, 39–40.

x Blessed are the peacemakers

1 Norman Thomas, "Memorandum on the Communist Problem in the Committee for a Sane Nuclear Policy" [1961] (typescript at Duke); Barbara Deming, "The Ordeal of SANE," *Nation*, CXLII (March 11, 1961), 200–205.

2 *New York Times*, April 22, 1962, p. 2; June 21, 1962, p. 10.

3 Norman Thomas, "The Dangers of Political Zionism" [1948] (typescript at Duke). Norman Thomas to Rabbi Elmer Berger, February 4, 1944; Norman Thomas to Simon Davis, September 14, 1956; Norman Thomas to the Editor, *Manchester Guardian*, November 5, 1956; Norman Thomas to Hugh Gaitskell, November 5, 1956; Norman Thomas to Jacob Javits, November 7, 1956; Norman Thomas to Dwight D. Eisenhower, November 12, 1956; Norman Thomas to Reinhold Niebuhr, December 4, 1956; in NT Papers. Norman Thomas, "Impressions of Israel," *Jewish Newsletter*, XIV (January 13, 1958), 1; Norman Thomas, "The Middle East: Perils and Prospects," *Commonweal*, LXVI (May 16, 1958), 175; *Socialist Call*, December 12, 1936, March 24, 1944.

4 Norman Thomas, "The Return to Religion, Sermon at Unitarian Church of Germantown, June 7, 1953" (Tamiment); Norman Thomas, "Religion and Civilization," *Atlantic Monthly*, CLXXX (August 1947), 33–36.

5 Norman Thomas to Royal W. France, December 16, 1952 (NT Papers); Norman Thomas to Darlington Hoopes, October 30, 1956 (NT Papers); *New York Times*, June 8, 1963, p. 52, December 16, 1963, p. 5.

6 Norman Thomas to Chester Bowles, July 5, 1960; Norman Thomas to David Susskind, September 2, 1960; Bill Biggs to Norman Thomas, October 1, 1960; Norman Thomas to A. Philip Randolph, September 20, 1960; at Duke.

7 Norman Thomas to the Reverend Tansel Butler, May 19, 1948 (NT Papers); Norman Thomas to Maxwell W. Rabb, February 20, 1956 (NT Papers); Norman Thomas, "Why Socialism?" [1963] (typescript at Tamiment).

8 *New York Times*, May 30, 1964, p. 14.

9 *New York Times*, March 27, 1964, p. 26, September 10, 1964, p. 34, May 20, 1966, p. 16, June 1, 1966, p. 15, June 3, 1966, p. 13, February 20, 1967, p. 18, February 22, 1967, p. 17.

10 Norman Thomas to M. Bracke, February 2, 1947 (NT Papers); Norman Thomas to Leon Blum, February 3, 1947 (NT Papers); "Statement by Norman Thomas for the Celebration of Vietnam Independence," September 28 [1948] (typescript in NT Papers); Harold L. Orams to Norman Thomas, April 2, 1956 (NT Papers); *New York Times*, January 3, 1965, sec. IV, p. 8, April 14, 1965, p. 3, May 18, 1965, p. 3, June 9, 1965, p. 4, August 1, 1965, sec. IV, p. 11, August 29, 1965, p. 69, November 29, 1965, p. 3, November 30, 1965, p. 5, January 31, 1966, p. 31, January 11, 1968, p. 7.

11 *New York Times*, March 26, 1968, p. 20, June 18, 1968, p. 35, August 22, 1968, p. 36, November 21, 1968, p. 51.

12 *New York Times*, November 21, 1965, p. 60; *New York Times Magazine*, January 23, 1966, p. 2; *New York Times*, May 5, 1966, p. 27, March 31, 1967, p. 36, October 30, 1967, p. 1, November 12, 1967, p. 6, November 15, 1967, p. 34, November 21, 1968, p. 51, December 20, 1968, pp. 1, 43.

XI Full circle

1 Homer C. Zink to Norman Thomas, June 24, 1932 (Duke); Norman Thomas to Israel Knox, November 27, 1942 (NT Papers); Claude Moore Fuess, "Norman Thomas, Socialist Crusader," *Current History*, XXXVII (October 1932), 2; Bryn Hovde, quoted in "The Election of Norman Thomas," *Christian Century*, LXXXVI (January 8, 1969), 37.

2 Roger N. Baldwin, "Norman Thomas: A Combative Life," *New Republic*, CLVIII (January 13, 1968), 11–12.

3 *Ibid.*, p. 12; "The Election of Norman Thomas," p. 36.

4 Norman Thomas to H. Gordon Rogers, November 2, 1934 (NT Papers); Edwin P. Hoyt, *The Tempering Years* (New York, Scribner, 1963), p. 336; "The Meaning of Norman Thomas," *America*, CXX (January 4, 1969), 5.

5 Daniel W. Hoan to James Oneal, June 30, 1933 (Hoan Papers); *Der Tog* (*The Day*, Yiddish daily), August 12, 1961.

6 "The Election of Norman Thomas," p. 36.

7 Interview with Norman Thomas, October 1963.

8 Norman Thomas to Daniel Bell, November 10, 1947 (Tamiment); Norman Thomas to Tucker P. Smith, January 5, 1956 (NT Papers); "My Forty Years in Politics," (typescript in NT Papers), pp. 4, 6, 8; Hentoff, *Peace Agitator: The Story of A. J. Muste*, p. 235.

9 Norman Thomas, *The Choices* (New York, Washburn, 1969), pp. 76, 81, 84–85.

Index

A note on the author

Bernard K. Johnpoll was born in New York and studied at Boston University. After working as a newspaperman with the *Pittsburgh Post Gazette*, the *Erie Dispatch Herald*, and the *Boston Record-American*, he returned to school and received an M.A. degree from Rutgers University and a Ph.D. from the State University of New York. Since that time he has taught political science and written *The Politics of Futility*. He is now Associate Professor of Political Science in the Graduate School of Public Affairs at the State University of New York, Albany.

45401